Wissenschaftliche Untersuchungen
zum Neuen Testament · 2. Reihe

Begründet von Joachim Jeremias und Otto Michel
Herausgegeben von
Martin Hengel und Otfried Hofius

42

The Secretary in the Letters of Paul

by

E. Randolph Richards

*cf. review in JThS 43(1992) 618-20
(H.D. Betz)*

J.C.B. Mohr (Paul Siebeck) Tübingen

CIP-Titelaufnahme der Deutschen Bibliothek

Richards, Ernest Randolph:
The secretary in the letters of Paul / by E. Randolph Richards. –
Tübingen : Mohr, 1991
  (Wissenschaftliche Untersuchungen zum Neuen Testament : Reihe 2 ; 42)
  ISBN 3-16-145575-4
  ISSN 0340-9570
NE: Wissenschaftliche Untersuchungen zum Neuen Testament / 02

© 1991 by J.C.B. Mohr (Paul Siebeck), P.O. Box 2040, D-7400 Tübingen.

This book may not be reproduced, in whole or in part, in any form (beyond that permitted by copyright law) without the publisher's written permission. This applies particularly to reproductions, translations, microfilms and storage and processing in electronic systems.

The book was typeset by Computersatz Staiger in Ammerbuch-Pfäffingen using Bembo-Antiqua typeface, printed by Gulde-Druck in Tübingen on acid free stock paper from Papierfabrik Niefern and bound by Heinr. Koch in Tübingen.

Printed in Germany.

To
Stacia, Joshua and Jacob

Preface

It is surprising that a topic as potentially significant as secretarial mediation in the Pauline letters has gone largely undeveloped. This work will hopefully move Pauline studies a step closer toward an understanding of how Paul used his secretary.

Although many have contributed throughout the process, a few deserve special mention. Thanks are due first of all to my loving wife, Stacia. I am also appreciative particularly to three professors at Southwestern Baptist Theological Seminary: Earle Ellis, a true gentleman-scholar, who encouraged me to pursue the publication of my dissertation; Bruce Corley, who had first introduced me to a subject that I had dreaded for years: Pauline studies; and James Brooks, who most importantly taught me to love the study of the Greek New Testament.

Finally I am grateful to Profs. Martin Hengel and Otfried Hofius for accepting this work for publication in *Wissenschaftliche Untersuchungen zum Neuen Testament*, and to Ilse König and the rest of the editorial staff of J.C.B. Mohr-Siebeck.

All classical works are cited by the now standard abbreviations listed in the *Oxford Classical Dictionary*. Commonly cited periodicals, reference works, serials, Pseudepigraphal and early Patristic works, the Dead Sea Scrolls (and related texts), orders and tractates in the Mishnah (and related texts), and the Nag Hammadi tractates were always abbreviated using the list provided in *JBL* 99 (1980): 83–97. Collections of papyri were abbreviated following the list provided by Chan-Hie Kim, "Index of Greek Papyrus Letters," *Semeia* 22 (1981): 107–12. The bibliography contains the full form of all abbreviated material.

All quotations from classical works depend on the editions and translations of the Loeb Classical Library unless stated otherwise. The text of the Greek New Testament is that of *Novum Testamentum Graece*, ed. E. Nestle and K. Aland, 26th ed. (Stuttgart: Deutsche Bibelgesellschaft, 1979). All translations from scripture are my own unless stated otherwise. Statistical information concerning the Greek New Testament was calculated with the assistance of the computer concordance of *GramCord* (© copyright 1986, Project GramCord/Trinity Evangelical Divinity School) and is used by personal license.

Bandung, Indonesia, Christmas 1989　　　　*E. Randolph Richards*

Table of Contents

Preface V

List of Tables XI

Introduction

1. Statement of the Problem 1
2. Methodology 2
   a) Terminology 2
      aa) Three Related Roles 2
          Copyist — Letter Carrier — Reader
      bb) Definition and Ancient Terms 10
   b) Primary Sources 11

Chapter One
The Secretary in Greco-Roman Antiquity

1. The Prevalence of the Secretary 15
   a) Official or Business Correspondence 15
      aa) Imperial 15
      bb) Business 18
   b) Private Correspondence 18
      aa) The Upper Classes 18
      bb) The Lower Classes 20
2. The Employment of a Secretary 23
   a) The Secretary as a Recorder 24
      aa) *Syllabatim* 25
      bb) *Viva voce* 26
          Evidence for Shorthand in Antiquity (Latin — Greek)
          Prevalence of the Use of Shorthand in the First Christian Century
   b) The Secretary as an Editor 43
      aa) The Secretary's Use of the Author's Draft 44
      bb) The Secretary's Use of the Author's Instructions 44

    c) The Secretary as a Co-author 47
    d) The Secretary as a Composer 49
    e) Related Issues 53
        aa) Responsibility 53
        bb) Training 57
        cc) Practical Considerations 62

Chapter II
The Role of the Secretary in a Particular Letter

1. Criteria for Detecting the Use of a Secretary in a Particular Letter . . 68
   a) Explicit Evidence 68
      aa) References by the Author 68
      bb) References by the Secretary 73
          Illiteracy Formulae – Secretarial Remarks
      cc) Changes in Handwriting 76
          Autograph – Annotations in a Copy – Remarks in the Text
   b) Implicit Indications 80
      aa) The Presence of a Postscript 81
          Summary Subscriptions – Additional Material
      bb) The Preference of the Author 90
      cc) The Particular Letter-type 91
      dd) Stylistic Variations in an Authentic Letter 92

2. Situational Considerations for Determining the Secretarial Method
   Employed in a Particular Letter 97
   a) An Author-Controlled Letter 98
      aa) The Secretary as a Recorder 99
          Syllabatim – Viva voce
      bb) The Secretary as an Editor 102
          Author's Draft – Author's Instructions
   b) A Secretary-Controlled Letter 105
      aa) The Secretary as a Co-author 106
          Involuntary – Voluntary
      bb) The Secretary as a Composer 107

3. Differences Resulting from the Use of a Secretary 111
   a) Differences Possible in Any Type of Secretary-Assisted Letter . . 111
   b) Differences Possible From a Specific Secretarial Method 118
      aa) Differences Possible in an Author-Controlled Letter 118
      bb) Differences Possible in a Secretary-Controlled Letter 123

Table of Contents IX

Chapter III
The Role of the Secretary in the Letters of Paul

1. Preliminary Considerations 129
   a) Paul's Relation to the Greco-Roman Letter Tradition 129
      aa) The Greco-Roman Letter 129
          Purpose – Structure – Content (Stereotyped Formulae – Epistolary Rhetoric)
      bb) The Pauline Letter 136
          Purpose – Structure – Content (Stereotyped Formulae – Epistolary Rhetoric)
      cc) The "Jerusalem or Tarsus" Debate: the Question of the Educational Background of Paul 144
   b) Συνεργοί 153
   c) Παραδόσεις and Μεμβράναι 158
      aa) Paul's Use of Παραδόσεις and Μεμβράναι 158
      bb) Implications of the Use of Παράδοσις and Μεμβράναι in the Composition of a Letter 160

2. Paul's Employment of a Secretary 169
   a) Explicit Evidence 169
      aa) References by the Author 169
      bb) References by the Secretary 169
          Illiteracy Formulae – Secretarial Remarks
      cc) Changes in handwriting 172
          Autographs – Annotations in a Copy – Remarks in the Text
   b) Implicit Indications 175
      aa) The Presence of a Postscript 176
          Summary Subscriptions – Additional Material
      bb) The Preference of Paul 181
      cc) The Particular Letter-Type 182
      dd) Stylistic Variations in an Authentic Letter 183
          Establishing a Pauline Standard of Form, Style, and Diction – Deviating Letters That Contain Argumentations, Tone, or Content Suggesting Paul – Deviating Letters That Match the Style of a Trusted Colleague

3. An Evaluation of Paul's Use of a Secretary 189
   a) The Pauline Letters Written with Secretarial Assistance 189
   b) Toward an Analysis of Paul's Method of Using a Secretary . . . 194

Conclusion

1. The Role of the Secretary in Greco-Roman Antiquity 199
2. The Role of the Secretary in the Letters of Paul 201

Appendix

A. Types of Letters 202
B. Examples of Various Locations for Introductory Formulae 203
C. Various Types of Stereotyped Formulae 204
D. The Greeting Formulae 206
E. Examples of Chiasmus in Paul 207
F. Examples of Tribulation Lists 209
G. The "Literary or Non-Literary" (Deissmann) Debate:
   The Problem of Classifying the Letters of Paul 211
H. Criteria for Detecting Παράδοσις and Μεμβράναι
   in the Pauline Letters 217

Sources Consulted 222

Indices 243

Subjects 243
Modern Authors 244
Ancient Authors 248
Papyri and Inscriptions 249
References 250

List of Tables

1. Clause-Endings in Selected Letters of Cicero and Others 122
2. "I" vs. "We" Uses in 2 Corinthians 157
3. A Presentation of Gordon Bahr's Analysis of the Letter
   Body Written by a Secretary to the Postscript by Paul 177
4. The Evidence for the Use of a Secretary in the Letters of Paul 190

Introduction

The primitive Christian church used two basic literary tools: the gospel and the letter. The gospel may be indigenous to the Christian community, but letters were immensely popular in the first century Greco-Roman world. The nature of letter writing in the first century has received much modern attention.[1]

1. Statement of the Problem

Despite the interest in letter writing in general, the role of the amanuensis[2] or secretary has received scant attention. Although many works note the possible influence of a secretary, particularly in the letters of Paul, there has been no inclusive study of the various roles of a secretary and the possible effects of secretarial mediation on a letter.

---

[1] *E.g.*, two important series, Guides to Biblical Scholarship and Library of Early Christianity, selected works on letter writing for inclusion; hence, Wm. Doty, *Letters in Primitive Christianity* (Philadelphia: Fortress, 1973); and Stanley K. Stowers, *Letter Writing in Greco-Roman Antiquity* (Philadelphia: Westminster, 1986). A few other important works are: Heikki Koskenniemi, *Studien zur Idee und Phraseologie des griechischen Briefes bis 400 n. Chr.*(Helsinki: Suomalainen Tiedeakatemia, 1956); Francis X. J. Exler, *The Form of the Ancient Greek Letter: a Study in Greek Epistolography* (Washington, DC: Catholic University of America, 1922); Otto Roller, *Das Formular der paulinischen Briefe* (Stuttgart: W. Kohlhammer, 1933); Paul Schubert, *The Form and Function of the Pauline Thanksgiving* (Berlin: Alfred Topelmann, 1939); and Adolf Deissmann, *Light from the Ancient East*, trans. L. R. M. Strachan (London: Hodder & Stoughton, 1910). Two articles together cover the discipline well: C. Dziatzko, "Der Brief", in *PW*, 3: 836–38; and J. Sykutris, "Epistolographie", in *PWSup*, 5: 185–220.

[2] 'Amanuensis' is probably the most popular term in modern studies to denote the ancient secretary. In antiquity, however, it was perhaps the *least* common term (see below, p. 11). Therefore throughout this work, the modern English equivalent, 'secretary,' is used.

2. Methodology

To classify the possible roles of a secretary, an inductive examination is made of the primary material, Greek and Latin private letters, for traces of a secretary. The resulting descriptions of secretarial roles are placed on a spectrum composed of four basic categories, ranging from more author-controlled to more secretary-controlled roles. With the aide of letters in which the author is more explicit about his use of a secretary, criteria are developed for detecting the presence of a secretary in letters where it is less evident. The results are applied to the letters of Paul. In many ways still a *prolegomenon* to the role of the secretary in Paul, this work attempts to set the general parameters and to suggest the probable secretarial role in the individual letters of Paul. Yet, in prolegomena style, it engages little in any detailed analyses of the individual letters nor in the ramifications for other issues of Pauline study.

a) Terminology

An analysis should begin with a definition of an ancient secretary, and the best way to begin this definition is to describe three peripheral tasks often performed by a secretary that are not germane to his role and therefore will not be considered elsewhere: copying, carrying the letter, and reading (orally) for the recipient.

aa) Three Related Roles

Copyist

A copyist is not treated as a secretary. This is actually an artificial distinction.[3] As a professional writer, secretaries were often hired to copy existing material. For example, Cicero informs Atticus that his latest work is almost finished: "tantum librariorum menda toluntur".[4] He calls these copyists *librarii*, a term he also uses for his personal secretary. Yet for the purpose of this research, only those scribes who are functioning as letter writing secretaries are considered.[5]

---

[3] The same word is used for a secretary and a copyist in Hebrew (סוֹפֵר), Greek (γραμματεύς) and Latin (*librarius*).

[4] Cicero *Epistulae ad Atticum* 13.23 (July 10, 45 B.C.); "There is [left] only the correction of the copyists' mistakes." Also Cic. *Epistulae ad Quintum Fratrem* 3.6.6.

[5] It was because of this equivocation that the term 'scribe' is rejected in favor of 'secretary'. The former can connote less than intended, as in a mere copyist, or more than in-

This is not to say that the fact that a scribe often had the dual roles of a secretary and a copyist is not significant. Rather the production and use of copies impacts letter writing. From remarks by ancient authors, primarily in the letters of Cicero,[6] it appears that copies of letters were used for four reasons: (1) a copy was made to be retained by the author; (2) a copy was made to share with another; (3) multiple copies were sent via different carriers to help insure the arrival of the message; and (4) a copy was made in order to use all or part in another letter.

(1) There are numerous references that indicate the author retained a copy for himself, usually prepared by the secretary. Cicero tells Fadius Gallus:

> You are sorry the letter[d] has been torn up; well don't fret yourself; I have it[e] safe at home; you may come and fetch it whenever you like.
>
> [d Probably the preceding letter, in which Tigellius was severely criticized.]
> [e No doubt a copy of it.][7]

In a letter to his brother, Cicero relates a mishap with a letter to Caesar. The packet of letters had become wet so that Cicero's letter to Caesar was destroyed. Yet there was no real loss, for he tells, "itaque postea misi ad Caesarem eodem illo exemplo litteras".[8] Cicero agrees to send Dolabella a copy of a small speech. He thought little of it; yet evidently he still had a copy of it with him in his residence in Pompeii.[9] He chides a young lawyer-friend for making multiple copies of a letter in his own hand, seeming to imply that he considered this secretarial work.[10] He remarks casually in a note that he was writing a copy of the letter into his 'notebook' while at the meal-table.[11] Evidently he or more likely his

---

tended, as in an expert in the Jewish law. The New Testament use of γραμματεύς is always in the sense of an expert in religious law with one exception (Acts 19:35) where it refers to a government official. See J. Jeremias, "γραμματεύς", *TDNT*.

[6] The practice, however, was not exclusively Cicero's. Many of the references are from letters *to* Cicero. Nevertheless the limitation of evidence to the collection of his letters was unfortunate but largely unavoidable. The papyrus letters are too abbreviated and stereotyped to speak much of incidental matters. Pliny's letters, for example, are also rather artificial. Yet Cicero wrote many letters and often spoke of such ordinary matters of everyday life.

[7] Cic. *Epistulae ad Familiares* 7.25.1 (LCL 2: 101).

[8] Cic. *QFr.* 2.12.4; "So later on I sent Caesar an exact duplicate of my letter."

[9] Cic. *Fam.* 9.12.2.

[10] Cic. *Fam.* 7.18.2.

[11] Cic. *Fam.* 9.26.1. This was a quick note that he dashed off (*exaravi*) in the midst of a meal; yet still a copy was retained for his notebook (*in codicillis*).

secretary kept copies of his letters in notebooks.[12] He advises his brother Quintus to destroy any letters he wrote that were unbecoming of a man in his position. This must refer to copies that Quintus had retained because later in the same letter, Cicero repeats his advice and also tells him to request that the recipients also destroy their letters (the dispatched copies).[13]

(2) A copy of a letter was often appended to another letter to someone else, with whom the author wished to share the original letter. Frequently the copy was of another letter by the same author but to a different recipient.[14] For example, Pollio writes to Cicero, "I am sending you for your perusal a letter that I have written to Balbus".[15] Cicero ends a letter to Atticus with "I have sent you a copy of the letter I wrote to Pompey".[16] Elsewhere he notes, "Your letter and the enclosed copy of one of my brother Quintus' letters show me...."[17] Although the reasons are different, an interesting parallel to Col. 4:16 may be seen in a request of Cicero: "Be sure you send me a line as often as you can, and take care that you get from Lucceius the letter I sent him".[18] Evidently copies were shared among friends. Brutus advises Cicero "I have read the short extract from the note which you sent to Octavius: Atticus sent it to me".[19] One may infer that Cicero *usually* shared with Atticus the letters that he received from others, because Curius specifically asks Cicero not to let Atticus read that particular letter.[20] Finally Cicero mentions in a

---

[12] Cic. *Att.* 13.6.3. This passage indicates that Tiro, Cicero's trusted secretary, kept copies of the letters, which he published after Cicero's death; so also R. Y. Tyrrell and L. C. Purser, *The Correspondence of M. Tullius Cicero*, 7 vols., 3d rev. ed. (London: Longmans, Green, & Co., 1901–33), 5: 18 n. 3; 5: 379 n. 5. See also *Att.* 16.5 where συναγωγή is used for the corpus of letters.

[13] Cic. *QFr.* 1.2.8, 9. He also mentions that he had also seen one, probably a circulated copy.

[14] Moreover, presumably the second letter (the one that contained the copy) was not written *before* he sent the original letter. Thus the author must have retained a copy of the first letter that served as the exemplar for the copy appended to the second.

[15] Cic. *Fam.* 10.32.5. Obviously this 'letter' that he is including must have been a copy.

[16] Cic. *Att.* 3.9.

[17] Cic. *Att.* 1.17; see also *Fam.* 3.3.2; 10.12.2; 10.33.2; and *Ad Brutum* 1.16.1.

[18] Cic. *Att.* 4.6.

[19] Cic. *Br.* 1.16.1. Ever since James Tunstall (Cambridge, 1741), this letter's authenticity has been questioned mainly because its pettiness was deemed unworthy of Brutus. However Tyrrell and Purser, *Cicero*, accept it as does M. Cary in the Loeb edition (see the discussion by Cary, LCL 4: 619). Other examples are found in Cic. *Fam.* 3.3.2; 10.12.2; and *Br.* 1.6.3.

[20] Cic. *Fam.* 7.29.2, and vice versa: "I was the man – I don't think I am boasting unduly in saying to you privately, especially in a letter which I would rather you didn't read to anyone" (Cic. *Att.* 1.16).

letter to Caecina that he would be speaking personally with Furfanius soon and therefore Caecina would not need a letter of recommendation. Nonetheless he has sent Caecina with one that was *sealed* to deliver to Furfanius. Yet because Cicero wants Caecina also to know the content of the letter of recommendation, he appends a copy of it to the letter he sent Caecina.[21]

(3) Multiple copies of important letters were often made and dispatched by different carriers (with different routes) to help ensure the safe delivery. Whether this has relevance to more ordinary personal letters is questionable.[22]

(4) This last reason for making copies is related to the first. By retaining copies of his own letters, an author was able to reuse all or part of a letter in a different letter to another. Cicero observes "The letter contained the same passage about your sister that you wrote to me". Apparently Atticus had used the same passage in letters to Cicero and to another man, who happened to share his version of the letter with Cicero. In two letters to different men, Cicero begins each with a clever and witty reference to Caesar's assassination and Anthony's survival.[23] The young Quintus (Cicero's nephew) had sent both Cicero and Atticus a long letter. Apparently he was pleased with the letter (or perhaps was trying to kill two birds with one stone) and had sent them both the same letter, although the one to Atticus was evidently abbreviated.[24] It seems to have been quite acceptable to use the same material, theme, or argument in more than one letter, if the recipients were different.[25]

---

[21] Cic. *Fam.* 6.8. He no doubt wished the family to know what a kind letter he had sent.

[22] A few references will suffice: Cic. *Fam.* 9.16.1; 10.5.1; 11.11.1; 12.12.1; and 12.30.7. It is unlikely Paul took such precautions over the delivery of one of his letters, particularly if he retained a copy.

[23] Cic. *Fam.* 10.28.1; "How I should like you to have invited me to that most gorgeous banquet on the Ides of March! We should have left no leavings [Anthony]" and *Fam.* 12.4.1; "I should like you to have invited me to your banquet on the Ides of March; there would have been no leavings."

[24] Cic. *Att.* 13.29; "I am sending you young Quintus' letter... I have sent you half the letter. The other half about his adventures I think you have in duplicate."

[25] A good piece of prose was worth sharing with others. Is there a parallel in the Colossians and Ephesians problem? Reusing material, however, was not always appropriate. *Cf. Att.* 16.6 where Cicero sheepishly confesses to Atticus that he had carelessly used the same preface in two different works, admitting that he kept a notebook of prefaces from which he selected. The works were too similar to allow this. Is it possible that others such as Paul kept notebooks of material, such as *testimonia* or doxologies? The possible relevance of the μεμβράναι (parchment notebooks) of 2 Tim. 4:13 is discussed below, pp. 164–68.

6   Introduction

Copies of letters were a desirable thing in the ancient world.[26] Cicero frequently read some of his letters to his dinner guests, both the ones he wrote and the ones he received. If a guest particularly enjoyed a letter, he would request a copy.[27] Cicero is dumbfounded as to how one of his works became so widely copied, despite his efforts to keep it secret.[28] It appears that at least in certain circles people actively sought copies of pieces that they liked. This has immediate relevance to Paul. Those asserting an early collection of Paul's letters often maintain that the churches shared copies of their letters.[29] This would not have been unusual. There is an alternative explanation, however, and it may be the most significant aspect of the secretary also serving as a copyist. The secretary retained copies. Tyrrell and Purser observe:

> For there seems considerable evidence that the senders of letters, or, at all events, Cicero and Tiro, were accustomed to keep copies of letters, even, perhaps, letters which might seem to us to be of no great importance; and this is probably one of the reasons why we have such a rich collection of the correspondence of Cicero.[30]

The collection of Paul's letters may have begun much earlier, with Paul himself. If he employed a secretary to write the letter, then a copy was likely retained.[31] Perhaps the letters were collected not by gathering

---

[26] They were also used by historians as primary sources; see *e.g.*, Plutarch *Alexander* 47.3; 54.2; 57.4; 60.1.

[27] Cic. *Att.* 8.9.

[28] Cic. *Att.* 13.21a.

[29] See Harry Gamble, *New Testament Canon: Its Making and Meaning*, Guides to Biblical Scholarship, New Testament Series (Philadelphia: Fortress, 1985), 36–43. Also see idem, "The Redaction of the Pauline Letters and the Formation of the Pauline Corpus", *JBL* 94 (1975): 403–18.

[30] Tyrrell and Purser, *Cicero*, 1: 59. Note also that when Alexander sets fire to Eumenes' (his secretary's) tent, he regrets that the letter-copies are destroyed. Consequently he orders all his correspondents to send copies back to replace the lost ones; Plut. *Eumenes* 2.2–3. Evidently he anticipated that all of his recipients retained their letters as well. Of course these were probably more official correspondences.

[31] That Paul retained copies of his letters seemed a matter of course to Hermann von Soden, *Griechisches Neues Testament* (Göttingen: Vandenhoeck & Ruprecht, 1913), VII. So also T. Henshaw, *New Testament Literature* (London: Hodder & Stoughton, 1963); and L. Hartman, "On Reading Others' Letters", *HTR* 79 (1986): 139. *Cf.* O. Roller, *Formular*, 260.

The theory may be applied to the severe letter of 2 Corinthians. It was quite possibly written without secretarial assistance. (*Cf.* the harsh letter Cicero wrote and then tried to intercept and destroy; *Att.* 8.5.) If it was written in anger and without a secretary, then it is less likely that a copy was retained. Is this the reason it is now lost?

them from the churches but by using the copies Paul had kept.[32] All the aspects of a secretary serving also as a copyist may merit future attention but is not central to the initial investigation of the role of the secretary in Paul. Hence a copyist is not included in the definition of a secretary.

Letter Carrier

Although a secretary could be asked also to deliver the letter, this request was independent and therefore also will not be considered part of the secretarial task.[33] Nevertheless this is not to downplay the importance of the letter carrier (*tabellarius*[34]). He was often a personal link between the author and the recipients in addition to the written link. Commonly the oral remarks from the carrier were preferred. When Cicero was trying to discover what was happening in Rome during his temporary exile, he notes that he often trusted "the remarks of those who travelled by this route [from Rome]..." more than the news in the letters.[35] Occasionally a letter and a personal report could conflict. Cicero explains:

> Decius the copyist [*librarius*] paid me a visit and entreated me to make every effort to prevent the appointment for the present of anybody to succeed you; now although he impressed me as being an honest fellow and on friendly terms with you, still, having a clear recollection of the purport of your previous letter to me, I did not feel quite convinced... [After checking with other sources, I was persuaded, but] what gave me the most trouble was to compel... all the others to whom you had written to believe me rather than the letter.[36]

---

[32] If only Luke was with Paul when he died (2 Tim. 4:11), then it is quite likely that he inherited the copies. This idea is discussed more fully below, p. 165 n. 169.

[33] The two tasks are not mutually exclusive; however, they are also not mutually dependent. If a letter refers to the carrier, this is no indication of the secretary's identity: the carrier may or may not have been the secretary. Probably a public (hired) secretary was rarely used for this. Furthermore it seems unwise to 'waste' a secretary's time in this way, but see John White, *Light from Ancient Letters*, Foundation and Facets Series (Philadelphia: Fortress, 1986), 216.

[34] For the use of this term, see Cic. *Fam.* 2.7.3; 2.29.1; 9.15.1; 14.1.6; 14.18.2; *Att.* 1.18; Plut. *Cicero* 15.2–3. See also the discussion in O. Roller, *Formular*, 68 and 474 n. 314. For a brief discussion of the postal system, see J. White, "The Greek Documentary Letter Tradition, Third Century B.C.E. to Third Century C.E.", *Semeia* 22 (1981): 89–106, and more recently, idem, *Light*, 214–15.

[35] Cic. *Fam.* 5.4.1. A living person communicates with more than words, is easier to catch in a lie, and can be questioned further. Also see 2.29.1. *Cf.* his exclamation "If only I could talk with you instead of writing!" (*Att.* 11.4).

[36] Cic. *Fam.* 5.6.1. It is interesting to see Cicero's struggle: the man appears reliable and friendly (*n.b.*), but the letter is unambiguous.

Evidently an oral supplement could call an undisputed letter into question, but it was difficult to overturn a letter's message, because the letter was assumed also to be the author's wishes.[37]

The carrier became a vital link in the writing process; therefore he had to be trustworthy.[38] At the end of private letters, if the carrier was not a mere employee, it was not unknown to note that the carrier was trustworthy and deserving of any assistance the recipient could offer.[39] Yet why did carriers need to be so reliable? There was the obvious problem of the letter not arriving. An interesting example is provided by comparing two of Cicero's letters to Atticus. In the first one, he notes that he is planning to give the letter to the first available person as compared to waiting for a trusted one.[40] The following letter to Atticus begins with a lament over the news that his previous letter had not arrived.[41] If *Cicero* had difficulty with a carrier not bothering to deliver a letter, how much more would a less prominent man?

The failure of the carrier to deliver the letter was not the only cause of a lost letter. Evidently carriers could actually lose a letter in transit. Cicero explains to Atticus:

> [I heard] that some slaves had come from Rome. I called them and inquired if they had any letters. "No", they said... Frightened to death by my voice and look, they confessed they had been given one, but it had been lost on the way. As you may suppose, I was wild with annoyance.[42]

Notably, Cicero is not amazed that they could lose a letter, but only annoyed that they had.[43]

---

[37] Cicero tells Cassius (*Fam.* 15.14.2–3) that he wishes "that I might congratulate you in person... since that has not come to pass, we will avail ourselves of the boon of letters, and so secure almost the same objects in our separation as if we were together." See also Cic. QFr. 1.1.45. This aspect of a letter is discussed further below, p. 130 n.

[38] Cic. *Att.* 1.7.1; "And if I do [write letters] less frequently than you expect, the reason will be that my letters are not of such a nature that I can entrust them in a casual way to anybody. Whenever I can get hold of trustworthy men in whose hands I can properly put them, I shall..." See also Cic. *Fam.* 1.9.23 and the complaints of the lazy carrier in 8.12.4.

[39] Often either to introduce the carrier or to assure the recipient that he could trust any additional information the carrier gave. See, *e.g.*, the letters of Ignatius discussed below, pp. 70–71.

[40] Cic. *Att.* 2.12.

[41] Cic. *Att.* 2.13. Incidentally, it is quite noteworthy that this earlier letter (2.12) is *in* the collection. *This illustrates that the collection was compiled from Cicero's copies and not by gathering them from all the recipients. Cf.* the relevance to the formation of the Pauline corpus suggested below, p. 165 n. and p. 188 n.

[42] Cic. *Att.* 2.8.

[43] One carrier carelessly allowed some of his letters to become soaked with water, effectively losing the letter, since the ink washed off. See Cic. QFr. 2.12.4.

Sometimes the loss of a letter was not the carrier's fault. During the breakdown of the Republic during the Spring of 43 B.C., Pollio complains to Cicero that brigands were stopping the letter carriers.[44] Lepidus was known to detain, read, or even destroy letters.[45] Yet he was not alone in this vice. Cicero on occasion intercepted letters.[46]

Cicero states a second reason for a trustworthy carrier:

> but I have been rather slow about sending one, for lack of a safe messenger. There are very few who can carry a letter of weight without lightening it by a perusal.[47]

A third reason for needing a trustworthy carrier was because he often carried additional information. A letter may describe a situation briefly, frequently with the author's assessment, but the carrier is expected to elaborate for the recipient all the details.[48]

The oral message that the carrier had may also have been confidential and perhaps even have been the real message. Brutus plainly reveals this in a request to Cicero.

> Please write me a reply to this letter at once, and send one of your own men with it, if there is anything somewhat confidential which you think it necessary for me to know.[49]

Since the role of the carrier is not to be discussed further, a concluding observation may be made. The availability of a messenger often prompted the writing of a letter. A papyrus letter states, "As an opportunity was afforded me by someone going up to you I could not miss this chance of addressing you".[50] Alan Samuel argues that the absence of

---

[44] Cic. *Fam.* 10.31.1. During a period of political intrigue, Cicero is afraid of his letters being intercepted; therefore he used pseudonyms and only the most trusted carriers; Cic. *Att.* 2.19.

[45] Cic. *Fam.* 10.31.4.

[46] He confesses to this once (Cic. *Att.* 11.9) because he wished Atticus to go ahead and deliver them. Although these situations require opponents and conflicts, they may still be relevant to Paul. Apparently Paul's opponents were not above forgery (2 Thes. 2:2).

[47] Cic. *Att.* 1.13.

[48] This is the clear implication of Cicero's complaint (*Fam.* 4.2.1): "I received your letter ... and on reading it I gathered that Philotimus did not act ... [on] the instructions he had from you (as you write) ... [when] he failed to come to me himself, and merely forwarded me your letter; and I concluded that it was shorter because you had imagined that he would deliver it in person." See also Cic. *Fam.* 3.5; 10.7; 1.8.1; 3.1.1. In *Fam.* 7.18.4, the carrier tells Cicero that the author wishes the letter destroyed after he reads it. See also John White, *Light*, 216 (and *PCol.* 3.6 [p. 34]).

[49] Cic. *Fam.* 11.20.4. Cicero also does this (*Fam.* 11.26.5).

[50] *POxy.* 123 (third to fourth Christian century).

a state postal system for ordinary private correspondences affected a letter's contents.[51] Many letters appear to have been written more from the opportunity provided by an available carrier than from an actual need.[52] The financial status of men like Cicero allowed the extravagance of dispatching slave carriers when needed.[53] This luxury was certainly not available to most, including Paul. However someone like Paul was not left entirely to the whims of chance. If he is responding to a church's letter, then the one who delivered the letter could return it.[54] A letter could also be seen as vital to his mission and hence worthy of a special dispatch.

Reader

On occasion a secretary was also used as a reader (*lector*). According to servile custom, these roles were separated, but even the wealthiest of the upper classes found it too convenient to blend the roles.[55] Apparently a recipient often preferred to have the letter read to him.[56] Little privacy was lost since even private reading was aloud, and it afforded some relief for the eyes.[57] Since this role is also independent, it is not considered further.

bb) Definition and Ancient Terms

To say what an ancient secretary was *not* is only a partial definition. For the purposes here, he was a person employed to write out correspon-

---

[51] In an unpublished paper on Hellenistic epistolography, "The Mechanics of Letter Writing", read at the SBL Annual Meeting (1973). See the brief discussion in J. White, "The Ancient Epistolography Group in Retrospect", *Semeia* 22 (1981): 2.

[52] See the discussion in John White, *Light*, 215 (and *PMich*. 8.490 [p. 162]).

[53] The wealthy Epicurean Papirus Paetus kept at least two slaves solely for carrying letters; see Cic. *Fam*. 9.15.1.

[54] If a letter was not occasioned by the church (perhaps Romans?), then the availability of a messenger may have been more of an influence.

[55] So argues A. N. Sherwin-White, *The Letters of Pliny: a Historical and Social Commentary* (Oxford: Oxford University, 1966; reprint with corr., Oxford, Oxford University, 1985), 225 n. 15 and 515–16.

[56] See esp. Pliny *Epistulae* 8.1, who laments at length the temporary loss of his reader. Cicero kept a reader, although perhaps only for Greek texts, judging from the reader's Latinized Greek title (*anagnostes*).

[57] A statement like "I read your letter" in no way implies that a reader was not used. E.g., Plutarch relates that Alexander "read" the inscription on Cyrus' tomb. Yet certainly he did not: "After reading (ἀναγνούς) the inscription upon this tomb, he ordered it to be repeated below in *Greek letters*" (Plut. *Alex*. 69.2) [italics are mine].

dence for another, whether as a professional or only as an amateur, whether with or without financial compensation, whether maintained full-time by one individual or used only for one assignment, and whether used throughout the entire letter writing process or only for preparing the final draft. This definition includes everyone from the public secretaries usually hired in the agora, to the private secretaries usually retained by wealthy persons, to the friend who writes out a letter for another.[58] His skills could range from a minimal competency with the language and/or the mechanics of writing to the highest proficiency at rapidly producing an accurate, proper, and charming letter.

Greek writers use the same term, γραμματεύς, to describe several positions. A γραμματεύς could mean a secretary, public or private, or a government official.[59] The Latin language is more specialized: *scriba* denotes a public or official secretary, *librarius*, a private secretary as does the rarer term *amanuensis*, and *notarius*, a shorthand writer.[60]

b) Primary Sources

Greek and Latin private letters are the primary sources for this investigation,[61] although ancient discussions about secretaries and letter writing are also used. The greatest concentration will be given to the sources closest to the first Christian century, but materials from the third century B.C. to the third Christian century are used.[62]

Chance may have dictated that more Latin letters survived by literary transmission than did Greek letters, but can their inclusion be justified?

---

[58] Contracts, bills of divorce, etc., were also written by secretaries, but the task at hand is to investigate the secretary's role in *letter* writing.

[59] In the LXX and the New Testament a third possibility exists: an expert in religious (Jewish and Christian) law. See LSJ, s.v. "γραμματεύς"; J. H. Thayer, ed., *A Greek-English Lexicon of the New Testament* (New York: Harper & Bros., 1887), s.v. "γραμματεύς"; BAG, s.v. "γραμματεύς"; and J. Jeremias, "γραμματεύς", *TDNT*.

[60] *Oxford Latin Dictionary*, ed. P. G. W. Glare (Oxford: Clarendon, 1968–82), s.v. "amanuensis", "librarius", "notarius", "scriba"; and *Harper's Latin Dictionary*, rev. ed. C. T. Lewis and C. Short (New York: Harper & Bros., 1879), s.v. "amanuensis", "librarius", "notarius", "scriba". E.g., see Seneca *Apocolocyntosis* 9.2, Pliny *Naturalis Historia* 7.25.91, Pliny *Ep.* 3.5.11, Suetonius *Titus* 3.2, and Cic. *Att.* 8.13.1.

The existence and use of shorthand is discussed in detail below, pp. 26–43.

[61] This includes both letters preserved by literary transmission and extant originals in the papyri, ostraca, and inscriptions.

[62] These are well-recognized and widely used parameters. See Wm. Doty, "The Epistle in Late Hellenism and Early Christianity: Developments, Influences, and Literary Form" (Ph.D. diss., Drew University, 1966), 51–52; and Stanley Stowers, *Letter Writing*.

As Abraham Malherbe explains, Greek private letters were an established form and had been absorbed by Rome: "what is significant is that Greek and Latin epistolography are of a piece, and that the latter bears testimony to the development of epistolary theory".[63] As his analysis alludes, the surviving Latin letters in actuality are often better examples of the Greek private letter than are most of the surviving Greek letters. A. N. Sherwin-White, although approaching the subject from the other direction (the study of Latin letters), echoes the same conclusion:

> The surviving Greek letters are mostly addresses and long essays meant for publication... But the Roman letter, as it emerges full-grown in the correspondence of Cicero and his friends, is the private letter of genuine intercourse, whether concerned with *res domesticae* or *res publicae*.[64]

Certainly the Greek letters preserved in the papyri were not intended for publication; yet they too reveal only a part of the spectrum comprising Greek private letters.[65] To have a more complete picture of letter writing in Paul's world, Latin letters must be considered.

Thus the letters of Cicero, the younger Pliny, Seneca, and others are included in the study. One may question if the letters of Cicero, for example, are analogous enough to Paul's letters to warrant their use.[66] Nevertheless it must be remembered that the argument is not that Cicero's *letters* are analogous to Paul's but that their uses of a *secretary* have points of comparison.[67]

---

[63] A. Malherbe, "Ancient Epistolary Theorists", *Ohio Journal of Religious Studies* 5 (1977): 5–6. Latin letters have been included in the study of Greek epistolography without debate since Klaus Thraede confirmed their relation; *Grundzüge griechisch-römische Brieftopik*, Monographien zur klassischen Altertumswissenschaft, no. 48 (Munich: Beck, 1970). See also H. Koskenniemi, "Cicero über die Briefarten (*genera epistularum*)", *Arctos* (1954): 97–102.

[64] Sherwin-White, *Letters of Pliny*, 1.

[65] So Stowers, *Letter Writing*, 18–19; C. H. Roberts and T. C. Skeat, *The Birth of the Codex* [*Codex*²] (London: Oxford University, 1983), 35; and E. A. Judge, *Rank and Status in the World of the Caesars and St. Paul*, University of Canterbury Publications, no. 29 (Christchurch, NZ: University of Canterbury, 1982), 7. Pace Wm. Doty, "Epistle", 10; Heikki Koskenniemi, *Studien*, 205; W. Hershey Davis, *Greek Papyri of the First Century* (New York: Harper & Bros., 1933), XXVII; and H. G. Meecham, *Light from Ancient Letters* (New York: Macmillan, 1923). The problem of classifying the Greek letters, especially with respect to the papyri and their relation to the Pauline letters is discussed below, pp. 129–43 and in detail in Appendix G.

[66] There are more points of commonality than scholars traditionally (since Deissmann) have been willing to allow. See the discussion of Deissmann in Appendix G.

[67] Even this is not assumed but is tested in Chapter Three. But also see Sherwin-White, *Letters of Pliny*, 1–3; Pliny the Younger, *Letters and Panegyricus*, ed. and trans. B. Radice,

Furthermore many of the Latin writers, especially Cicero, by virtue of their love for letter writing, leisure time, financial freedom, and even propensity for verbosity provide useful information. In their quest for topics to discuss,[68] they occasionally even write of such a mundane matter as how they were using their secretary. Hence these Latin letters often provide the best starting point, since a method of secretarial use may be discussed in enlightening detail.[69] Once provided with a more accurate description, the same secretarial procedure is often seen in the Greek letters.

---

2 vols., in LCL, 1: XV; Stowers, *Letter Writing*, 19; and C. Salles, "Le genre littéraire de la lettre dans l'antiquité", *Foi et Vie* 84/5 (1985): 41–47.

[68] Evidently it was a problem; *e.g.*, "When you have nothing to write, write and say so" (Cic. *Att.* 4.8a). See also Cic. *Fam.* 2.4; 4.13.

[69] Again, the restriction of most descriptions to the letters contained in the collections of Cicero is unfortunate. Other sources are examined, but usually his letters provide the best illustrations. The possibility that a practice could be singular to Cicero is always considered, and thus attestation outside his letters is required.

Chapter One
The Secretary in Greco-Roman Antiquity

Before an examination can begin, some clarifications must be made. A secretary was often used differently in various types of letters, and therefore the problem of classifying secretarial usage is tied to the lingering problem of classifying the letters themselves.

Ever since Adolf Deissmann's use of *Brief* versus *Episteln*,[1] scholars have had difficulty finding an acceptable way to categorize the Greco-Roman letters.[2] A method in vogue today is to speak of literary versus non-literary letters.[3] Yet this is not an entirely successful solution.[4] Some ancient letters are clearly situational and pragmatic in purpose, apparently intended for a private audience, while others by the same author are equally clearly intended for publication. This ambiguity, however, exists not merely between a given author's letters but frequently within a letter itself. Some seemingly private letters apparently were written for publication. Letters could frequently blend genres, combine stylistic/rhetorical devices, and display a frustratingly hybrid nature.[5]

Since this work endeavors to investigate the role of the secretary and not letter writing *per se*, a slightly different approach is used. Since the

---

[1] This is discussed in Appendix G.

[2] John White suggests that a primary problem in any study of letter writing is still "the ambiguity of the category"; John White, "Retrospect", 6. *Cf.* also *Der kleine Pauly*, ed. Konrat Ziegler and Walther Sontheimer, 5 vols. (Stuttgart: Druckenmüller, 1964–75), s.v. "Epistolographie", by Peter L. Schmidt, 2: 324–27.

[3] In his dissertation, an excellent work on Greco-Roman letters, William Doty opted for a less finely distinguished scale, using a public vs. private polarity within the common category of letter; Doty, "Epistle".

[4] Stanley K. Stowers, in his recent work, however, criticizes this as an overlaying of a modern category upon an ancient system. The public and private realms were not so well differentiated. Many public matters were administrated through private channels. Moreover many letters, especially the letters of Paul, cannot be classified well. His letters would be called 'private'; yet they are addressed to a community and are encouraged to be read to other communities; Stowers, *Letter Writing*, 19. In a sense, Paul's letters are no less public than Cicero's were originally intended to be.

[5] White, "Retrospect", 6.

purpose is to examine the use of a secretary by Paul, the classification of official or business letters versus private letters will be used.[6] There is, of course, still some blurring of categories since many private letters also handled an item or two of business.

1. The Prevalence of the Secretary

The prevalence of secretarial assistance in antiquity is investigated within the two categories of official or business and private letters.

a) Official or Business Correspondence

aa) Imperial

Evidently secretaries were used down the spectrum of public life, from royal secretaries to the agora secretaries. They were a vital part of the administrative structure of the Greco-Roman world, at least in Ptolemaic Egypt. Apparently (since ecological factors have prevented the preservation of any papyrological evidence), the 'central office' in Alexandria maintained hordes of secretaries who kept the main accounting and record-keeping. From Alexandria there was a hierarchical structure of secretaries, finally reaching down to the local village secretary. Yet these secretaries were more like modern "clerks"; they were the record-keepers for the massive bureaucratic government.[7]

---

[6] The category of private letter includes the hybrid "public/private" letters as well because this distinction is based more upon the purpose than the audience.

[7] The system probably even predates the satrap, Ptolemy I. See Roger S. Bagnall and Peter Derow, eds., *Greek Historical Documents: the Hellenistic Period* [GHD], SBLSBS, no. 16 (Chico, CA: Scholars, 1981), Appendix 1, 253–54. The essential foundation for administration in Egypt was the nome, the administrative district. All Egypt was divided into nomes, whose number and individual sizes varied from time to time. Nome administration fell under three branches: the bureaus of the nomarch, οἰκόνομος, and βασίλικος γραμματεύς.
In theory the nomarch was in charge of agricultural production (the major reason the Greco-Roman world was interested in Egypt). He distributed responsibility through a hierarchy to his various subordinates: the toparchs and the komarchs. The οἰκόνομος supervised finances through his network of clerks (ἀντιγράφεις). The βασίλικος γραμματεύς, "royal scribe", kept the necessary records, particularly of land productivity (see GHD, nos. 77, 80, 86, 91, 93, 95, 100, 110, 138). His subordinates were the τοπογραμματεύς, "local scribe", (see GHD, nos. 68, 91, 110) and κομογραμματεύς, "village scribe", (see GHD, nos. 68, 70, 80, 85, 90, 91, 96, 98, 109, 110). For a glimpse of the dynamics of

This is not to say, however, that government officials did not have traditional secretaries in the sense of letter writers. Quite to the contrary, officials from the emperor down evidently made extensive use of secretaries.[8] An inscription containing the request of the priests of Isis at Philae reads:

> Since those travelling to Philae — strategoi and epistatai and Thebarchs and basilikoi grammateis and ... all other officials and their accompany escorts ... — compel us to extend hospitality to them against our will, whence it has come to pass that our sanctuary is impoverished ... we ask of you, greatest gods, if it seem best to you to instruct Noumenios, your kinsman and epistolographos, to write to Lochos, your kinsman and strategos of the Thebaid, not to harass us...[9]

This inscription is typical of most inscriptions from this period,[10] and indicates several things. One, a distinction is made between an ἐπιστολόγραφος ('a letter writer') and a βασίλικος γραμματεύς ('a royal scribe'). Two, the βασίλικος γραμματεύς is called an official and listed before the police commander, indicating a position of some rank. Three, the priests of Philae request the king to have his ἐπιστολόγραφος write a letter. Four, since the ἐπιστολόγραφος is cited by name and called a kinsman (*i.e.*, an official of rank), he probably is an official in charge of a department of letter writing secretaries.[11]

---

this system, see the memorandum of various instructions from a διοικήτης to an οἰκονόμος in the Fayum; Stanley M. Burstein, ed., *The Hellenistic Age from the Battle of Ipsos to the Death of Kleopatra* VII, Translated Documents of Greece and Rome Series, no. 3 (Cambridge: Cambridge University, 1985) no. 101, esp. *ll.* 44–46 and 259–60.

[8] For examples of professional secretaries in official business, see *inter per multi* PZen. 56 and 122.

[9] Burstein, *Hellenistic Age*, no. 108. It is actually a painted "inscription" which contains the response of the king as well as a copy of this original request.

[10] The purpose for these inscriptions may be seen in the advice of Antiochus I to Meleagros, governor of the Hellespontine satrapy: "You, however, would do well ... and to make a copy of the terms of his grant and inscribe it on a stele and place it in the sanctuary in order that you may retain securely for all time what has been granted. Farewell" (Burstein, *Hellenistic Age*, no. 21). Evidently, the original letter was considered temporary until the document could be inscribed: "A sealed copy of the treaty [is to be given] to the Rhodian [ambassadors] in order that it may be preserved until it is copied onto the stelae" (ibid., no. 37).

[11] Since it is only tangential to the topic and will not be discussed elsewhere, perhaps a word should be said here about the role of the secretary in writing inscriptions. First, if a secretary composed the original letter recorded in a given inscription, which is likely, it is not ascertainable from the inscription, for usually all but the essential epistolary elements are stripped away (see *e.g.*, ibid., no. 9, which has a bare address and a final ἔρρωσο). Furthermore, royal letters speak with a strong imperial presence, having no signs of personal distance; *e.g.*, "I, the king, say" or perhaps "the king says".

Many of the commemorative stelae include at the end of the decrees instructions that the

In an incidental comment during Suetonius' discussion of the morning routine of Vespasian (emp. A.D. 69–79), "... then after reading his letters and the reports of all the officials, he admitted his friends",[12] the clear implication is that someone else, certainly a secretary, had written at least that draft of the letter. This implied use of a royal secretary is confirmed by Plutarch (fl. A.D. 50–120), who even discusses the life of Alexander's secretary, Eumenes, at length,[13] although no doubt because Eumenes had assumed military significance after the death of his master. Plutarch describes Alexander's secretary as eloquent, particularly in writing, a requirement no doubt of an imperial secretary. Evidently Eumenes was used extensively by Alexander to write letters, for Plutarch declares: "θαυμάσαι δὲ αὐτὸν ἔστιν ὅτι καὶ μέχρι τοιουτῶν ἐπιστολῶν τοῖς φίλοις ἐσχόλαξεν, ..."[14]

The more exact nature of the position of royal secretary is described in, among other places, a note on *amicitia principum* in the classic commentary on the Letters of Pliny the Younger (ca. A.D. 61–112) by A. N. Sherwin-White:

---

proceedings shall be recorded by the secretary. "This decree shall be inscribed by the secretary for the prytany on a stone stele and set up on the Akropolis, and for the inscribing of the stele there shall be paid out by the exetastes and the trittyarchs 20 drachmas" (ibid., no. 4); see also ibid., nos. 6, 8.2, 11, 13, 17, 62, 100 *inter alii*. The secretary is spoken of as responsible for the recording of the official decree, usually meaning the creation of the stelae, "... this decree shall be inscribed by the secretary and placed..." See ibid., nos. 4.4.27; 6.53; 11.68; 13.4; 31.3; 32.7–9; 55.6–7; 56.42–43, 64–65; 59.11; 77.9.

Although the inscriptions do seem to imply that the secretary was to record the decree, an inscription clarifies, as might be expected, that the 'secretary' was the title for the official responsible for overseeing the work, not the one actually inscribing the stone: "Since the sanctuary of Athena Lindia, being very ancient and distinguished, has been adorned with many fine dedications ... but since it happens that the most ancient dedications ... have been destroyed because of time ... it has been resolved ... two men shall be chosen, ... they shall prepare a stele of Lartian stone, in accordance with the architect's specifications, and they shall record on it this decree, ... and they shall prepare the account in the presence of the secretary..." (ibid., no. 46A.2–7).

[12] Suet. *Vespasian* 21.

[13] Plut. *Eum.* 11.1–2; "Eumenes, however, although closely besieged in a stronghold which had grain, water in abundance, and salt, but no other edible, not even a relish to go with the grain, nevertheless, with what he had, managed to render the life of his associates cheerful, inviting them all by turns to his own table, and seasoning the meal thus shared with conversation which had charm and friendliness. For he had a pleasant face, not like that of a war-worn veteran, but delicate and youthful, and all his body had, as it were, artistic proportions, with limbs of astonishing symmetry; and though he was not a powerful speaker, still he was insinuating and persuasive, as one may gather from his letters".

[14] Plut. *Alex.* 42.1; "And it is astonishing that he [Alexander] had time to write so many letters for his friends. ..." See also Plut. *Alex.* 22.1–2; 29.3; 29.4; 34.1; 37.2; 39.3; 42.1.

To the prefects of the *vigiles, annona,* fleet or fleets, and praetorian guard, with the head librarian and Greek secretary, Trajan added the imperial secretaries *ab epistulis* and *a rationibus,* offices now promoted to equestrian status.[15]

The royal secretary was usually an official who oversaw a staff of secretaries, although he might well be skilled in the art himself. Despite the usurpation of the title by the controlling official, these references clearly indicate that secretaries were heavily used by the emperor and his subordinate officials.

bb) Business

Even a cursory examination of the papyri reveals a widespread use of secretaries in the business sector. For example, a first century papyrus contains a letter from Eudaemon, of Marcus Antonius Spendon, a collector.[16] The use of all three names indicates that Eudaemon was a slave-secretary and was used to write the business letter for his master.[17] Furthermore, the use of the illiteracy formulae in the predominant number of papyrus business letters indicates the pervasive use of a secretary in the business sector.[18]

b) Private Correspondence

In the Greco-Roman world, the private sector consisted of two definite socio-economic divisions: the upper classes and the lower classes. The use of secretaries by these two classes, because of their concurrent economic variables, are considered separately.

aa) The Upper Classes

Clearly the upper classes could afford to use a secretary. The questions are whether they preferred to use one and how pervasive was the practice. In a pseudonomous letter of the early second Christian century,

---

[15] Sherwin-White, *The Letters of Pliny,* 222. In a note to letter 3.5.7, he explains that the *amici principis* formed the advisory circle of the emperor (see also his note to letter 1.17.2 and Juvenal's parody, *Sat.* 4).

[16] *POxy.* 3273.

[17] So argues J. A. Strauss, "Notes sur quelques papyrus concernant l'escalvage dans l'Egypt romaine", *Zeitschrift für Papyrologie und Epigraphik* 32 (1978): 259–62.

[18] Many more papyri can be cited to indicate the widespread use of secretaries in the business sector, but this point is not disputed. For a fuller discussion of the illiteracy formula and its implications for the role of the secretary; see below, pp. 73–76.

'Speusippus' reports that his health is poor but that he is still able to 'write' because "my tongue and the faculties of my head are intact..."[19] Thus to write a letter, the author needed his *tongue* and not his *hand*.

The author of a letter requesting his two recipients to send someone to help him during his recovery from a serious accident[20] evidently uses a secretary, either amateur or professional. The letter appears to end with the customary greetings; then an additional note, a postscript, is appended still in the original hand. The indication of a secretary comes, however, with the inclusion of a closing health-wish in a second hand, the hand no doubt of the author.

This may appear to be a simple example of the use of a secretary by a relatively illiterate person; however, the discussion of finances for the trip as well as the fact that the author was injured while riding horseback suggests a person of the upper classes who most likely then was literate. The author probably *chose* to employ a secretary, whether as the result of customary preference or because of his accident. Yet because he did not mention his use of a secretary, it may be assumed that it was not considered unusual.

When Clodius became tribune (*ca.* 58 B.C.), he wanted Cato the Younger out of Rome and removed as an influence so that he, Clodius, might further the plans of Caesar, his ally and Cato's opponent. Concerning this plan Plutarch states:

ἐξιόντι δὲ οὐ ναῦν, οὐ στρατιώτην, οὐχ ὑπηρέτην ἔδωκε πλὴν ἢ δύο γραμματεῖς μόνον, ὧν ὁ μὲν κλέπτης καὶ παμπόνηρος, ἅτερος δὲ κλωδίου πελάτης.[21]

The obvious tone is that Clodius was doing all he could to hinder the effectiveness of Cato. Evidently by sending unreliable γραμματεῖς ('secretaries'), Clodius was hobbling the work of Cato, not because Cato was illiterate or even unfamiliar with letter writing,[22] but rather because Cato customarily made extensive use of his secretaries.

---

[19] Pseudo-Socrates and the Socratics *Epistle* 31 (hereafter Ps-Socr. *Ep*.). The texts and translations of all the Cynic letters are from *The Cynic Epistles: a Study Edition*, ed. A. Malherbe, SBLSBS, no. 12 (Missoula, MT: Scholars, 1977). The letter is pseudonomous and hence of little relevance for the time of Socrates, but it was forged during the time period under consideration (*ca.* A.D. 200 [see A. Malherbe, "Introduction", in *The Cynic Epistles*, 28–29]) and thus is appropriate here.

[20] *POxy.* 3314 (fourth Christian century).

[21] Plut. *Cato Minor* 34.3; "Moreover, when Cato set out, Clodius gave him neither ship, soldier, nor assistant, except two clerks, of whom one was a thief and a rascal, and the other a client of Clodius".

[22] See, *e.g.*, Plut. *Cat. Min.* 24.1–2.

Therefore one may conclude that the use of secretaries among the upper classes was pervasive.[23] This may be supported *via negativa* by remarks in Cicero (106—43 B.C.) who comments with pride that he writes to his friends in his own hand.[24] Gordon Bahr uses this text to argue that the upper classes did not prefer to use a secretary.[25] Yet if this were a point of pride, then it could hardly have been usual custom among their peers.

bb) The Lower Classes

The situation among the lower classes is more complex. While one may assume that a member of the upper classes was literate, a member of the lower classes was more likely to be illiterate; yet even this is not always the case.[26] John Winter discusses a papyrus letter evidently written by a son to his mother.[27] Additionally, the son evidently knew his mother could not read and also anticipated that his other brother probably would be reading the letter to her, because he appends to the letter to his mother a confidential note to his brother, offering filial advice concerning his mother.

Another example of literacy among the lower classes is a papyrus of the second Christian century in the Michigan collection.[28] It has been labelled the most illiterate letter in the collection, for the spelling and grammar are quite poor. Doubtlessly, it was written by the sender herself, for a professional scribe would not have such an awkward hand, to say nothing of the marginal literacy.

---

[23] Quintilian *Institutio oratoria* 10.3.19 denonces the fashionable use of a secretary. The works of both Plinys, Cicero, Atticus, Seneca, Cato, *et alii*, indicate the widespread use of secretaries. It was not, however, unheard for a member of the upper classes to write personally, especially if the letter was quite personal; see Plut. *Demosthenes* 29.3—4.

[24] Cic. *Att.* 2.23.1.

[25] Gordon J. Bahr, "Paul and Letter Writing in the First Century", *CBQ* 28 (1966): 468. He also cites Sen. *Ad Lucilium epistolae morales* 26.8, but the appropriateness of this text is not clear.

[26] Exler, *Form*, 126, cautions "The papyri discovered in Egypt have shown that the art of writing was more widely, and more popularly, known in the past, than some scholars have been inclined to think". See *e.g.*, PZen. 6, 66, POxy. 113, 294, 394, 528, 530, 531, and esp. 3057.

[27] John G. Winter, *Life and Letters in the Papyri* (Ann Arbor: University of Michigan, 1933), 48—49. The papyrus was published in H. I. Bell, "Some Private Letters of the Roman Period from the London Collection", *Revue egyptologique*, n.s., 1 (1919): 203—6.

[28] *PMich.* 188. See also Winter, *Life and Letters*, 90.

Despite instances of literacy among the lower classes, the preponderance of evidence indicates that most members were functionally illiterate. For example, a second Christian century letter from Oxyrhynchus discusses the inability of a couple, the senders, to fill a friend's request for roses for a wedding.[29] In the modern editors' judgment, the style is rather high and contains several phrases either rare or unknown in the papyri. The papyrus concludes with a customary health-wish, in the plural, written in a second hand, indicating that the letter proper was written by a secretary.

In addition to longer, more elaborate, or more important letters, apparently the lower classes on occasion used secretaries to write even minor letters.[30] Several papyri from Oxyrhynchus are small letters of invitation.[31] Having only the barest epistolary framework and containing only the scantest of stereotyped text on a shred of papyrus, one might expect such notes to be written personally by the sender if he were able to write at all. Yet in *POxy.* 1487 the date Τῦβι η was changed to Τῦβι Θ by a second hand. Who besides the original scribe is likely to correct (or change) the date of a wedding except the author? Thus at least in this instance, one may conclude that even this little note was written with the use of a secretary.

In an opisthograph (an ancient document containing writing on both sides) found among the Oxyrhynchus papyri, the recto (the 'front' side of the sheet) contains a government record; yet apparently once disposed, the papyrus was garnered and reused. The verso (the 'back' side) contains a letter to a brother.[32] Oddly, the health-wish, in a second hand, is a *verbatim* repetition of the last line of the letter:

	ἐρρῶσθαι σε εὔχομαι ἀδελφέ.
2nd hand	ἐρρῶσθαι σε εὔχομαι ἀδελφέ.

---

[29] *POxy.* 3313. Other aspects of this papyrus are discussed in E. A. Judge, *Rank and Status*, 25.

[30] Pace J. A. Eschlimann, "La rédaction des epîtres pauliniennes: d'après une comparison avec les lettres profanes de son temps", *RB* 53 (1946): 186, who argues that "Souvent ils [ancient writers] les ecrivaient de leur main. Ainsi faisaient les gens trop pauvres pour se payer un scribe". Although a reasonable conjecture, the evidence does not support his claim.

[31] *POxy.* 1484–1487.

[32] *POxy.* 1491.

While it could be pure coincidence that the secretary and the author both chose the same formula, it is unusual for a secretary to include a closing wish if the author himself intends to do so, as indicated by the usual presence of only one closing health-wish even if the letter evidences two hands. A reconstruction suggests itself: the author is functionally illiterate and requests a secretary to write the letter. The secretary, knowing his employer is illiterate, includes a customary closing. The sender, for whatever reason — authentication? — wishes to add something in his own handwriting but is not sure of his skill; therefore he copies the secretary's formula.

One may conclude that the use of a secretary was prevalent among both the upper and lower classes, although perhaps for different reasons.[33] Both the upper and lower classes made widespread — almost exclusive — use of a secretary in the composition of business and official letters. Both upper class members and those of the lower class who were literate used a secretary in the writing of private letters, although at times they would send private letters in their own hand as well.[34]

Yet here there may be one noticeable difference: the practice of the illiterate person. It has already been noted that they appear to make equal use of a secretary in business and official correspondence; yet this could be considered required or unavoidable correspondence. What is striking is the relative lack, at least among the Oxyrhynchus papyri, of private letters from illiterate persons, that is, a letter written strictly for private, non-business reasons by a secretary for an illiterate person. This may be explained in two ways. (1) Perhaps it is a false impression. In actuality there are private letters from illiterates, but because they could not write at all, there is no change in handwriting to evidence a secretary.[35] Since illiteracy formulae were usually reserved for legal documents,[36] the secretary did not need to indicate his presence. Although there are other indicators of a secretary,[37] a limited examination of the private letters in only one hand reveal no other signs of a secretary. (2) A second explana-

---

[33] The situations engendering the use of a secretary are discussed below, pp. 97—111.

[34] For literates who used a secretary, see, *e.g.*, Cicero also *PZen.* 88 and *POxy.* 2985, and possibly *PZen.* 74 and *POxy.* 118. For literates who did not use a secretary, see, *e.g.*, (the well literate) *POxy.* 3057, (the fairly literate) *POxy.* 113, 394, 530, 531, *PZen.* 6, and (the marginally literate) *PZen.* 66, *POxy.* 294, 526, 528.

[35] A simple EPP or ερρω (ἔρρωσο), however, was quite sufficient, and evidently easily within the grasp of many illiterates. See, *e.g.*, *POxy.* 2983, also 2860, 3063, and 3066.

[36] The illiteracy formulae are discussed below, pp. 73—76.

[37] They are discussed in detail below, pp. 68—97.

tion is possible: an illiterate person did not send such types of letters. If they had such messages, they must have sent then orally.

Several factors suggest that illiterate persons preferred to send simple personal letters orally. (1) The cost of hiring a secretary plus the cost of the materials was a significant sum for a member of the lower classes, particularly since illiterates frequently found themselves near the poorer end of their class. (2) The expense required to contract a scribe or the time needed to visit an obliging friend might have been seen as frivolous when the letter was not "required". (3) Even in modern times those who cannot read or write often prefer oral messages, trusting less the medium they cannot understand (or control). Lastly, (4) the types of philophronetic (personal) messages common to a private letter could as easily be given and conveyed orally, and due to the use of carriers, was perhaps as likely to arrive. If the message was lost or forgotten in transit, the loss probably would not have been serious. Consequently, when an illiterate man sent a simple personal letter, he easily might have preferred an oral message since it was considerably less expensive, much more convenient, and probably as reliable as one in writing.

2. The Employment of a Secretary

The use of a secretary is complicated further by the flexibility available to the sender. He could grant to the secretary complete, much, little, or no control over the content, style, and/or form of the letter. Moreover in modern studies secretarial usage in antiquity has been mainly speculation and conjecture, with little concrete evidence on which to base a conclusion.

The examination of ancient letters below reveals the role of the secretary may be categorized into four general practices.[38] (1) He dictated the letter that was then recorded *verbatim* by the secretary. If a final secretarial draft were written later, the contents remained unchanged.[39] In this role the secretary was a "recorder". (2) The writer recited his letter while the secretary made extensive notes, or he gave a rough draft to the secre-

---

[38] John McKenzie, *Light on the Epistles: a Reader's Guide* (Chicago: Thomas More, 1975), 14–15, rejecting the existence of shorthand, suggests three otherwise (somewhat) similar uses. Otto Roller, *Formular*, 5, lists three uses roughly parallel to recording, editing and co-authoring.

[39] See, e.g., Cic. *Att.* 5.12; 7.13a; 8.15; 12.32.1; 13.32; *Fam.* 11.32.2; and *QFr.* 2.2.1; 2.15b.1; 2.16; 3.1.

tary.[40] In this role the secretary was an "editor", because he was responsible for the composition of the final draft and thus minor decisions about syntax, vocabulary, and style. He remained, however, within the strict guidelines of the writer's oral or written draft. The secretary could also work as (3) a "co-author", employing the same type of procedure as (2) except that the resulting secretarial notes were far less extensive.[41] The form, syntax, vocabulary, and style as well as specific pieces of content may be contributed by the secretary, who usually was more experienced in matters of epistolary expression, while the general content and perhaps argumentation remained the author's. Finally, (4) in some instances the secretary was the "composer". In this role, the author instructed his secretary to send a letter without specifying the exact contents.[42] This method was possible because of the highly stereotyped nature of most Greco-Roman letters, including personal letters.

a) The Secretary as a Recorder

The composition[43] of letters in antiquity by dictation[44] is not disputed.[45] McKenzie plainly states:

> Dictation ... was the normal means of producing letters. Many of the ancient letters which have been preserved were letters of the poor, so dictation was not the luxury which it is in modern times.[46]

The question concerning dictation is not its existence but its nature. Was it dictation *syllabatim*, or was it dictation *viva voce*? In other words, was the text dictated at the speed of normal handwriting, or was the text dictated at the speed of normal speech? Obviously there is a considerable

---

[40] See, *e.g., PZen.* 111 and *PTebt.* 13.

[41] See, *e.g., PZen.* 57; also see Cic. *Att.* 11.5.

[42] See, *e.g.*, Cic. *Att.* 3.15; 11.3.

[43] Around the turn of the century, E. I. Robson drew a distinction between composition and dictation. In 'dictation' Robson meant the author drafted the letter by speaking extemporaneously, and in 'composition' he wrote personally the drafts. Since the aim of the present study is the recording of the letter and not the method of composition, Robson's distinction will not be pressed. E. Iliff Robson, "Composition and Dictation in New Testament Books", *JTS*, o.s., 18 (1917): 288–301.

[44] Again not dictation in Robson's meaning (see n. 43 immediately above), but in the usual sense of the oral recitation of a text for the purpose of having it recorded by another.

[45] There are many references to dictation, particularly in the letters of Cicero. *E.g.*, Cic. *Att.* 5.12; 7.13a; 8.15; 12.32.1; 13.32; *Fam.* 11.32.2; *QFr.* 2.2.1; 2.15b.1; 2.16; 3.1. See also Pliny *Ep.* 3.5 [concerning the elder Pliny] and Plut. *Caesar* 17.3–4.

[46] John McKenzie, *Light*, 13–14.

difference in speed. Furthermore, probably any secretary — or for that matter, anyone who could write — could take dictation *syllabatim*, but a specially prepared secretary trained in a complex technique was needed to take dictation *viva voce*.

aa) Syllabatim

In a passing description of curriculum requirements in ancient Athens, C. E. Robinson comments:

> Schooling began when a boy was six, and its elementary stage lasted until he was fourteen. In the grammar-school he would learn to write with a metal instrument on a tablet of soft wax. *Lessons in dictation followed.*[47]

Although he offers no explanation of what he meant by 'dictation', no doubt it probably meant a drill, in which a teacher slowly read a text while the students wrote. Thus it is not incorrect to assume that anyone who could write probably also could take dictation recited *syllabatim* ('syllable by syllable').

Cicero explains to Atticus that when he composed a letter to Varro "... dictavi ... Spintharo syllabatim."[48] Such a procedure was naturally rather slow. Consequently, it must be this form of dictation to which Seneca was referring, when he advises Lucilius that it is better to say a thing properly than to say much, adding:

> Aliquis tam insulsus intervenit quam qui illi singula verba vellenti, tanquam dicaret, non diceret, ait, "Dic, numquid dicas".[49]

Pliny the Elder (A.D. 23/24—79) states that Julius Caesar (102?-44 B.C.) was of the habit of dictating to his secretaries (*librariis*) four letters at once, if the matters were serious, and seven letters at once if he was at leisure.[50] Gordon Bahr argues that this probably refers to dictation *syllabatim*, for he "could not have been dictating fluently as we are accustomed to doing it, but if he did it word for word, or syllable by syllable,

---

[47] C. E. Robinson, *Everyday Life in Ancient Greece* (Oxford: Clarendon, 1933), 139. [Italics are mine.]

[48] Cic. *Att.* 13.25.3; "... I dictated it to Spintharus syllable by syllable".

[49] Sen. *Ep.* 40.10; "Although someone without taste may come along, like the person who said when he [Vinicius, the stammerer] was pulling out individual words, as if he were dictating, not speaking, 'Tell me, you do not actually have anything to say, do you?'" So also argues Bahr, "Letter Writing", 470.

[50] Pliny *H.N.* 7.25.91.

then a man of Caesar's ability would be able to dictate several letters at once".[51]

The existence in antiquity of dictation at the speed of writing is thus substantiated, and probably has never really been doubted. It is the art of dictation *viva voce* that is usually debated.

bb) Viva Voce

The use of dictation at the speed of speech in Greco-Roman antiquity requires the existence of a secretarial system capable of recording text at that speed, or to use modern terms, the existence of a practical system of shorthand.[52]

The history of shorthand, or tachygraphy as it is often called, in classical and even post-classical antiquity, has been shrouded in obscurity and attended by several difficult problems. There is a thorough knowledge of the Roman system of shorthand, *notae Tironiannae*, but even the very existence of a contemporaneous Greek system is uncertain. Were there three different systems of Greek shorthand, as the scanty evidence may suggest, or only one system which underwent three stages of development? How was the Greek system related to the Roman? Was the Greek system a genuine tachygraphic system, that is, could it record *viva voce*, or was it only a method of cryptic or economical script?[53]

Perhaps the place to begin is to define what was meant here by 'tachygraphy' or shorthand. The term may refer only to an *Engschrift*, a brachygraphy, a script made up of abbreviations designed apparently for the main purpose of conserving space.[54] In the sense here, however, it will denote:

---

[51] Bahr, "Letter Writing," 470–71. It must be remembered, however, that the pivotal issue is not Caesar's ability but the statements of Pliny. Since Pliny is known for preferring facts that are extraordinary if not hyperbolic (e.g., *H.N.* 7.21), it is questionable whether dictating seven letters *syllabatim* qualifies.

[52] Since the ultimate intention is to consider the possibility of Paul's use of dictation *viva voce*, the task is actually more specific: to demonstrate a system of *Greek* shorthand available in the first Christian century, a system prevalent enough to have been available to Paul.

[53] Although not germane to the question of the role of a secretary, one might further ask: was the Greek system phonetic, syllabic, alphabetic, *ad verbum*, or phraseologic? See the excellent albeit now outdated article by F. W. G. Foat, "On Old Greek Tachygraphy", *JHS* 21 (1901): 238.

[54] *Cod. Vat. Gr.* 1809 is a good representative.

a means merely or primarily of gaining speed, by the use of either purely sematographic forms, or of some method of systematically reducing the extent of outline required for the representation of the spoken sound, a true tachygraphy.[55]

Therefore to clarify the term 'tachygraphy', the following parameters are used. One, since brevity normally is directly proportional to rapidity, the term tachygraphy includes brachygraphy with the exception of those systems of very small script designed solely for extreme compactness, since such efforts at minute writing surely hindered speed. For example, the elder Pliny contends:

Oculorum acies vel maxime fidem excedentia invenit exempla. in nuce inclusam Iliadem Homeri carmen in membrana scriptum tradit Cicero.[56]

Two, cryptographs are excluded. While perhaps shorter than the corresponding word, they are frequently far more cumbersome to write and thus more time consuming.[57] Three, quasi-tachygraphic systems are excluded, that is, those systems that employ a limited number of symbols within the usual script. Symbols were frequently used to replace common declensional or verb endings. While they were certainly tachygraphic, their use was too limited and hence the script as a whole would not have been fast enough. Finally, four, with some reservation syllabic systems are excluded. Because of their very nature, they were faster than the common hand but could not have reached the speed of speech.

With these parameters in mind, tachygraphy is used in the present work for all systems of continuous nonstandard writing employed in an-

---

[55] Foat, "Greek Tachygraphy", 239. This would be a functional equivalent of modern shorthand or the Greek shorthand known from the tenth century MS *Cod. Paris Graec.* 1056 that claims (according to the reading of Michael Gitlbauer, *Die drei Systeme der griechische Tachygraphie*, Denkschriften der kaiserliche Akademie der Wissenschaften, no. 44 [Vienna: C. Gerold's Son, 1896], 25) that the text (a tachygraphic text) was written down at the rate of 27, 290 words an hour, three times the rate of usual speech! The writer himself appends: ε γαϱ ψε γαϱ μα τα ες τα να γον στυ κον δυ α ε Θυ μυσυ α τα α πε Θα να (that is, εγϱαψε γϱαμματα ες ταναγνωστου κονδυα ε – Θημισεα αυτα απιΘανα – ενακοσια or "that he wrote a passage 900 times by the water clock five times replenished".) See Foat, "Greek Tachygraphy", 239. Regardless of how one views this [impossible] claim, it implies the existence of some form of functional tachygraphy.

[56] Pliny, *H.N.* 7.21; "Keenness of sight has achieved instances [of minute writing] transcending belief of the highest degree. Cicero records that a parchment copy of Homer's poem *The Iliad* was enclosed in a nutshell." See also Pliny *Ep.* 3.5.17. These parameters and resulting definition of tachygraphy are modified from Foat, "Greek Tachygraphy", 238–40.

[57] The cryptographs in the magical papyri, for example, were part of a well developed system; yet, surely they could not have been faster than the common hand.

tiquity to increase the speed (and concomitantly the ease) of writing, with the goal of attaining at least the speed of speech.[58] Thus dictation *viva voce* required the reproduction of the spoken text by some means of tachygraphy. It was in this sense that H. G. Liddell and R. Scott define a ταχυγράφος as a shorthand writer.[59]

The existence of a working system of *Latin* shorthand by the first Christian century capable of recording dictation *viva voce* is indisputable. Five examples are sufficient. (1) In a letter discussing the marvelous things invented by slaves, Seneca speaks of a shorthand system certainly capable of recording a speech: "Quid verborum notas quibus quamvis citata excipitur oratio et celeritatem linguae manus sequitur?"[60]

(2) The same idea is clearly implied by Seneca's remark that when Janus addressed the Senate the speech was so eloquent "quae notarius persequi non potuit".[61] Since Seneca's purpose is to impress the reader with the oratorical skill of Janus, it must be presumed that a secretary could have followed a normal speech without difficulty. Thus unquestionably by the middle of the first Christian century, there was a working system of Latin shorthand that was so efficient that a secretary could even record a speech in the Roman Senate,[62] a considerably more difficult task than merely recording a dictated letter.

---

[58] Perhaps the best singular work on the history and development of shorthand from ancient until modern times is Chr. Johnen, *Geschichte der Stenographie: im Zusammenhang mit der allgemeinen Entwicklung der Schrift und der Schriftkürzung*, (Berlin: F. Schrey, 1911). Each section includes a comprehensive (albeit rather dated) bibliography. E. M. Thompson, *An Introduction to Greek and Latin Paleography* (Oxford: Oxford University, 1912; reprint, New York: Burt Franklin, 1973), 71*ff*. has a short discussion on tachygraphy and a good German bibliography, although pre-1906. See also H. W. Johnston, *Latin Manuscripts: an Elementary Introduction to the Use of Critical Editions*, The Inter-Collegiate Latin Series (Chicago: Scott, Foresman & Co., 1897), 27*ff*.

[59] LSJ, s.v. "ταχυγράφος". The earliest evidence they cite is Lydus, Joannes Laurentius (Historicus) *de Magistratibus populi Romani* (6th Christian century), ed. R. Wünsch (Leipzig: n.p., 1903).

[60] Sen. *Ep.* 40.25 (*ca.* A.D. 63/4); "What about signs for words, with which a speech is taken down, however rapid, and the hand follows the speed of the tongue?"

[61] Sen. *Apolocol.* 9.2, written shortly after the death of Claudius in A.D. 54; "... that the secretary is not able to follow him".

For the use of the term *notarius* for a shorthand writer, see also Sen. *Ep.* 90.25; Suet. *Tit.* 3; Paulus, *Digesta* 29.1.40 (*ca.* A.D. 210); Ausonius, *Epigrammata* 146 († *ca.* A.D. 395); and PW, s.v. "Kurzschrift", by Weinberger, 11/2: 2217−31.

[62] So Arthur Mentz, *Die tironischen Noten: eine Geschichte der römischen Kurzschrift* (Berlin: de Gruyter, 1944), 66 and Arthur Stein, "Stenographie", 182. Other references, which alone are questionable, may be cited for additional support: Manilius, *Astronomicon* 4.197−99; Martial, *Epigrammata* 14.208 (*ca.* A.D. 84/85); and Quint. *Inst.* 10.3.19.

(3) In his discussion of the daily life of Julius Caesar, Plutarch relates:

... ὠχεῖτο δὲ μεθ' ἡμέραν ἐπὶ τὰ φρουρία καὶ τὰς πόλεις καὶ τοὺς χάρακας, ἑνὸς αὐτῷ συγκαθημένου παιδὸς τῶν ὑπογράφειν ἅμα διώκοντος εἰθισμένων, ἑνός δ' ἐξόπισθεν ἐφεστηκότος στρατιώτου ξίφος ἔχοντος.[63]

(4) Plutarch further lauds Caesar by exclaiming:

ἐν ἐκείνῃ δὲ τῇ στρατείᾳ προσεξήσκησεν ἱππαζόμενος τὰς ἐπιστολὰς ὑπαγορεύειν καὶ δυσὶν ὁμοῦ γράφουσιν ἐξαρκεῖν, ὡς δὲ Ὄππιός φησι, καὶ πλείοσι· λέγεται δὲ καὶ τὸ διὰ γραμμάτων τοῖς φίλοις ὁμιλεῖν Καίσαρα πρῶτον μηχανήσασθαι, τὴν κατὰ πρόσωπον ἔντευξιν ὑπὲρ τῶν ἐπειγόντων τοῦ καιροῦ διά τε πλῆθος ἀσχολιῶν καὶ τῆς πόλεως τὸ μέγεθος μὴ περιμένοντος.[64]

(5) Where Suetonius recounts the multitudinous virtues and expertises of Titus, he adds:

E pluribus comperi, notis quoque excipere velocissime solitum, cum amanuensibus sius per ludum iocumque certantem, imitarique chirographa quaecumque vidisset, ac saepe profiteri maximum falsarium esse potuisse.[65]

Yet the existence of Latin shorthand may probably be pushed back into the first century B.C. The earliest important text is found in Plutarch's discussion of the speech of Cato the Younger, which was delivered on December 5, 63 B.C.:

Τοῦτον μόνον ὧν Κάτων εἶπε διασώζεσθαί φασι τὸν λόγον, Κικέρωνος τοῦ ὑπάτου τοὺς διαφέροντας ὀξύτητι τῶν γραφέων σημεῖα προδιδάξαντος ἐν μικροῖς καὶ βραχέσι τύποις πολλῶν γραμμάτων ἔχοντο δύναμιν, εἶτα ἄλλον ἀλλαχόσε τοῦ βουλευτηρίου σποράδην ἐμβάλοντος· οὔπω γὰρ ἤσκουν οὐδ' ἐκέτηντο τοὺς καλουμένους σημειογράφους, ἀλλὰ τότε πρῶτον εἰς ἴχνος τι καταστῆναι λέγουσιν· ...[66]

---

[63] Plut. *Caes.* 17.4–5: "Most of his sleep, at least, he got in cars or litters, ... and in the daytime he would have himself conveyed to garrisons, cities, or camps, one slave who was accustomed to write from dictation as he travelled sitting by his side, and one soldier standing beside him with a sword". The brevity of Plutarch's remarks prevent the use of this passage as certainly indicating the taking of dictation *viva voce*.

[64] Plut. *Caes.* 17.4–5; "Horsemanship, moreover, had been easy for him from boyhood; ... And in the Gallic campaigns he practiced dictating letters on horseback and keeping two secretaries at once busy, or, as Oppius says, even more. We are told, moreover, that Caesar was the first to devise intercourse with his friends by letter, since he could not wait for personal interviews on urgent matters owing to the multitude of his occupations and the great size of the city". A similar reference has been construed by some to mean dictation *syllabatim*; see above, p. 26 n. 51.

[65] Suet. *Tit.* 3.2; "I have heard from many sources that he used also to write shorthand with great speed and would amuse himself by playful contests with his secretaries; also that he could imitate any handwriting that he had ever seen and often declared that he might have been the prince of forgers".

[66] Plut. *Cat. Min.* 23.3–5; "This is the only speech of Cato which has been preserved,

Plutarch's use of the term σημειογράφος indicates that he was familiar with the practice of shorthand.[67] The historicity of Plutarch's account is not disputed.[68] This text is dated *ca.* A.D. 100 but his sources may be much earlier. Plutarch uses in his discussion the terms, φάσι and λέγουσιν, expressions he employs frequently to indicate his use of sources. Indeed, since Plutarch makes extensive use of Thrasea Paetus as a source in the following chapters, *Cat. Min.* 25 and 27, and since Paetus similarly uses Munatius Rufus, a personal friend of Cato, Bahr thinks that "the material in Plutarch rests ultimately on an eyewitness account".[69] Bahr, however, argues that this particular text need not refer to true shorthand. He supposes that Cicero uses several secretaries to record the speech, because one secretary would not have been sufficient.[70] That is, secretaries did not yet possess the tools necessary to record something *verbatim*. Several secretaries were used so that Cicero could then compare their texts and thereby, perhaps also with the aide of his own recollection, virtually recreate the original speech.

Several points may be made against Bahr's assertion. (1) The speech is introduced with the words: "... εὐθὺς ἵετο τῷ λογῳ μετ' ὀργῆς καὶ πάθους ..."[71] Taking shorthand from a passionate and angry speaker was quite difficult, a problem recognized more than a hundred years later by Seneca.[72] (2) Cicero was a man of considerable financial resources, and the employment of more than one secretary could easily

---

we are told, and its preservation was due to Cicero the consul, who had previously given to those clerks who excelled in rapid writing instruction in the use of signs, which, in small and short figures, comprised the force of many letters; these clerks he had then distributed in various parts of the senate-house. For up to that time the Romans did not employ or even possess what are called shorthand writers, but then for the first time, we are told, the first steps toward the practice were taken". See also Arthur Stein, "Die Stenographie im römischen Senat", *Archiv für Stenographie* 56 (1905): 177–86, and Otto Morgenstern, "Cicero und die Stenographie", *Archiv für Stenographie* 56 (1905): 1–6.

[67] So argues also Mentz, *Noten*, 83. Although Plutarch does define the term here, it is probably only another example of his tendency to explain offices and functions.

[68] It was well established by Hermann W. G. Peter, *Die Quellen Plutarchs in den Biographien der Römer* (Halle: Waisenhaus, 1865) 65–68, and is also discussed in Mentz, *Noten*, 39.

[69] Bahr, "Letter Writing", 471. He briefly discusses this entire topic.

[70] For further evidence of the use of several secretaries at once, see Cic. *Pro Sulla* 41–42 and Suet. *Caes.* 55.

[71] Plut. *Cat. Min.* 23.1; "... Cato arose to give his opinion, and launched at once into a passionate and angry speech..."

[72] Sen. *Apocol.* 9.2 (*ca.* A.D. 54). See below, p. 51 n. 70. The existence of Latin shorthand by this time is not disputed.

have been a safety factor. In letter writing if a secretary missed something, he could ask the author to repeat it. One could not, however, stop a Roman orator, especially since recording the speech would have been seen as the most peripheral of events; the delivery was everything. This brings up the third point. (3) Plutarch is discussing *Cato* delivering a *speech* in the Roman Senate, not Julius Q. Publius dictating a *letter* to a secretary. Surely there would have been a difference in the speed of delivery, not to mention the diction, and that would have made it difficult for one to keep up for a sustained period. (4) While Plutarch mentions only the recording of Cato's speech (a natural enough occurence since he was discussing the life of Cato), the text could mean that Cicero was recording the entire meeting, that is, all the speeches. If this were the case, the employment of more than one secretary is certainly understandable. Nevertheless whether Cato's speech represents the true use of Latin shorthand, the recording of Cicero's speech in defense of Milo, eleven years later, is widely accepted as an instance of functional shorthand.[73]

Cicero apparently strongly propagated the use of Latin shorthand. In a letter to Atticus, he mentions that he is dictating the letter rather than writing it with his own hand.[74] He includes the observation that he usually wrote personally to *Atticus*, thereby implying that he commonly dictated his letters to others.[75] His connection to the rise of Latin shorthand is further strengthened by the strong tradition that his freedman and personal secretary, Tiro, was the inventor of the Latin system.[76] Tiro's name has since become synonomous with a system of Latin shorthand, Tironian Notes.[77]

---

[73] Bahr, "Letter Writing", 472. He also cites Asconius Pedianus who in his discussion of this same speech adds "Manet autem illa quoque excepta eius oratio". *In Milonianum* 36.27—28 (*ca.* A.D. 57/8).

[74] Cic. *Att.* 2.2.1: "...ut dictarem hanc epistulam et non, ut ad te soleo, ipse scriberem".

[75] See, *e.g.*, Cic. *Att.* 10.8 that appears to be *ippsissima verba Ciceroni* and yet apparently was written by a secretary. This letter is discussed below, pp. 167—68.

[76] Eusebius *Chronica* 156 and Isidor (*ca.* 602—36) *Etymologiae* 1.22.1; Isidor notes that the system employed in his day had undergone revision since its invention by Tiro. See also Bahr, "Letter Writing", 472, n. 52. Dio Cassius *Roman History* 55.7 credits Maecenas, the friend of Augustus, with the invention of a system of σημεῖα for speed writing. Dio is probably correct that Maecenas used such a system, but the texts dating the invention earlier to Tiro are to be preferred.

[77] Arthur Mentz, *Die Geschichte der Kurzschrift* (Wolfenbüttel: Heckners, 1949), 18—19, in his discussion of the Tironian notes indicates that Jacques Gohory, a French scholar, first coined this term in 1550. The notes were first published in 1603 by Gruter, *Notae Roma-*

How does a demonstrated system of Latin shorthand relate to the investigation of a corresponding system of Greek shorthand? In his article on Greek tachygraphy,[78] Foat addresses this problem in two ways: he first examines the evidence for Greek shorthand, and then he argues, through analogy from the Latin system, that a Greek system predates the Latin.

The last century saw the labors of Kopp, Blass, Gardthausen, Schmitz, Wattenbach, Lehmann, Ruess, Giry, Tardif, Chatelain, and especially Gomperz, Gitlbauer, and Wessely among others[79] attempt to clarify the nature and development of Greek tachygraphy. Yet they had no evidence earlier than late Byzantine manuscripts. In 1883, however, a marble slab found on the Acropolis, dated to the fourth century B.C., gave concrete evidence that some early form of Greek tachygraphy existed in pre-Christian times.[80] A comparison with similar systems in the tenth Christian century showed in the opinion of some that it contained a syllabic system of shorthand.[81] This has, however, been disputed. Notably Mentz argues that the inscription is not an example of tachygraphy but rather an early attempt, during the tumultuous times surrounding the Pelopponesian War, to reform the Greek language. "Es handelt sich freilich nicht, wie einige gemeint haben, um eine Kurzschrift". He supposes that these early efforts at language reform had been forgotten because they had failed.

... Beide Reformversuche haben, soviel wir wissen, keinen Erfolg gehabt, nicht einmal einen vorübergehenden. Und das ist erklärlich. Die Schrift der delphischen Tafeln bedeutete eine Erschwernis des Erlernens, die Schrift des Akropolissteines machte das Wiederlesen unsicherer, da kürzere und gleichmäßiger gebildete Zeichen einer Schrift weniger gut voneinander zu unterscheiden sind als umständlichere mit mehr Merkmalen versehene, die möglichst verschiedenartig geformt sind".[82]

---

norum Veterum quibus litera verbum facit, Tulii Tironis et Annaei Senecae erutasque nunc primum editaeque. See also Mentz, *Noten*. Examples may be seen in Foat, "Greek Tachygraphy", 261 n.3; and in Isaac Pitman, *A History of Shorthand*, 3rd ed. (London: Isaac Pitman & Sons, 1895).

[78] Foat, "Greek Tachygraphy", 242–61.

[79] Complete bibliographic data can be found in the comprehensive bibliography in ibid., 265–67.

[80] The text is published in Arthur Mentz, "Die Grabschrift eines griechischen Tachygraphen", *Archiv für Stenographie* 54 (1902): 49. A fascimile with an edited text is given in Foat, "Greek Tachygraphy", 246.

[81] The debate over its nature is summarized in V. Gardthausen, "Tachygraphie oder Brachygraphie des Akropolis-Steines", *Archiv für Stenographie* 56 (1905): 81–84.

[82] Mentz, *Kurzschrift*, 10–12.

If the Acropolis stone is uncertain evidence, papyrus fragments from the Fayum, Egypt, dated to the fifth (sixth?) century B.C.[83] have since provided additional examples of a Greek syllabic system of shorthand.

These early texts, however, can be used only to indicate that early *attempts* were made at developing a functional Greek tachygraphic system; they cannot be used as evidence for a working system of tachygraphy, for they are syllabic systems. Foat, in his evaluation of syllabic systems, concludes:

> Indeed, for syllabic representation, [it] presents one of the most concise systems ever invented, being obviously superior within those limits to the favourite modern English system, 'Phonography', which uses *detached* vowel-signs. But no sooner are these limits passed than the impracticability of all three alike is manifest. And here we are face to face with *the false assumption that full syllabic representation can be the method of a practical tachygraphy*. Its formal disproof would be out of place here, but this is hardly necessary, with the example of the 'Tironian' and modern systems before us.
>
> . . .
>
> Supposing, however, that the list [of syllabic symbols] was once complete, to what extent was it [a syllabic system] capable of writing Greek *rapidly*? As already stated, it could never have been of service for verbatim 'reporting' of ordinary speech.[84]

The remaining evidence available to these nineteenth-century scholars was too tenuous. The quip by Diogenes Laertius [early 3d Christian century] that Xenophon [426?-354 B.C.] was "the first to use signs to represent spoken words"[85] is intriguing but too ambiguous to use for evidence of a shorthand system capable of taking dictation *viva voce*. This same ambiguity pertains to the use of ὀξυγράφος in the LXX version of Ps. 45:2.[86]

Thus, because he had no conclusive evidence for a functional system of Greek shorthand in the first Christian century, Foat resorts to a secondary line of argument. Although he must rely upon classical references

---

[83] *PRain.* 13.444; 3.9, 10.

[84] Foat, "Greek Tachygraphy", 248, 252. [Italics are his.]

[85] *Vitae Xenophon* 2.48; "πρῶτος ὑποσημειωσάμενος τὰ λεγόμενα εἰς ἀνθρώπους ἄγαγεν, Ἀπομνημονεύματα ἐπιγραψας". R. D. Hicks (LCL 1: 179) translates this more generally: "He was the first to take notes of, and to give to the world, the conversation of Socrates, under the title of *Memorabilia*." See also *The Oxford Classical Dictionary*, 2d ed., ed. M. Cary, N. G. L. Hammond and H. H. Scullard (Oxford: Clarendon, 1970), s.v. "Tachygraphy" by F. G. Kenyon.

[86] H. J. M. Milne, *Greek Shorthand Manuals: Syllabary and Commentary* (London: Oxford University, 1934), 1, the noted authority on Greek shorthand, likewise considers these two passages too cryptic to be decisive.

because there were no extant Greek tachygraphic texts from that period, his argument was nevertheless still rather compelling, particularly when it is further developed.

Although Plutarch claims that Cicero introduced (Latin) shorthand at Rome, he does not speak of it as an innovation but only as something new to the Romans: "οὔπω γὰρ ἤσκουν οὐδ᾽ ἐκέκτηντο τοὺς καλουμένους σημειογράφους, ἀλλὰ τότε πρῶτον εἰς ἴχνος τι καταστῆναι λέγουσιν."[87] Moreover, Plutarch uses *Greek* terms for this practice: σημειόγραφος and σημεῖον,[88] implying that the Latins borrowed the art from the Greeks.[89] One may contend that the Greek terms are a necessary anachronism by the Greek writer Plutarch, but Cicero also uses a *Greek* description for shorthand in a *Latin* letter to Atticus: "διὰ σημείων".[90] Surely a Latin innovation would not be described by a Greek name. Moreover, he employs the phrase like a *terminus technicus*, strongly indicating the use of an established form of Greek shorthand. This is by the middle of the first century B.C.[91]

An argument that Cicero borrowed and modified a Greek system is strengthened by demonstrating more than a casual connection between Cicero —a Latin writer — and the Greek language. Several examples may suffice. (1) Plutarch, in his life of Cicero, mentions an interesting interchange, on one of Cicero's tours of Greece, between Cicero and Apollonius, a Greek rhetorician:

λέγεται δὲ τὸν Ἀπολλώνιον οὐ συνιέντα τὴν Ῥωμαϊκὴν διάλεκτον δεηθῆναι τοῦ Κικέρωνος Ἑλληνιστὶ μελετῆσαι· τὸν δ᾽ ὑπακοῦσαι προθύμως, οἰόμενον οὕτως ἔσεσθαι βελτίονα τὴν ἐπανόρθωσιν·[92]

---

[87] Plut. *Cat. Min.* 23.3–5: "For up to that time the Romans did not employ or even possess what are called shorthand writers, but then for the first time, we are told, the first steps toward the practice were taken".

[88] This is the earliest known occurrence of σημειόγραφος, according to Chr. Johnen, *Allgemeine Geschichte der Kurzschrift*, 4th ed. (Berlin: F. Schrey, 1940), 20; see also idem, *Stenographie*, 130. LSJ, s.v. "σημειόγραφος," and "σημεῖον" define them as 'shorthand writer' and 'a shorthand symbol', respectively.

[89] Milne plainly evaluates the Cato incident in this way: "And who more fit than he [Cicero], *utriusque linguae peritus*, to sponsor the transfer of a Greek invention to the Roman use?" *Greek Shorthand Manuals*, 1. He further notes five points of similarity between the two systems of shorthand to support his contention that the Latin system was borrowed from the Greeks (ibid., 2).

[90] Cic. *Att.* 13.32.

[91] So also argue Bahr, "Letter Writing", 474; Milne, *Greek Shorthand Manuals*, 4–5; and V. Gardthausen, "Zur Tachygraphie der Griechen", *Hermes* 2 (1876): 444–45.

[92] Plut. *Cic.* 4.4–5; "Apollonius, we are told, not understanding the Roman language, requested Cicero to declaim in Greek, with which request Cicero readily complied..."

Cicero's willing compliance was warranted according to Plutarch, for Apollonius commended Cicero, regretting only that it was not a native Greek who had spoken so eloquently. (2) To illustrate Cicero's wit, Plutarch mentions several of Cicero's Latin puns that actually required a play on the Greek equivalents. (3) Plutarch also speaks of Cicero as being the man who supplied the Romans with appropriate Latin terms for Greek philosophical thoughts.[93] (4) Cicero occasionally himself writes sections of his letters in Greek, particularly when writing to his Greek friend, Atticus. Lastly, (5) Tiro, his trusted secretary, apparently wrote frequently in Greek, if he was not a Greek himself. For example, after Tiro returned from visiting Atticus, Cicero writes to Atticus and notes "Tiro ἐνερευθέστερον te sibi esse visum dixerat".[94] It is reasonable to infer that Cicero was giving the term Tiro himself had used, ἐνερευθέστερον.[95]

Foat's argument for the existence of Greek shorthand by the first Christian century may be extended. It is generally agreed that there was no such system during the time of Alexander the Great († 323 B.C.). W. W. Tarn comments,

> Speaking generally, one expects a speech in any ancient historian to be a fabrication, either composed by the historian himself or by a predecessor, or else some exercise from one of the schools of rhetoric which he had adopted. But, very occasionally, one does meet with a speech which is genuine. 'Genuine', of course, does not imply a verbatim report; *no such thing was known.*[96]

Yet Tarn considered one of Alexander's speeches (that Arrian reported) to be authentic for four reasons. One, Arrian introduced it as "ταῦτα εἰπών" rather than with his customary "τοιαῦτα" or "ταῦτα καὶ τοιαῦτα." Two, the speech contained words and phrases that would have been appropriate for Alexander, such as addressing his men as "Μακεδόνες". Three, the described situation was accurate and the speech might plausibly have been the subject of notes. Four, the style of the speech was Macedonian and not Greek.[97]

---

[93] Plut. *Cic.* 25.4 and 40.1–2, respectively.

[94] Cic. *Att.* 12.4; "Tiro had said you looked to him rather flushed".

[95] It is quite likely that Tiro's claim to fame with regard to shorthand ought to be the adaptation of an established Greek system of tachygraphy into Latin instead of the creation of a Latin system *de novo*.

[96] W. W. Tarn, *Alexander the Great. II: Sources and Studies* (Cambridge: Cambridge University, 1948), 286. [Italics are mine.] Tarn proposed that this particular speech, whose occasion and general content are authentic, was drawn by Arrian from an ἀπομνημονεῦμα.

[97] Ibid., 290–95.

This same rationale applies to Arrian's *Discourses of Epictetus*. One, the speeches are reported by Arrian (*ca.* A.D. 96–180) as Epictetus' (*ca.* A.D. 50–120). Two, they seem to be more in the style of Epictetus than in the well-established style of Arrian. Three, they reflect a situation where one would expect note-taking, that is, a classroom.[98] Four, they are in the koine Greek while Arrian wrote in Attic Greek.

This reapplication of Tarn's argument about Alexander's speeches broadens an existing discussion concerning the nature of the Discourses of Epictetus. Like many ancient teachers, Epictetus wrote nothing for publication,[99] but his faithful pupil, Arrian, also an accomplished historian, recorded many of his discourses and informal conversations. Extant today are four books of Διατριβαί, or *Discourses*, out of the original eight. They are not a formal presentation of Stoic philosophy or a formal curriculum for a philosophic school, but they are rather the friendly personal pedagogical interchanges between the teacher and his students, that is, they appear to be the actual "classroom" teachings of Epictetus to his students: important points received frequent repetition, a necessary practice in spoken instruction but redundant in written works, and some comments seemed little more than *obiter dicta*.

In a classic work on the nature of the *Discourses*, Hartmann argues forcibly, based upon an analysis of Arrian's extant works, that Arrian was incapable of producing a work like the *Discourses* from mere recollection.

> Fragen wir aber nach der Art der Festlegung jener 'Gespräche', so führt angesichts der riesigen Ausdehnung einzelner Kapitel, der außerordentlichen Buntheit des Inhalts mit seinen vielen Bildern, Zitaten und Anspielungen —Faktoren, die ein nachträgliches Aufzeichnen aus dem Gedächtnis höchst unwahrscheinlich, wenn nicht unmöglich erscheinen lassen — zu einer befriedigenden Lösung nur die naheliegende Annahme, daß der junge Arrian auch in der Tachygraphie, einer in Hellas seit Jahrhunderten, in Rom seit mindestens einem Jahrhundert eingebürgerten Kunst, Tüchtiges geleistet hat.[100]

---

[98] An earlier parallel exists if Diogenes Laertius (early third century A.D.) can be trusted. Xenophon (*ca.* 428–354 B.C.) took notes of the teachings of Socrates (ὑποσημειωσάμενος τὰ λεγόμενα), publishing them as the ἀπομνημονεύματα of Socrates. See Diog. *Vit. Xen.* 2.48.

[99] Oldfather suggests that Epictetus may have composed personal notes for the purpose of elaborating his arguments, for he praised Socrates for such a practice and spoke of it as customary for a philosopher; Epictetus, *The Discourses as Reported by Arrian, The Manual, and Fragments*, ed. and trans. W. A. Oldfather, 2 vols., in LCL, 1: XII.

[100] Karl Hartmann, "Arrian und Epiktet", *Neue Jahrbücher für das klassische Altertum, Geschichte und deutsche Literatur und für Pädogogik* 8 (1905): 257.

He adds that only in this way could such a philosophical layman as Arrian have reproduced the truth, freshness and color-fidelity of Epictetus' teachings as well as retained accurately the details. Arrian's other works forbid an appeal to a great memory.[101] Hartmann supports his position by noting Arrian's ability to take dictation *viva voce*. In an excursus, he addresses the expected question of whether Arrian could have known Greek shorthand:

> Finden wir nun auch schon in Jahrzehnten vor Arrian, das Lob der Stenographie selbst von Dichtern[a] besungen und von Philosophen (Seneca, *Ep.* 90.25) erörtert und betrachten Reste griechischer und römischer Stenographie nichtamtlichen Inhalts (Faulmann a. a. O.), so dürfen wir mit vielen Gebildeten seiner Zeit wohl auch unseren Arrian in Besitz der Kunst denken.
>
> [a Manilius, *Astr.* 4.197; Martial. 14.208.][102]

Hartmann was not the only scholar to hold this opinion. W. A. Oldfather, the Loeb translator of Epictetus, concludes, "That Arrian's report is a stenographic record of the *ipsissima verba* of the master there can be no doubt".[103] His reasons are (1) Arrian wrote in Attic, while the discourses are in the koine, (2) there was a marked difference in the style, especially in the use of several prepositions, and (3) the complete and utter difference in the spirit and tempo between the *Discourses* and the works of Arrian.

With this additional argument from Epictetus Foat may have been able to strengthen his conclusions. Nevertheless, he concludes that, despite the lack of primary evidence:

---

[101] Although after Hartmann's day, such a position is asserted by Brunt in his introduction: "Before his public career began [before Trajan's death in 117], Arrian had attended the classes of the Stoic teacher, Epictetus, at Nicopolis in Epirus, and was so impressed that probably at the end of each day he wrote down extensive notes of his master's lectures or sermons, trying to preserve what had been said word for word..." Arrian, *Anabasis Alexandri*, ed. and trans. P. A. Brunt, 2 vols., in LCL, 1: IX-X. Clearly Brunt had recognized the difference in their styles and credits it to a "word for word" recollection. He offers no further defense – his work was on Arrian and not Epictetus. The theory of Hartmann seems more plausible.

[102] Hartmann, "Arrian und Epiktet", 275.

[103] Oldfather, *Epictetus* (LCL), 1: XIII. He adds "We have, accordingly, in Arrian's *Discourses* ... the actual words of an extraordinarily gifted teacher upon scores, not to say hundreds, of occasions..." Whitney J. Oates, ed. and trans., *The Stoic and Epicurean Philosophers: the Complete Extant Writings of Epicurus, Epictetus, Lucretius, Marcus Aurelius* (New York: Random House, 1940), XXII, expresses a similar sentiment: "The so-called *Discourses* of Epictetus are ... an apparently almost stenographic record of his lectures and informal discussions taken down and compiled by one of his pupils, Arrian..."

There did exist in post-classical, and accepting a reasonable hypothesis, also in classical times, a Greek tachygraphy. Its invention was thus, probably, anterior to that of the Roman system, which, with the accretions and corruptions of the Middle Ages, has descended to us as the *'notae Tironiannae'*; and there are reasonable grounds for the belief that the original Roman system was directly derived from the hypothetical oldest Greek system.[104]

Although he had reservations about the speed of such a system, he does concede that it would have been as efficient as the Roman system.

As a result of these investigations, the existence of Greek shorthand in the first Christian century may be asserted with at least some force, albeit perhaps limited to the upper classes. As Foat himself recognized, some form of primary evidence was vitally needed, not only as evidence, but also to substantiate the secondary arguments.

Once again the papyri from the Egyptian sands have supplied the missing piece of data. A papyrus contract from Oxyrhynchus, dated A.D. 155, records that a former official apprenticed his slave, Chaerammon, to Apollonius, σημειογράφῳ (a writer of shorthand). This very significant text reads:

Πα[ν]εχώτης ὁ καὶ Πανάρης τῶν κεκοσμητευκότων τῆς Ὀξυρυγχειτῶν πόλεως διὰ Γεμέλλου φίλου Ἀπολλωνίῳ σημειογράφῳ χαίρειν. συνέστησά σοι Χαιράμμωνα δοῦλον πρὸς μάθησιν σημείων ὧν ἐπίσταται ὁ υἱός σου Δι[ο]νύσιος ἐπὶ χρόνον ἔτη δύο ἀπὸ τοῦ ἐνεστῶτος μηνὸς Φαμενὼθ τοῦ ὀκτωκαιδεκάτου ἔτους Ἀντωνίνου Καίσαρος τοῦ κυρίου μισθοῦ τοῦ συμπεφωνημένου πρὸς ἀλλήλους ἀργυριου δραχμῶν ἑκατὸν εἴκοσι χωρὶς ἑορτικῶν, ἐξ ὧν ἔσχες τὴν πρώτην δόσιν ἐν δραχμαῖς τεσσαράκοντα, τὴν δὲ δευτέραν λήψῃ τοῦ παιδὸς ἀνειληφότος τὸ κομεντάρ[ι]ον ὅλον ἐν δραχ[μ]αῖς τ[εσσ]αράκοντα, τὴν δὲ τρίτην λήψομαι ἐπὶ τέλει τοῦ χρόνου τοῦ παιδὸς ἐκ παντὸς λόγου πεζοῦ γράφοντος καὶ ἀναγεινώσ[κον]τος ἀμέμπτως τὰς {δὲ} λοιπὰς δραχμὰς τεσσαράκοντα. ἐὰν δὲ ἐντὸς τοῦ χ[ρ]όνου αὐτὸν απαρτισῃς οὐκ ἐκδέξομαι τὴν προκειμένην προθεσμ[ί]αν, οὐκ ἐξόντος μοι ἐντὸς τοῦ χρόνου τὸν παῖδα ἀποσπᾶν, παραμενεῖ δέ σ[ο]ι μετὰ [τὸ]ν χρό[νον] ὅσας ἐὰν ἀργήσῃ ἡμέρας ἢ μῆνας. (ἔτους) ιη Αὐτοκράτορος Καίσαρος Τίτου Αἰλίου Ἁδριανοῦ Ἀντωνείνου Σεβαστοῦ Εὐσεβοῦς Φαμενὼθ ε.[105]

---

[104] Foat, "Greek Tachygraphy", 264.

[105] *POxy*. 724; "Panechotes also called Panares, ex-cosmetes of Oxyrhynchus, through his friend Gemellus, to Apollonius, *writer of shorthand*, greeting. I have placed with you my slave Chaerammon to be taught the signs which your son Dionysius knows, for a period of two years dating from the present month Phamenoth of the 18th year of Antonius Caesar the lord at the salary agreed upon between us, 120 drachmae, not including feast-days; of which sum you have received the first instalment [*sic*] amounting to 40 drachmae, and you will receive the second instalment [*sic*] consisting of 40 drachmae when the boy has learnt the whole system, and the third you will receive at the end of the period *when the boy writes fluently in every respect and reads faultlessly*, viz. the remaining 40 drachmae. If you make him perfect within the period, I will not wait for the aforesaid limit; but it is not

Fortunately, the owner of the slave was careful to state his expectations and payment schedule. Payment was to begin as soon as Chaerammon started learning the signs (σημείων). The last payment would not be made until "the boy writes fluently in every respect and reads faultlessly". Although this text is from the mid-second century, a reasonable period of development that allows for proliferation to provincial Egypt and the establishment of an apprenticeship system requires a florishing practice of Greek shorthand in the first century. Furthermore, although this legal contract carefully explains many details, it interestingly does not define the term σημειόγραφος. The evidence of this papyrus is undergirded by various wax tablets from the second and third centuries.[106]

Although this Oxyrhynchus papyrus is usually cited as the oldest certain evidence of Greek shorthand,[107] this may not be the case. A gravestone inscription described by Arthur Mentz in an earlier work appears to mark the grave of a σημειόγραφος.[108] The date of the gravestone is the problem. From internal evidence it can be dated to the reign of either Hadrian or Aurelius,[109] and because of this uncertainty, it cannot be cited as evidence earlier than the Oxyrhynchus papyrus. A second early piece of evidence reported by Arthur Mentz in a much later discussion of Greek shorthand in the first Christian century is unfortunately hard to confirm. He contends "der älteste bekannte stenografische Papyrus, der jetzt in Bremen ist, aus der Zeit zwischen 113 und 120 stammt".[110] Yet he offers no bibliographic information to support his claim. Although a lack of documentation does not need to invalidate the claim of this respected scholar, fortunately other early evidence in now available.

Various Jewish letters dating to the second Jewish revolt have been discovered in the Judean wilderness at Wadi Murabbaʿāt. While reading

---

lawful for me to take the boy away before the end of the period, and he shall remain with you after the expiration of it for as many days or months as he may have done no work. The 18th year of the Emperor Caesar Titus Aelius Hadrianus Antoninus Augustus Pius, Phamenoth 5". [Italics are mine.]

[106] F. G. Kenyon, "Tachygraphy", *OCD*, 1033–34. Also *POxy.* 42 (A.D. 323) has three lines of shorthand at the end of this (apparent) rough draft of a letter. The editors do not translate them (p. 89 n. 10).

[107] So Bahr, "Letter Writing", 473; Ernst Haenchen, *Die Apostelgeschichte* (Göttingen: Vandenhoeck & Ruprecht, 1959), 39 n. 3; Otto Roller, *Formular*, 306–07; and A. Mentz, *Geschichte der Stenographie*, 2d ed. (Berlin: Gerdes & Hödel, 1907), 19–20.

[108] A. Mentz, "Grabschrift", 49–53. The inscription can also be found in *CIG* 3902d.

[109] Mentz, "Grabschrift", 53; thus, A.D. 117–138 or 180–192.

[110] Idem, *Kurzschrift*, 22.

through these predominantly Hebrew letters, this writer came across a parchment containing Greek tachygraphic symbols.[111] The editors had noted its stenographic nature but did not make any further textual analysis, deferring the topic to scholars in that field. To this writer's knowledge, however, no further work has been done on the parchment.[112]

In its present state, the parchment is in two pieces, and it is not certain whether it was originally one piece. The two pieces apparently had been commandeered, probably from the scrap pile, and sewn together on three sides to form a pouch no doubt to hold papyrus letters, which was a common enough practice.

Without a translation and analysis of the text, any conclusions remain tenuous. Nonetheless, two points may be made with reasonable certainty. One, the date of the parchment is most probably contiguous with the other papyrus letters found in the Wadi, that is, they probably date to the second Jewish revolt in the *early* second century. With typical scholarly reserve, Benoit and his associates conclude:

> Si nos pièces, comme il est au moins vraisemblable, sont contemporaines de l'ensemble des documents trouvés à Murabbaʿât, c'est-à-dire appartiennent au IIe siècle après J.-C., leur importance peut être grande.[113]

This certainty concerning the date is possible because of the nature of the finds in Wadi Murrabbaʿât. It was a barren place of refuge for Jews fleeing from the Romans, and thus the vast bulk of the Judeo-Greco-Roman material discovered there dates to the period surrounding the revolt.[114]

---

[111] *PMur.* 164. The parchment (with a drawing of the text) is described in Benoit, *et al., Les grottes de Murabbaʿât*, DJD, no. 2 (Oxford: Oxford University, 1961), 275–79. Since this parchment was uncovered after Mentz wrote, it cannot be the same piece to which he referred.

[112] The recent loss of Père Benoit was felt here as well. I asked a colleague, Daniel Schwartz, a lecturer in Hebrew History at the Hebrew University in Jerusalem, to inquire of the Museum where the pieces are stored to see if they knew of anyone who had worked on the fragments. To our knowledge, there has been no further work on them.

Obviously this would be a very worthwhile endeavor for any of the many papyrologists who can read Greek shorthand (!?). If further motivation is needed, the occurence of a *Chi-Rho* in the text provides it (*PMur.* 164a, *l.* 11).

[113] Benoit *et al., Murabbaʿât*, 277.

[114] The evidence is overwhelmingly from the *early* second century. There were a few Roman coins from the late second century, apparently lost by Roman soldiers garrisoned there. Since the parchments were recycled, to assume a date nearer the early end of the spectrum is very reasonable.

Two, while the content of the parchment texts remain unascertained, its stenographic nature is certain.[115] Thus a stenographic parchment is found in the remote Judean wilderness implying a widespread use of Greek shorthand by the late first century. While because the parchments were recycled it is likely that they originated elsewhere and were lost in the wilderness (by a soldier), probability prevents an argument that these are the earliest examples of Greek shorthand, imported directly from Greece or Rome.[116]

The arguments for the use of Greek shorthand in the first Christian century may thus be summarized. (1) Indisputably Latin shorthand existed by the first Christian century and was capable of recording speech. (2) The Latin system most probably was derived from a similar earlier Greek system. (3) There are ancient references that strongly imply the use of Greek shorthand before the Christian era. (4) There are several extant fragmentary texts of Greek shorthand that may be dated to the *early* second century. Finally (5) the early evidence has a very wide geographical distribution: Rome, Greece, Asia Minor, the Judean desert, and Provincial Egypt.

Since Greek shorthand existed in the first Christian century, how prevalent was its usage? Several factors argue for the fairly widespread use of shorthand.[117] First and most important, Quintilian (35/40–95?) writes

---

[115] A comparison of the symbols of the text to Milne, *Greek Shorthand Manuals*, reveals numerous symbols in common as well as a similarity in general appearance to known Greek shorthand texts. The editors (*Murabba'āt*, 276–77) agree: "En résultat nous obtenons respectivement 24 et 23 lignes d'une écriture qui relève manifestement de la tachygraphie, et très probablement de la tachygraphie grecque. Non seulement on y descerne des lettres grecques ... mais encore on y reconnaît bien des tracés qui s'apparentent au systeme tachygraphique grec déjà connu".

[116] The Roman soldiers that captured and later garrisoned in the wadi were from the X Fretensis Legion that had been stationed in Jerusalem since its fall in A.D. 70.

[117] *Pace* scholars such as McKenzie, *Light*, 14, who asserts boldly "no generally used method of shorthand is attested for ancient times". Of those who recognize the existence of shorthand, not all share the view that shorthand was fairly common, notably Otto Roller, *Formular*, 333 and F. R. M. Hitchcock, "The Use of *graphein*", *JTS*, o.s., 31 (1930): 273-74. Bahr, "Letter Writing", 468, correctly cites Roller as concluding that dictation was a rarity; however, he incorrectly states that Hitchcock disagrees and asserts that dictation was common. Bahr misunderstands him, failing to notice that the initial section of Hitchcock's article is an extended excerpt that Hitchcock intends to refute. While Hitchcock disagrees with Roller concerning the use of a secretary – Hitchcock contends that Paul never used one – they *both* maintain that dictation was uncommon. By dictation, however, they mean dictation *syllabatim* not *viva voce*. Certainly dictation *syllabatim* was uncommon being too impractical. This distinction was discussed above, pp. 24–28.

against the fashionable practice of dictation.[118] Second, the numerous references to dictation in the writings of Cicero indicate his preference for using a secretary capable of recording rapid speech.[119] Seneca, Pliny the Younger, and others, mention the use of dictation, particularly in private letters. Yet was dictation the option only of the most elite of Romans? Similar remarks are absent generally from the papyri, however so are any other references to the manner of writing, with the single exception of the illiteracy formula, which was required in legal documents. Thus the lack of references to dictation in the papyri should not be understood as significant. Third, the discovery in Oxyrhynchus of a *teacher* of shorthand as well as a stenographic text in the remote Judean desert indicate a wide distribution of the art, particularly since the other references are predominantly from Rome, Greece, or Asia Minor. Fourth, references arise across the spectrum of social prominence: from the very elite upper class in the heart of the empire down to minor officials in provincial Egypt.

A less direct argument for the prevalence of Greek shorthand may also be noted. In a Socratic letter, *Ep.* 14, dated about A.D. 200,[120] Aeschines supposedly is recounting to Xenophon the events surrounding the death of Socrates, particularly the trial. He describes how the prosecutor arose and gave a very poor speech. He then adds:

> But Socrates had intended anything but that he should make such a speech — for you know how he spoke — with a seriousness mixed with laughter he smiled and said the things which your sons have written down...[121]

Obviously such a comment has no value for the time of Socrates, being no doubt anachronistic. Yet it may still contain implications for the present discussion. The forger of the letter mentions the speech presumably to provide the opportunity later to forge it. For the speech, which was "taken down", to be represented as the words of Socrates, it needs to be portrayed as being recorded *verbatim*.[122] For the forger to

---

[118] Quint. *Inst.* 10.3.19.

[119] He notes *once* (*Att.* 13.25.3) that he chose specially to dictate *syllabatim*, indicating that usually he does not, preferring to dictate to Tiro who recorded "whole sentences". See also *Att.* 2.23.1; 4.16.1; 5.17.1; 7.13a.3; 8.12.1; 8.13.1; 10.3a.1; 13.25.3; 14.21.4; 16.15.1; *QFr.* 2.2.1; 3.1.19; 3.3.1. Note also *Att.* 6.6.4, where Cicero mentions a letter from Atticus that was dictated.

[120] So dated by A. Malherbe, "Introduction", 28–29.

[121] Ps-Socr. *Ep.* 14.4.

[122] This may be reading too much into the text; however, in the responding letter, *Ep.* 15.2, 'Xenophon' commends these 'Friends of Socrates': "You do well to have

make such an anachronism, it is quite unlikely that Greek shorthand was a recent innovation known only in elite Roman circles. Because he makes such a mistake and because it remained unnoticed apparently, one may infer that the art of taking dictation *viva voce* was well established and pervasive by the forger's time.

One final caution is needed concerning tachygraphy. Shorthand frequently can use one sign for several syllables or words.[123] Similarly difficult words can be recorded by a simpler synonym. Stock phrases, articles, and other common words are frequently noted by a short stroke or sign. In other words, the conversion of a tachygraphic text into longhand requires, as it does now, some recall on the part of the tachygrapher. A shorthand text of one writer was not always convertible by another, as perhaps illustrated by Cicero:

Et quod at te de decem legatis scripsi, parum intellexisti, credo, quia διὰ σημείων scripserum.[124]

Nevertheless a competent stenographer in antiquity was able to convert his own text "flawlessly",[125] especially if converted immediately. Were the text exceptionally long, however, or were there a delay between recording and drafting, the quality of reproduction must inevitably have suffered. The result, though, still should have been near verbatim.

b) *The Secretary as an Editor*

In much the same way as an executive secretary today, the secretary in antiquity could serve as an editor of the author's work. Logically the se-

---

Aeschines among you so that he can write to me. I think that we certainly need to record what that man said..." What does 'Xenophon' mean? Surely Aeschines was not the only one there capable of writing a letter. Rather perhaps he means that they were fortunate to have someone like Aeschines who could record what Socrates said, *viz.*, a tachygraphist.

[123] *E.g.*, the first letter of a word can be used to represent an entire word with appended dots to indicate the declensional ending, or the first and last letter can represent an entire phrase as in ἐ(ν Σαλαμῖνι ναυμαχί)α. Milne, *Greek Shorthand Manuals*, 5–6. See also A. Mentz, *Kurzschrift*, esp. the diagrams on pp. 15, 17, and 21, and idem, *Geschichte und Systeme der griechischen Tachygraphie* (Berlin: Gerdes & Hödel, 1907), 43, 54.

[124] Cic. *Att.* 13.32; "What I said about the ten legates, you did not fully understand. I suppose because I wrote it in shorthand". Cicero probably tried to disguise the meaning of the text from interceptors by using 'signs' that he thought Atticus (or Alexis?) would understand. There is no other discernible reason why Cicero (or Tiro?) would have left this part of the text in shorthand.

[125] "ἀμέμπτως", according to the requirements of *POxy.* 724. See above, p. 38.

cretary could be working in two ways: (1) from the author's draft, or (2) from the author's instructions. Ultimately the secretary's role as an editor was the same for both procedures; yet since the manner of presentation by the author is different, some preliminary distinctions are needed.

aa) The Secretary's Use of the Author's Draft

When the secretary is working from the draft of the author, the draft must be 'rough' in some sense, that is, the secretary must be doing more than merely preparing another copy of the text. Although this was a legitimate task for an ancient scribe, for the purpose here, such a scribe is designated a mere copyist and therefore not considered here.

How and why a writer might employ a rough draft is discussed later.[126] At this point, the task at hand is to investigate if secretaries made minor corrections of an author's work, that is, if secretaries were used as editors of a author's draft.

bb) The Secretary's Use of the Author's Instructions

When editing from the author's instructions, the secretary could be used exactly the same way as with a written text. Thus corrections to his text are done with the author's consent — actually it was often done at the author's request. Yet what if the author preferred the text exactly as he stated it, but for some reason he is unwilling either to dictate it *syllabatim* or to write it himself? His only option then is to dictate it *viva voce*. But what if that particular secretary is unable to take shorthand — a reasonable enough possibility? The secretary is forced then to take notes as extensively as he can and to try to recreate the text. The observation of John McKenzie mentioned earlier: "Dictation ... was the normal means of producing letters"[127] probably pertains more to this process than to strict recording. Obviously, in a letter of any length, inevitably the secretary will introduce minor changes in vocabulary, syntax, and style, but probably not in content. Consequently, the use of a secretary as an editor theoretically could occur either intentionally, at the author's request, or unintentionally, due to the limitations of the secretary.

---

[126] See below, pp. 102–4 and 162.
[127] McKenzie, *Light*, 13–14; or see above, p. 24.

Is there any evidence that secretaries edited the work of their employers? Obviously, since shorthand was not so pervasive that all secretaries took shorthand and since many letters were not worth the time and labor of either dictating *syllabatim* or writing oneself, cases of unintentional changes must have occurred. Equally obviously, such cases are quite difficult to detect for one is seeking letters that show a change from an oral original.[128] In the former case, that of intentional changes, however, the situation is different because the author desires the secretary to correct a *faux pas* if he finds one. There is ample evidence for such a practice as indicated in the following examples. In a letter that Cicero wrote to Tiro, his secretary, who was elsewhere convalescing, he laments:

> Innumerabilia tua sunt in me officia, domestica, forensia, urbana, provincialia; in re privata, in publica, in studiis, in litteris nostris.[129]

What are these 'irreplaceable services' of Tiro? No doubt these services correspond to those mentioned in this later letter:

> Etsi opportunitatem operae tuae omnibus locis desidero, tamen...[130]

What skill does Tiro possess that makes him so valuable? Certainly it is *not* his ability to take shorthand. Plutarch has already indicated that Cicero had several tachygraphists available for his use.[131] Cicero had come to rely upon the editorial skill of Tiro. Certainly this is Cicero's meaning in his unexpected use of the term κάνων in another letter to Tiro. It appears that Tiro, being sick, wrote and assured Cicero that he would care 'faithfully' for his health. Cicero writes back chiding Tiro good-naturedly for his improper use of the word 'faithfully' (*fideliter*).

> Sed heus tu, qui κανών esse meorum scriptorum soles, unde illud tam ἄκυρον, *valetudini fideliter inserviendo*?[132]

---

[128] This is not an impossible task, albeit difficult. If one has sufficient examples to determine an author's preferences, then deviations can be noted.

[129] Cic. *Fam.* 16.4.3; "Your services to me are past all reckoning — at home, in the forum, in the City, in my province, in private as in public affairs, in my literary pursuits and performances". Note the odd switch from singular to plural within the same sentence: "in me ... litteris notris". W. G. Williams (the LCL translator) apparently considers it an editorial plural. See also 16.3.2.

[130] Cic. *Fam.* 16.11.1; "Although I miss your timely assistance at every turn, ..."

[131] Plut. *Cat. Min.* 23.3–5. It is less likely that Tiro's 'skill' lay outside the usual secretarial repertoire. Slave duties were strictly defined. There were lectors (readers), nomenclators (men who walked with their masters and supplied the names of other men who approached them), etc., and their duties were not commonly combined; see Sherwin-White, *Letters of Pliny*, 225 n. 15.

[132] Cic. *Fam.* 16.17.1 (July 29, 45); "But look you here, sir, you who love to be the 'rule'

Surely Tiro's role as Cicero's κανών was that of a correcting editor, particularly since Cicero offers it as ironic justification for *his* correction of Tiro.

In an earlier letter, Cicero declares to Tiro:

> Litterulae meae, sive nostrae, tuui desiderio oblanguerunt. ... Pompeius erat apud me, cum haec scribebam, ... Et cupienti audire nostra dixi sine te omnia mea muta esse. Tu Musis nostris para ut operas reddas.[133]

A request like Pompey's customarily was for a work recently finished. It is not that Cicero, the great orator, is unable to read but that evidently he does not have anything recently written that is in suitable form to present to a peer like Pompey. It is less likely that Cicero was experiencing a brief period of unproductiveness than that the absence of Tiro prevented any recent works from being checked and ready for presentation. Although Cicero on occasion does employ an editorial 'we', the concessive use of *nostrae* here is a further indication.[134] Perhaps Cicero preferred for Tiro to examine his work and perhaps prepare a nice draft before he presented it to a peer.[135] Apparently therefore Tiro often had an editorial role as Cicero's secretary. It is possible of course that Cicero's relationship to Tiro was unique; however, Cicero on occasion compares his relation to Tiro with Atticus' relation to his secretary, Alexis.[136]

Plutarch relates an interesting interchange in his Life of Eumenes, the former secretary of Alexander:

---

of *my* writings, where did you get such a solecism as '*faithfully ministering to your health*'?" [Italics in text and translation are the editor's.]

[133] Cic. *Fam.* 16.10.2; Apr. 17, 54/53. "My poor little studies (or if you like *ours*) have simply pined away from longing for you ... Pompey is staying with me as I write these words; ... When he expresses a desire to hear something of mine, I tell him that, without you, I am altogether dumb. Please be ready to render due service to our Muses".

[134] See also Cic. *Fam.* 16.4.3 (p. 45 n. 129 above).

[135] Works were often written for such occasions. Cicero apparently worried excessively about the quality of his work. E.g., *Att.* 2.1; "My book ... has exhausted all the scent box of Isocrates, and all the rouge-pots of his pupils, and some of Aristotle's colours too ... I should never have dared to send it to you [Atticus], if I had not revised it with leisure and care". Yet it was Atticus to whom he usually sent his works to be checked before publishing. Note that when Cicero prepared a Latin and a Greek version of his consulship, he sent the Greek version to Atticus to be edited by him ("If there is anything in it which to your Attic taste seems bad Greek or unscholarly ... [correct it, for I wish there to be no] barbarisms and solecisms as a clear proof that it was the work of a Roman"; *Att.* 1.19, 20). Quintus once asked his brother Cicero to edit one of his works (Cic. *Att.* 2.16).

[136] See Cic. *Att.* 5.20: "Tiro who is my Alexis"; 12.10: "Let us take care of Alexis, the living image of Tiro"; also 7.2: "Talking of Alexis, I left Tiro sick at Patrae".

He [Antigonus] therefore cherished no longer an inferior hope, but embraced the whole empire in his scheme, and desired to have Eumenes as friend and helper in his undertakings. Accordingly, he sent Hieronymus to make a treaty with Eumenes, and proposed an oath for him to take. This oath Eumenes corrected and then submitted it to the Macedonians who were beseiging him, requesting them to decide which was the juster form.[137]

There is easily a risk of reading too much into this account. Nevertheless, interestingly it is a former secretary who thinks to edit a document before considering it finished.

c) The Secretary as a Co-author

A distinction is made here between co-authors of a letter and using the secretary as a co-author. Evidently an ancient letter from more than one sender is uncommon.[138] The practice is not unknown, however, if Cicero's ascription can be trusted, for he observes that Atticus wrote a letter together with others.

Equidem ex tuis litteris intellexi, et eis, quas communiter cum aliis scripsisti, et eis, quas tuo nomine, ...[139]

In such a case of multiple authors, Gordon Bahr postulates that this could have occurred in one of two ways. Either the authors discussed and determined the content which one then dictated *verbatim* to a secretary, or the authors discussed the content together with a secretary and then allowed the secretary to draft the letter. Yet, in either case, the vocabulary, grammar, and style are of one individual, although the thought of all senders could be expressed.[140] This however may be mis-

---

[137] Plut. *Eum*. 12.1–2.

[138] With two clear exceptions: one, a letter from a community, such as the priests at Philae or the Jews of Alexandria, and two, a letter from a husband and wife. Yet it is questionable how much these 'co-authors' contributed. Otherwise the practice seems rare. Cicero, Pliny, and Seneca wrote none. I found 6 among the 645 papyrus letters from Oxyrhynchus, Tebtunis, and Zenon: *POxy*. 118, 1158, 3094, 3313, 3064 (all third century) and 1167 (*n.b.*, A.D. 37–41) [using the list provided by C.-H. Kim, "Index of Greek Papyrus Letters", *Semeia* 22 (1981): 107–12]. *PZen* 35 may be from two persons but the text is too fragmentary to be certain. Yet none of these letters are analagous to Paul's letters. His inclusion of other writers in his letter addresses is investigated in Chapter Three below, pp. 153–58.

[139] Cic. *Att*. 11.5.1; "For my part I have gathered from your letters – both that which you wrote in conjunction with others and the one you wrote in your own name – ..." Bahr, "Letter Writing", 476, mistakenly describes this as the solitary reference to the practice.

[140] Bahr, "Letter Writing", 476

leading. In both cases if all the senders are present during the drafting of the letter, then their influence could be felt even in more minor elements, such as diction, argumentation, or organization.

For the purposes here, though, co-authorship is limited to mean that the secretary took an active role in the composition of the letter. This is more than the correction of grammar or phraseology, more than mere editing, for the letter would reflect, in at least some way, the thought of the secretary as well as that of the author.[141]

In their effort to determine the role of Tiro in the composition of Cicero's letters, several writers propose methods that correspond with this category. For example, Bahr suggests:

> Probably Tiro, who had served his master and friend so long that the two almost thought alike, did not take dictation literally, but freely altered the terminology of the letter. That is, Tiro took part in the composition of the letter.[142]

This conclusion, however, may have been reached *a priori*. These writers, particularly the earlier ones, do not allow for the possibility of dictation *viva voce*. Consequently, by 'dictation', they mean dictation *syllabatim*. In this respect they are probably correct: Cicero's letters were not dictated (*syllabatim*), for even a cursory reading of most of his letters reveal a spontaneity not restricted by the labored style required with slow dictation.[143] Furthermore, the letters demonstrate throughout a Ciceronian character. Therefore, if one asserts that Tiro had a part in the composition of the letters, 'freely altering the terminology', then one must conclude "the two almost thought alike". While this is plausible, it falls to Occam's razor. It is not necessary to assert that Tiro and Cicero are so familiar that they almost thought alike in order to explain the internal consistency of Cicero's letters: Cicero usually dictated his letters which were recorded in shorthand, with minor corrective editing by Tiro on occasion.

Evidently then, irrespective of the verdict concerning the particular role of Tiro, secretaries were used as co-authors. The very nature of the ancient letter, with its rigid structure, frequently predetermined arrangement of the content, and stereotyped formulae, almost necessitates the inclusion of a secretary's expertise, particularly for the marginally lite-

---

[141] Could this have ramifications for structural analysis?

[142] Bahr, "Letter Writing", 470; see also Roller, *Formular*, 307–8 and Otto Morgenstern, "Cicero und die Stenographie", 2–4.

[143] *E.g.*, the spontaneous clarification of an antecedent in Cic. *Fam.* 9.6.1; "Well then, his arrival – I mean Caesar's – is being eagerly awaited".

rate. With official letters, this may not be surprising, but even personal letters suffered from what many modern people might call a decidedly impersonal nature.[144]

d) The Secretary as a Composer

Ancient letter writers had a fourth option in how they used a secretary. They could request him to send a letter to someone without specifying its contents. This procedure was possible because of the nature of the ancient Greco-Roman letter, because the letters, especially official and business letters, had a very set form, vocabulary, and style.[145] For example, an author could request a letter to be written to a local official assuring him of compliance with the latest ordinances. The secretary would then compose a suitable letter. In this role the secretary is actually the author of the letter, although the stated author assumes responsibility for it.

How private letters made use of such a procedure may be less apparent; however, they are in many ways no less stereotyped than the official and business letters. Although written for philophronetic reasons,[146]

---

[144] An examination of the papyrus letters demonstrates their stereotypical nature. See also Doty, *Letters*; Stowers, *Letter Writing*, 17−26; and White, "Retrospect", 10.

[145] Perhaps the best examples of these were the *litterae commendaticae*. These letters of recommendation were written by a person of note and carried by the recommended person to serve as a letter of introduction, guarantee of character, request for assistance, etc. John White, "Greek Documentary Letter Tradition", 95−97, offers a convenient summary of the structure, essential elements and distinctives of this type of letter.

Cicero, as may be expected of a person of his fame, wrote many letters of recommendation. In fact, *Fam.* 13, with the singular exception of *Ep.* 68, consists of nothing else. The unavoidable monotony inherent in such letters is acknowledged by Cicero in a recommendation letter (*Fam.* 13.27.1) sent to a colleague to whom he had already sent a number of such letters for others: "It is inexcusable to use exactly the same terms over and over again in sending you letters of this kind, thanking you for so punctiliously attending to my recommendations; I have done so in other cases, and shall do so, I foresee, ever so often; but for all that I shall make every effort to do in my letters what you lawyers habitually do in your *formulae*, and that is, '*to put the same case in a different way.*'" [Italics are the editor's.] Clearly Cicero is trying to vary his letters, indicating that such letters were usually the same. Because the phrases were so stereotyped, they had already lost their impact. *E.g.*, when in one letter (*Fam.* 13.69.1) Cicero apparently *truly* meant what he is saying, he is forced to add "Haec ad te eo pluribus scripsi, ut intellegeres, me non vulgari more, nec ambitiose, sed ut pro homine intimo ac mihi pernecessario scribere".

[146] Heikki Koskenniemi uses the term "philophronesis" to denote the desire of the sender to establish, strengthen, or restore his personal relationship with his recipient; *Studien*, 115−27. Paul Dion, "The Aramaic 'family letter' and Related Epistolary Forms in other Oriental Languages and in Hellenistic Greek", *Semeia* 22 (1981): 59−76; and idem,

they usually employed stereotyped health-wishes, affirmations of prayers and offerings to the gods on the recipient's behalf, and assurances of the well-being and concern/love of the sender.

Was this practice, though, employed by literate persons, who could and did write their own letters on other occasions? Because, as has been seen, the secretary wrote on behalf of the author, references to this practice within the letters themselves naturally are rare. Presumably one did not wish his recipient to know that a secretary, not he, wrote the letter. Nonetheless, instances of and allusions to this practice are not unknown. Four examples will suffice.

(1) During one period in his life, Cicero repeatedly asks Atticus to write to their various friends in *Cicero's* name.

> Tu velim et Basilo, et quibus praeterea videbitur, etiam Servilio conscribas, ut tibi videbitur, meo nomine.[147]

Any confusion about Cicero's meaning is removed by the additional instructions he gives to Atticus: "Si signum requirent aut manum, dices me propter custodias ea vitasse".[148] Clearly Cicero intends for Atticus to write letters for him that the recipients will believe are from Cicero.

(2) Cicero himself may have performed the same task for L. Valerius, an intimate friend. Evidently Cicero was asked by Valerius, who was currently in Cilicia, to write on his behalf to Lentulus, the then proconsul. Writing on his behalf need not mean at all that Cicero *composed* a letter for him as his 'secretary'. Cicero's reply, however, implies that he did that very thing: "Lentulo nostro egi per litteras tuo nomine gratias diligenter".[149] This particular reference, though, is too laconic to be certain.

(3) Cicero's brother, Quintus, apparently employed his secretary in this way, although it may have been limited to more official correspondence.[150] Cicero, in a lengthy letter of advice to his brother who was on

---

"Tentative Classification of Aramaic Letter Types", *SBLASP* 11 (1977): 417, 430–32, notes that Aramaic letters often had this intent, even employing similar conventions. For instance Cicero, *Fam.* 4.9 and 4.10 were apparently written purely for philophronetic reasons.

[147] Cic. *Att.* 11.5; "I should like you to write in my name to Basilius and to anyone else you like, even to Servilius, and say whatever you think fit". Also see *Att.* 3.15; 11.2; 11.7.

[148] Cic. *Att.* 11.2.4: "If they look for [my missing] signature or handwriting, say that I have avoided them because of the guards".

[149] Cic. *Fam.* 1.10; "I have heartily thanked our friend Lentulus by letter in your name" (so LCL). Or can it mean, "... Lentulus in your name by a letter"?

[150] This limitation is not indicated in the texts and may be inappropriate, for as a Roman

his first Roman appointment, discusses Quintus' customary methods of using his trusted secretary, Statius.

> Statius mihi narravit, scriptas ad te solere afferri, ab se legi, et, si iniquae sint, fieri te certiorem; antequam vero ipse ad te venisset, nullum delectum litterarum fuisse; ex eo esse volumnia selectarum epistularum, quae reprehendi solerent.[151]

The implication is that Quintus had various secretaries compose letters for him. He then had Statius, probably in a role as chief secretary, read the letters, checking for inconsistencies and advising him. What is notable here is that he is not criticized by Cicero for using secretaries to compose letters but rather for not having the letters checked. He was responsible for them.

(4) Rufus, a friend of Cicero, makes an interesting arrangement for him while Cicero was banished from Rome in 51 B.C. Rufus had promised to keep Cicero abreast of even the smallest happenings in Rome. In his letter to Cicero, he outlines how he intends to fulfill his promise:

> As you were leaving me, I promised to write you a very careful and full account of all that happened in the city; well, I have been at some pains to get hold of a man who would report every detail — so minutely, indeed, that I fear you will regard his efforts in that line as a mere excess of loquacity. Although I know how keenly interested you are, and what pleasure it gives all who are abroad to be informed of even the most trivial transactions at home, still, as to this particular arrangement, I implore you not to condemn this way of discharging my duty as savouring of superciliousness, simply because I have delegated the task to another.
>
> It is not that anything in the world would be more delightful to me, busy as I am, and the laziest of letter-writers, than to refresh my memories of you. But the packet I send you herewith itself explains my conduct. It would require I don't know how much leisure, not only to write out all this, but even to cast an eye over it [*Nescio cuius oti esset, non modo perscribere haec, sed omnino animadvertere*]. Decrees of the Senate, edicts, gossip, rumours — they are all there. If you are not altogether pleased with this sample be sure you let me know, so that I may not exhaust your patience and my purse at the same time.
>
> Should anything of unusual political importance be transacted, which those scribes [*operarii*] of mine cannot adequately explain, I will send you a full and accurate account of the way it was done, what was thought of it afterwards, and what anticipations it has aroused.[152]

---

official all correspondence, no matter how philophronetic, may have carried official connotations. See Stowers, *Letter Writing*, 19.

[151] Cic. *QFr.* 1.2.8; "Statius told me that they were often brought to your house ready written, and that he read them and informed you if they contained anything inequitable, but that before he entered your service there had never been any sifting of letters, with the result that there were volumes of dispatches picked out which lent themselves to adverse criticism".

[152] A letter from Rufus recorded in Cic. *Fam.* 8.1.1.

Several observations may be made. First, assuming that Rufus' statements are not mere rhetoric to absolve himself of the guilt of a delay, he evidently had difficulty finding a secretary capable of composing suitably a record of all the affairs of Rome or at least a record worthy of the eyes of Cicero. Second, a secretary was able to compose a very lengthy work, so long a work that Rufus does not even trouble to read over it.[153] Third, since Rufus specifically states that he did *not* check the secretary's work, one may infer that usually the author did. Fourth, the cost was high enough that Rufus is willing to admit that he did not wish to spend the money unnecessarily. Fifth, apparently Rufus considered the task of gathering all the "decrees, edicts, gossip, and rumors" and composing them into a pleasing account to be a task within the grasp of a good secretary. That he was willing to send the first sample without checking it may also indicate his confidence in the ability of the secretary. Lastly, allowing the secretary to compose on his behalf may have implied a slight to the recipient as unworthy of his personal attention. Rufus was at pains to insure Cicero that it was his concern for fulfilling his promise to Cicero and not laziness that prompted him to delegate the task to a secretary.[154]

Since a writer usually does not reveal that his letter was actually composed by a secretary, one may doubt whether certain routine correspondences are in fact from the pen of the busy author himself even though they appear to be so. Such skepticism may lie behind a remark by Philostratus of Lemnos who, in the third Christian century, wrote a handbook for scribes.

Τὸν ἐπιστολικὸν χαρακτῆρα τοῦ λόγου μετὰ τοὺς παλαιοὺς ἄριστά μοι δοκοῦσι διεσκέφθαι φιλοσόφων μὲν ὁ Τυανεὺς καὶ Δίων, στρατηγῶν δὲ Βροῦτος ἢ ὅτῳ Βροῦτος εἰς τὸ ἐπιστέλλειν ἐχρῆτο, βασιλέων δὲ ὁ Θεσπέσιος Μάρκος ἐν οἷς ἐπέστελλεν αὐτός, πρὸς γὰρ τῷ κεκριμένῳ τοῦ λόγου καὶ τὸ ἑδραῖον τοῦ ἤθους ἐντετύπωτο τοῖς γράμμασι, . . . [155]

---

[153] Again assuming that this was not mere rhetoric to accentuate the extent of his efforts. The same assumption applies to his perhaps embarassing reference to the expense.

[154] This probably was mere rhetoric. Nevertheless either way the possibility for insult remained.

[155] Philostratus of Lemnos, *Flavii Philostrati Opera*, ed. C. L. Kayser, 2 vols. (Leipzig: Teubner, 1871), 2.28. The text is reprinted in A. Malherbe, "Theorists", 40–41, with this translation: "Those who, next to the ancients, seem to me to have used the epistolary style of discourse best are, of the philosophers [Apollonius] of Tyana and Dio, of military commanders Brutus or the person Brutus employed to write his letters, of the emperors, the divine Marcus when he himself wrote (for in addition to his distinction in speech, his firmness of character, too, had been imprinted in his letters)".

Whether this reflects an ancient tradition about the secretarial practices of Brutus or merely skepticism in general is not clear. Interestingly however, Philostratus, presumably speaking as an ancient expert on secretaries, could differentiate between the letters of Marcus written by Marcus himself and those written by a secretary.

There is ample evidence, therefore, that secretaries in antiquity were employed in the four ways described above. Some blending of these roles, however, should be allowed. Since the distinctions between these roles are, of course, artificial, the uses are frequently separated more by gray areas than by hard and fast lines. How an author used his secretary depended upon how much control he exercised at that particular moment in that particular letter. Moreover, he was not restricted to one type of use even within the same letter.[156]

e) Related Issues

This section discusses several remaining miscellanea related to the general use of a secretary that has not already been discussed under the framework of the four roles of a secretary. Three main questions are addressed: (1) Who was responsible for the content of the letter? (2) What was the customary training that a "professional" secretary received? (3) What practical issues are involved in using a secretary to write a letter?

aa) Responsibility

Even though a secretary is the one actually writing down the letter, the author speaks as the writer, not just the author. For example, Cicero writes "Quo die haec scripsi, Drusus erat..."[157] The author assumes full responsibility for the purpose, content, style, and perhaps even the form of every letter whether actually from his pen or not. When responding to a recent letter from Appius Claudius, Cicero states:

> Vix tandem legi litteras dignas Appio Clodio,... Nam... ad me litteras misisti,... legi pirinvitus.[158]

---

[156] *E.g.*, Cic. *QFr.* 3.1, contains sections from his own hand as well as parts he dictated. This letter is discussed below, pp. 113–14.

[157] Cic. *QFr.* 2.16.3.

[158] Cic. *Fam.* 3.9.1; "At last, after all, I have read a letter worthy of Appius Claudius... For the letters you sent me en route... I have read with much pain..."

Apparently Claudius had sent several letters that implied some unfriendliness toward Cicero. Cicero was willing to allow that a return to the intellectual atmosphere and leisure of Rome had restored Claudius to his senses. Yet, notably Cicero never suggested the secretary as a possible excuse for his friend to use, that is, Cicero did not state "How could you have permitted your secretary to use such phrases?" Rather he lamely suggested that the rigors of provincial life had affected his friend's perception. Evidently one assumed that the author was responsible for every phrase and nuance contained in his letter no matter how much the secretary actually formulated.

Again, in a reply to a private letter from Pompey, Cicero writes that he felt snubbed because Pompey's letter contained "but a slight expression of your regard for me". To offer an excuse for Pompey, he comments "I can only suppose that you omitted any such reference because you were afraid of wounding anybody's feelings".[159] Once again, he never suggests the possibility that the scribe merely failed to include those remarks. He considered the contents, even to the point of omissions, to be exactly what the author intended.[160]

When Cicero wishes to disclaim the phrasing of several remarks in a particular letter, he is forced to disclaim the *entire* letter:

> Stomachosiores meas litteras quas dicas esse, non intelligo. Bis ad te scripsi, me purgans diligentur, te leniter accusans in eo, quod de me cito credidisses;... Sed si, ut scribis, eae litterae non fuerunt disertae, scito meas non fuisse.[161]

Of course this is mere rhetoric and not true confusion on the part of Cicero.[162] He is using the opportunity to re-express the intention of his previous statements. Nevertheless it is notable that he does not blame the secretary, apparently because this was not an acceptable excuse. Cicero is forced to revert to what he knows is an obviously weak explanation.

---

[159] Cic. *Fam.* 5.7. Of course, these remarks like the previous are steeped in rhetoric with political overtones and subtle inuendos, the full implications of which are quite outside this writer's purview; nevertheless, the basic point, I think, is still pertinent.

[160] Thus in *QFr.* 2.15b.2, Cicero feels justified in expressing his indignation over the form and content of a letter from his brother, for whom he knew Statius often wrote: "Verum attende nunc, mi optime et suavissime frater, ad ea dum rescribo, quae tu in hac eadem brevi epistula πραγματικῶς valde scripsisti".

[161] Cic. *Fam.* 3.11.5; "What letter of mine it is you describe as unduly choleric I cannot make out. I wrote to you twice, clearing myself carefully, and mildly rebuking you for having too readily believed what was said of me;... But if, as you write, the letter was badly expressed, you may be sure I never wrote it".

[162] He admits this later in the letter, chiding an earlier writer Aristarchus for the same thing (Aristarchus tries to argue that a poor line from Homer was not Homer's).

The Employment of a Secretary

Why were appeals to secretarial errors not valid in letter writing? The author was *expected* to check the final draft of the secretary. That this was the practice of official correspondence has already been demonstrated by Cicero's discussion of his brother Quintus' use of his secretary[163] and by the imperial routine of Vespasian.[164] In a costly example, evidently Cicero and Quintus were to inherit a portion of the estate of a man named Felix.[165] Apparently however Felix filed an incorrect (older) copy of his will that did not include them.

> De Felicis testamento tum magis querare, si scias. Quas enim tabulas se putavit obsignare, in quibus in unciis firmissimum locum tenemus (lapsus est per errorem et suum et Sicurae servi), non obsignavit; quas noluit, eas obsignavit. 'Αλλ' οἰμωζέτω! nos modo valeamus.[166]

Carelessly Felix had signed (sealed) an incorrect copy. Although apparently his slave (secretary?) was partly to blame, Felix was responsible, and thus the older will stood uncontested.

Official letters were proofread. Is the same true for private letters? Obviously "responsibility" was more casual. The evidence is also less abundant. Among some wedding invitations discovered at Oxyrhynchus, one had the date corrected by a second hand,[167] indicating that the text had been checked after the invitation was prepared. This text, though, typifies the problem of differentiating authorial corrections from mere changes. Wedding dates did — and do — change. The correction may have precipitated from a change of wedding plans and not from the correction of the final draft.

Perhaps an analogy may be drawn from a related issue with the letter carrier, mentioned in a reply of Cicero to a question of his brother:

> I come now to your letters, which I received in several packets when I was at Arpinum ... the first thing you noticed was that my letter to you bore an earlier date than that to Caesar. That is what Oppius occasionally cannot help doing —

---

[163] Cic. *QFr.* 1.2.8 (see above, p. 51).

[164] Suet. *Vesp.* 21 (see above, p. 17).

[165] One source of revenue for prominent Romans was wills. Evidently obscure "millionaires" enjoyed giving a portion of their estates to famous men they did not even know. It honored the giver (although it perhaps cheated the rightful heirs).

[166] Cic. *QFr.* 3.9.8; "About Felix's will, you would complain still more bitterly, if you only knew the facts. The document he thought he was sealing, in which we most certainly have a place as heirs to a twelfth of his estate (his slip was due to a mistake on his own part as much as on that of his slave Sicurra), he did not seal; the document he didn't want to seal, he sealed! But let him go hang, so long as we keep our health". Whether his reconstruction is accurate or only wishful thinking does not alter the point.

[167] *POxy.* 1487 (see above, p. 21).

I mean that, when he has decided to send letter carriers and has received a letter from me, something unexpected hinders him, and he is unavoidably later than he intended in sending the carriers; while I, when once the letter has been handed to him, do not trouble about having the date altered.[168]

Cicero's effort to explain his custom implies perhaps that usually one corrected the date of the letter, presumably because, like the other parts of the letter, the author is responsible, even though such peripheral details were handled customarily by the secretary.

One situation that was possible in more official contexts appears to contradict the assertion that the author was solely responsible for the content. At the end of Cicero's term as a provincial governor, he turned in the official "books", accounting for all the financial dealings during his term. A controversy arose concerning some alterations, or to be more direct, Cicero was accused of "fixing the books". Cicero defends himself in a letter,[169] and it becomes apparent that some persons — quite probably those friendly to him and wishing to acquit him of a crime that they believed he probably did — had suggested that the alterations were actually done by his secretary and were unknown to him. Such a defense would not absolve him from responsibility but at least would not impugne his character as severely: it is better to be thought careless than a thief. Cicero indignantly replies that he had, *according to custom*, checked all the work his secretary had done. He also defends the changes, which he asserts that he himself had made, and also defends fervently the unimpeachable character of Tiro, his secretary. The hushed nature of the entire affair may be construed from Cicero's reply near the end of the letter: "There is no reason why I should wish this letter to be torn up".[170]

---

[168] Cic. QFr. 3.1.8. The final line reads "... neque nos datis iam epistulis diem commutari *curemus*". The LCL translator (W. Glynn Williams) renders it with a singular. While Cicero frequently employs an editorial 'we', he has been speaking here in the singular, and further one would not expect a plural in such a statement. Is he saying that neither he nor his secretary cared to make such a correction?

[169] Cic. Fam. 5.20.

[170] Cic. Fam. 5.20. There are instances of where a dead official's (former) secretary was procured by devious individuals to alter the dead man's records to their advantage, since the handwriting of these corrections would be the same as that of any original corrections. E.g., Cic. Att. 14.18: "he [Dolabella] has freed himself from enormous debts by the handwriting of Faberius". E. O. Winstedt (the LCL translator) explains that Faberius was Caesar's secretary and was used by Dolabella to alter some of Caesar's records about the public treasury. See also Cic. Att. 7.3.

bb) Training

Probably the average secretary did not attend any special school. He learned the necessary basic skills within the established educational system. Any special skills were acquired by apprenticeship, if *POxy.* 724 is representative.[171] While this typical reconstruction is probably correct, several questions may be asked: (1) Is there any evidence that secretaries were trained in any special way? (2) What constituted a basic education? (3) Are there ancient textbooks for secretaries, and if so, what did they teach? These questions have been explored indepth elsewhere;[172] nevertheless, a brief summary is useful here.

John White notes the scholarly consensus as to the highly standardized character of certain parts of the ancient letter.[173] This conformity most likely was caused by widespread elementary training in letter writing, in the same way as training today accounts for the pervasive use of a standard format for business letters. More specifically, Abraham Malherbe argues that the essential continuity found in the basic form and style of the Greek private letter across several *centuries* indicates that literacy included rudimentary instruction in letter writing.[174]

Usually Greek and Roman education is described as progressing through three stages: elementary school, secondary school under the *grammaticus*, and rhetorical training. Stan Stowers, however, recently countered that such a picture is seriously misleading.[175] First, the availability of all three types of education was greatly affected by local needs and resources. Smaller cities frequently offered only elementary and secondary levels and often only elementary education plus whatever additional skills in which the local teacher was competent.

Second, these supposed "stages" were generally not sucessive but socially differentiated tracks, especially in the larger cities. Thus elementary school, taught by a 'teacher of letters', was for those of the lower classes and was usually all the education they received. Boys from the upper classes received their elementary instruction in their homes from a tutor or by the *grammaticus* himself before progressing to secondary material.

---

[171] See above, p. 38.
[172] See esp. Abraham Malherbe, "Theorists", 7–14, who presents the more traditional view; also John White, "Retrospect", 9–10, idem, "Greek Documentary Letter Tradition", 90, *et permulti*. But *cf.* Stanley Stowers, *Letter Writing*, 32–34, who disagrees slightly with the traditional understanding.
[173] White, "Retrospect", 10.
[174] Malherbe, "Theorists", 4–5.
[175] Stowers, *Letter Writing*, 32.

58   *The Secretary in Greco-Roman Antiquity*

They might then advance to the teacher of rhetoric. According to Stowers, there usually was no advancement from a teacher of letters to a *grammaticus*, that is, boys from the lower classes did not usually advance to secondary education, which centered on the analysis and imitation of the classics.[176]

In Egypt, teachers used model letters, which the students copied, to instruct in basic letter writing.[177] No doubt this practice was not limited to Egypt but was the general practice for Greek teachers. The widespread use of these collections, or handbooks, of elementary model letters may be seen in the bilingual Bologna Papyrus.[178] While not a handbook itself, it appears to be a student's exercises in writing various letters, following a handbook. Each letter was copied in Greek and Latin. The writer had only modest linguistic skills.

It is not certain the extent to which these collections were a part of the elementary school curriculum, but probably basic letter writing was taught by model letters in the early secondary stage.[179] Many of the *grammatical* handbooks used in the secondary stage, for example, those of Dionysius of Alexandria (first Christian century) and Apollonius Dyscolus (second Christian century),[180] clearly presuppose a knowledge of basic letter forms. This presupposition prompts Malherbe to conclude "... a knowledge of basic forms ... must therefore have been learned very early in secondary education".[181] He adds that the majority of papyrus letters also point to rudimentary instruction in letter writing early in secondary education.[182]

---

[176] Ibid.

[177] Model letters discovered in the Egyptian desert have been dated as early as 164/3 B.C.; see A. Erman, *Die Literatur der Aegypter* (Leipzig: Teubner, 1923), 252, 257, and 260; see also *PParis* 63 which contains four model letters.

[178] *PBononiensis* 5, probably from the third or fourth Christian century. The text is translated by Benjamin Fiore in Malherbe, "Theorists", 43.

[179] W. Schubart, *Einführung in die Papyruskunde* (Berlin: Weidmann, 1918), 397; also Donald L. Clark, *Rhetoric in Greco-Roman Education* (New York: Columbia University, 1957), 60–62.

[180] See G. A. Gerhard, "Untersuchungen zur Geschichte des griechischen Briefes, I. Die Anfangsformel", *Philologus* 64 (1905): 27–65. See also H. I. Marrou, *A History of Education in Antiquity*, trans. George Lamb (New York: Sheed & Ward, 1956), 235–37, 369–71. *Cf.* H. Rabe, "Aus Rhetoren-Handschriften", *Rheinisches Museum für Philologie*, n.s., 64 (1909): 290 n. 1, who denied that the handbooks in secondary education were used to *teach* letter writing; yet he suggests no other plausible purpose.

[181] Malherbe, "Theorists", 12.

[182] This instruction may have been even earlier, in late elementary school, if S. Stowers is correct that most students never advanced to secondary education. See above, p. 57.

The level at which basic letter writing was learned may have been more flexible. In the smaller cities where only primary education was available, the teacher of letters often supplemented the curriculum with whatever additional skills he was competent to teach.[183] Quite possibly he taught the rudimentary principles of letter writing to those of the lower classes during their primary — and only — education, thus accounting for the poor educational level indicated in many of the papyrus letters. Most of these letters were written in the language characteristic of persons of average superficial education, struggling to mimic the style of the well educated.[184]

Letter writing was also of interest to the rhetoricians, although it was omitted from consideration in the rhetorical handbooks of Cicero and Quintilian. Theoretical discussions of letter writing, however, are found in other writings of Cicero as well as such rhetorically cultured writers as Philostratus and Gregory of Nazianzus.[185] Although they must have known of the handbooks of rudimentary letters, they do not speak of them, no doubt because they did not need their guidance.[186]

Greek sophists frequently held the position of *ab epistulis* in chanceries.[187] Aspasias of Ravenna, who was serving as the *ab epistulis graecis* in the first half of the third Christian century, was unable to write a letter properly according to a contemporary and antagonistic sophist, Philostratus of Lemnos. Philostratus wrote a short work on proper letter writing techniques aimed at Aspasias.

Discussions of letter writing were not limited to dialogical works among sophists. Rather, handbooks were composed for the purpose of

---

[183] This point, although less certain, may be held with the arguments of M. Fuhrmann, *Das systematische Lehrbuch* (Göttingen: Vandenhoeck & Ruprecht, 1960), who reasons that even the handbooks represented by *PBon.* 5 were used *after* the most basic form of the letter had already been mastered.

[184] A famous and oft-cited example is the letter, *POxy.* 119, from Theon, a school-boy, to his father who was travelling to Alexandria. The atrocious spelling and grammar — not to mention the line of argument — indicate his poor educational level. The letter is discussed by Adolf Deissmann, *Light,* 201—4.

[185] Hermann Peter, *Der Brief in der römischen Literatur* (Leipzig: Teubner, 1901), 22—24, asserts that Cicero knew a well-rounded Greek system of letter writing. Indeed, Cicero wrote of his frustration over the lack of an appropriate letter type for one situation; *Fam.* 4.13.

[186] Koskenniemi, *Studien,* 62—63 correctly points out that the rhetorical handbooks presuppose some rhetorical skill and deal mainly with the subtleties.

[187] See Malherbe, "Theorist," 7; Philostratus *Vitae Sophistarum* 590, 607; Eunapius *Vitae Sophistarum* 497; and G. W. Bowersock, *Greek Sophists in the Roman Empire* (Oxford: Clarendon, 1969), 44, 50—57.

advanced instruction in letter writing. The prologue of one manual, credited to Demetrius of Phaleron and dated at least pre-Christian and probably around 100 B.C.,[188] indicated that the work was written to serve as an instructional guide in letter writing:

Τῶν ἐπιστολικῶν τύπων, ὦ Ἡρακλείδη, ἐχόντων τὴν θεωρίαν τοῦ συνεστάναι μὲν ἀπὸ πλειόνων εἰδῶν, ἀναβάλλεσθαι δὲ ἐκ τῶν ἀεὶ πρὸς τὸ παρὸν ἁρμοζόντων, καὶ καθηκόντων μὲν ὡς τεχνικώτατα γράφεσθαι, γραφομένων δ' ὡς ἔτυχεν ὑπὸ τῶν τὰς τοιαύτας τοῖς ἐπὶ πραγμάτων ταττομένοις ὑπουργίας ἀναδεχομένων, θεωρῶν σε φιλοτίμως ἔχοντα πρὸς φιλομάθειαν ἐπραγματευσάμην διά τινων συστήσειν ἰδεῶν καὶ πόσας καὶ ἃς ἔχουσι διαφοράς, καὶ καθάπερ δεῖγμα τῆς ἑκάστου γένους τάξεως ὑποδέδειχα προσεκθέμενος μερικῶς τὸν περὶ ἑκάστου λόγου, . . .[189]

As Malherbe notes, the manual in its present form is not merely a collection of sample letters, but it addresses more often the selection of the proper style and tone for a particular epistolary situation. "It is aimed at meeting the practical needs of its readers, who are assumed to be accomplished stylists, and not to be in need of instruction in basic rhetorical technique".[190] The prologue contains Demetrius' critical observation that many (most?) of the professional secretaries lack the awareness to select properly the appropriate letter style and tone and thus need the training he is providing. Because of his remarks and because, in contrast to the collections of model letters used at the more rudimentary level, the purposes of the sample letters in his handbook are (1) to provide instruction in the proper selection of the style appropriate to various epistolary occasions, (2) to serve as a guide for the correct tone in which the letter

---

[188] Demetrius *On Style*, and so dated by Malherbe, "Theorists", 8 and Stowers, *Letter Writing*, 34. See also L. Brinkmann, "Die älteste Briefsteller", *Rheinisches Museum für Philologie*, n.s., 64 (1909): 310–17, who conservatively dates the manual 200 B.C. to A.D. 50.

[189] Demetr. *Style* 1. Valentin Weichert, ed., *Demetrii et Libanii qui feruntur* ΤΨΠΟΙ ΕΠΙΣΤΟΛΙΚΟΙ *et* ΕΠΙΣΤΟΛΙΜΑΙΟΙ ΧΑΡΑΚΤΗΡΕΣ (Leipzig: Teubner, 1910) also cited in Malherbe, "Theorists", 29 with his translation: "According to the theory that governs epistolary types, Heraclides, they can be composed from a great number of specific types [of style], but take their shape from among those which always fit the particular circumstance [to which they are addressed]. While [letters] ought to be written as skillfully as possible, they are in fact composed indifferently by those who undertake such services for me in public office. Since I see that you are eager in your love to learn, I have taken it upon myself, by means of certain forms of style, to organize them and what they are, and have sketched a sample, as it were, of the arrangement of each kind".

[190] Malherbe, "Theorists", 8–9.

should be written, and (3) not to teach basic letter types, the apparent audience for the handbook was the professional secretary.[191]

Although a person of the social class able to attend a secondary and especially a tertiary school would be unlikely to choose a career as a professional secretary, professional secretaries evidently were exposed to at least some of the subjects learned in secondary and tertiary education. For many secretaries, this no doubt occurred not through regular enrollment under a *grammaticus* or a teacher of rhetoric but usually through apprenticeship to a skilled secretary or perhaps through enrollment in a special school specifically for the training of secretaries.[192]

One last observation concerning the training of a secretary may be made. Although it is uncertain how much of the standard general curriculum a secretary might receive in his specialized training, it is quite likely he received some training in the *progymnasmata*.[193] These elementary exercises in rhetoric should have occurred under the teacher of rhetoric; however, as the curriculum of the rhetoric schools became more complex, frequently responsibility for some of the *progymnasmata* was assumed by the *grammaticus* in the secondary curriculum. If a secretary received any instruction in the *progymnasmata*, it probably included the exercises in *prosopopoeia*, that is, characterization or impersonation,[194] especially since, according to Theon, a contemporary of Quintilian, letter writing was good practice for *prosopopoeia*.[195] Thus secretarial training may well have included training in the art of mimicking the style of another. Tiro, who had a great deal of practice writing for Cicero, was able to mimic, at least superficially, the style of his master. As has been discussed above, many modern writers comment to the effect that Cicero and Tiro had worked so much together that their styles had become alike, a kind of passive acquisition. It is, however, probably a case of *active* acquisition. As a good secretary, Tiro worked to mimic the style of the author.[196]

---

[191] See J. White, "Greek Documentary Letter Tradition", 90 and Schubart, *Einführung*, 198–99, 248.

[192] *E.g.*, the apprenticed slave in *POxy.* 724; see p. 38.

[193] For information on the *progymnasmata*, see Marrou, *Education*, 238–40. More recently, see Ronald F. Hock and Edward N. O'Neil, *The Chreia in Ancient Rhetoric; vol. 1: the Progymnasmata*, SBLTTS, no. 27 (Chico: Scholars, 1986). The *progymnasmata* were a series of graded exercises, carefully progressing from easier to more difficult, building upon the skills just learned (in much the same way as 'programmed instruction' today).

[194] *Cf.* Cic. *Att.* 15.4.

[195] See the discussion in Malherbe, "Theorists", 5.

[196] If a professional letter writer was trained to mimic style and thus when writing more than a mere stereotyped letter, he attempted to mimic the author's style as far as conven-

cc) Practical Considerations

A final issue relating to the use of a secretary are practical matters involved in employing a secretary to write a letter. There were evidently several common reasons for using a secretary. (1) A secretary was useful if the writer was in less than good health. For example, letters from Atticus's own hand indicated his good health.[197] (2) A secretary saved time, allowing the writer more time for other business. For example, Cicero tells his brother Quintus

> Occupationem mearum tibi signum sit librari manus. Diem scitp esse nullum, quo die non dicam pro reo. Ita, quidquid conficio aut cogito, in ambulationis fere tempus confero.[198]

(3) The savings in time referred only to the author's time. Using a secretary actually required more elapsed time, but less of the author's time. When a letter was needed in haste, Cicero wrote in his own hand.[199] Finally, (4) evidently business was often used as an excuse for another common reason for using a secretary, laziness. Cicero confesses to his old friend Atticus: "Nam illam νομαίαν ἀργίας excusationem ne acceperis".[200]

Elsewhere he admits:

> Noli putare pigritia me facere, quodnon mea manu scribam, sed mehercule pigritia. Nihil enim habeo aliud, quod dicam. Et tamen in tuis quoque epistulis Alexim videor adgnoscere.[201]

---

tions and propriety allowed, then it might be incorrect to *expect* a dramatic shift in style in a letter where parts were written by a secretary, especially if the secretary knew the author's style well. Of course, minute points of style were more difficult to mimic, such as an authorial preference in phraseology.

[197] Cic. *Att.* 4.16. See Cic. *Att.* 7.2: "I like Alexis' hand [Atticus' secretary]; it so closely resembles your own script [coincidence?], but there is one thing I do not like about it — it shows that you are ill". See also Cic. *Att.* 8.13.1; 7.13a.3; 8.12.1; 10.14.1; 10.17.2; *QFr.* 2.2.1 (all caused by an inflammation of the eyes); *Att.* 6.9.1 (fever); and *Att.* 7.2.3 (general debilitation).

[198] Cic. *QFr.* 3.3.1; "The handwriting of my secretary should indicate to you the pressure of my engagements. I assure you that there is never a day on which I don't speak on behalf of some defendent, with the result that whatever I compose or think out, I generally pile on to the time for my walks". Note his distinction: "conficio aut cogito". Also he later adds: "cum haec scribebam", although he was actually dictating. See also Cic. *QFr.* 2.16.1. Other letters also indicate how a busy schedule prompted the use of a secretary; see Cic. *QFr.* 2.2.1; *Att.* 2.23.1; 4.16.1.

[199] Cic. *Fam.* 3.6.2; 15.18.1–2. But these are a short note and a not well-composed letter.

[200] Cic. *Att.* 5.11; "I won't ask you to accept the lazy man's stock excuse, my business".

[201] Cic. *Att.* 16.15; "Don't think it is laziness that prevents my writing myself; and yet,

Obviously dictating a simple letter was easier than penning it, and this appealed to a lazy nature.

There are other considerations. First, the writer and his regular secretary frequently had a personal relationship despite their divergent social classes. In addition to the famous relationship of Cicero and Tiro, one may note that of Quintus and Statius, and of Atticus and Alexis.[202] In Plutarch's discussion of the life of Eumenes, Alexander's secretary, he observes:

μετὰ δὲ τὴν ἐκείνου τελευτὴν οὔτε συνέσει τινὸς οὔτε πίστει λείπεσθαι δοκῶν τῶν περὶ Ἀλέξανδρον ἐκαλεῖτο μὲν ἀρχιγραμματεύς.[203]

The concessive tone implies that Eumenes' prestige was unusual for his position and due to his personal merits. Normally a chief secretary would not enjoy such privileges, but they are granted because of the favor Alexander bestowed on him. Evidently it was possible for a secretary to become a trusted friend of the king, suggesting a working relationship rather than merely that of another attending servant. Of course, a personal and trusted working relationship is possible only in those situations where the author has an established secretary. No such relationship is expected between a letter writer and an unknown secretary contracted in the agora.

Trusted secretaries probably functioned as administrative assistants as well. Like executive secretaries today, they may have been used to read, evaluate, sort, and present pertinent received correspondences for their masters. When Plutarch is building the suspense factor for his discussion of the murder of Julius Caesar, he includes the story of a man who purportedly carried a warning of the plot to Caesar.

Furthermore, Artemidorus, a Cnidian by birth, a teacher of Greek philosophy, and on this account brought into intimacy with some of the followers of Brutus, so that he knew most of what they were doing, came bringing to Caesar in a small roll the disclosures which he was going to make; but seeing that Caesar took all such rolls and handed them to his assistants, he came quite near, and said, "Read this, Caesar, by thyself, and speedily; for it contains matters of importance and of concern to thee". Accordingly Caesar took the roll and would have read it, but was prevented by the multitude of people who engaged his attention, although he

---

to be sure, it is nothing but laziness, for I have no other excuse to make. However, I seem to recognize Alexis' hand in your letters too".

[202] See above, pp. 51 and 46, respectively.

[203] Plut. *Eum*. 1.2; "After Philip's death Eumenes was thought to be inferior to none of Alexander's followers in sagacity and fidelity, and though he had only the title of chief secretary".

set out to do so many times, and holding in his hand that roll alone, he passed into the senate.[204]

Presumably the assistants who were handling his correspondences are secretaries. Moreover, they probably were used also to evaluate what were important matters of correspondence and then to compose and present replies for their masters to check (possibly to correct), and to seal. Earlier in his discussion of the events leading to the death of Caesar, Plutarch relates the following:

> Moreover, on the day before [the Ides of March], when Marcus Lepidus was entertaining him at supper, Caesar chanced to be signing letters, as his custom was, while reclining at table, and the discourse turned suddenly upon the question what sort of death was the best.[205]

In this passage he indicates that Caesar often used mealtimes as an opportunity to check the final drafts prepared by his secretaries.

Writers often combined letter writing with other activities. Pliny the Younger discloses the preferences of his famous uncle and namesake, Pliny the Elder.

> Before daybreak he used to wait upon Vespasian, who likewise chose that season to transact business. When he had finished ... he returned home again to his studies. After a short and light repast at noon ... he would frequently in the summer ... repose himself in the sun; during which time some author was read to him from whence he made extracts and observations, as indeed this was his constant method whatever book he read ... Then, as if it had been a new day, he immediately resumed his studies till dinnertime, when a book was again read to him, upon which he would make some running notes.[206]

The Elder Pliny was assisted by a *notarius* as well as the *lector*, when reading a book. The *notarius* was used to take down the Elder's reflections, resulting in immense collections of notes and excerpts of selected passages.[207] These anthologies were often used later in the composition of major works.

---

[204] Plut. *Caes.* 65; "... ὁρῶν δὲ τὸν Καίσαρα τῶν βιβλιδίων ἕκαστον δεχόμενον καὶ παραδιδόντα τοῖς περὶ αὐτὸν ὑπηρέταις". For other examples of Caesar sending and receiving letters, see 17.4–5; also 23.4; 24.2; 30.2; 31.1; 48.2; 49.4.

[205] Plut. *Caes.* 63.4.

[206] Pliny *Ep.* 3.5; "... Super hanc liber legebatur, adnotabatur et quidem cursim".

[207] Sherwin-White, *Letters of Pliny*, 224–25 n. For the use of a *notarius* to record notes from readings, see also Pliny, *Epp* 9.29.2; 36.2. Evidently Pliny adopted this practice from the Elder: "posco librum T. Livi ... excerpo" (*Ep.* 6.20.5).

Like Caesar, apparently the Elder liked to use mealtimes for literary endeavors, enjoying the recitation of books during his meals,[208] presumably also, as was his custom elsewhere, having a secretary at hand to record his notes and extracts. This use of a secretary, however, was not the undesirable result of the cramped schedule of a busy man, for the Younger also discusses the daily routine of his uncle while at leisure in his country home. There also the Elder spent the majority of his time in literary pursuits, including, to the exasperation of his nephew, his time at bath. Pliny exclaims that while his uncle did not work during his bath, he meant only that time he was actually in the water, "nam, dum destringitur tergiturque, audiebat aliquid aut dictabat".[209]

The home was not the only place where secretaries were used. Pliny notes another of his uncle's customs:

> In his journeys, as though released from all other cares, he found leisure for this sole pursuit. A shorthand writer, with book and tablets, constantly attended him in his chariot, who, in the winter, wore a particular sort of warm gloves, that the sharpness of the weather might not occasion any interruption to his studies; and for the same reason my uncle always used a sedan chair in Rome.[210]

This passage affords several observations. First, the Loeb translator renders *notarius* as "shorthand writer", a choice well justified by the context. Second, the remark about the cold of winter implies that anything that hindered the *notarius* was an interruption of the Elder's studies. The *notarius* was an indispensable part of his work. Third, Sherwin-White observes that the use of only a *notarius* indicates that there must not have been room in the litter for a *lector* as well. The *notarius* was forced to do both duties.[211] Fourth, the mention of the codex notebook (*pugillaribus*) in addition to the roll implies they had different functions. Finally, using a secretary to write while in litter must have been a convenient process, since the Elder chose to use a carriage similarly in Rome, where not only was it unnecessary but may have been viewed contemptuously.

The convenience of having a secretary in the litter was preferred by others also. While discussing the routine of Caesar, Plutarch observes that Caesar frequently sought ways to improve the use of his time. He

---

[208] Pliny *Ep.* 9.36.4.

[209] Pliny *Ep.* 3.5; "for all the while he was rubbed and wiped, he was employed either in hearing some book read to him, or in dictating himself".

[210] Pliny *Ep.* 3.5; "... ad latus notarius cum libro et pugillaribus, cuius manus hieme manicis muniebantur, ..."

[211] Sherwin-White, *Letters of Pliny*, 225.

often slept in a litter, thus using his rest time for transportation as well. Also to save time, according to Plutarch, Caesar:

... ὠχεῖτο δὲ μεθ' ἡμέραν ἐπί τὰ φρουρία καὶ τὰς πόλεις καὶ τοὺς χάρακας, ἑνὸς αὐτῷ συγκαθημένου παιδὸς τῶν ὑπογράφειν ἅμα διώκοντος εἰθισμένων, ἑνὸς δ' ἐξόπισθεν ἐφεστηκότος στρατιώτου ξίφος ἔχοντος.[212]

His preference for the efficient use of secretaries, according to Plutarch, was not limited to the litter:

ἐν ἐκείνῃ δὲ τῇ στρατείᾳ προσεξήσκησεν ἱππαζόμενος τὰς ἐπιστολὰς ὑπαγορεύειν καὶ δυσὶν ὁμοῦ γράφουσιν ἐξαρκεῖν, ὡς δὲ Ὄππιός φησι, καὶ πλείοσι. λέγεται δὲ καὶ τὸ διὰ γραμμάτων τοῖς φίλοις ὁμιλεῖν Καίσαρα πρῶτον μηχανήσασθαι, τὴν κατὰ πρόσωπον ἔντευξιν ὑπερ τῶν ἐπειγόντων τοῦ καιροῦ διά τε πλῆθος ἀσχολιῶν καὶ τῆς πόλεως τὸ μέγεθος μὴ περιμένοντος.[213]

Since the context is the excellence of Caesar's horsemanship, it is quite plausible that what Plutarch considers incredible were: one, Caesar's ability to dictate *on horseback* and two, Caesar's ability to dictate to more than one secretary at the same time. Thus, dictating to one secretary while strolling about, reclining at meal, or sitting by the roadside would hardly be considered worthy of praise. Similarly in a letter to his wife, Cicero indicates that being aboard ship is no barrier to writing: "Navem spero nos valde bonam habere; in eam simultatque conscendi, haec scripsi. Deinde conscribam ad nostros familiares multas epistulas, ..."[214]

Although a secretary was sometimes used while actually travelling, for instance, in a litter, the variety of potential projects was limited. Caesar apparently composed administrative dispatches and possibly short personal letters. Pliny the Elder used his secretary for recording notes and transcribing excerpts. Thus simple tasks were possible, but were more complex literary attempts possible under these conditions? Pliny the Younger, who adopted many of his uncle's customs, comments in a letter to a friend:

---

[212] Plut. *Caes.* 17.3—4; "... and in the day-time he would have himself conveyed to garrisons, cities, or camps, one slave who was accustomed to write from *dictation* as he travelled sitting by his side, and one soldier standing behind him with a sword". [Italics are mine.]

[213] Plut. *Caes.* 17.4; "And in the Gallic campaigns he practiced dictating letters on horseback and keeping two scribes at once busy, or, as Oppius says, even more. We are told, moreover, that Caesar was the first to devise intercourse with his friends by letter, since he could not wait for personal interviews on urgent matters owing to the multitude of his occupations and the great size of the city".

[214] Cic. *Fam.* 14.7.2.

In via plane non nulla leviora statimque delenda ea garrulitate, qua sermones in vehiculo seruntur, extendi. His quaedam addidi in villa, cum aliud non liberet.[215]

Pliny considers this work he did *in via* as negligible and of no consequence, while in an earlier letter,[216] he remarks that an excellent time for composing good material was *ad retia*. As might be expected, compositions of a serious sort, including lengthy letters like the Younger composed, required more concentration then could be given while actually travelling, even with the use of a secretary.[217]

Thus, in conclusion, a secretary was used for letter writing in several ways and in a host of situations, whether he was an amateur secretary or one who was very well trained. Regardless of when, where, or through whom a letter was written, however, the sender was held completely responsible for the content and the form of the letter.

---

[215] Pliny *Ep.* 9.10; "I composed, indeed, a few trifles in my journey hither, which are only fit to be destroyed, as they are written with the same negligence and inattention that one usually chats upon the road. Since I came to my villa, I have made some few additions to them, not finding myself in a humor for work of more consequence".

[216] Pliny *Ep.* 1.6.

[217] On the day Cicero was beginning a journey, he decides to arise before dawn, to write an important letter to his brother. This may indicate the problems with writing while travelling, since he preferred writing before dawn. Cic. *QFr.* 2.5.5: "A. d. III. Id. April. ante lucem hanc epistulam conscripseram, eramque in itinere, ..." The availability of a letter carrier, however, could be an issue here as well.

Chapter Two
The Role of the Secretary in a Particular Letter

The previous chapter addressed the secretary in categorical terms and from a more general viewpoint. The present chapter examines the secretary from a more practical viewpoint, that is, his role in a particular letter. It inquires into potential influences of a secretary in the writing of a given letter. The first task at hand, however, is to determine whether or not a secretary was in fact used.

1. Criteria for Detecting the Use of a Secretary in a Particular Letter

Criteria for detecting a secretary's presence may be divided into two groups, based on their nature and reliability: (1) explicit evidences and (2) implicit indications of the presence of a secretary.

a) Explicit Evidence

Explicit evidence falls into three categories: (1) references by the author, (2) references by the secretary, and (3) changes in handwriting.

aa) References by the Author

These are the simplest and most reliable indicators of the use of a secretary. Unfortunately, as may be suspected, they are also probably the least common, perhaps because an author often did not care especially to draw attention to his employment of a secretary, for, understandably, he might not wish to advertise his inability or unwillingness to write the letter himself.

Of the extant letter writers, Cicero is perhaps the most open to remarks of this type. For example, he opens a letter to his brother Quintus with:

Non occupatione, qua eram sane impeditus, sed parvula lippitudine adductus sum, ut dictarem hanc epistulam et non, ut ad te soleo, ipse scriberem.[1]

No doubt Cicero begins with this explanation because his brother would notice that the handwriting was not Cicero's. Consequently, one may conjecture that had the intended recipient been someone who would not have recognized Cicero's handwriting, he would not have bothered to mention it. There are many other examples of Cicero indicating directly or indirectly that he was using a secretary.[2]

Surely it is not coincidence that in the fourteen letters where Cicero specifically indicates that he is using a secretary (dictating), all are written to either his brother or his closest friend Atticus.[3] These two men are perhaps the only recipients, whom Cicero would particularly wish not to offend and who would certainly recognize that the handwriting was not Cicero's. Furthermore, apparently these references by the author almost always occur at the *beginning* of the part where a secretary was used. Nine of the fourteen occurrences in Cicero begin the letter; the other four occurrences that can be ascertained for certain begin a section in which evidently a change in secretarial usage occurs. As far as these limited examples indicate, ancient authors appear not to make references to their use of a secretary in the *middle* of the section to which such usage pertains. If an author chooses to refer at all to his employment of a secretary, he does so at the onset. The apparent exception, a remark like "I have dictated the previous parts but am now writing the rest in my own hand", is no exception at all, for it serves as the introductory explanation for an autographed section.[4]

The decision to exclude one type of apparent authorial reference may raise eyebrows. The formula "γράφω διά..." appears to be evidence of a secretary. Such a statement by a letter writer may well indicate that the person who is mentioned by name is the secretary. This formula is ex-

---

[1] Cic. QFr. 2.2.1; "It is not the pressure of business (though I am sorely hampered in that respect), but a slight imflammation of the eyes that induced me to dictate this letter instead of writing it, as I generally do when corresponding with you, with my own hand".

[2] See *e.g.*, Cic. QFr. 2.16; 3.1; 2.15b.1; Att. 5.12; 7.13a; 8.15; 12.32.1; 13.32; Fam. 11.32.2.

[3] Att. 2.23.1; 4.16.1; 5.17.1; 7.13a.3; 8.12.1; 8.13.1; 10.3a.1 (he refers to dictating another); 13.25.3; 14.21.4; 16.15.1; QFr. 2.2.1; 3.1.19; 3.3.1; also see Att. 6.6.4. Bahr, "Letter Writing", 469 also notes this correlation.

[4] Cic. QFr. 3.1.19 is more complex and difficult to classify. He notes at the beginning of a section how the preceding section was done. See below, p. 193. But *by far* the references by an author open the section. The fact that Cicero feels the need in this letter to explain *so carefully* all changes may indicate that he was not following the usual pattern.

cluded, however, because it does not *always* refer to the process of writing but may more often refer to the transporter of the letter. In other words, "γράφω διὰ Μάρκου" probably means merely that Markus is the carrier of the letter and *not necessarily* that Markus is the secretary.

Two examples — albeit perhaps significant ones — should be sufficient when examined carefully: the letters of Ignatius of Antioch and the Philippian letter of Polycarp. According to Eusebius, Ignatius went to Rome to be martyred. On the journey he visited various churches in Asia. While in Smyrna, he wrote letters to the churches in Ephesus, Magnesia, Tralles, and Rome. Later, while in Troas, he wrote to Philadelphia and Smyrna, and to Polycarp.[5] In the letter to the Philadelphians 11:2, Ignatius comments:

ἀσπάζεται ὑμᾶς ἡ ἀγάπη τῶν ἀδελφῶν τῶν ἐν Τρωάδι· ὅθεν καὶ γράφω ὑμῖν διὰ Βούρρου πεμφθέντος ἅμα ἐμοὶ ἀπὸ Ἐφεσίων καὶ Σμυρναίων εἰς λόγον τιμῆς.

Kirsopp Lake, the translator of the Loeb edition, renders the phrase "ὅθεν καὶ γράφω ὑμῖν διὰ Βούρρου" as "and I am writing thence to you by the hand of Burrhus".[6] Apparently Lake understands Burrhus to be the secretary through whom Ignatius wrote the letter. Certainly Burrhus, a deacon, was a significant character in the present ministry of Ignatius, for he is described in glowing terms by Ignatius in his letter to the Ephesians:

Περὶ δὲ τοῦ συνδούλου μου Βούρρου, τοῦ κατὰ θεὸν διακόνου ὑμῶν ἐν πᾶσιν εὐλογημένου, εὔχομαι παραμεῖναι αὐτὸν εἰς τιμὴν ὑμῶν καὶ τοῦ ἐπισκόπου· [7]

Burrhus is called a σύνδουλος, a term that incidentally Paul uses to describe Epaphras (Col. 1:7) and Tychicus (Col. 4:7), both of whom traditionally are considered to be the carriers of the letter and not the secretaries.

Ignatius closes his letter to the Smyrnaeans in the same fashion as the Philadelphian letter but with an additional remark:

Ἀσπάζεται ὑμᾶς ἡ ἀγάπη τῶν ἀδελφῶν τῶν ἐν Τρωάδι, ὅθεν καὶ γράφω ὑμῖν διὰ Βούρρου, ὃν ἀπεστείλατε μετ' ἐμοῦ ἅμα Ἐφεσίων, τοῖς ἀδελφοῖς ὑμῶν, ὃς κατὰ πάντα με ἀνέπαυσεν· καὶ ὄφελου πάντες αὐτὸν ἐμιμοῦτο, ὄντα ἐξεμπλάριον θεοῦ διακονίας. ἀμείψεται αὐτὸν ἡ χάρις κατὰ πάντα.[8]

---

[5] Eusebius *Historia ecclesiastica* 3.36.3–10.
[6] Ignatius *Phld.* 11:2.
[7] Ign. *Eph.* 2:1.
[8] Ign. *Smyrn.* 12:1; "The love of the brethren who are at Troas salutes you, whence I am writing to you by Burrhus, whom you together with the Ephesians your brothers sent with me, and he has in every way refreshed me. Would that all imitated him, for he is a pattern of the ministry of God. In all things grace shall reward him".

Like Kirsopp Lake, Camelot, the translator for the Sources chrétiennes edition, understands the phrase "ὅθεν καὶ γράφω ὑμῖν διὰ Βούρρου" to mean "c'est de la que je vous ecris par l'intermediaire de Búrrhus".[9]

Again, with wording strikingly similar to the Smyrnaean letter, Ignatius includes in the farewell greetings to the Magnesians:

Ἀσπάζονται ὑμᾶς Ἐφέσιοι ἀπὸ Σμύρνης, ὅθεν καὶ γράφω ὑμῖν, παρόντες εἰς δόξαν θεοῦ, ὥσπερ καί ὑμεῖς οἳ κατὰ πάντα με ἀνέπαυσαν ἅμα Πολυκάρπῳ, ἐπισκόπῳ Σμυρναίων.[10]

Why, in a passage virtually identical to *Smyr.* 12:1, would Ignatius mention Burrhus to the Smyrnaeans and not to the Magnesians? Furthermore, in *Smyr.* 12:1, Ignatius commends Burrhus at length: "he has refreshed me in every way. Would that all imitated him, for he is a pattern of the ministry of God. In all things, grace will reward him". Again nothing precludes Burrhus from being the secretary, but is this what the formula is indicating? Furthermore, customarily a secretary was not commended, while frequently the carrier was commended at such length and in such a manner as a way of introduction.[11]

The deciding factor is provided by Ignatius' closing farewell greetings in his letter to the Romans:

Γράφω δὲ ὑμῖν ταῦτα ἀπὸ Σμύρνης δι᾽ Ἐφεσίων τῶν ἀξιομακαρίστων. ἔστιν δὲ καὶ ἅμα ἐμοὶ σὺν ἄλλοις πολλοῖς καὶ Κρόκος, τὸ ποθητόν μοι ὄνομα.[12]

Although he uses the same formula, it is quite unlikely — if not impossible — that an entire group of persons served as his secretary.[13] Rather the clear meaning here is that he is sending the letter to the Romans by means of the Ephesians who were with him.[14] Walter Bauer argues that

---

[9] P. Th. Camelot, ed., *Ignace d'Antioche*, 4th corr. ed., SC, no. 10 (Paris: Les editions du Cerf, 1969), *Smyrn.* 12:1 (p. 143). Inexplicably, Lake is more ambiguous in his translation here: "whence also I am writing you by Burrhus" (LCL 1: 265).

[10] Ign. *Magn.* 15:1.

[11] Such introductions/endorsements also helped to certify any additional insights the carrier provided. These commendations, of course, were limited to letters dispatched by assigned carriers, hence eliminating most common papyrus letters (which usually made haphazard use of travelers) and most offical correspondences (which used the official post). For examples, see Cic. *Fam.* 16.21.8 (a letter from Cicero's son to Tiro); *Fam.* 3.1.2; and the host of *litterae commendaticae* in Cic. *Fam.* 13, such as 13.6a.

[12] Ign. *Rom.* 10:1.

[13] The logistic problems and the fact that, as far as I know, the practice was unknown, rule against the possibility. That it could refer to co-authorship is very unlikely especially since the letter to the Romans was such a personal and self-effacing letter of martyrdom. Letters however were carried by groups of persons; see, *e.g.*, Cic. *Fam.* 15.17.1−2.

[14] Walter Bauer, *Die Briefe des Ignatius von Antiochia und der Polykarpbrief*, vol.2, in *Die*

since Ignatius presumably used an amanuensis for all of his letters, the references, which are found in only half of his letters, to people 'through' whom he is writing must mean the carriers.[15]

If then the references are to the carriers, what *Sitz-im-Leben* can explain why only some of the letters mention the carriers? The following reconstruction may explain. Bauer contends that the letters to Ephesus, Magnesia, and Tralles, all written from Smyrna, were carried by the very ones who came to visit Ignatius and thus did not require an introduction for the carrier.[16] According to *Eph.* 2:1, Burrhus was originally from Ephesus and probably was supported by the church at Ephesus, thus explaining Ignatius' prayer in *Eph.* 2:1, "I pray that he may stay longer for the honor of you and your bishop". While in Smyrna, Ignatius sends a letter to the Romans carried by the group of Ephesians (*Rom.* 10:1), but the group does not include Burrhus.[17] While in Troas, the last stop in Asia, Ignatius sends Burrhus home to Ephesus with various letters to deliver on the way. He was to stop in Philadelphia and deliver the letter, which contains a brief introduction explaining his relation to Ignatius and to Smyrna and Ephesus. He was then to drop off the letter to Smyrna, which contains a word of thanks for their contributing to Burrhus' support, "he has refreshed me in every way. Would that all imitated him..."[18]

The second example that demonstrates that the formula "γράφω διά..." need not refer to a secretary comes from Polycarp's letter to the Philippians. This letter concludes in a very similar manner to Ignatius' letters:

Haec vobis scripsi per Crescentem, quem in praesenti commendavi vobis et nunc commendo. Conversatus est enim nobiscum inculpabiliter; credo quia et vo-

---

Apostolischen Väter, 3 vols. in 1, HNTSup (Tübingen: Mohr, 1920), 254, concludes: "Mit διά bei γράφειν können Persönlichkeiten eingeführt werden, die mehr oder weniger bei der Abfassung des Schriftstücks beteiligt gewesen sind (s. zu 1 Peter 5:12, Dionys von Corinth bei Euseb. *H.E.* 4.23.11), anderseits auch — *und das ist die Regel* — der Überbringer (Polyc. ad Phil. 14, Unterschriften paulinischer Briefe: διὰ Φοίβης, διὰ Τίτου usw. Tischendorf, *NT*[8] 2:457, 568, 662, usw.). In diesem Sinne ist die Präposition gewiß an unserer Stelle verwendet". [Italics are mine.]

[15] Ibid.

[16] Ibid. See also Wm. R. Schoedel, *Ignatius of Antioch*, in the Hermeneia Series (Philadelphia: Fortress, 1985), 191.

[17] This is arguing predominantly *e silentio*, but the prayer may indicate that the Ephesian church wished Burrhus home and thus he was not sent to Rome.

[18] Ign. *Smyrn.* 12:1. Schoedel agrees that Smyrna was also contributing to the support of Burrhus and his companions, since *Phld.* 11:2 describes Burrhus as "sent with me by the Ephesians and Smyrnaeans as a mark of honor".

biscum similiter. Sororem autem eius habebitis commendatam, cum venerit ad vos.[19]

The conclusion to his letter is extant only in the Latin version, but clearly "*scripsi per...*" is the Latin equivalent of "γράφω διά..." Crescens is the *carrier* here, because Polycarp commends him and then adds that his sister will likewise receive a commendation when she *comes* to Philippi.[20]

The two foregoing – rather extended – examples demonstrate that the formula "γράφω διά..." or its Latin equivalent "*scripsi per...*" probably refers to the letter carrier and not to the secretary. Hence it is not explicit evidence of the use of a secretary.[21]

bb) References by the Secretary

As a statement by the author that he used a secretary is explicit evidence, certainly also is a similar statement by the secretary. Secretarial references fall into two broad categories: (1) the illiteracy formulae and (2) secretarial remarks in the text.

Exler in the classic study of the illiteracy formula,[22] notes that official communications and contractual/business letters apparently required an explicit notation if the document was written by someone other than the stated writer (sender), in a sense attesting to the identity of the sender and his concurrence with the document in much the same way as a no-

---

[19] Polycarp *Phil.* 14:1, "I have written this to you by Crescens, whom I commended to you when I was present, and now commend again. For he has behaved blamelessly among us, and I believe that he will do the same with you. His sister shall be commended to you when she comes to you".

[20] Again, this does not preclude Crencens from being the secretary as well, but the formula indicates only that he was the carrier.

[21] The same must be contended for Silvanus in 1 Pet. 5:12. Pace E. G. Selwyn, *The First Epistle of St. Peter*, 2d ed. (London: Macmillan & Co., 1947; reprint, Grand Rapids: Baker, 1981), 9–11. Certainly Selwyn is correct that the text reads ἔγραψα not ἔπεμψα διὰ Σιλουανοῦ, but it has now been shown that ἔγραψα διὰ is a formula identifying the letter carrier. Lightfoot's identification of Silvanus as the bearer of the letter is correct (see the discussion in Selwyn, *1 Peter*, 10 n. 1). But *cf.* Theodor von Zahn, *Die Apostelgeschichte des Lukas, Kap. 1–12*, Kommentar zum Neuen Testament, 5/1 (Leipzig, Deichert, 1922), on Acts 15:23. If this did not refer to the carriers as he contends, then he must argue that γράψαντες διὰ χειρός is the full form of what is abbreviated *everywhere else*. Yet the opposite would be more likely: χειρός was included to prevent misunderstanding this as the usual carrier-formula.

[22] Exler, *Form*, esp. pp. 124–27.

tary public today.[23] Occasionally this statement is in the third person, but customarily after stating his name, the scribe adds in the first person that he is writing the document because of the unfamiliarity with, or the total ignorance of, writing on the part of the person for whom he was writing.

Obviously complete illiteracy prompted the most occasions for the need of a secretary and the use of an illiteracy statement. Thus statements of total illiteracy are the most common, hence the most formulaic. The earlier formulae use a prepositional construction, such as "διὰ τὸ μὴ εἰδέναι (ἐπίστασθαι) αὐτὸν γράμματα". Although this formula evidently remains in use until the second Christian century, from the beginning of the Christian era, the participial construction becomes far more common: "ἔγραψα ὑπὲρ αὐτοῦ μὴ εἰδότας γράμματα".[24] Illiteracy formulae were also used when the author was not completely illiterate. Deissmann discusses a quasi-personal letter from Thebes, dated in the Ptolemaic period, which concludes:

> Written for him hath Eumelus the son of Herma..., being desired so to do for that he writeth somewhat slowly.[25]

An interesting variation occurs in a wax tablet,[26] containing a request for the official registry (A.D. 145) of twin sons born (illegitimately) to a Roman father. The official request naturally is in Latin. A Greek subscription follows apparently written by the father who claims only to be the appointed guardian and who is writing for the mother "because she did not know letters". Apparently the father is acting somewhat as a "secretary" for the mother who is illiterate; yet, evidently even he could not write Latin. The official request had to be written by another. Evidently, though, because of the appended Greek subscription which contains an illiteracy (and an attestation) formula, it was not necessary for the Latin secretary to append his own.

In his discussion of the formula, Exler observes:

> It is remarkable, also, how well most letters are written.... One of the reasons for this remarkable correctness of expression and spelling may be the employment of professional scribes. Not a few papyri have been found which were written in

---

[23] There is some similarity also to the later colophons appended to Biblical MS copies by the copyist. Frequently he included his name, occasionally the date or place of production, as a guarantee of correctness – or at least of accountability. Since secretaries often both wrote letters and prepared copies, is there a connection?

[24] Exler, *Form*, 126–27. Examples date 136 B.C. to A.D. 306.

[25] Deissmann, *Light*, 166–67.

[26] The tablet is discussed by Winter, *Life and Letters*, 54–55.

the same hand yet addressed by and to entirely different persons. In purely private letters the scribe or whoever wrote the letter did not need to declare that he, and not the person whose name was found on the document, was the writer.[27]

John White later makes the same observation: "this convention is not employed in ordinary private correspondence..."[28] Thus in a private letter the lack of an illiteracy formula is not necessarily an indication that the author himself wrote the letter. It is possibly here that Otto Roller errs, leading him to the faulty conclusion that dictation was rare in antiquity. He asserts:

> Soviel uns Überlieferung und erhaltene Originale zeigen, kann man wohl sagen, daß ein Schreibkundiger kleine Briefchen von nur wenigen Worten oder Zeilen, wie es die meisten der erhaltenen Papyrus-Originale sind, wohl einmal eigenhändig niederschrieb, und viele, aber durchaus nicht alle der uns erhaltenen, meist von Angehörigen der breiteren Mittelschichten stammenden kurzen Originalpapyrusbriefe dürften eigenhändig sein, soweit es die mitgeteilten Faksimile erkennen lassen. Auch ohne diese ausdrückliche Feststellung ist das eine sofort klar und bedarf keines Beweises, daß jeder, der schreiben konnte und auf Sparsamkeit angewiesen war, seine Briefe, damals wie heute, selbst niederschrieb.[29]

Although he himself later notes the problem: should the presence of only one handwriting be taken as evidence for the author writing personally?[30] he apparently understands many papyrus letters as having been *eigenhändig*. The problem is difficult. Is the one handwriting that of the author's? Yet as Exler observes, "Not a few papyri have been found which were written in the same hand yet addressed by and to entirely different persons".[31] Thus the avoidance of the formula in private letters is not maintained entirely *e silentio*. Consequently, for ascertaining the use of a secretary in a private letter, the absence of an illiteracy formula is *not* significant. While the presence of the formula certainly indicates

---

[27] Exler, *Form*, 126.
[28] White, "Greek Documentary Letter Tradition", 95.
[29] Roller, *Formular*, 4. The condition "jeder der schreiben konnte" is severely limiting. Furthermore, frugality is an issue only if the secretary was paid, which probably was not the case with Paul. His contention for the rarity of dictation has a second element. He only allows for dictation *syllabatim*, which as he argues well was terribly impractical.
[30] Ibid., 252 n. 9: "Dieses Urteil über *Eigenhändigkeit* vieler erhaltener Originalbriefe beruht auf der Gleichheit der Schrift im Briefkontext und in der Unterschrift, ist aber nicht sicher, nachdem Wilcken an diesem Brief gezeigt hat, daß auch in Privatbriefen bei Schreibunfähigkeit des Absenders der Schreiber für denselben den ganzen Brief, einschließlich der Unterschrift ohne weitere Bezeichnung der Stellvertretung in der Unterfertigung, schreiben konnte".
[31] Exler, *Form*, 126.

the employment of a secretary, the absence of the formula does not imply in any way the lack of a secretary.

The second type of secretarial reference that qualifies as explicit evidence are remarks made by the secretary somewhere in the text of the letter. Cicero is returning a greeting from Atticus' secretary in the closing greetings of his responding letter:

> Alexis quod mihi totiens salutem adscribit, est gratum; sed cur non suis litteris idem facit, quod meus ad te Alexis facit?[32]

Cicero requests a more expensive alternative to what was probbably the more usual procedure: the secretary inserts greetings of his own, if he also knows the recipient, usually within the letter's closing greetings.

Possibly it was a greeting from Tiro inserted into Cicero's letter to Marcus Curius, Cicero's banker, that prompted this closing remark in the short reply letter from Curius:

> Ego, patrone mi, bene vale, Tironemque meum saluta nostris verbis.[33]

cc) Changes in Handwriting

Obviously a shift in handwriting indicates a change in writers. When a letter body is written in one script and the closing ἔρρωσο ('*vale*') is in the script of another, the final handwriting is assumed to be the author's and the handwriting of the text that of his secretary, whether amateur or professional.

In today's cursive script, handwriting is quite distinctive, but was this the case in Greco-Roman times when writing was usually in a careful uncial script? Anyone familiar with edited collections of papyri is aware that editors often note when the handwriting changes. Yet to say that something is discernible under the scrutiny of a careful scholar is not to say that handwritings were quite distinct. There is, however, evidence that the ancients noticed changes in handwriting. Five examples will suffice.

(1) An early account of political deceit is related by Plutarch:

> οὗτος ἀγορανομίαν μετιὼν ἡττᾶτο συμπαρὼν δὲ ὁ Κάτων προσέσχε ταῖς δέλτοις μιᾷ χειρὶ γεγραμμέναις· . . .

---

[32] Cic. *Att.* 5.20; "I am pleased that Alexis so often sends greetings to me; but why cannot he put them in a letter of his own, as Tiro, who is my Alexis, does for you?"

[33] Cic. *Fam.* 7.29.2; "Well then, patron mine, a hearty farewell to you, and mind you salute my dear Tiro in my name". This is of course a conjecture. If Curius is not returning a greeting, however, then why is a banker greeting a former slave?

Discerning that the handwriting was the same on all the tablets enables Cato to label the election a fraud.[34]

(2) Ovid asks a friend why he has not written for two years. He adds that whenever he opens a letter, he hopes that it will contain the name of his friend.[35] Bahr maintains that Ovid needed the name, because he would not have recognized the handwriting of the letter, since it would have been written by a secretary.[36]

(3) It will be recalled that when Cicero requests Atticus to send letters in his name, he advises him:

Si signum requirent aut manum, deces me propter custodias ea vitasse.[37]

(4) Suetonius in his description of Titus includes among Titus' skills:

... imitarique chirographa quaecumque vidisset, ac saepe profiteri maximum falsarium esse potuisse.[38]

Not only does this indicate that ancients noticed handwriting, but also that someone who could forge handwriting could find gainful employment.

(5) In a letter to Tiro, his beloved secretary, Cicero expresses his concern over Tiro's extended illness and the lack of recent news. He complains that although a messenger brought news that his fever had abated, he was expecting Hermia to arrive with more recent news. Evidently after Cicero closes the letter, Hermia arrives; therefore Cicero adds this postscript:

---

[34] Plut. *Cat. Min.* 46.2; "He [Marcus Favonius] was being defeated in a candidacy for the aedileship, but Cato, who was present, noticed that the voting tablets were all inscribed in one hand;..." In actuality the interpretation of this passage is more complicated. Its historicity is frequently questioned on the very strong ground that usually votes were recorded not by inscribing a tablet but by turning in the appropriate tablet. A senator had three tablets, corresponding to 'yes', 'no', and 'abstain'. Irrespective, the fact that Plutarch uses the story suggests that it was reasonable in his day to assert that someone noticed the handwriting.

[35] Ovid *Tristia* 4.7.7–8.

[36] Bahr, "Letter Writing", 467. He is probably correct, although Ovid's expression may have been idiomatic.

[37] Cic. *Att.* 11.2.4; "If they look for [my missing] signature or handwriting, say that I have avoided them because of the guards". Cicero took advantage of an opportunity of having Atticus' secretary present and had the secretary write a letter in Atticus' name. Thus the handwriting would not be questioned; Cic. *Att.* 6.6.4.

[38] Suet. *Tit.* 3.2 (see above, p. 29).

Vale. Scripta iam epistula, Hermia venit. Accepi tuam epistulam, vacillantibus litterulis.[39]

This familiarity with handwriting went both ways. In another letter to Tiro, Cicero states:

Ego hic cesso, quia ipse nihil scribo; lego autem libentissime. Tu istis, si quid librarii mea manu non intellegent, monstrabis. Una omnino interpositio difficilior est, quam ne ipse quidem facile legere soleo, de quadrimo Catone.[40]

In addition to being able to discern between different handwritings, an ancient could also tell aberrations in the handwriting of someone with whose handwriting he was familiar.

For the purposes of a modern detection of the use of a secretary, a change in handwriting can be noted in three ways: (1) a discernible change in an extant autograph, (2) a copy containing an annotation of a change, and (3) remarks in the text about a change.

The most obvious way to discern a shift in handwriting is to examine the autograph. Adolf Deissmann, in his classic work, comments that *many* letters were written in two hands.[41] Moulton and Milligan cite — with obvious motive — the Rainier Papyrus 215, where two of the signatures are in a larger hand than the rest of the script.[42]

Because original autographs are not available in most situations, other means of detecting shifts in handwriting are needed. In modern texts, editors note a change frequently by "[2d hand]" or more recently

---

[39] Cic. *Fam.* 16.15.2; "Farewell. Since the above was written, Hermia has turned up. I have gotten your letter, though your poor handwriting is very shaky".

[40] Cic. *Fam.* 16.22.1:
"I am idling here, because I am not writing anything myself, but reading is a great pleasure to me. Being where you are, I am sure you will explain anything the copyists cannot make out on account of my handwriting. There is certainly one rather difficult inserted passage, which even I myself always find it hard to decipher, about Cato at the age of four.[a]

[[a] The story was in all probability that told of Cato Uticensis when a boy, by Plutarch (*Cat. Min.* 2)... This is the story which Cicero added to his work on Cato the Younger, written in 46, but in so cramped a hand that he always found it hard to make out what he had himself written" (LCL 3:371).]

This passage demonstrates that Cicero does on occasion write works in his own hand. Yet this is probably because of the seriousness of the composition (*i.e.*, it could not be dictated extemporaneously) and also perhaps because Tiro was absent.

[41] Deissmann, *Light*, 166–67 n. 7.

[42] J. H. Moulton and G. Milligan, "Lexical Notes from the Papyri", *The Expositor*, 7th ser., 6 (1908): 383.

"[M²]". In the case of a copy, the ancient copyist could mark the change, unfortunately they did not employ such a convention.[43]

Thus in the case of a copy of a letter, authenticity was more difficult to ascertain for even the ancient reader, because any trace of an authenticating signature in the author's own hand was gone. For example, Cicero criticizes his brother for carelessly writing letters to other people which were harsh and insensitive. To make his point, he cites an example. Quintus had written a letter to C. Fabius, whom Cicero did not know, which someone else was showing to others. Cicero was stunned when he read the letter and writes that he hopes that Quintus was not serious in his request for Fabius to have the accused parties burned. He then concludes:

> Hae litterae abs te per iocum missae ad C. Fabium, si modo sunt tuae, cum leguntur, invidiosam atrocitatem verborum habent.[44]

He must have been shown a copy,[45] because Cicero could not be positive the letter was from Quintus, and he knew the handwriting of his brother as well as no doubt the handwriting of Statius, Quintus' secretary.

Because of the problems with copies, the only other reasonably reliable method for detecting a change in handwriting besides an autograph are remarks in the text. Although this criterion is very similar to the criterion 'references by the author', an (artificial) distinction is maintained because the references are not *directly* to the process of using a secretary, such as "I am dictating this...",[46] but rather to a change in handwriting. Four examples will show the various types of remarks commonly found.

(1) Some remarks are simple and straightforward. In a letter to Atticus, Cicero appears to close with greetings after only about one-sixth of the letter. The remaining (larger) section begins with a remark about

---

[43] With the exception discussed below, p. 83, where notations were made in *copies of legal documents* to explain the lack of a different handwriting in the subscription.

[44] Cic. *QFr.* 1.2.6; "That letter you sent by way of a jest to C. Fabius (if indeed it is yours) conveys to the reader an impression of brutality of language".

[45] It is unlikely that they could have secured the original, and making copies of letters to share with others was a common practice. See *e.g.*, Cic. *Att.* 8.12; 13.22; 16.16; and *PTebt.* 32. Also see above, pp. 4–5.

[46] See, *e.g.*, Cic. *Att.* 14.21.

the change in handwriting: "Piliae et Atticae salutem... Haec ad te mea manu".[47]

(2) Some remarks indicate the reason for using another to write down the letter. Cicero's brother begins a letter:

> Cum a me litteras librari manu acceperis, ne paullum quidem oti me habuisse indicato, cum autem mea, paullum.[48]

(3) Personal reasons may also be included in a remark about a change in handwriting. In a letter to Atticus, Cicero acknowledges "Lippitudinis meae signum tibi sit librarii manus".[49]

(4) Another type of remark about a change in handwriting is notable. Because of its "third person" nature, however, it is of less value in a decision about a particular letter. This "third person" remark occurs when a letter comments about a *different* letter containing a change in handwriting. For instance, Cicero tells Atticus that he received a letter from Pompey that contains a postscript in Pompey's own hand.[50] Obviously, unless Pompey's letter is extant and can be ascertained with reasonable certainty, the remark of Cicero is of little assistance. Nevertheless all these various remarks clearly indicate the use of a secretary.[51]

b) Implicit Indications

In addition to the explicit criteria that clearly evidence the use of a secretary in a particular letter, there are indicators in Greco-Roman letters which may imply the use of a secretary. These indicators however only mean that secretarial assistance should be *suspected*. Furthermore, since these indicators are only suggestive, they have varying degrees of reliability, ranging from scarcely more than guesswork up to *but not including* certainty. There are four general types of implicit indicators, ranked somewhat in ascending order of reliability: (1) the presence of a postscript, (2) the preference of the author, (3) the particular letter type, and (4) stylistic variations in an authentic letter.

---

[47] Cic. *Att.* 12.32.1; "Greetings to Pilia and Atticus... The rest I write to you in my own hand."

[48] Cic. *QFr.* 2.16.1; "When you receive a letter from me in my secretary's hand, you may be sure that I have not had a bit of free time; but if in my own hand, just a little".

[49] Cic. *Att.* 8.13.1: "Let my secretary's handwriting be an indication to you of the inflammation of my eyes".

[50] Cic. *Att.* 8.1.1. See also Cic. *Fam.* 16.15.2 (p. 78 n. 39 above).

[51] See also Cic. *QFr.* 3.1.19; 3.3.1; 2.2.1; *Att.* 2.23.1; 4.16.1; 7.13a.3; 8.12.1; 19.14.1; 10.17.2.

aa) The Presence of a Postscript

In a Greco-Roman letter, there are two types of postscripts when categorized by content: summaries and additional material. Gordon Bahr offers an excellent discussion of summary postscripts.[52] He prefers to call these postscripts "summary subscriptions". His work has at its foundation the separation and subsequent reconciliation of the differences between Greco-Roman letters and records.[53] For his purposes — and the purpose here — a record is differentiated from a letter by defining a record as an instrument not specifically designed to communicate between two parties but to recount by a third party the oral agreement reached by the original two parties. Thus a record is a secondary type of document, being merely the fixed form of the oral agreement.[54] The Greeks call a record a ὑπόμνημα (a reminder). When two parties made an oral agreement, a third party recorded it. Consequently this third party served as a secretary, whether amateur or professional. Because the record was a legal document, it was usually written by a professional secretary, for he knew the appropriate form and language. After writing the record, one or more signatures were afixed, depending upon the nature and requirements of the type of agreement.

At this point, the format of ancient records diverges radically from our own, for more than a name was required as a signature in antiquity. The signature was really a summary of the body of the document; by giving this summary, the signator made the contents of the body of the record his own and bound himself to the stipulations of the written form of the oral agreement.[55]

A translated example of a typical record will serve to illustrate the purpose of the subscription (ὑπογραφή). A contract for the sale of a loom from Oxyrhynchus, dated A.D. 54, is commonly cited.

Ammonius, son of Ammonius, to Tryphon, son of Dionysius, greeting. I agree that I have sold to you the weaver's loom belonging to me, measuring three weavers' cubits less two palms, and containing two rollers and two beams, and I acknowledge the receipt from you through the bank of Sarapion, son of Lochus, near the Serapeum at Oxyrhynchus, of the price of it agreed upon between us, namely 20 silver drachmae of the Imperial and Ptolemaic coinage; and that I will

---

[52] G. J. Bahr, "The Subscriptions in the Pauline Letters", *JBL* 87 (1968): 27–41; see also idem, "Letter Writing", 467–68.

[53] His thesis is only summarized here. Because his conclusions are tied to the Pauline letters, he is critiqued in Chap. 3 below, pp. 176–78.

[54] This definition is Bahr's who adapts it from Otto Gradenwitz, *Einführung in die Papyruskunde* (Leipzig: S. Hirzel, 1900), 123–24.

[55] Bahr, "Subscriptions", 28; also Gradenwitz, *Einführung*, 143, 146–50.

guarantee to you the sale with every guarantee, under penalty of payment to you of the price which I have received from you increased by half its amount, and of the damages. This note of hand is valid. The 14th year of Tiberius Claudius Caesar Augustus Germanicus Imperator, the 15th of the month Caesareus.

[2d hand] I, Ammonius, son of Ammonius, have sold the loom, and have received the price of 20 drachmae of silver and will guarantee the sale as aforesaid. I, Heraclides, son of Dionysius, wrote for him as he was illiterate.[56]

It is noteworthy that the subscription typically repeats the important points. The subscription, however, could vary considerably, ranging from an elaborate and thorough summary of the body[57] to only a very brief sketch[58]. The important and distinguishing characteristic of the summary subscription, though, is that it rarely contains anything not found in the body and normally repeats the points in the same sequence.[59]

This role of the subscription in verifying and legalizing a record is not limited to Greek sources.[60] Although evidence for Latin documents is not as common,[61] Ludwig Mitteis argues:

> Das ganze klassische Altertum kennt nicht den Satz, daß die eigenhändige Niederschrift des bloßen Namens unter einer Urkunde als Willenserklärung gilt. Bloße Namensunterschriften sind daher durchaus unerhört, vielmehr besteht die Unterschrift immer in einer kürzeren oder längeren Erklärung des Inhalts, daß man der in einer Urkunde niedergelegten Erklärung beistimme.[62]

---

[56] POxy. 264.

[57] E.g., BGU 910 (Aug. 23, A.D. 71); BGU 183 (A.D. 85); BGU 526 (Oct. 12, A.D. 86); Paul M. Meyer, *Griechische Papyrusurkunden der Hamburger Staats- und Universitäts-bibliothek*, I, no. 30 (Aug. 30, A.D. 89). See Bahr, "Subscriptions", 28 n. 6.

[58] E.g., BGU 713 (A.D. 41/2); BGU 636 (Nov. 5, A.D. 20); *Select Papyri* [PSel.], ed. A. S. Hunt and G. C. Edgar, 2 vols., in LCL, no. 51 (A.D. 47); and Meyer, *Papyrusurkunden*, 64 (Sept. 6, A.D. 104). Brevity had even reached the rare extreme of "as above"; see BGU 526 (Oct. 12, A.D. 86). See also Bahr, "Subscriptions", 29 nn. 7–8.

[59] So Bahr, "Subscriptions", 29; also O. Gradenwitz, *Einführung*, 148: "Sie gibt nie mehr, als in der Urkunde steht", also n. 1. There are exceptions (*e.g.*, POxy. 255, PGiess. 97), but it remains a rather reliable distinction.

[60] Bahr, "Subscriptions", 29–32, cites several pieces of Tannaitic literature. Although he notes that the legalizing aspect in the Jewish subscriptions is the appended signatures of witnesses and not the summaries, he argues that they are somewhat parallel to subscriptions. It seems more likely, however, that the Jewish literary custom arose from the older oral requirement of two witnesses to verify an account, including alterations. The location of the signatures at the end of the record, hence in a "subscription", is only natural.

[61] But see the wax tablet discussed above, p. 74.

[62] L. Mitteis, *Römisches Privatrecht bis auf die Zeit Diokletians*, 2 vols. (Leipzig: Duncker & Humblot, 1908), 1: 304–5.

Furthermore a remark by Apuleius suggests the same. When confronting Aemilianus over whether he had written a letter, Apuleius asks "Estne haec tua epistola?" He further demands "estne tua ista subscriptio?"[63] Evidently something about the subscription, the handwriting no doubt, convinced Apuleius that Aemilianus was the author.

The summary subscription serves the important role of authenticating the agreement, which a secretary has written in the appropriate legal form. The subscription is a recasting of the agreement in the words of one or both of the parties involved, and their handwriting, or the handwriting of their agent, is the seal of their acceptance of the terms of the subscription and hence the body of the document that the subscription reflects. This important role of the handwriting in a subscription prompted an unusual practice in making copies of records. The copyist usually titled a copy with "ἀντίγραφον". Frequently in the case of a document with a subscription, however, the copyist would *repeat* the notation, "ἀντίγραφον," before copying the subscription[64]. Obviously this was done to remind the reader why this (copy of the) subscription is not in a different hand.

Although Bahr will be criticized for blurring the distinctions between records and private letters, this point is well made: the presence of a summary subscription indicates the use of a secretary in the composition of the body of a *record*.[65]

The second type of postscript are those that contain additional material. In Greco-Roman letters this material usually takes two forms: (1) new or forgotten material or (2) secretive or sensitive material. The premise for using a postscript of new or forgotten information as a possible indication of a secretary arises from the time delay usually implied by such a postscript. For example, in a letter from Cassius to Cicero, a postscript begins: "Since writing this letter I have been told..."[66] There has obviously been a time delay of sufficient length to allow the receipt and synthesis of new information, prompting an addition to the letter. Although the letter has apparently been finished, it has not been sealed and dispatched and thus is available for postscripting new material.

---

[63] Apuleius *Apologia* 69 (second Christian century).

[64] *POxy.* 1453. Mitteis, *Privatrecht*, 1: 305, offers additional examples.

[65] That this same point does not pertain to private letters is discussed in Chap. 3 below, pp. 176–78.

[66] Cic. *Fam.* 12.12.5. Many postscripts by the author (as evidenced by a change in handwriting) may be seen in the papyri, where the author appended an ἔρρωσο to the secretarial draft and then added a line or more of additional material; *e.g., POxy.* 2985, also *POxy.* 113, 394, 530.

One possible explanation for a delay is the time required for a secretary to draft the final copy. Cassius may have written the letter using a secretary, who had left then to prepare the final copy. In the interim Cassius receives the new information that he adds when the secretary later returned with the final copy for Cassius to check and to 'sign'. The nature of a 'signature' is not in the modern sense; rather an ancient writer, to close a letter, frequently adds, in his own hand, a healthwish[67] and/or a closing greeting, and occasionally also a date and/or the place of writing. This practice no doubt had an authenticating function. Afterwards he folded and sealed the letter.[68] This example has no closing healthwish before the postscript, while the postscript does conclude with a healthwish and a date, indicating perhaps that such expressions were not added until the letter was ready to seal.[69]

Letters *to* Cicero often contain this type of postscript. In a reply, Cicero mentions:

Extrema pagella pupugit me tuo chirographo Quid ais? Caesarem nunc defendit Curio?[70]

The content of the note as well as Cicero's response implies it was a new development hurriedly scratched into the letter.

In a letter to his young protégé Trebatius, Cicero comments:

Your letter, delivered to me by L. Arruntius, I have torn up, though it did not deserve such a fate; for it contained nothing that might not have been quite pro-

---

[67] Usually the healthwish at the end was merely a *façon de parler* and not an expression of any geniunely occasioned concern.

[68] Tyrrell and Purser, *Cicero*, 7: 98 note that '*signare*' means 'to seal' not 'to sign' but with the same result. The letter was folded repeatedly forming a long narrow strip which was then folded double and usually tied with a string or shred of papyrus. A seal, if used, was impressed in wax covering the knot. According to Meecham, *Light*, 154–55, the two main ideas in sealing were (1) security, the supposition being that if the seal were broken it could not easily be replaced (see *POxy*. 116; 117; 528; 1062; 932; 1293; 1677; Dan. 6:17; Mt. 27:66; akin to security is secrecy, see Rev. 10:4; 22:10); and (2) authentication, the supposition being only the author had his seal (see Cic. *Att*. 11.9; 1 Kg. 21:8; Neh. 9:38; Jer. 32:14; Rom. 4:11; akin to this is ownership; see 1 Cor. 9:2; Eph. 1:13; 2 Cor. 1:22; 2 Tim. 2:19). When Cicero sent a letter to Brutus via Atticus, he wanted Atticus to know its contents. The only way to do this and still leave the letter in deliverable form was to send *another* copy of the letter; Cic. *Att*. 12.18.

[69] Cic. *Att*. 12.18a implies that the date was added when dispatched, meaning that the letter was not sealed until then. New information certainly caused the postscript in Cic. *Att*. 5.19. In Cic. *Br*. 1.2.1, Cicero added a 'postscript' to a *sealed* letter, but he had to use a separate sheet.

[70] Cic. *Fam*. 2.13.3; "The postscript in your own handwriting gave me a twinge of pain. What's this? 'Curio is now defending Caesar'".

perly read out, even at a public meeting. But not only did Arruntius say that such were your instructions, but you yourself added a note [*tu ascripseras*] to that effect. But let that be.[71]

Furthermore, Cicero's claim to have received a letter with a postscript in the hand of Pompey[72] also demonstrates that a postscript could indicate the use of a secretary for the body of the letter.

Not only do the correspondents of Cicero indulge in postscripts, but Cicero does as well. After finishing a letter, he evidently receives a letter with additional details that elicit more discussion: "Scripta iam epistolam superiore, accepi tuas litteras de publicanis, ..."[73] In a letter to Marcellus, a consul in 51 B.C., Cicero apparently intended to end the letter after the second section, for it concludes "Take care of your health, and show your regard for me and defend me in my absence".[74] He uses this verbatim expression, "... me absentum diligas atque defendas", to close his two previous letters to Marcellus.[75] Thus every letter (three in all) written to Marcellus during this time period ends with the same expression.[76] Yet in this third letter, after apparently closing, Cicero adds a short note about why he did not discuss the Parthians. As if after checking the letter, he reconsiders and decides to explain his omission of the topic.

This type of postscript, that is, one of new or forgotten material, is labelled only an implicit indicator and the poorest one at that. What is the problem with using it to indicate the use of a secretary? The problem can be illustrated with three types of examples. (1) A private letter from Oxyrhynchus[77] from an incapacitated man requests the two recipients to send someone to assist him during his recovery. The letter appears to end with the customary greetings. After a slight gap, there follows a postscript advising the recipients what to do if they need funds. This postscript ends with a healthwish. Based on the foregoing argument, one would surmise that a secretary wrote the body of the letter and the man appended the postscript. Yet because it is an autograph, the handwriting can be used to check the accuracy of this conclusion. Indeed the final healthwish is in a second hand, evidencing the use of a secretary;

---

[71] Cic. *Fam.* 7.18.4.
[72] Cic. *Att.* 8.1.1.
[73] Cic. *Fam.* 1.9.26.
[74] Cic. *Fam.* 19.9.2.
[75] Cic. *Fam.* 15.7–8; all written in September 51 B.C.
[76] This pattern is noted by no one else but appears justified.
[77] *POxy.* 3314; fourth Christian century.

however, the *postscript* is in the secretary's hand. It is not unreasonable then to argue that if the man was able — or willing — to write the letter himself, it might still have contained the postscript.

(2) The problem with using postscripts of new or forgotten material as an indicator of a secretary can be illustrated by a different type of example: the letters of Plato.[78] Before these letters are discussed, a general observation should be made. Surely the goal of the forgeries was to appear as letters written by Plato. The letters contain no explicit evidence of the use of a secretary, presumably because the forger wished them to appear as being from the hand of Plato himself. If the forger designed much intermediation, it would defeat the purpose of the exercise.

Among the letters of Plato, *Ep.* 1 is "certainly spurious" and probably dates no later than the first Christian century and possibly earlier.[79] This forgery concludes with "Farewell [ἔρρωσο]. May you realize how much you have lost in me and conduct yourself better toward others".[80] Plato's second letter, also spurious and from the same time period,[81] concludes with ἔρρωσο and then additional remarks.[82] The tenth letter, which is probably also spurious,[83] again concludes with ἔρρωσο, and then a brief platitude of encouragement.

Notably, as the unquestionably spurious letters all contain a word of farewell and then a postscript of some type, both unquestionably genuine letters, *Epp.* 7 and 8,[84] have no word of farewell and no postscript.

---

[78] Doty correctly concludes that most — if not all — of Plato's letters are forgeries. Moreover, the letters of Plato were to be models of style and thinking, not epistolary form, and therefore should not be used as examples of letter writing in the time of Plato (Doty, "Epistle", 53; see also Sykutris, "Epistolographie", 217). Yet he does not use the letters as evidence for the period in which they were forged. He even quips that *Epp.* 6 and 8 are not like Plato but are more like later letters. They are later letters! As progymnasmatic forgeries, they may be taken as "school examples" of a proper letter during the time they were actually written.

[79] Glenn R. Morrow, *Plato's Epistles: a Translation with Critical Essays and Notes* (Indianapolis: Bobbs & Merrill, 1962), 191; also Plato *Epistles*, in *The Works of Plato*, vol. 7, ed. and trans. R. G. Bury, in LCL, 393.

[80] Plato *Ep.* 1.310b.

[81] So Morrow, *Plato's Epistles*, 196 n. 3; and Bury, *Epistles of Plato* (LCL), 399.

[82] The additional remarks include references to the carrier, "You will then send Archedemus back to me" and incidental remarks, "There is something wrong with the globe; and Archedemus will point it out to you when he arrives" (*Ep.* 2.312d).

[83] Bury, *Epistles of Plato* (LCL), 597, contends "There need be no hesitation, therefore, in rejecting this letter also as a spurious composition". Morrow, *Plato's Epistles*, 259 n. 1, is less certain due to the brevity of this commendation letter.

[84] Morrow, *Plato's Epistles*, 44–60, "certainly genuine"; so also Bury, *Epistles of Plato* (LCL), 463–75.

Two other letters are probably authentic, *Epp.* 3 and 6,[85] and neither contain a word of farewell nor a postscript. The authenticity of *Epp.* 4, 5, 9, 11, and 12 is debated; yet none have a postscript and only three contain any word of farewell (εὐτύχει). The thirteenth letter is probably a clever forgery,[86] and contains an extended postscript.

If this analysis is correct, then the first century forgeries contain postscripts, a practice apparently not employed by Plato himself.[87] For a forger to make such a mistake, one must assume that postscripts were an established and accepted part of epistolary convention during the time of the forger (the first Christian century). Furthermore, if the letters were forged to appear as autographs of Plato, then apparently in the first century it was quite acceptable for an author to append a postscript, particularly one of lesser matters, to a letter written with his own hand.[88]

In addition to these first two weaknesses for using a postscript to indicate the use of a secretary (that is, there are rhetorical and organizational reasons for placing certain types of material in a postscript), a third weakness exists: the 'time-delay' can have alternative causes. There would of course be a delay between writing and dispatching when a secretary was used. There are, however, other situations that could cause a sufficient time delay. Most notably, the departure of the carrier could be delayed. Furthermore the author may have chosen to compose his letter over several days or longer, leaving it open for later additions.

Thus, in summation, a postscript of new or forgotten material may certainly indicate the use of a secretary, but it is not a reliable indicator. This one point, however, may be made, if the letters of Cicero are representative: if one has already ascertained that a secretary was used, then a postscript may indicate where the author began writing in his own hand.

In a letter to his brother, Cicero is making some final miscellaneous observations. After commenting upon some writer, whom apparently Quintus has written that he is enjoying, Cicero adds: "Sed quod ascribis,

---

[85] Morrow, *Plato's Epistles*, 200 n. 2, and 214 n. 6 (respectively), defends their geniuneness. Bury, *Epistles of Plato* (LCL), 422–23, and 454–55 (respectively), is more skeptical but allows that the cases against them are weaker.

[86] Bury, *Epistles of Plato* (LCL), 613.

[87] I found no one who suggests this line of argument, but it has promise.

[88] Ps-Socr. *Ep.* 9, dated *ca.* A.D. 200, contains about 17 lines of general philosophical reflection. This section concludes with ἔρρωσο. About 25 lines follow with more specific remarks of a more practical (and personal) and less philosophical nature, exhorting the recipient toward a cynic lifestyle and to seek the counsel of "Simon the Shoemaker". See also Ronald F. Hock, "Simon the Shoemaker as an Ideal Cynic", *GRBS* 17 (1976): 41–53.

aggrederisne ad historiam?"[89] Why Quintus reserved such a remark for a postscript is less clear. While this certainly may be merely another example of relegating new or forgotten material to a postscript, it may also be an example of the second type of postscript containing additional material, that is, it may be a postscript of secretive or sensitive material. Quintus may not have wished to announce his literary ambitions to his secretary or whomever else was present. Although still a postscript of additional material, this type does not fall prey to all the weaknesses of postscripts of new or forgotten material.

In the opening discussion of a letter, Cicero states "Haec negotia quomodo se habeant, ne epistula quidem narrare audeo".[90] He goes on to discuss a little of the matter then interrupts himself, "Sed haec ipsa, nescio, rectene sint litteris commissa; quare cetera cognosces ex aliis".[91] These two examples illustrate the two kinds of secretive or sensitive material: (a) information too sensitive to risk a lost or intercepted letter, thus usually politically sensitive material; and (b) information that one does not wish to become public knowledge or even household gossip, thus usually more confessional material.

In the middle of a letter to Atticus, Cicero notes:

> But here I take the pen myself; for I shall have to deal with confidential matters![92]

In a long letter of advice to his brother, Cicero cautions Quintus about using slaves in his work:

> Of course, if anyone of your slaves stands above the rest in trustworthiness, employ him in your domestic and private affairs; but with matters belonging to your office as governor, or with any State department, – with such matters don't let him meddle. For there are many things which may quite properly be entrusted to honest slaves, but which, for all that, in order to avoid tittle-tattle and fault-finding, should not be so entrusted.[93]

How is it that such information could become household gossip? Attending servants could be dismissed temporarily. Obviously, though, a

---

[89] Cic. *QFr.* 2.12.4; "But about your postscript – do you really intend taking up history?"

[90] Cic. *Fam.* 2.5.1; "What the state of affairs is here I dare not tell you even in a letter".

[91] Cic. *Fam.* 2.5.2; "But I am not sure that it is safe to have entrusted to a letter even what I have just written; so you will be told all the rest by others".

[92] Cic. *Att.* 11.24. Why explicitly state this? The handwriting would reveal it. Perhaps he wished to give Atticus warning, if he was using a reader.

[93] Cic. *QFr.* 1.1.18; "... tamen sermonis et vituperationis vitandae causa committenda non sunt".

secretary who records (or composes) the letter would know of the matter. This problem of gossiping secretaries is explained more fully in another letter:

> Neque enim sunt epistulae nostrae eae quae si perlatae non sint, nihil ea res nos offensura sit; quae tantum habent mysteriorum, ut eas ne librariis quidem fere committamus, lepidum quid ne quo excidat.[94]

Suetonius tells that when Caesar wrote personal letters to Cicero and his other friends, he usually did so in his own hand, and when he had anything confidential to say, he wrote it *"per notas."*[95] Likewise, in a letter to Atticus Cicero ventures his opinion about the activities of some other important figures and declares that he thought it wise to write the letter in his own hand.[96]

A letter from Brutus to Cicero includes an engaging statement, "Quae tibi superioribus litteris mea manu scripsi, terrendi tui causa homines loquuntur".[97] It implies that Brutus has added a postscript in his own hand containing some accusations (or whatever) that he either (1) learned later, (2) remembered later, or (3) did not wish the secretary to know. Considering the circumstances and the brevity of the letter, the third possibility is the most probable. Brutus did not wish the secretary and/or others present to know of the slander (or whatever) brought against Cicero. In a similar manner, Cicero announces to Trebatius, his often wayward protégé:

> And so, since what you lawyers term 'guarantees' don't hold water, I have sent you a 'guarantee' in Greek of a sort, — and in my own handwriting.[a]
>
> [a This probably means that Cicero had sent Trebatius a private letter of instructions as to his behaviour towards Caesar, and that, to insure secrecy, he had written it in such Greek as he could command, and in his own hand.][98]

---

[94] Cic. *Att.* 4.17.1; "For our letters are not such that it would do no harm to us if they are not delivered. They are full of secrets that we cannot even trust an amanuensis as a rule, for fear of some jest leaking out". Interestingly the risk was not from enemy interception but from indifferent gossip.

[95] Suet. *Caes.* 56.6; "with signs".

[96] Cic. *Att.* 15.20.4. Cicero tells Atticus (8.12) that he dictated the letter because his eyes were still troubling him, but "yesterday I wrote myself to the best of my ability a letter containing prognostications". Why write personally if his eyes were bothering him? This previous letter is extant (8.11) and contains some very sensitive material.

[97] Cic. *Fam.* 11.23.2: "What I wrote to you with my own hand in my last letter is only what people are saying with the object of intimidating you".

[98] Cic. *Fam.* 7.18.1 (LCL 2: 57).

Consequently, if a letter contains a postscript that includes *secretive* or *sensitive* material *not* discussed in the body of the letter — that is, the postscript is not merely a summary — then it may well be an indication of an autographic postscript appended to a letter body written by a secretary. For if the entire letter is from the pen of the author, then there was no reason to reserve such material for a postscript. This argument gains strength significantly if the body of the letter alludes to or discusses matters that should have precipitated the material reserved for the postscript, thereby insuring the material in the postscript was not merely new or forgotten.

In summary, the presence of a postscript may imply the use of a secretary, but there are limitations. Summary postscripts are strong indicators in legal records, but the practice does not appear to extend to private letters. Both types of postscripts of additional material also have limitations. There are other valid reasons for reserving new or forgotten material to a postscript that do not involve a secretary. Certainly secretive or sensitive material may be placed in an autographed postscript to protect it from the eyes and ears of others. Yet determining what qualifies is difficult.[99] Therefore, while a postscript may indicate the use of a secretary in the writing of a letter, it is the weakest indicator.

bb) The Preference of the Author

The individual preference of the author concerning the use of a secretary in writing his private letters is a much stronger indicator. In a letter to Atticus, Cicero claims:

> Numquam ante arbitror te epistulam meam legisse nisi mea manu scriptam. Ex eo colligere poteris, quanta occupatione distinear. Nam, cum vacui temporis nihi haberem, et cum recreandae voculae causa necesse esset mihi ambulare, haec dictavi ambulans.[100]

---

[99] It is not impossible. For example, Cicero wrote eight letters to Atticus during his exile from Rome until his return in Jan. 57 B.C. (*Att.* 3.10–17). It is quite possible that the secretarial drafts ended in these letters with a formulaic request to be kept informed (so in seven of the eight letters; 3.14 ends with travel plans and a formulaic note that he will *send* news). Thus the additional remarks found in two letters (3.13 and 3.15) that *follow* the formulaic request are quite possibly autographed postscripts by Cicero.

[100] Cic. *Att.* 2.23.1; "I don't think you ever before read a letter of mine which I had not written myself. That will show you that I am plagued to death by business. As I haven't a moment to spare, and must take some exercise to refresh my poor voice, I am dictating this as I walk".

Bahr contends that Seneca also claimed to write his letters in his own hand, citing *Ep.* 26.8.[101] This text, "Desinere iam volebam et manus spectabat ad clausulam; ...", however, does not require such an interpretation.[102]

Authorial preference can only suggest a secretary because authors were not unfailingly consistent. While Cicero's confession to Atticus (quoted above) certainly should apply to his previous letters, one must allow for rhetorical exaggeration and slips of memory.[103] Furthermore, preferences are not invariable. As a matter of point, Cicero later writes to Atticus that on the previous day he dictated two letters to him *and* wrote another in his own hand.[104] Evidently Atticus writes some letters in his own hand[105] and others with a secretary[106].

The vacillations of some authors stand in contrast to the consistency of others. The statement by Suetonius that Caesar wrote to his friends in his own hand should be a fairly reliable indicator. Furthermore, albeit with less certainty, the increasing frequency of Cicero's references to using a secretary because of the crush of his daily schedule should be considered when examining similar letters from the same time period. Therefore if an author is shown to prefer the use of a secretary during a particular time, then one may assume the same of his other similar letters in which a secretary is less evident, provided such things as his personal, epistolary, geographical, or financial situation has not changed dramatically.

cc) The Particular Letter-type

It has been noted before in a different context that certain types of letters, mainly official and business letters, are so bound by conventional forms and formulae that to insure a proper letter the writer needed to be

---

[101] Bahr, "Letter Writing", 468.

[102] Sen. *Ep.* 26.8; "I was just intending to stop, and my hand was making ready for the closing sentence;..." This text *may* mean he was writing personally, but in no way implies a customary practice.

Is Bahr's reference in Seneca misprinted? Yet I could find no alternate text, although *Ep.* 8.1–2 *might* imply that Seneca wrote personally.

[103] However tempting, such a remark must not become a litmus test of authenticity. *Cf.* 2 Thes. 3:17.

[104] Cic. *Att.* 10.3a.1.

[105] Cic. *Att.* 6.9.1 and 7.3.1.

[106] Cic. *Att.* 7.2.3 and 6.6.4.

trained. Moreover, it has already been shown that most individuals lacked the necessary education to write such letters without assistance.

Letters were expected to comply with the traditionally ascribed forms, as illustrated in these three examples. (1) Winter notes two papyri[107] where a royal secretary has been promoted temporarily to a higher rank. Meanwhile it became necessary for a letter to be written to this higher position. Consequently the secretary writes a letter *to himself* with all the customary honorific titles. (2) In a very rhetorical letter to Curio[108] Cicero complains that he has nothing to write and supports his complaint by demonstrating that there was no letter type available to express what he wished to say. As a result, Cicero writes a letter about nothing rather than branch into a new type of letter. (3) The writer of a papyrus letter severely chides his recipient for having sent an improperly written letter.[109] In order to avoid this type of embarrassment, secretaries were customarily used for writing these types of letters. Thus when one of these specialized types of letters appears having an untrained person for the author, then one may readily assume that a secretary was used.[110] The limitation of this indicator for the purposes here is that most types of private correspondences do not fall within those which usually necessitated the use of a secretary.

dd) Stylistic Variations in an Authentic Letter

This indicator may be the most reliable, but it is also fraught with difficulties, the major one being the determination of the authenticity of the letter. The letter must be determined or assumed to be authentic prior to the application of this criterion. However many modern techniques may fail to recognize the possible influences of a secretary upon their analyses.

How did the ancients determine authenticity? Cicero demonstrates the major method, *via negativa*, when in a politically dangerous period he at-

---

[107] Wilcken, *Archiv für Papyrusforschung* 4.123 and *PL*. 69.508; see Winter, *Life and Letters*, 25.

[108] Cic. *Fam.* 2.4.

[109] *POxy*. 1837 (early sixth century); "No one who wishes to make a charge or a complaint writes it at the beginning of his letter, lest he who reads should be annoyed and they should not read the letter, but you wrote your beginning in the form of a plea..." See also *POxy*. 928 (second or third century).

[110] If Galatians is a highly structured apologetic letter (as suggested by H. D. Betz), then either a well trained secretary was used or Paul himself received a high level of education in Hellenistic rhetoric. This is discussed below, p. 182.

tempts to represent some of his letters as *inauthentic*, trying to disguise them in case they are intercepted. Therefore he advises Atticus:

> However, I have written this in a hurry, and, I may say, in a fright too. Some time I will give you a clear account if I find a very trustworthy messenger; or if I veil my meaning you will manage to understand it. In these letters I will call myself Laelius and you Furius and convey the rest in riddles.[111]

After a day's thought, he realizes that his original strategy was faulty and in the next letter he offers this revision:

> I said I would call you Furius in my letters, but there is no need to alter your name. I will call myself Laelius and you Atticus, and I won't use my own handwriting or seal, at any rate if the letters are such that I should not like them to fall into a stranger's hands.[112]

In order to hide his identity, Cicero does not write in his own hand, showing that, for the ancients, authenticity was usually determined by the handwriting.

Cicero also mentions that he would not use his seal. "The seal was looked on as the formal guarantee of genuineness for the handwriting was generally that of a slave, if the writer possessed sufficient means to keep a *servus a manu* or *ab epistulis*".[113] The importance of the seal may be seen in another of Cicero's misadventures. He took wrongful advantage of an opportunity to intercept two letters which he suspected spoke badly of him to others. After reading them, he realizes that they would have done him no harm and therefore sends them to Atticus, with the notation that Atticus could proceed to deliver them. Cicero adds "Though the seals are broken, I think Pomponia has his signet".[114]

What did an ancient do, however, when the letter was not in a recognizable hand or the seals were already broken, for example, when a copy of a letter was circulating? In other words, when faced with a situation like that of the modern investigator, how did an ancient determine a letter's authenticity? Two ancient criteria for authenticity may be inferred *via negativa*: (1) although a letter deviates in diction, phraseology, or grammar from the author's custom, the style,[115] tone, or argument is re-

---

[111] Cic. *Att.* 2.19; July 59 B.C.
[112] Cic. *Att.* 2.20.
[113] Tyrrell and Purser, *Cicero*, 1: 56.
[114] Cic. *Att.* 11.9.
[115] The term "style" is used more loosely here in a more encompassing sense, as in Webster's definition "a manner of expression characteristic of an individual, period, school, or nation", such as the proclivity for the diatribe, the manner or extent of the ci-

cognizably the author's; and (2) although the letter deviates also from the author's customary style, tone, or argument as well as his diction, phraseology, or grammar, the letter is recognizably from the pen of a trusted colleague who was unlikely to have written in the author's name without his permission or direction. Albeit perhaps unusual in nature, there is evidence that the ancients used these two criteria to determine a letter's genuineness.

Three examples will demonstrate the use of the first criterion: a letter is still accepted as genuine, although it deviates from the author's customary diction, phraseology, or grammar, when it is recognizably in the author's larger style, tone, or method of argumentation. (1) Cicero wrote a speech that he later wished to have represented as inauthentic or pseudonomous. He considers this possible not because the diction or grammar was unusual for him, but because the tone, style, and argument was not typical of his works.

> Your news too that my speech has been published is a blow to me. Heal the wound, if possible, as you propose. In my indignation I paid him back in his own coin: but I had suppressed it so carefully that I thought it would never leak out. How it has, I can't imagine. But since it so happens that I have never said a word against him, and this appears to me to be more carelessly written than my other speeches, I should think it could be passed off as someone else's work. If you think my case is not hopeless, please pay attention to the matter; . . .[116]

It is Atticus, an ancient publisher, who first suggests the ploy, and Cicero apparently believes that it will work. (It may well have.[117])

(2) This criterion was used to ascertain that a letter purportedly from Caesar was in fact a forgery. Atticus shared a copy of the letter from Caesar with Cicero, and he apparently sent the copy to Cicero without comment perhaps to see if Cicero would also raise objections to the letter's genuineness. He does, declaring:

---

tation of authorities, or, as possibly in the letters of Epicurus, the readdressing of the recipient before closing imperatives.

[116] Cic. *Att.* 3.12. He usually carefully edited his material. Does he mean a lack of editing when he states that it was "more carelessly written"?

There is actually another element at work as well: inconsistency with known works of the author.

[117] Cic. *Att.* 3.15; "Sed quid Curio? an illam orationem non legit? quae unde sit prolata, nescio".

...the letter you send does not give me any consolation. For it is grudgingly written, and raises great suspicion that it is not by Caesar; I expect you noticed that too.[118]

Cicero makes no appeal, for instance, to deviations in vocabulary or grammar as evidence of the letter's inauthenticity. Rather he appeals to its "out of character" nature.

(3) Tyrrell and Purser, authors of the monumental commentary on Cicero's letters, use this argument to reject the supposed letter of Cicero to Octavian:

> That this letter is the work of a rhetorician, and a very foolish one too, is evident. The complete lack of dignity, the feeble impotent abuse, and the utter aimlessness of the whole production stamp it at once as entirely alien from Cicero's style.[119]

Again, such things as *hapax legomena*, variations in diction, or deviations from established phraseology are not considered. The reason is clear: a secretary can easily account for such differences. Hence such differences may not indicate a forgery. This is, however, a one-way street. Diction, grammar, and phraseology can be used to support a letter's authenticity (and that it probably had little or no secretarial mediation), but they cannot be used to deny its authenticity.

Consequently, if a letter is already suspected to be authentic for various reasons including perhaps the presence of the author's tone or argument, yet the diction, phraseology or grammar is not typical for the author, the use of a secretary should be considered, probably in the role of an editor or perhaps a co-author. It is this variability that allows Cicero to ask Atticus to send simple letters in his name. How could Atticus otherwise hope to succeed in this little ploy? Surely Cicero's friends were not so unfamiliar with his style, nor was Atticus able to mimic Cicero's style well enough to fool their close friends. Variations in style were simply not items of suspicion, because of the influences of a secretary.

The second test for authenticity involves a letter that deviates from the author in both minor ways, such as diction, and major ways, such as style or argumentation. All these factors point to a forgery. Yet the letter is recognized as from the hand of a trusted collegue. Presumably he would not have written in the author's name without his consent and probably his direction. Apparently the author's consent may be assumed

---

[118] Cic. *Att.* 11.16; "... Nam et exigue scripta est et suspiciones magnas habet non esse ab illo;..."

[119] Tyrrell and Purser, *Cicero*, 5: 338–39.

when a trusted colleague (or secretary) ventures to compose in his name. Two examples will suffice.

(1) Atticus insistently asks Cicero to write a speech for publication in Brutus' name (not for deceit but to aid their common cause). Atticus wishes to put the best possible speech on the lips of the visible leader of their cause. Initially Cicero responds:

> I want to assist Brutus in every way that is possible. I see you have the same opinion of his harangue as I have. But I don't quite understand why you want me to write a speech attributing it to Brutus, when he has published his own. How could that be proper?[120]

When Atticus insists, Cicero balks because again Brutus had already written on the subject and because Brutus has not *asked* Cicero.

> You are very insistent about Brutus' speech, since you say so much about it again. Am I really to plead the same case as that he has written about? Am I to write without being asked by him? One could not put one's oar in more rudely.[121]

(2) A letter from Pompey but actually written by another is considered by Cicero to be Pompey's even though Cicero knows it is from the pen of Sestius.

> Scriptae enim et datae ita sunt, ut proponerentur in publico. In quo accusavi mecum ipse Pompeium, qui, cum scriptor luculentus esset, tantas res atque eas, quae in omnium manus venturae essent, Sestio nostro scribendas dederit. Itaque nihil umquam legi scriptum σηστιωδέστερον.[122]

Although Pompey is himself a good writer, he delegates the task of composing this very important letter to a colleague, Sestius. The style is obviously — at least to Cicero — not Pompey's, but Cicero assumes that Pompey approved of and probably even suggested the contents. Notably, it is because Cicero recognizes the style of Sestius[123] and *not* because the letter does not match the style of Pompey[124] that he suspects that the

---

[120] Cic. *Att.* 15.3.

[121] Cic. *Att.* 15.4.

[122] Cic. *Att.* 7.17: "You should know already the reply that Pompey is sending by Lucius Caesar, and the nature of his letter to Caesar; for it was written and sent on purpose to be published. Mentally I blamed Pompey who, though a clear writer himself, gave Sestius the task of drawing up documents of such importance, which were to come into everyone's hands. Accordingly I have never seen anything more Sestian in its style".

[123] Cicero knew Sestius because he had defended Sestius in 56 B.C.; see Cic. *Pro Sestio*. *Cf.* Catullus 44 (84–54 B.C.) for comments on Sestius' style.

[124] Cicero knew Pompey's style as well. Despite his affirmation here that Pompey is a clear writer, he elsewhere considers Pompey to be a careless writer: "Please note his [Pompey's] careless style and my careful answer" (*Att.* 8.11).

letter was not from the actual pen of Pompey. Accordingly, because Sestius is a known associate of Pompey and thus deemed unwilling to write pseudonymously, Pompey's letter is not considered a forgery by Cicero. Rather the letter is treated as authentic because the actual writer is assumed to be acting as the stated author's secretary, serving in the role of a co-author or perhaps a composer. Therefore a letter written by a trusted colleague should be considered authentic, that is, the letter may be deemed at least to be consonant with the thoughts and sentiments of the author by virtue of the trust that exists between the stated author and the actual author.

Although both ancient criteria for authenticity are substantiated only from examples *via negativa*, they nevertheless indicate that because of the use of secretaries, letters were not rejected on the basis of style analyses alone.[125]

2. Situational Considerations for Determining the Secretarial Method Employed in a Particular Letter

After a letter is determined — or even suspected — to have been written with the aid of a secretary, there still remains to ascertain in what role the secretary was used, that is, was the secretary employed to record, edit, co-author, or compose the letter? While an author may on occasion specify how he is employing his secretary, most are not so helpful.

Several ancient writers, notably Cicero, occasionally carefully elucidate how they are specifically employing their secretary for a particular letter and thus provide an established point of departure. Moreover, since many of these letters, especially Cicero's, are also very self-revelatory, much of the ancient situation immediately surrounding the writing of that letter can be reconstructed. When these two factors, the stated role of the secretary and the epistolary situation are correlated, one finds that a particular epistolary situation was more likely to precipitate a certain usage of the secretary.

With some secretarial methods the epistolary situation could be surmissed *a priori*, that is, the reason for their use is self-evident. In fact, the entire procedure (correlating a stated secretarial method to a stated [or inferred] epistolary situation) runs the risk of often only concluding the

---

[125] The inappropriateness of stylistic analysis for determining authenticity is argued forcibly by Roller in his first chapter; *Formular*, 1−33.

obvious, for after the method and situation are correlated, many of the conclusions will correspond to what was suspected anyway. Nonetheless the few exceptions may be significant. The goal of the investigation into the epistolary situations, however, is to be able then to work the procedure in reverse, that is, to use known epistolary situations to suggest possible secretarial roles. In many letters, especially those of Paul, great efforts have already been expended, for other reasons, to discern their epistolary situation. Armed with such an analysis, one can conjecture the secretarial usage most likely to have been employed in that situation.

The four secretarial roles will be discussed separately but grouped under two more general headings[126]: author-controlled letters, that is, those letters where the secretary records or edits the letter of the author; and secretary-controlled letters, that is, those letters where the influence of the secretary is considerably more, that of a co-author or even a composer.[127]

a) An Author-Controlled Letter

While a certain situation may precipitate an author-controlled letter, there are frequently too many other variables to suggest specifically whether the secretary is merely recording or also editing. For example, when a letter of Cicero[128] contains several *very* subtle plays on words, one should assume the text is author-controlled, since a secretary is less likely to be able to handle such witticisms. When another letter of Cicero[129] has a haphazard structure, leaping from one idea to another and possessing a very "chatty" character, then the secretary probably also was recording or only slightly editing the letter, for any editing apparently did not extend to an improvement in the organization of the letter. Differentiating between a secretary used as a recorder and one used as an editor was not always merely a modern problem. Often the limitations of the secretary determined how the author used him. The author may prefer the secretary only to record the letter. The secretary, however,

---

[126] There is actually an initial secretarial category that is not discussed: "no secretary". A letter writer could choose not to use a secretary, because either there was no secretary readily available and the author could himself write, or the author *preferred* to write himself, perhaps for convenience, economy, or secrecy.

[127] The two more general headings are employed because at times it becomes impossible to differentiate between two closely related uses by situational considerations alone.

[128] Cic. *Fam.* 5.5.2.

[129] Cic. *Fam.* 8.9.

may be forced by his own lack of recording skill into a reconstruction — hence editing — of the author's text.

aa) The Secretary as a Recorder

The familiar passage about Cicero dictating to Spintharus *syllabatim* but to Tiro in whole sentences should be reexamined with more contextual attention.

> But pray tell me, were you very pleased with my letter to Varro? May I be hanged if I ever take so much trouble with anything again. So I did not even dictate it to Tiro, who can follow whole sentences as dictated, but syllable by syllable to Spintharus.[130]

This passage is often cited to argue for the limited availability of secretaries skilled in shorthand. Cicero is forced to use someone who is able only to take dictation at the speed of script, a less desirable situation. Yet the situation suggests otherwise. Varro was an influential and powerful man in Roman life, whose respect Cicero coveted. In three different letters Cicero refers to Varro in terms of respect. To improve their relationship, he dedicates the *Academica* to Varro and alters the content to make Varro the principal figure.[131] Cicero, though, still fretted over how Varro might receive it, expressing his misgivings to Atticus.[132] Nevertheless he continued and less than a week later sent the work to Rome to be copied onto fine large paper (*macrocolla*) as a gift for Varro.[133]

When he sent the corrected work,[134] Cicero composed a letter to accompany it, and it is this letter that contains the passage about dictating *syllabatim*. Cicero claims to have spent an inordinate amount of time on the composition of this letter. He was quite proud of it.[135] Because he has spent much time on the planning and composition of the letter, naturally he wishes the secretarial copy to be precisely what he planned. Why did he not dictate it to Tiro? He states that it is because Tiro records entire sentences, no doubt meaning some form of shorthand. This implies however that the result of Tiro's work may not always have been *preci-*

---

[130] Cic. *Att.* 13.25.
[131] This edition (in four volumes) is known as *The Academica Posteriora*.
[132] Cic. *Att.* 13.14.
[133] Cic. *Att.* 13.21; 13.25.
[134] See Cic. *Att.* 13.23.
[135] See Cic. *Att.* 13.25. Apparently Varro was not an easy man to please. Cicero did not welcome a visit from Varro, who arrived like the *lupus in fabula*. Yet Cicero courted Varro's favor. See Tyrrell and Purser, *Cicero*, 5: xx.

sely what Cicero said. It should be recalled that Cicero could, on occasion, debate the use of a preposition in a letter.[136] Thus to insure that the letter to Varro was exactly what he wanted, he dictates it syllable by syllable to Spintharus. Why did he not dictate slowly to Tiro? He may not have wished to offend the sensitivities of his friend by besmirching his abilities. Although dictation could be done at the speed of script or at the speed of *vivae vocis*, this text may imply that *precise ipsissima verba* requires the former. The difference, however, is probably negligible, and thus this text reflects more Cicero's nervousness concerning Varro than any significant differences. Irrespective of Cicero's apprehension, though, the implication remains that when Cicero wished the letter to be reproduced verbatim, exactly how he stated it, he dictated to a secretary *syllabatim*.

If Cicero was concerned about the letter to this extent, why did he not write the letter personally? Since he expended so much effort on the letter, one may presume that he used some form of rough draft and did not compose extemporaneously. The answer may lie in the matter of handwriting. If Cicero was willing to pay to have his work for Varro copied on the finest material, he may also have wished the accompanying letter to have a pleasing appearance, written in a fine, careful hand. Therefore he used Spintharus who perhaps had a better hand than Cicero (or Tiro). This is certainly not the only case where the issue of handwriting caused the use of a secretary.[137]

If the need for precise reproduction could cause the use of a secretary to record at the speed of script, what could prompt the use of a secretary to record at the speed of *vivae vocis*? Convenience is a powerful motivator. Bahr states it plainly, "Secretaries were just very convenient people to have at one's disposal".[138] Cicero notes how one could save time.

Cum a me litteras librari manu acceperis, ne paullum quidem oti me habuisse iudicato, cum autem mea, paullum.[139]

---

[136] Cic. *Att.* 7.3.

[137] See *inter permulti* Deissmann, *Light*, 166–67: "Written for him hath Eumelus the son of Herma..., being desired to do so for that he writeth somewhat slowly". Deissmann has a similar understanding of Gal. 6:11; see *St. Paul: a Study in Social and Religious History*, trans. L. R. M. Strachan (London: Hodder & Stoughton, 1912), 51 and below, pp. 174–75.

[138] Bahr, "Letter Writing", 469.

[139] Cic. *QFr.* 2.16.1; "When you receive a letter from me in my secretary's hand, you may be sure that I have not had even a moment's leisure; if in my own, that I have had just a little". See also 3.3.1; 2.2.1; and *Att.* 2.23.1; 4.16.1.

Rhetorical aspects aside, Cicero is indicating that using a secretary saved a considerable bit of time. He must therefore be speaking of dictating *viva voce* for he indicated in the Varro incident that dictating *syllabatim* was very time consuming.

Convenience extended beyond a mere savings in time. By using a secretary Cicero was able to dictate during meals.[140] With a secretary he could also dictate while walking or travelling.[141] A secretary permitted a letter to be sent with little or no premeditation, such as Cicero's letter to the younger Curio on the death of the elder Curio. He advises Curio that he had prevented Curio's agent from ordering the customary spectacles for his father's funeral. He announces that he will not explain his reasons until he met Curio face to face. He then immediately begins explaining himself but then stops and observes:

> But I am not acting as I declared I would; I am entering upon a reasoned explanation of my views; so I postpone all discussion of this until you arrive.[142]

Although the opposite attitude prevails in modern times, the ancient writer practiced and valued oral delivery over a written presentation. In his recent discussion of letter writing, Stowers notes:

> The highest level of linguistic and literary achievement came to those who completed the secondary stage of education and then studied with a teacher of rhetoric. Greco-Roman culture regarded the well-delivered and persuasive speech as the most characteristic feature of civilized life. In contrast to our own culture, linguistic skill focused on oral speech; the written word was secondary, derived from primary rhetoric.[143]

When composing a rhetorical piece, therefore, an author could have *preferred* to deliver the letter *viva voce*, assuming a competent secretary was available. Being forced to deliver a rhetorical letter *syllabatim* may have been a challenge indeed. Letters for an ancient rhetorician were to be dictated at the speed of speech. It is with this in mind that the younger Pliny, while making a point about the improvement of oratorical prowess, advises another orator to relax from the serious work of the courts by doing various exercises that will nonetheless improve his oratorical

---

[140] Cic. *QFr.* 3.1.9; *Att.* 14.21.4; 15.13.5, 27.3.

[141] Cic. *Att.* 5.17.1; also Pliny *Epp.* 9.36 and 3.5 (where he is speaking of the Elder's literary habits).

[142] Cic. *Fam.* 2.3.1–2. There is some rhetoric in this. See also 8.14.4, where Caelius in a letter to Cicero writes near the end of his rambling letter, "I nearly forgot what I had expecially wanted to write".

[143] Stowers, *Letter Writing*, 33–34.

skills: reading works written in good style and letter writing.[144] Surely Pliny means that dictating a letter *viva voce* could improve one's oratorical skills, how else could letter writing be good practice for an experienced orator?[145]

Evidently then two situations often prompted an author to use a secretary to record dictation at the speed of speech: (1) when the author valued convenience more than precise reproduction, and (2) when he preferred to deliver the contents *viva voce*. Obviously he needed a secretary capable of recording dictation at these speeds. In the first instance, however, if such a secretary was unavailable, he was probably more likely to use his secretary as an editor than to revert to dictating at the speed of script. In other words, he would have preferred the inevitable editing (that resulted from the use of non-shorthand notes) to the loss of time.

In the second instance, he preferred to dictate the letter rapidly, perhaps because the letter was intended to resemble a speech (or a sermon). This procedure does not exclude the use of a rough draft or at least precomposed sections. He merely desired to present the final draft to the secretary as a speech than as a written document.

bb) The Secretary as an Editor

In the second type of author-controlled letter the author permits (or asks) the secretary to make minor corrections or changes in his content, form, or structure. He is using the secretary to edit his rough draft. Why would an author present a "rough" draft?[146] Two reasons are possible: he was *unwilling* to prepare the final draft, or he was *unable* to prepare or polish the final draft.

If the author is unwilling, or to say it another way, if he is willing for the secretary to prepare the draft, the situations are usually the same as those when a secretary is merely copying the draft without editing. An author could permit the secretary to prepare the final draft if he was unwilling to expend the necessary labor himself, whether due to laziness, the length of the piece, or his poor level of dexterity. This was more likely when the letter or other project was not seen as significant enough

---

[144] Pliny *De orat.* 2.51–62.

[145] Practice in composition is better done by composing literary pieces and poems not letters. His letters evidence that he made extensive use of a secretary who no doubt took shorthand. Note that he calls his secretary a *notarius*; see *Ep.* 3.5.11.

[146] By definition they must be 'rough'; otherwise the secretary is merely preparing a copy (*i.e.*, he is only a copyist).

to merit his personal effort. Obviously a casual letter qualified as did routine official or business correspondences.

Cicero's son provides another example. He was studying philosophy in Athens. Like many sons today attending college and living on an allowance, his father was not always pleased with his son's performance, dedication, or extracurricular activities. The younger Cicero wrote to Tiro, through whom he apparently responds in a manner to his father's complaints. Interestingly, he ends the letter with this request:

> Sed peto a te, ut quam celerrime mihi librarius mittatur, maxime quidem Graecus; multum mihi enim eripitur operae in exscribendis hypomnematis...[147]

The younger Cicero is more than willing to allow a secretary the freedom to record the lecture notes, which, unless the secretary was a tachygraphist, involved some editing. He does not perceive the notes as significant enough to merit his personal efforts, although this does not preclude his overseeing the production nor proofreading the final copies.

An author was often unwilling to prepare the final copy, not because of the labor involved, but because he thought his own penmanship is unsatisfactory. Either (1) for that particular letter the writer wished a prettier, more professional hand, as perhaps in the case of Cicero's use of Spintharus,[148] or (2) the writer's hand was generally difficult to read.[149]

Personal desires did not always play a role. The author was often *unable* to prepare or polish the final draft. If he prepared the *rough* draft, then his inability to prepare a *final* draft was not from illiteracy but rather was probably from his lack of epistolary expertise in the required letter

---

[147] Cic. *Fam.* 16.21.8:
"But I beg of you to see that a secretary is sent to me as quickly as possible — best of all a Greek; for that will relieve me of a lot of trouble in writing out lecture notes.[c]
[c A characteristic request.]"
The LCL editor's note is not clear. Was it 'characteristic' to record lecture notes (*cf.* Epictetus and Arrian), or was it 'characteristic' to request a secretary for that purpose?

[148] Cic. *Att.* 13.23; see the discussion above, pp. 99–100.

[149] As evidenced in some of the illiteracy formulae; see above, pp. 73–76. Perhaps also Cic. *Fam.* 16.22.1 (see p. 78 above). The line of distinction between unwilling and unable may be blurred here. *POxy.* 119, the filial letter, evidences such deplorable handwriting (and grammar) that for an important (non-family) letter a secretary probably would have been used.

McKenzie strongly asserts "Even people who could read and write did not think of submitting their readers to unprofessional penmanship. It was probably not even a concern for legibility, but rather a concern for beauty, or at least for neatness, which imposed dictation as a social canon" (*Light*, 14). His contention, however, should be limited to the more public types of letters. The ordinary papyri rarely portray a "beauty" or "neatness" of the caliber of these other letters.

structure or formulae. He knew what he wished to say but was unable to present the material in the manner prescribed by the appropriate literary conventions. Thus when one encounters a letter written in a *form* which probably should have been unfamiliar to the author, yet the letter has *content* which appears like that of the author's, then a secretary may be suspected of acting as an editor.

In addition to editing the author's rough draft, a secretary also worked from the author's oral instructions.[150] This is distinguished from recording, taking dictation *viva voce*, only by the incompleteness of the notes. In this situation the text (notes) that resulted were not the same as the finished letter. This could be of course the result of the author: he recited an incomplete text. Yet it could also be the fault of the secretary. If the secretary was not a tachygraphist, then even when the author presented a finished form as far as his preparation and delivery are concerned, the resulting notes were less complete. Since many secretaries were unable to record *viva voce*, many letters were probably prepared in this manner. In fact many authors no doubt prepared their material with this in mind. Attention to minor details were wasted effort in the first presentation, unless one deliberately slowed down and used the secretary to record *syllabatim*. The minor details, however, were not necessarily lost. They were often corrected or added when the letter was checked.[151] The presence of corrections in the papyri attest to such a practice.

The secretary often acted as an editor, even if he was a tachygraphist. Although he took dictation, the author's oral presentation still needed minor editing. Frequently however, the author's ignorance was even more extensive. An author often chose an oral presentation because he was functionally illiterate. Indubitably many personal letters among the papyri that evidence (by handwriting) the use of a secretary fall into this category. The secretary edited the oral instructions of the author into an acceptable letter form. The more extensive was the author's ignorance; the more extensive was the required editing, extending finally as far as making the secretary a co-author.

Not only did the author's ignorance create the need for secretarial editing, but so also did his carelessness. In his haste, unconcern, or inatt-

---

[150] The recitation could be extemporaneous or from notes. The secretary, however, receives only the oral delivery.

[151] McKenzie, *Light*, 14–15 argues that a secretary familiar with the author could still produce a quasi-verbatim text in this situation by virtue of his ability to parody the author. The letter would need to be very standardized, or the secretary would need to be *very* familiar with the author.

entiveness, he erred in his grammar, presentation, or in any of the items controlled by literary conventions. The secretary, usually trained in such matters, noticed and corrected such *faux pas*. This was probably an expected advantage of employing a professional secretary.

'Carelessness' need not be limited to accidental errors. The author may not have 'cared' to edit the letter himself. Cicero's letter to Quintus concerning the use of secretaries in administative affairs has already demonstrated that officials trusted some editorial and organizational duties to a reliable secretary. This practice probably extended to personal letters as well. Cicero, in a playful exchange with Tiro, reminded him that it was Tiro who usually served as Cicero's κάνων.[152] Here Cicero had found their roles reversed. He was serving as Tiro's editor, catching a *faux pas* — at least in his eyes — of Tiro. Cicero stricken by the irony was enjoying the opportunity to be the corrector. Nevertheless, evidently this task customarily fell to Tiro, who, acting as a good secretary, edited a draft letter when Cicero's "carelessness" required it. An author may have *consciously* chosen to leave such details to his secretary. Especially in an established relationship, the author did not trouble himself with the task of carefully guarding what he said, trusting his secretary to notice and correct any inconsistencies. Consequently a letter written for a busy author by a trusted and competent secretary had an increased probability that the secretary was used as an editor.

b) A Secretary-Controlled Letter

The remaining two roles in which a secretary acted are termed "secretary-controlled", because he influenced both the diction, grammar, syntax, and other 'minor' elements of style and also the more 'major' elements of style, such as the form, method of argumentation, and even perhaps some *content*. In a secretary-controlled letter, the author details to varying degrees the content of a letter, leaving the final composition to a secretary. Thus a spectrum of secretarial control is possible, stretching from filling in the author's detailed instructions to fleshing out the most skeletal of directions, and even to the complete assumption of the contents by the secretary. This range of possibilities is further complicated by another variable: the letter cannot be treated as an indisoluble unit. The author perhaps dictated an important section of the letter to insure the complete accuracy of his intentions and then gave little direction as to the composition of the rest. The author may leave certain parts of

---

[152] Cic. *Fam.* 16.17. See the text and discussion above, pp. 45–46.

the letter entirely in the hands of his secretary, while choosing to control tightly the content of other parts. He may dictate one part, give detailed instructions as to another, and offer only the scantest direction for the remainder, trusting his secretary's familiarity and competency with the subject. If an author is known or suspected to be incapable of the quality of a letter's composition or even parts of a letter bearing his name, the letter, or parts of the letter are not necessarily pseudonymous but may have been controlled by the secretary.

aa) The Secretary as a Co-author

Here also one type of co-authorship must be excluded from any correlation to an epistolary situation. In a letter from Atticus and others,[153] evidently they wrote attempting to persuade Cicero to action, and the multiple senders were probably used to show unanimity as to the content. Neither the letter nor the situation indicates if one wrote and all agreed, or if all or part contributed to the composition. Irrespectively, the secretary presumably was not among the co-authors. Regardless of how the various co-authors drafted the letter, the secretary was still employed in an author-controlled manner. If however the secretary was included among the co-authors (*i.e.*, he was allowed some control of the letter), then the number of additional authors is irrelevant. The same situations would precipitate this usage whether or not there were other contributers than the secretary.

Logically an author chose to employ a secretary as a co-author for two reasons: (1) if he lacked the knowledge or literary skill to complete the letter, or (2) if he chose to delegate the completion to the secretary. In the former case, the extent of secretarial co-authorship is proportional to the author's ignorance. Perhaps he knew the specific (or general) content he desired but was unable to express it correctly, or knew perhaps only what he wished to accomplish, such as the acknowledgement of some item of business, a social invitation or petition, congratulations or condolences, or merely the rekindling of a relationship (philophronesis), and thus entrusted the secretary to find the proper manner of expression.

The first situation is caused by the inadequacies of the author, the second situation is volitional. The ancient author, if he was busy and considered the composition of the entire letter to be unworthy of his time, delegated much of the work to his secretary, giving his secretary suffi-

---

[153] Cic. *Att.* 11.5. See above, pp. 47–48.

cient direction to insure the proper expression of the essential message but leaving the actual composition to the secretary, even including expressions of intimacy. This saved considerable time, albeit at the expense of personableness. Obviously the more routine was the correspondence, the more likely was the author to use this method.[154]

A saving of time is apparently not the only situation that precipitated secretarial co-authorship. Although the secretary was rarely considered a peer, it is quite possible that he was well acquainted with the topic at hand and was capable of valuable input. Similarly to when Pompey chose to use Sestius to compose an important letter,[155] an author assumed that the secretary was sufficient, especially with certain parts or ideas of the letter. Obviously if the secretary was somehow a participant in the matter, then the author was more likely to use this method.[156]

bb) The Secretary as a Composer

The previous role of the secretary (as a co-author) is only an extreme development or extension of his role as an editor. In this case, however, the secretary is not left merely to flesh out a letter but actually to compose it. Even the content is completely controlled by the secretary. The author determines only the nature of the letter, such as an invitation, congratulations, recommendation, or philophronesis, and the choice of the recipient.

What type of situation caused an author to reliquish complete control of a letter yet still desire the letter to be written in his name? When Rufus sought to fulfill his ambitious promise to Cicero (keeping him abreast of all the events of Rome during his absence), he soon realized the immensity of such an endeavor.[157] He requests Cicero not to think that he is shirking responsibility when he delegates the task to a secretary, arguing that the secretary was far better equipped to handle the task, having more time to investigate and write. Thus although Rufus allowed the secretary to compose the document, he admitted it freely to Cicero. One should perhaps then expect that when an author sent a letter in his own name that was actually composed by a secretary he would likely indicate

---

[154] There are among the papyri examples of an author's sketchy outline draft of a letter for the secretary to flesh out; see *PZen.* 57, also perhaps *PZen.* 111 and *PTebt.* 13.

[155] See above, pp. 96–97.

[156] *E.g.*, were Paul's secretary an active and competent member of the Pauline missionary band or a part of the church or conflict to which Paul was responding, he is more likely to be permitted input in the letter.

[157] Cic. *Fam.* 8.1. See the discussion above, pp. 51–52.

this, *unless* there was some reason for hiding the fact.[158] Be that as it may. Evidently one situation that prompted the use of a secretary as a composer was that of practicality, meaning only that the author thought the secretary was somehow better equipped to write the letter.

Nonetheless, was the use of a secretary as a composer primarily based on a desire to deceive? An ancient author was not exempt from the tedious duty of "required" correspondences. Cicero repeatedly asked Atticus to write such letters in his name.[159] Bahr cites these requests as evidence of the practice but does not note the epistolary situation,[160] although this can lead to the seriously misleading conclusion that the author's use of a secretary to compose a letter in the author's name, with the intention of representing it as the work of the author, was a common or at least an acceptable practice. This may *not* have been the case. Cicero clearly indicates that he wishes the recipient to be deceived into thinking that the letters are from him,[161] and concomittantly that the letters represent his concern/regard for the recipient, because supposedly he has personally troubled to write.

Are these the customary arrangements of a busy man and thus to be taken as examples of a widespread practice? The answer lies in the epistolary occasion. These requests occur during the period of Cicero's life which is considered to be the time of his greatest despair. He not only concedes his wretched condition but acknowledges that this was the reason he made the request:

> I am so fearfully upset both in mind and body that I have not been able to write many letters; I have only answered those who have written to me. I should like you to write in my name to Basilius and to anyone else you like, even to Servilius, and say whatever you think fit.[162]

His request was not an example of an acceptable literary practice but the orders of a tired old man who had despaired of his life's situation.[163]

---

[158] It is always a dubious practice to generalize from one example, but it is necessary here if the role is to be maintained at all. This is the only example I found of the use of a secretary as a composer where the author was *not* intending deceit. Yet it is even questionable if the resulting "letter" — Rufus calls it a "packet" (Cic. *Fam.* 8.1.1) — was sent in Rufus' name.

[159] Cic. *Att.* 3.15; 11.2; 11.5; 11.7. See above, p. 50.

[160] Bahr, "Letter Writing", 467.

[161] In *Att.* 11.2, Cicero offers an explanation — an outright lie — for Atticus to use to insure the reception of these letters as Cicero's.

[162] Cic. *Att.* 11.5 (see above, p. 50).

[163] See also Cic. *Att.* 11.11: "Worn out as I am by the agony of my grevious sorrows I should not find it an easy task to write to you, ..."; in *Att.* 11.3, "Grief prevents me from

Forgotten is the meticulousness of a literary giant who defends a letter's use of a preposition. Now he wishes only to be freed from the responsibilities of his high position. He asks Atticus, probably the only man with whom he could be so candid, to assume some of his most tedious duties. He even delegates the choice of recipients to Atticus!

Based on the epistolary situation represented by Cicero, it is tempting to conclude that an author-initiated request for deception was rare indeed, perhaps singularly restricted to Cicero and to this time in his life. An exception, however, exists in Cicero's practice: a letter dated Sept. 17, 58 B.C., where apparently to improve his standing at home Cicero asks Atticus, "Si qui erunt, quibus putes opus esse meo nomine litteras dari, velim conscribas curesque dandas".[164] Evidently then such tactics were used by Cicero before the time of his great depression, and therefore his depression cannot be used as the sole etiology for his using a secretary as a composer. Certainly his depresssion prompted the renewed requests, but he evidently had employed the procedure previously. No doubt he believed that Atticus was better equipped to write such letters, being present in Rome and familiar with current events. Nevertheless, even in this earlier letter to Atticus Cicero is clearly asking him to deceive the recipients. Apparently therefore author-initiated requests for the use of a secretary as a composer *for the purpose of deception* was used by ancient writers — at least Cicero. These requests primarily were the discouraged instructions of a writer apathetic of life wishing to escape undesired letter writing responsibilites but perhaps also were a means of delegating a task to someone more qualified.

The requests for a secretary to compose did not always originate with the author. The deception apparently could be secretary-initiated. The one actually writing the letter initiates the task of composing a letter for the "author". Yet this was not typical pseudonymous letter writing for apparently the author's knowledge (and thus permission) was required. When Atticus attempts to persuade Cicero to take the initiative and to write a speech for Brutus,[165] it is Cicero's uncertainty that Brutus would approve that causes him to hesitate.

---

writing more. If there is anything you think should be written to anyone in my name, please do so as usual".

[164] Cic. *Att.* 3.15; "If there is anyone to whom you think a letter ought to be sent in my name, please write one and see that it is sent". Since *Att.* 11.3 (see the note immediately above) refers to the practice "as usual", it is possible that the practice began at this earlier time and continued throughout. But this would require Cicero allowing years to pass without mentioning the practice in any letter and then suddenly speaking of it repeatedly.

[165] Cic. *Att.* 15.3—4 (see above, p. 96).

Cicero is seen taking the initiative and composing for Atticus. He apparently desires the favor of Caelius for his friend Atticus. Therefore he dictates to the copyist of Atticus, who happened to be with him, a letter in praise of Caelius Caldus that he then read to Caelius, representing it as a letter he received from Atticus. He then writes to Atticus "ad te apud eum, di boni! quanta in gratia posui, eique legi litteras non tui sed librari tui".[166] Judging from his ready willingness to tell Atticus, Cicero surely acted because he knew his friend would approve.[167]

Using a secretary to compose in order to deceive the recipients apparently arose therefore from two different situations: (1) when the author needed a letter to be sent but was unwilling to write it himself, that is, it was author-initiated, and (2) when the secretary initiated the deception, representing his work as the author's. The resulting letter remains distinct from a pseudonymous work, however, because the secretary anticipated and usually sought, albeit sometimes belatedly, the author's permission.

Although these situations prompted the employment of a secretary as a composer *for the purpose of deception*, two serious restrictions must be noted. First and foremost, the term 'secretary' had to be used in its broadest sense. In *every* case the 'secretary' was not the typical professional or even amateur secretary — a very serious restriction. Rather he was a colleague, friend, and peer of the author. Nowhere was there *any* indication that an ordinary secretary was asked, much less presumed, to compose a letter for the author.[168]

Second, the evidence limits the practice to Cicero. Although the later letters of Cicero indicate that Atticus suggests on occasion that Cicero permit him to compose for Cicero, the earlier letter (*Att.* 3.15) places the initiative with Cicero. Because Cicero was known to practice other unethical activities with respect to letters,[169] one cannot assume that his use

---

[166] Cic. *Att.* 6.6.4. I owe Tyrrell and Purser, *Cicero*, 1: 49 for this reconstruction.

[167] This may also be Cicero's subtle request for belated permission. It cannot be ignored that all these incidents were part of the complex web of influence and deception that engulfed Rome as men jockeyed for position and power during the dangerous years of the first triumvirate.

[168] This restriction, however, does not eliminate this role from consideration with respect to Paul. A fellow member of the Pauline band might meet this qualification. (Again, it must be recalled that "compose" does not include co-authorship. Many ordinary secretaries acted as extensive co-authors, working from the scantest of instructions.)

[169] *E.g.*, the interception and reading of another's mail; see Cic. *Att.* 11.9 (or p. 164 above). The ethics of a man embroiled in the tumultuous struggle of the first triumvirate (and a man endorsing the assasination of Caesar) may not reflect accurately those of the common man (and *ad maiorem* those of Paul).

of such a questionable secretarial method is indicative of an acceptable custom of the day. Because this role of a secretary (using a secretary to "compose" for the purpose of deception) has these serious restrictions, it ought not to be considered a representative usage. Therefore the only remaining situation that prompted the use of a secretary as a composer is the one represented by Rufus, who it will be recalled stated at the outset that he was using a secretary and specifically detailed how. Moreover it is uncertain if the resulting "letter" was sent in Rufus' name.[170] Because of the uncertainties and restrictions surrounding both circumstances, there is serious question whether there are any normal situational criteria for determining the employment of a secretary as a composer, especially since (1) in the only example where deception was not intended the author explicitly stated that he was employing this method and (2) more importantly there is such extremely limited evidence for the use of the method in general.[171] Therefore, without an explicit reference to the use of a secretary as the composer of a letter, this secretarial method probably should not even be considered a valid option, for there is not an epistolary situation that by itself is sufficient to suggest this role of the secretary.

3. Differences Resulting from the Use of a Secretary

Regardless of the role of the secretary, the resulting letter was different than if it had been written by the author *eigenhändig*. The differences are divided into two types: those that result from all types of secretarial mediation and those related to a specific role of a secretary.

a) Differences Possible in Any Type of Secretary-Assisted Letter

When a secretary was used to write a letter, the possibility increased considerably for certain types of changes. In the case of complex compositions even the very presence of a secretary can be a disadvantage, for as Quintilian notes, silence and privacy were essential for the proper production of any serious work.[172] Naturally for an author like Quintilian, this applies only to using a secretary to record or perhaps to edit. It is

---

[170] It is even uncertain if it should be called a letter; see p. 108 n. 158 above.
[171] J. N. Sevenster, *Do You Know Greek? How Much Greek Could the First Jewish Christians Have Known?* NovTSup, no. 4 (Leiden: Brill, 1961), 12, observes in passing that the use of a secretary to compose was not common.
[172] Quint. *Inst.* 10.3.22. See also Sen. *Ep.* 56.1.

quite doubtful that Quintilian would view a typical secretary as capable of acceptable input in a serious work and thus would not consider using him as a co-author. This effect, that of the secretary being an undesirable, perhaps disruptive, influence during a serious composition, should be limited then to author-controlled situations. The secretary's influence, after all, was usually desired in a secretary-controlled letter. Thus if the ancient writer had previously decided to use a secretary and the work was serious in nature, then he was wise to compose first notes or a rough draft in privacy. To invert this, one may say: if a letter is a serious work and yet evidently was written with a secretary, then the possibility is increased that a rough draft of at least part of the letter was used.

Another difference possible from the use of a secretary is the letter's length. Cicero claims "Plura scriberem, si ipse possem".[173] The clear impression is that an author tended to write long letters in his own hand, or possibly, that the use of a secretary tended to decrease the letter length. Gordon Bahr reaches this conclusion.[174] The matter however is more complex. Bahr's point is certainly based on the plain meaning of Cicero and suggests that there is a positive correlation between the length of Cicero's letters and writing in his own hand. This correlation however is skewed by a third determinant: Cicero's motivation. Cicero repeatedly notes that he is using a secretary because of his busy schedule. Hence, conversely, a letter in his own hand probably indicates leisure time.[175] The availability of extra time no doubt had a great deal to do with the length of the letter.[176] Therefore the use of a secretary *per se* cannot be blamed for a letter's brevity.

Another remark about letter length indicates a different type of motivation. Cicero apologizes "Si scriberem ipse, longior epistula fuisset..."[177] This appears to be the same situation, but he continues "... sed dictavi propter lippitudinem".[178] His discomfort apparently affected the letter's length, particularly since it was compounded by another problem. This letter was written Jan. 23, 49 B.C., and it is quite

---

[173] Cic. *Att.* 8.15; "My letter would be longer, if I could write myself".

[174] Bahr, "Letter Writing", 475.

[175] Cicero himself admits that a letter in his own hand indicates that he had "a little" time; Cic. *QFr.* 2.16.1.

[176] Note Cicero's friendly defense of his letters: "If I had as much time as you have, or if I could bring myself to write such short letters as you generally write, I could ... write far more frequently ... but on top of my inconceivable stress of work..." (*Att.* 1.19).

[177] Cic. *Att.* 7.13a; "Were I writing myself, this letter would have been longer".

[178] Cic. *Att.* 7.13a; "... but I dictate it owing to inflammation of the eyes".

likely that Tiro was absent. Thus Cicero was using another secretary and probably an unfamiliar one.[179] That personal discomfort could cause both a shortened letter and the use of a secretary is stated explicitly in another letter of Cicero:

Lippitudinis meae signum tibi sit librarii manus et eadem causa brevitatis".[180]

Since these shortened letters have alternative explanations than the mere use of a secretary, one may conclude that the use of a secretary did not produce a consistent effect on the length of a letter.

Quintilian notes a potentially significant effect that a secretary had upon a letter: if the secretary was a slow writer or had poor comprehension, then the author, if working orally, was forced to slow down, perhaps even to a syllable-by-syllable rate.[181] This reduction in speed could have several effects: (1) the thread of ideas could be broken, resulting in a more disjointed letter, particularly when using more oratorical style arguments; (2) the letter could be drawn to a close more quickly, resulting in an abbreviated argument; or (3) the drafting of the letter could be broken up over several sittings, resulting in possible disjointments and creating the potential for changes in the author's mood or tone. For example, Cicero wrote to his brother Quintus a letter that was written in several sittings.[182] He began dictating the letter[183] and discussed various topics at great length. Evidently he was working through the letters received from his brother, answering them in order: after discussing business at home, he states "I come now to your letters, ..."; then "I have answered your longest letter; now hear what I say about your very little one, ..."; then "I come to your third letter"; then "your fourth

---

[179] Tiro was still recuperating at an earlier stop on their journey. Cicero certainly had other secretaries, but he was travelling at the time and would not have brought along extra ones. Whether because of Cicero's illness or the unfamiliar secretary, this particular letter is rather "flat" stylistically, lacking his customary *viva vox* energy, the anacolutha, exclamations, short quotations, or witticisms. He probably wrote only because he and Atticus were corresponding daily and they needed to keep the carriers moving.

[180] Cic. *Att.* 8.13; "Let my secretary's handwriting be proof that I am suffering from inflammation of the eyes, and that is my reason for brevity". Apparently the discomfort of writing aboard ship prompted the brevity of Cic. *Att.* 5.12. Tiro had been left ill in Athens, and inclement weather had insured his continued absence; therefore Cicero was probably writing in his own hand. But another letter (*Fam.* 14.7.2) indicates that he did write letters on another occasion at sea (perhaps when he had a secretary?).

[181] Quint. *Inst.* 10.3.20.

[182] Cic. *QFr.* 3.1.

[183] He does not explicitly state this but he notes that the next section (3.1.19) was written in his own hand (see n. 186 immediately below).

letter..."; then "I have also received a very old letter..."[184] After this long section of the letter, he adds "Just as I was in the act of folding this letter, there came letter-carriers from you and Caesar... How distressed I was! And how I grieved over Caesar's most charming letter [about the death of Caesar's daughter Julia]!"[185] Since the letter has no closing remark at this point, Cicero must have meant by "the act of folding it" the entire process of dispatching the final secretarial draft: checking of the draft, appending of any subscription or closing health-wish, dating the letter, folding, and sealing. His short remark about Caesar was written in his own hand, for he mentions at the beginning of the next section:

> Cum scripsissem haec infima, quae sunt mea manu, venit ad nos Cicero tuus ad cenam.[186]

Apparently the disturbing news of the death of Caesar's daughter and an additional letter from Quintus had prompted Cicero to retain the letter and to append immediately a 'postscript' in his own hand. Again it appears that Cicero had intended to end the letter after this 'postscript', but the visit of the younger Cicero, who had yet another letter from Quintus, prompted Cicero to continue the letter. Yet he mentions that his visitor came during dinner, and consequently he notes: "Hoc inter cenam Tironi dictavi, ne mirere alia manu esse".[187] In this long complicated letter, Cicero had begun by dictating a long letter to answer several letters from his brother. Before dispatching it, he received disturbing news from Caesar as well as another letter from his brother. The situation prompted him to add immediately a postscript (in his own hand). Before dispatching the modified letter, he again received visitors, his nephew Cicero, who arrived during dinner with another letter from Quintus. He dictated a postscript in response to this letter. He then finally concludes the letter:

> Quod multos dies epistulam in manibus habui, propter commorationem tabellariorum, ideo multa coniecta sunt, aliud alio tempore, velut hoc:...[188]

---

[184] The parallel to 1 Corinthians is obvious and may reflect a typical approach when responding to a letter.

[185] Cic. *QFr.* 3.1.1–7, 8, 11, 12, 13, 14, 17 (respectively). Answering a letter point by point was common in antiquity. *E.g.*, note the recurring *de* ... *de* ... in a reply to a letter from Cornificius (Cic. *Fam.* 12.30).

[186] Cic. *QFr.* 3.1.19; "After I had written these last words, which are in my own hand, your son Cicero came in and had dinner with me".

[187] Cic. *QFr.* 3.1.20; "I dictated this to Tiro during dinner, so do not be surprised at its being written in a different hand".

[188] Cic. *QFr.* 3.1.23; "Because I have had a letter on my hands for many days on account

Quintilian also notes the possibility of a secretary having the opposite effect.[189] If the secretary was a skillful writer, especially if a tachygraphist, then the author might feel pressure to keep his dictation quick, lest he appear hesitant or unsure. The effects on the letter could only be adverse. Yet again, the effect probably is limited more to an author like Quintilian, a skilled Roman orator. The average author was less likely to feel such pressure or to be concerned over his hesitancy. He was probably worried more about embarrassing himself with a linguistic *faux pas* from haste than with any hesitation in thought.

It has been noted repeatedly that another effect of using a secretary (in any manner except as a recorder) is variation in the language, style, or content of the letter. The more freedom that the secretary was given, the more variance that was possible. With a marginally literate man, these differences were noticeable and desirable; yet with any writer there were differences. Philostratus of Lemnos in his handbook for secretaries lists the writers with excellent epistolary styles and includes:

Βασιλέων δὲ ὁ Θεσπέσιος Μάρκος ἐν οἷς ἐπέστελλεν αὐτός, πρὸς γὰρ τῷ κεκριμένῳ τοῦ λόγου καὶ τὸ ἑδραῖον τοῦ ἤθους ἐντετύπωτο τοῖς γράμμασι, ...[190]

At least to Philostratus there was a noticeable difference in the style between Marcus and Marcus via a secretary.

In Cicero the use of a secretary appears to have influenced his style. This effect was mentioned in the earlier discussion of effects on a letter's length, but it has a corollary. During a time when Tiro was absent (ill) and Cicero himself was physically ailing, his letters appear short and flat. On March 12, 49 B.C., however, Cicero was beginning to improve and undertook a letter to Atticus in his own hand.[191] It is an odd letter. He

---

of delay on the part of the letter-carriers, many things have been jumbled up in it, written at various times, as, for instance, this: ..." Another postscript followed, for another letter had arrived. Cicero blames the disjointed nature of the letter on delays in dispatching. Presumably had the carriers been ready Cicero would have made each addition a separate letter, a viable option for a man of Cicero's wealth. Carriers themselves could be cantankerous. Cicero complains to Cassius of the pressures that carriers placed on him to write quickly so they could be on their way (Cic. *Fam.* 15.17.1–2). See also Cic. *Fam.* 3.7.1.

A delay in the departure of one of Paul's carriers could provide a time lapse in, *e.g.*, 2 Corinthians. Fueled by some intervening annoyance, Paul could have picked up the letter again and added additional remarks (chs. 10–13?). Evidently such long additions were not unknown. This is discussed further below, pp. 180–81.

[189] Quint. *Inst.* 10.3.19–20.
[190] Philstr. 2.257.29–258; "the divine Marcus when he himself wrote (for in addition to his distinction in speech, his firmness of character, too, had been imprinted in his letters)".
[191] Cic. *Att.* 9.4.

bewails his plight, listing his woes and does so first in Greek and then in Latin. It is a very stylistic letter[192] and is quite similar to his orations. He had prefaced the letter by declaring that he was practicing his rhetorical technique. Possibly had Tiro been present this letter would not have been written. The use of a secretary perhaps prompted more pragmatic productions. One left experimentations and practice for autographs.[193]

There is another difference between secretary-assisted letters and autographed ones. In a letter to Atticus, Cicero had apparently offended him and is now writing to apologize. He is penitent and even adds "Scio te voluisse et me asinum germanum fuisse".[194] The very brief letter has no clear closing but goes straight into some incidental, usually postscripted, types of remarks, ending with "Bibliothecam mihi tui pinxerunt constructione et sillybis. Eos velim laudes".[195] Interestingly that same day (or perhaps the following) he sent another letter repeating the matter of Atticus' kind provision of the library slaves to organize his library:

> Postea vero quam Tyrannio mihi libros disposuit, mens addita videtur meis aedibus. Qua quidem in re mirifica opera Dionysi et Menophili tui fuit. Nihil venustius quam illa tua pegmata, postquam mi sillybis libros illustrarunt. Vale. Et scribas ad me velim de gladiatoribus, sed ita, bene si rem gerunt; non quaero, male si se gessere.[196]

This second letter expresses the same sentiments much more fully and eloquently, complete with mentioning the slaves by name. A reconstruction suggests itself. Cicero dashed off the first letter to apologize to his friend, even admitting a personal trait that he was less likely to state in front of a secretary. He also thanked his friend for the assistants, but like many powerful men he was unaware of the names of the workers. Later he sent a formal letter of thanks, no doubt telling the secretary to fill in the details, which included mentioning the workers by name.[197] The influence of the secretary accounts for the inclusion of such details.

---

[192] E.g., note the repetition of "εἰ ... εἰ ... εἰ ..."
[193] See Caesar's autographed experimentations below, p. 162.
[194] Cic. Att. 4.5; "I know you wished it, and I was a downright ass".
[195] Cic. Att. 4.5; "Your men have beautified my library by binding the books and affixing title-slips. Please thank them".
[196] Cic. Att. 4.8; "Since Tyrannio has arranged my books, the house seems to have acquired a soul; and your Dionysius and Menophilus were of extraordinary service. Nothing could be more charming than these bookcases of yours now that the books are adorned with title-slips. Farewell. Please let me know about the gladiators; but only if they are behaving well; if not, I don't want to know".
[197] The postscript in this letter was typical of Cicero who never summarized the content

Using a secretary to assist with a letter had another general effect. Apparently it could offend the recipient, if the author was capable of writing himself. This is inferred from the frequent apology an author added when he mentioned that he was writing with the aid of a secretary.[198] The practice of apologizing, however, may have become mere literary convention, since "being busy" is called "the lazy man's stock excuse".[199]

As mentioned before, the inclusion of secretive material could affect the letter's organization.[200] In some cases the use of a secretary may have prevented the inclusion of secretive material altogether. In the Cynic letter by pseudo-Heraclitus, supposedly discussing his eminent exile from Ephesus and return to Italy, Heraclitus concludes:

> Have done with them [the Ephesians]! But as for you, let me know the time of your departure. I especially want to meet you and briefly discuss many other matters as well as the laws themselves. I would write these things, except that I must, above all, keep them secret... Many people are not different from cracked vessels, since they cannot retain anything, but let everything leak out through their endless talking.[201]

Who are the "many people" that leaked a letter's secrets? Who would know the contents of a sealed letter?[202] Obviously the secretary (and the lector) would know.[203]

One final difference possible in any type of secretary-assisted letter was its general appearance. Although perhaps a minor matter, one aspect of the letter's appearance received the most notice in antiquity, judging from the frequency that it was mentioned. Using a secretary in any way resulted in a handwriting that the recipients did not recognize, unless the

---

but always stated some incidental matter or recent development. It was likely from his own hand.

[198] See Cic. QFr. 2.2.1 *inter alios*.

[199] Cic. Att. 5.11.

[200] I suggest that if an author included such secretive material he left it for a postscript in his own hand; see above, pp. 88–90.

[201] Pseudo-Heraclitus *Epistles* 8.3–4. Malherbe, "Introduction", 22–26, (following Jacob Bernays and most others) attributes the letter to a first Christian century untalented rhetorician. According to H. Attridge, *First Century Cynicism in the Epistles of Heraclitus*, Harvard Theological Studies, no. 29 (Missoula, MT: Scholars, 1976), 11–12, all the letters probably originated in the same rhetorical school.

[202] Notably Ps-Heraclides is not afraid of any illegal interception of the letter but the careless gossip of those who know its contents. See the similar situation described above, p. 9.

[203] That this letter is a forgery and hence only rhetoric does not preclude this. The forger considered it a viable reason for withholding the information.

author regularly used the same secretary as in the cases of Cicero, Atticus, and Quintus. Consequently if the author thought that the recipients needed authentication, he frequently appended a 'farewell', a health-wish, or perhaps a postscript in his own hand. Although pseudonomous letters *with forged handwriting* were known,[204] the typical writer had no reason to fear.

A secretary usually insured that the letter was neater and more pleasing in appearance. Apparently Quintus had complained to Cicero about the appearance of a letter from Cicero himself. His complaint drew this sarcastic response from Cicero:

> Calamo bono et atramento temperato, charta etiam dentata res agetur. Scribis enim, te meas litteras superiores vix legere potuisse; in quo nihil eorum mi frater, fuit, quae putas. Neque enim occupatus eram, neque pertubatus nec iratus alicui; sed hoc facio semper, ut, quicumque calamus in manus meas venerit, eo sic utar tamquam bono.[205]

b) Differences Possible From a Specific Secretarial Method
aa) Differences Possible in an Author-Controlled Letter

General effects of a secretary on the author's presentation have already been noted, but his ability to express his thoughts rapidly rather than at the slower speed required by personally writing had its own peculiar effects. Certainly verbosity was more likely as well as spontaneity. For example, a letter from Cicero reads "Est igitur adventus (Caesaris scilicet) in exspectatione".[206] While dictating Cicero realized that he had suddenly changed his subject and his antecedent was unclear. Therefore he immediately corrects himself. If he was writing in his own hand or if the draft

---

[204] Josephus *Bellum Judaicum* 1.31.1; Suet. *Aug.* 51.1. They were usually circulated to damage someone's reputation or cause. An autographed "signature" was the customary means of preventing this problem. Yet there were persons who were adept in the art of forging handwriting. See Suet. *Tit.* 3.2; *Vesp.* 6.4; also Joseph. *BJ* 1.26.3. The upper classes had the added advantage of seals, but *cf.* Cic. *Att.* 11.9 (p. 93 above). It is unlikely that someone like Paul was viewed as sufficiently significant to merit the effort (and expense) of forging his handwriting.

[205] Cic. *QFr.* 2.15b.1; "For this letter I shall use a good pen, well-mixed ink, and ivory-polished paper too. For you write that you could hardly read my last, but for that there were none of those reasons you suspect, my dear brother. I was not busy, nor upset, nor angry with someone, but it is always my practice to use whatever pen I find in my hand as if it were a good one". Note that the situations which Quintus apparently suggested are also those more likely to precipitate the author writing personally.

[206] Cic. *Att.* 9.6.1; "Well then, his arrival — I mean Caesar's — is being eagerly awaited".

was later edited he could merely have added the appropriate nominative. This wording rings of an extemporaneous correction recorded verbatim by a secretary.[207] This is not to imply that dictated letters were always entirely extemporaneous. Ancient writers often employed personal notes. Also many apparent indications of extemporaneous speech may have had rhetorical purposes. Tyrrell and Purser caution against reading too much spontaneity into Cicero:

> But it is a serious error to ascribe carelessness to them. His style is colloquial, but thoroughly accurate. Cicero is the most precise of writers... Every adjective is set down with as careful a pen as was ever plied by a masterhand; each is almost as essential to the sentence as the principal verb.[208]

When the secretary was used as an editor, the differences were usually corrections. Hence, the differences are actually more discernible when the secretary merely recorded the text or when the author himself wrote the letter. In the latter instance, while at sea Cicero personally penned a letter[209] that ends with a typical closing, "Please arrange my affairs". He then adds, "Oh I forgot to answer one question about the brickwork-..."followed by a sketchy bit of instruction. If a secretary had edited the final draft, he probably would have moved this section up into the letter body. There was sufficient time for a revision — Cicero was out to sea — but he had no secretarial help with him.[210]

In an author-controlled letter, presumably the secretary had little occasion to affect the letter. Consequently, one would expect an author-controlled letter to be quite similar if indistinguishable from a letter in the author's own hand. For example, in the letter of Ignatius to the Trallians the secretarial draft probably closed with 13:2, ἔρρωσθε ἐν Ἰησοῦ Χριστῷ. An exhortation, a brief confessional statement of weakness, and a request for prayer support follow. This brief postscript probably came

---

[207] See also Cic. *Att.* 1.16; "I was the man — I don't think I am boasting unduly in saying to you privately, especially in a letter which I would rather you didn't read to anyone — I was the man who..."

[208] Tyrrell and Purser, *Cicero*, 1: 76. See also Sen. *Ep.* 75.1: "Minus tibi accuratas a me epistulas mitti quereris". But Richard Gummere warns about this remark that by no means were Seneca's letters actually carelessly written: "... the ingenious juxtaposition of effective words, the balance in style and thought, and the continual striving after point, indicate that the language of the diatribe had affected the informality of the epistle" (LCL 1: x).

[209] Cic. *Att.* 5.12. He does not explicitly state this but it is ascertainable. See above, p. 113 n. 180.

[210] Cicero himself apparently recognized the poor state of the letter for he ends with "I will write a longer letter when I am on dry land. At present I am far out at sea".

from the hand of Ignatius himself. Yet as William Schoedel indicates, the self-deprecating language of this postscript is characteristic of the entire letter's style.[211] Thus this postscript is harmonious in thought, expression, and style with the main body.

Cicero mentions to Atticus (7.2) that he left Tiro sick in Patrae. Since the next letter notes that his additional travels had no long stops, it is quite improbable that Tiro recovered enough to journey and rejoined Cicero. Thus this letter (7.3) is probably from Cicero's hand, since it is unlikely he had taken an extra secretary with him when he left on the journey. This letter is rather long and contains many short quotations from Greek and Latin writers as well as several witticisms. It is very similar in style to a previous letter to Atticus (7.1). Since this earlier letter was written from Athens and thus before Patrae, presumably Tiro was with him and took down the letter. Hence in this case a letter from Cicero's own hand and a letter through the hand of his secretary were very similar.

Yet Cicero's letters are not all similar. There are in fact significant variations among his letters. Indeed, even to the casual reader, there are discernible differences.[212] For example, in a letter to his brother, Cicero claims to be busy; yet he writes a very fine letter.[213] It is sprinkled with allusions to Greek dramas, Greek expressions, and subtle plays on words. It is full of energy (*e.g.*, short staccato sentences), exclamations, excitement, satire, and so forth. Yet another letter to his brother[214] rambles through discussions, returning to old arguments and chasing rabbits. This letter shows a considerable lack of organization and theme (*e.g.*, near the end, he states "Aliud quid? Etiam. Quando...").

There is quite a difference between these two letters. Are these differences, however, to be credited to a secretary or to stylistic variations by the author? The disparity in style among Cicero's letters has not gone unnoted. Tyrrell and Purser discuss Cicero's use of the language of the comic stage, *viz.*, the familiar, conversational, more ordinary, everyday language, in many of his letters.[215] Jules Lebreton, in a classic work on

---

[211] Schoedel, *Ignatius*, 13.
[212] "Cicero's own letters vary greatly in style". J. P. V. D. Balsdon, "Cicero, Works, 24. Letters", *OCD*, 238.
[213] Cic. QFr. 2.16. No doubt "being busy" was merely a "stock excuse" here; see above, p. 117.
[214] Cic. QFr. 2.6.
[215] Tyrrell and Purser, *Cicero*, 2: LXV- LXVII.

Cicero's style,[216] would have taken objection to this, for his major point is that many of the letters are no different in language usage than his speeches. Tyrrell and Purser agree with Lebreton with one notation: one must differentiate between the letters of Cicero. Some letters truly are analagous to his speeches or philosophical treatises;[217] yet many others are far more conversational, far less formal and studied,[218] or to transfer descriptive terms from another language, they are more in the 'koine' Latin than in 'Attic' Latin. Tyrrell and Purser even conclude that Cicero's familiar letters are more like the letters of *other* writers than like his own orations![219]

Such a strong assertion requires the more thorough examination provided by the work of Tadeusz Zieliński.[220] Considered the most precise measure yet determined for Ciceronian style, Zieliński proposes that Cicero preferred to use particular types of clause-endings and avoided "poorly selected endings".[221] The proportion of each type of ending remained relatively constant. This celebrated law of clause-endings has been found to be remarkably accurate, that is, all the formal, carefully composed works of Cicero conform to a very significant degree, as may be seen in the compilation of statistical data in Table 1. Cicero's works are so consistent that Tyrrell and Purser assert that the law can be used to determine which of several variant readings is authentic.[222] From the same data (Table 1), it is evident that conformity is not universal for all writers. Other writers do not demonstrate a similar degree of agreement, and thus this law is an appropriate criterion for Cicero. The inter-

---

[216] M. Jules Lebreton, *Études sur la langue et la grammaire de Cicéron* (Paris: Bloud & Gay, 1901).

[217] *E.g.*, his first letter to Quintus, the famous letter to Lucceius (*Fam.* 5.12), and many of the consolation letters.

[218] Tyrrell and Purser, *Cicero*, 2: LXV-LXVII, cite the work of Lebreton who had catalogued some noticeable differences in the style and vocabulary between Cicero's more formal and more familiar letters. *E.g.*, (1) the use of *cum . . . tum* to note successive actions are frequent only in the more familiar letters; (2) the use of *ne feceris*, being a more absolute prohibition than *noli facere*, are more frequent in the familiar letters; (3) the familiar letters contain some "unusual alternations in tenses"; (4) the familiar letters use the present indicative instead of the deliberative subjunctive which is the common form in his formal writings; and (5) there are frequent uses of the common language, *e.g.*, *dicta dicere, facinora facere*, in his familiar writings.

[219] Ibid., 2: LXIX- LXX.

[220] T. Zieliński, *Das Clauselgesetz in Ciceros Reden: Grundzüge einer oratorischen Rhythmik*, Philologus, Supplementband, no. XIII, 1a (Leipzig: Dieterich, 1904).

[221] Tyrrell and Purser, *Cicero*, 2: LXVI- LXVII n.

[222] Ibid.

esting result is that although Cicero conforms to the law considerably in his speeches and in his more formal letters, his familiar letters usually show no more significant compliance than do the letters of *another* writer! Also notable is that the letters of Cicero to Tiro — letters that must have been written without secretarial assistance or perhaps more likely with an unfamiliar secretary — show a much larger proportion of the poor endings.[223]

Table 1

Clause-Endings in Selected Letters of Cicero and Others

	V(erae) Clausulae	L(icitae) Clausulae	Total	M(alae) S(electae) and P(essimae) Clausulae
Fam. 1.1–10 (incl. 9)	112	60	172	29
Fam. 1.9	58	36	94	7
Fam. 2.1–6	28	7	35	7
Fam. 5.12	20	13	33	5
Fam. 5.16–18	23	6	29	1
Fam. 7.1	9	3	12	2
Fam. 8.1–2 (Caelius)	4	2	6	14
QFr. 1.1	57	32	89	7
Cicero to Plancus	66	21	87	23
Plancus to Cicero and the Senate	42	27	69	56
Fam. 16.1–7, (Cicero to Tiro)	10	6	16	18
Fam. 6.6, (Cicero to Caecina)	13	7	20	8
Fam. 6.7, (Caecina to Cicero)	3	3	6	12
Att. 4.1–10	62	22	84	49

Source: Tyrrell and Purser, *Cicero,* 2: LXVII n.

---

[223] Is this because Tiro edited well his master's careless presentations or more likely because the other secretary could not record or recreate as accurately the text presented by Cicero?

Does Cicero merely write in two very different styles, or did the use of a secretary affect the letter? A familiar casual letter by its very nature incited Cicero to be less meticulous about the details. While he carefully oversaw the correct recording of every particle of an oration, a familiar letter to a close friend was less of a concern. Consequently more of the secretary's style was transmitted, obscuring the subtle unique aspects of Ciceronian style. Thus the letter becomes less distinguishable from the style of another author. Apparently when using a secretary there are enough minor changes that a highly specialized criterion, like clause-endings, can detect them, even though the letters are still quite Ciceronian in content and largely in style. Therefore, highly technical measures of style, such as a preference for a particular case or expression, cannot be used to indicate inauthenticity. Their presence may prove authenticity, but their absence cannot disprove authenticity.[224]

bb) Differences Possible in a Secretary-Controlled Letter

Sherwin-White examines the epistolary practice of emperor Trajan based on Trajan's replies to Pliny the Younger, replies that were included in the ancient collections of the letters of Pliny. From ancient references to customary imperial epistolary practices, Sherwin-White distils the most probable method employed by Trajan. From Suetonius' description of Vespasian and his co-regent Titus,[225] he suggests a schedule of arising before dawn, studying the letters submitted by the secretaries, possible discussions with the *amici*, and then the drafting of the replies or rescripts. Since, according to Suetonius, Titus dictated his replies to a secretary as probably also did his father, "patris nomine et epistulis ipse dictaret", Sherwin-White concludes that it was no doubt the usual procedure. Although purportedly Titus wrote (*conscriberet*) the replies for his father, this is not to be taken to mean with his own hand but rather that as co-regent he authored the replies for his father.[226] Severus, over a cen-

---

[224] Ancient writers argued for authenticity using issues like tone, method of argumentation, consistency with other writings, rhetoric, use of quotations, and genius.

[225] Suet. *Vesp.* 21; *Tit.* 6.1.

[226] Sherwin-White, *Letters of Pliny*, 536. Although a later source (Scriptores Historiae Augustae *Commodus* 13.6–7) contends that emperors wrote their own letters, this should not be taken literally, albeit they may have personally 'signed' some letters perhaps even appending a subscription in their own hand as Nero was reported to have done. See Suet. *Nero* 10.2; *cf.* S.H.A. *Carinus* 16.8: "in subscribendo tardus ... ut libellis una forma multis subscriberet", quoted in another context by Sherwin-White, *Pliny*, 717 n.

tury later, is said to use the same custom.[227] It is never stated nor directly implied that Trajan employed this method, but the overwhelming probability favors it.[228]

What was the nature of the secretarial assistance Trajan received for his replies to Pliny. He corresponded with Pliny through *epistulae* rather than by *libelli*; consequently, the letters should have passed through the hands of the secretary *ab epistulis*. Hermann Peter argues convincingly the quite reasonable position that Trajan himself did not draft the rescripts (reply letters) nor calculate the legal or administrative details required of such replies, including the search for precedents, because such duties were the work of a secretary.[229] Rather Trajan wrote the rescripts using his secretary as a co-author or possibly a composer, that is, these rescripts were secretary-controlled letters (my terms, not H. Peter's).

Sherwin-White attempts to outline the particular secretarial method employed by Trajan. He bases his conclusions on the excellent investigation by A. Henneman,[230] who seeks to establish the 'outer' and 'inner' styles apparent in these letters. By this distinction evidently Henneman is arguing that Trajan used his secretary as a co-author. Furthermore he argues that Trajan himself made the key decisions based upon the information provided by the secretary, who was then allowed to work up the reply, drafting an appropriate letter with Trajan's decision as its core. His reconstruction is based on the ability to discern an 'outer' and 'inner' style in the letters, that is, to discern between the remarks of Trajan (the inner style) and the secretarial dressing (the outer style). Although the letters are written in a uniform imperial style, the personal interventions and comments of Trajan are still discernible beneath the formal veneer. Henneman supports his conclusion using two main arguments. The first is rather typical of most form critical analyses: Henneman isolates a large amount of recurrent vocabulary and phraseology, both of common terms and administrative jargon, that he credits to the secretariat.[231] The second argument is somewhat similar: he demonstrates that the rescripts frequently follow very closely — sometimes practically verbatim — the

---

[227] Sherwin-White, *Letters of Pliny*, 536.
[228] This is also Sherwin-White's conclusion; ibid.
[229] H. Peter, "Der Brief", 123. See also Sherwin-White, *Letters of Pliny*, 536.
[230] A. Henneman, "Der äußere und innere Stil in Traians Briefen" (Ph.D. diss., Giessen, 1935), 28–33. His position is summarized by Sherwin-White, *Letters of Pliny*, 536–38, and this analysis is based on his summary.
[231] Sherwin-White, *Letters of Pliny*, 537, offers a brief list of examples.

diction, phraseology, and often the order of presentation of the original letter from Pliny. Apparently the secretary used the original letter to guide him in drafting the reply, particularly when the problem was rather complex or intricate. Henneman thus is able to assert strongly what parts are probably due to the authorship of the secretary.

Determining how much of the rescript that certainly were the thought or words of Trajan is more difficult; nevertheless, Henneman sought a method. In a few obvious instances, the direct intervention of Trajan is seen: when Trajan sharply refuses a not unreasonable request of Pliny,[232] or when he snaps at Pliny for countenancing a charge of *maiestas* or for not making his own decision,[233] or when Trajan is outraged with Pliny over the corruptions or disobedience he permitted, flailing Pliny with language that most probably a secretary would not have chosen.[234] Likewise an occasional commendation of Pliny is unlikely to have originated from anyone but Trajan.

These more obvious examples, however, arise from only a fraction of the letters. Henneman attempts to discover Trajan's hand by a stylistic comparison with other documents by Trajan. This comparison was not successful.[235] Sherwin-White suggests a different approach: an examination of the material content of the letters.[236] He contends that there are discernible principles that underlay the decisions of the Emperor, for example, equity toward the material interests of the provinces, severity toward malingerers, avoidance of dangerous precedents, suspicion of corporate bodies, and others. Both Henneman and Sherwin-White consider these principles to be easily detectable in certain parts of the letters. While Henneman concludes that such parts must then be the contribution of Trajan himself, Sherwin-White is more reserved: "these similarities do not suffice to prove that the decisions emanate in all cases, or even in most, from Trajan rather than from his advisors". Consequently Sherwin-White concludes that this method is also unreliable.[237] At this

---

[232] Pliny *Ep.* 40.3.
[233] Pliny *Ep.* 82, 117; respectively.
[234] Pliny *Ep.* 38: "sed medius fidius ad eadem diligentiam tuam pertinet inquirere quorum vitio ... tantam pecuniam Nicomedenses perdiderunt".
[235] The same opinion is shared by Sherwin-White, *Letters of Pliny*, 541: "The hand of Trajan cannot easily be detected by formal stylistic analysis..."
[236] Henneman alludes to such a possibility during his discussion of the 'inner' style and even occasionally discusses its indication of Trajan's hand but leaves it undeveloped as a technique.
[237] Sherwin-White, *Letters of Pliny*, 541. He does think a different approach may be possible in the case of Trajan. He suggests that since Trajan regularly consulted his *amici*

point, however, he diverges from our purpose here. He was ultimately trying to separate Trajan from even the input of his advisors. For such a goal, he is correct that this is not a reliable method. If however one is seeking only to separate the author — or the authors in the case of contributing advisors — from the secretary, then this method can be useful. In other words, in a secretary-controlled letter, the use of a secretary as a co-author may be detected by an analysis of the *content* of the letter, examining especially the handling of certain issues, the use of a particular type of argument, and so forth.

Thus a secretary-controlled letter can contain quite significant divergences from a letter written personally by the author. Obviously when the secretary composed — evidently a rare practice in private letters — the letters may have no points at all in common with the author's customary style. When the secretary was a co-author — a not so uncommon practice in private letters — the differences could still be significant. Furthermore these differences can and often do include those elements commonly considered in formal style analyses. Therefore a stylistic analysis can*not* be used to deny an authorial contribution. Despite the significant differences the presence of the author was not lost completely. Rather to the contrary, the input of the author — or the author and his advisors if regularly used — can be detected in recurrent themes, in argumentation, in even select phraseology or diction,[238] and perhaps in emotive outbursts and other nontemperate responses. Thus the differences that resulted from the commonly employed secretary-controlled method does *not* usually include the more significant aspects of the letter.

The presence of familiar authorial themes can indicate his contribution; yet the corollary is also possible. Sherwin-White notes in the case of Trajan that "when an unusual decision is made, when precedent is not followed, or a new one is set, it is likely that Trajan himself settled the issue with his characteristic independence of mind".[239] While this argument is reasonable, its major fallacy is that, when applied to another literary corpus, few internal criteria are left for the detection and rejec-

---

principis except when he was strongly moved by a particular subject, then an indication of personal — often emotional — intervention may evidence his personal input. Thus when a passage is highly charged then one should expect the content if not also the wording is probably Trajan's. Possibly Galatians 3 or 2 Corinthians 10—13 is analagous.

[238] The inclusion here of diction, for instance, is not contradictory, if extremely common formulae and other easily copied samples are excluded. The absence of an author's preferred terminology may be the result of secretarial intervention, while its presence may signal his contribution.

[239] Sherwin-White, *Letters of Pliny*, 542.

tion of a pseudonymous letter. Consequently for this corollary to be used, a prior determination or presumption of authenticity is needed.[240]

To summarize the possible influences of a secretary, it is clear that the use of a secretary to write a letter caused the letter to be different, regardless of how the secretary was used. The author was deprived of solitude with its advantages and disadvantages, and possibly was required to compose at a speed different from what he preferred. On the other hand, the author was relieved of the time, effort, and skill required of actual writing and could therefore concentrate his energies upon composition. The use of a secretary often led to the inclusion of additional details that the writer himself would not trouble to include. Freedom from the effort of actual writing could also prompt the author to include more preformed material, either presented in full or merely noted for the secretary to insert later into the draft.

In author-controlled letters specific types of differences were possible. Most notably for modern research, the letter could appear superficially to be in the author's style and yet vary considerably in more subtle ways. The content and style remained very much that of the author, but editorial corrections and changes were common, varying with the relative proficiency of the author and the secretary.

Secretary-controlled letters allowed the greatest amount of differences. It was possible for the letter to be quite different from any of the author's other works. Usually however the differences were far less extreme. One expected the content, including themes, purposes, and arguments, to be the same as or at least consistent with the author's (allowing for the new epistolary situation) but the form and style to vary considerably.

Irrespective of any secretarial influence, the author assumed complete responsibility for the content, including the subtle nuances. Because of his accountability, he checked the final draft.[241]

---

[240] Even an initial presumption of authenticity is not necessarily invalid. One may contend that if a letter claims for itself authenticity, the burden of proof lies with the dissenter. This one point may be said in support: all too frequently — particularly in the biblical field — a letter is *assumed* to be pseudonymous, unless strongly demonstrated otherwise, and even then, ironically, the letter is often subsequently dissected, without any external support, and various parts are rejected. Why is the simpler explanation (the influence of a secretary) not viable?

[241] It was because of this accountability that the marginally literate and illiterate used summary subscriptions in business letters to "insure" the letter body was accurate.

Chapter Three
The Role of the Secretary in the Letters of Paul

An examination of Paul's use of a secretary must begin by ascertaining what constitutes a letter of Paul. In other words, which of the thirteen traditional letters of Paul are actually Pauline? The authenticity of many letters in the Pauline corpus is rejected and the resulting list of "genuine" letters is disputed. Many scholars refer to the so-called "undisputed letters" (*viz.*, Romans, 1 and 2 Corinthians, Galatians, Philippians, 1 Thessalonians, and Philemon). Many include Ephesians and possibly 2 Thessalonians and Colossians, but few accept the Pastorals. Many of the criteria, however, used to reject these letters can be explained by the role of the secretary.[1] The *a priori* rejection of a letter on internal grounds, such as non-Pauline vocabulary or theology, would bias the investigation. Letters that usually are rejected must be included for the sake of scholarly thoroughness. The criterion for the selection of the letters for this study then should be broad: any New Testament letter that claims for itself Pauline authorship must be included. Thus because the role of the secretary may have implications for questions of authorship, the Pauline corpus is reopened to include the thirteen traditional letters of Paul.[2]

---

[1] So, *e.g.*, Alfred Wikenhauser, *Einleitung in das Neue Testament*, 2d ed. (Freiburg: Herder, 1953), 246: "Wenn bei der Abfassung eines Briefes ein Sekretär mitgewirkt hat, so können Differenzen in Wortschatz und Stil nicht als maßgebende Kriterien für die Entscheidung über seine Echtheit gelten".

[2] It is quite likely that this will still incur the criticism levelled against O. Roller: M. Dibelius and H. Conzelmann (*The Pastoral Epistles*, rev. ed., trans. P. Buttolph and A. Yarbro, in the Hermeneia Series [Philadephia: Fortress Press, 1972 (GE 1966)], 5) criticize him because "... he presupposes what is still to be demonstrated: the authenticity of all the canonical Pauline epistles". Yet what is the valid alternate starting-point, if a secretary could be responsible?

Cf. also A. Schweitzer's conclusion that Baur's criteria were applied most thoroughly by the ultra-Baurians who rejected them all; *Paul and His Interpreters*, trans. W. Montgomery (London: Adam & Charles Black, 1912), 12–21 and 118–20.

1. Preliminary Considerations

After the parameters for the corpus are set, a few preliminary issues must be briefly discussed: (1) the relation of Paul's letters to typical Greco-Roman letters in order to justify a comparison of their uses of a secretary; (2) the possibility and implications of Paul's use of συνεργοί (co-workers) in the composition of his letters; and finally (3) how Paul coordinated his use of a secretary with his inclusion of pre-formed material, both παραδόσεις (traditions) and previous notes, perhaps retainned in μεμβράναι (parchment notebooks).

a) Paul's Relation to the Greco-Roman Letter Tradition

Does the analysis of the use of a secretary in Greco-Roman letter writing have any relevance to Paul's use of a secretary? In other words, does Paul stand within the Greco-Roman letter tradition? It is unnecessary to offer a detailed analysis here, particularly since various aspects of this discussion have been adequately treated in depth elsewhere.[3]

Aside from the obvious but notable fact that Paul writes in Greek, are there other reasons for maintaining that Paul's letters stand within the Greco-Roman tradition? The issue may be approached by first querying, is there enough commonality among the Greco-Roman letters themselves to be able to speak of an established tradition and to justify comparing their own uses of a secretary?

aa) The Greco-Roman Letter

The affirmation of Greco-Roman scholarship concerning the unity of the letter tradition may be demonstrated by considering three related areas: purpose, structure, and content.[4]

---

[3] E.g., Stowers, *Letter Writing*; Doty, "Epistle", and idem, *Letters*.

[4] A casual acquaintance with much of this material was presupposed in the earlier descriptions of the use of a secretary in Greco-Roman letters.
This is not to imply that these three areas comprehensively cover the nature of the letter, but they are adequate for a comparison. William Doty, *Letter*, 49, lists four distinct elements: (1) stylistic and rhetorical features, (2) structural features, (3) formal and generic traits, and (4) the use of traditional materials including traditional forms and styles.

Purpose

In Roman times letter writing was popular. In the imperial court, letters were used extensively to spread not only official news but also gossip. Particularly with the publication of the letters of Cicero an important development occurred, for by his letters Cicero won the approval of educated men. As a result, letters became a means of expressing personal thoughts for public consumption in addition to their usual more circumstantial purpose. Thus there evolved both more literary and more occasional types of letters.[5]

Heikki Koskenniemi has isolated three purposes common throughout the diversity of letters:[6] (1) philophronesis (φιλοφρόνεσις), that is, the letter serves to express a "friendly relationship" between the sender and addressee (the expression is more in the act of sending the letter than in any content); (2) parousia (παρουσία), that is, the letter serves to revive the existence of an actual friendship and is the "presence" of the author, although physically separated;[7] and (3) homilia (ὁμιλία), that is, the letter is one-half of a conversation.[8] Within the framework of these three general purposes, the Greco-Roman letters, particularly the more occasional ones, may be further divided by purpose into business, official, public, 'non-real', and discursive letters, with ostraca forming a separate subgroup.[9]

Structure

Greco-Roman letters follow a definite structure of introduction, body, and conclusion. The introduction includes the names of the sender and the addressee, greetings, and often an additional wish (or prayer) for the recipient's good health. The body seeks/imparts information or re-

---

[5] The problems with this general classification will be pursued when the problems of classifying Paul's letters are discussed; see below, p. 136 and Appendix G.

[6] Koskenniemi, *Studien*, 34—47.

[7] The connection between actual presence and epistolary presence is illustrated in *PMich* 482 (A.D. 133): "Do not hesitate to write letters, since I rejoice exceedingly, as if you had come". J. L. White, "Epistolary Formulas and Cliches in Greek Papyrus Letters", *SBLASP* 14 (1978): 2: 307, is correct in maintaining that actual and epistolary presence "are integrally related and an extension of each other".

[8] This is a major point in Demetrius' [second or first century B.C.] description of a letter. In *On Style* 223, he attributes the concept to Artemon [*ca.* 2d c. B.C.], the editor of Aristotle's letters. Seneca, *Ep.* 75.1–2, also writes of the letter as a surrogate for spoken conversation.

[9] See Appendix A.

quests/orders something. The conclusion includes greetings to various persons, a second wish for the addressee's good health, perhaps also a summary subscription, a word of farewell (frequently merely ἔρρωσο or *vale*) and occasionally the date. The purpose of the letter often affects the length of the constituent parts. A business letter may have a minimal opening and closing, while a familial letter may contain little but these.

Content

For every assertion about the general contents of the two main types of letters, the more occasional letters or the more public epistles, an exception lurks around the corner. Nonetheless, a general observation concerning their relative contents is useful. The occasional letters usually reflect the concerns of the less educated, lower societal classes, while the literary epistles reflect more of the better educated, upper classes' concerns. The former tend to be more rigid, stereotypical, and formulaic, while the latter tend to be more rhetorical, less stereotypical, and perhaps less restricted to the formulae of the occasional letters. Although the occasional letters accomplished their purposes, they are hardly the paradigms of style and epistolary grace that the more public epistles often are. In the more occasional letters, the writer apparently felt limited in his freedom to substitute alternative phrases. Therefore, rather than having a kaleidoscope of style and vocabulary, one finds "a mass-produced print of stereotyped phrases, [with a] rigid external structure, of brevity and of detached impersonality matched only by our own most formal invitations and announcements".[10] The occasional letter typically lacks any of the personal qualities of modern letters. Except for stylistic references to good or bad health, wishes, and greetings, there are few mentions of personal details. A similar lack of personableness is found in the more literary epistles, which, while certainly models of rhetoric and style, often seem less an actual letter than a literary treatise adorned in epistolary garb. Yet despite this diversity, the *content* of the Greco-Roman letter may be characterized by two significant elements: stereotyped formulae[11] and epistolary rhetoric.

---

[10] Doty, *Letters*, 13.

[11] 'Formula' is used in a more general sense. There have been recent attempts to distinguish a 'cliché' from other formulae. Henry A. Steen, "Les clichés épistolaries dans les lettres sur papyrus grecques", *Classica et Mediaevalia* 1 (1938): 119–76, offers this distinction: 'clichés' are those expressions that either soften or intensify an epistolary function by modification or elaboration. Thus a cliché is an ornamental expression which, strictly

Stereotyped formulae. In the typical Greek letter — and in Paul — the main topics of the letter are frequently broached in some way as to establish mutual ground, such as by disclosing new information or recalling previous communication of which both parties are aware. This is a major role of the "introductory formulae", or as they are now called the "stereotyped formulae".[12]

John White has isolated six types of formulae: disclosure, request or petition, expression of joy, expression of astonishment, statement of compliance, and statement of report.[13] To these may be added four more: ironic rebuke, transition indicators, greetings, and thanksgiving. The formulae have a definite form and purpose, as well as a limited content, and thus they occur in the letters with very little variety.[14] Their use is more noticeable in the more occasional letters, due in part to the letter's brevity and commonality of purpose. Yet the formulae also occur in the more literary epistles. In these, however, more notable than their use of formulae is their frequent use of certain types of rhetoric, thus contributing to their perceived "higher" style.

Epistolary rhetoric. This type of rhetoric may be divided into two very general categories: literary devices and oratorical devices. Ancient letters contain not only literary devices but also oratorical devices, (a) because literary epistles were often 'speeches' cast into writing, (b) because more occasional letters are often a conversation put in writing, and (c) because some of the oratorical devices lend themselves easily to a written form.[15]

---

speaking, is not essential to the statement but which gives nuance. Because this is such a fine distinction and can be disputed (*e.g.*, J. White, "Greek Documentary Letter Tradition", 100 and esp. idem, *Light*, 211–13), it is not pressed here.

[12] The classic work in the field of epistolary formulae was by F. X. J. Exler, *Form*. He identifies the following formulae: opening, wish (three types), illiteracy, and oath. Subsequent work by others has only sharpened the definitions and supplemented the list.

T. Y. Mullins, "Formulas in New Testament Epistles", *JBL* 91 (1972): 386, argues for the term "stereotyped formulae" against the earlier term "introductory formulae" because, while these formulae often do appear near the opening or closing, they may appear anywhere. Furthermore, even when they do appear at the beginning, they seldom introduce the letter body. Examples of the various locations in which the so-called "introductory formulae" are found may be seen in Appendix B. A more recent summary has been given by White, *Light*, 198*ff.*

[13] J. White, "Introductory Formulae in the Body of the Pauline letter", *JBL* 90 (1971): 93.

[14] See Appendices B, C, and D.

[15] The difference between a letter and a speech was less pronounced in ancient times. Rudolf Hirzel claims that a letter was merely a speech caught in writing. They were so similar that an author might equally choose one or the other, to step into discourse or to write a letter. R. Hirzel, *Der Dialog: ein literarhistorischer Versuch*, 2 vols. (Stuttgart:

(1) Literary devices[16] may be distinguished from oratorical devices because of the medium in which they are created, that is, they are probably composed in a written form and are best noticed and appreciated there. Common literary devices include analogy, chiasmus (both in sense-lines and in thematic development), parallelism and antithesis, the grouping of items for dramatic effect,[17] and lists of virtues/vices and tribulations.[18]

(2) Oratorical devices were used frequently in speeches, both the more formal speeches in the forum and the more popular street preaching; yet they were used in letters as well. The examination of these devices is more complicated, since they are being preserved only in written forms. There are three major oratorical devices that appear in ancient letters: paraenesis, diatribe, and oration.

Paraenesis, from παραίνεσις meaning "exhortation", is usually associated with moral instruction. One particular method of propagating paraenesis was the use of *topoi*. A *topos* is "the treatment in independent form of the topic of a proper thought or action, or of a virtue or a vice, etc".[19] A *topos* is a type of stock response frequently used by the street preachers as an answer to a common question. "The *topoi* are miniature essays of stereotyped good advice".[20] When in series *topoi* are either arbitrarily connected or perhaps linked by catchword associations. These little essays adopted a standard form: injunction, rationale, discussion, and an optional analogous situation.[21]

S. Hirzel, 1895; reprint, Hildesheim: George Olms, 1963), 1: 305–6. So also the ancient epistolary theorists, Demetr. *Style* 228 and Isocrates *Epp*. 2.13 and 1.1–3. This is easier to understand if letters were often dictated *viva voce*.

[16] The use of "literary" may be unfortunate. It is meant to denote written rhetoric and not to imply a special connection to "literary epistles".

[17] Normally to imply relationship. Pleonasm would also be included. *E.g.*, Cic. *Att*. 10.8; "Could there be a crime, deeper, greater, or baser".

[18] *E.g.*, for a vice list, see Arr. *Epict. Diss*. 2.16.4: "Expel ... grief, fear, envy, malevolence, avarice, effeminacy, intemperance from your mind. But these can be no otherwise expelled than by looking up to God alone as your pattern". Tribulation lists which include beatings, shipwrecks, and nagging injuries may be found in Josephus, Nag Hammadi, the Mishnah, and Plutarch; see Robert Hodgson, "Paul the Apostle and First Century Tribulation Lists", *ZNW* 74 (1983): 59–80. See also Appendix F.

[19] David Bradley, "The *Topos* as a Form in the Pauline Paraenesis", *JBL* 72 (1953): 240.

[20] Doty, *Letters*, 39.

[21] The injunction urges the course of behavior to be followed or avoided. The rationale follows. The discussion covers the logical and practical consequences of the behavior, with a situation perhaps for illustration. See T. Y. Mullins, "Topos as a NT Form", *JBL* 99 (1980): 541–47. *E.g.*, Sir. 31:25–30; injunction, "Do not aim to be valiant over wine"; rationale, "for wine has destroyed many"; analagous situation, "fire and water prove the temper of steel"; discussion, "wine is like life..."

The second common oratorical device is the diatribe.[22] The modern debate over its nature began in 1887 when E. Weber published a study of the Cynic diatribe.[23] His description of the diatribe lies at the base of all later descriptions.[24] By the time of Eduard Norden's work, the diatribe was considered an established and well-defined *Gattung*, in which a declamation is staged by the speaker playing both his own part and that of the imaginary person with whom he is having his war of words.[25]

Understanding the diatribe as an established *Gattung* used by Cynic-Stoic preachers, Rudolf Bultmann wrote his dissertation relating it to Paul's letter to the Romans.[26] Examining Bion, Epictetus, and Seneca, Bultmann outlined five categories for the diatribe: dialogical character, rhetorical character, constituent parts and arrangements, manner of argumentation, and finally tone and mood. (He then described Paul with the same categories.) Bultmann further defined and clarified the diatribe's nature. He discovered that the "dialogue" aspect is maintained by giving a flowing speech that is "interrupted" by an imaginary opponent — representing an opposing philosopher or the *communis opinio* — who offers some anticipated objection.[27] For his defense the speaker calls upon dead heroes, personifications of the law and virtues, and the participation of the audience. His diction is conversational, yet provoking, and the syntax is λέξις εἰρομένη (a running style, that is, it is paratactic and also tends to string together short sentences). The progression of

---

[22] For the history and problems of the investigation of the diatribe, see esp. Stanley K. Stowers, *The Diatribe and Paul's Letter to the Romans*, SBLDS, no. 57 (Chico, CA: Scholars, 1981).

[23] E. Weber, *De dione Chrysostomo cynicorum sectatore*, Leipziger Studien, no. 9 (Leipzig: University, 1887).

[24] He offers formal categories, examples, and evidences for the diatribe. He lists 28 different stylistic characteristics, including the use of everyday language, comparisons and metaphors, proverbs and maxims, hyperbole, exempla, paradoxes, personifications, fictitious speeches by legendary persons, quotations from the poets, parody, short non-periodic sentences, asyndeton, and the use of ornamental rhetorical figures. He was the first to outline the major elements of the dialogue in the diatribe, including the imaginary opponent, objections, address to imaginary persons, short dialogical exchanges, and rhetorical questions.

[25] E. Norden, *Die antike Kunstprosa*, 2 vols. (Leipzig: Weidmann, 1898; reprint, Leipzig: Weidmann, 1958).

[26] R. Bultmann, *Der Stil der paulinischen Predigt und die kynisch-stoische Diatribe* (Göttingen: Vandenhoeck & Ruprecht, 1910).

[27] These objections are frequently in the form of questions, introduced by ἀλλά or τί οὖν. E.g., Epictetus' discussion on "Purity and Cleanliness" (Arr. *Epict. Diss.* 4.11.5): "What then (τί οὖν), would anybody have you dress yourself out to the utmost? By no means (μὴ γένοιτο), except..."; also 1.10.2.

thought is presented not by the subordination of logical relationships but generally by (1) a question and an answer, (2) an imperative followed by a statement or a question, (3) a statement followed by an imperative, or (4) some combination such as a statement and a question.[28] Thus the diatribe is marked by simplicity in style and syntax; yet it is strong, vigorous, and dynamic. The diatribe was used not for technical discourse on an abstract subject but usually for preaching to persuade the common man on the street to some philosophical or moral position. Its purpose was not so much intellectual enlightenment as conversion.

In more recent times, there has been a movement away from an understanding of the diatribe as an established *Gattung*. There is too much diversity in the style and elements that are considered to be a part of the diatribe. The category is too fluid and evasive to be classified so confidently.[29]

The third oratorical device common in letters is the oration or discourse (ὁμιλία or *disputatio*). It differs from the diatribe in that it is less conscious of an opponent. It presupposes the audience to be convinced rather than to need persuasion. They are not adversaries needing refutation but rather colleagues needing clarification. It is as much exegetical as hortatory.[30] An oration is characterized by repetition and — at least in a good oration — the effective presentation of the strong points and a clever covering of the weak.[31]

There are of course other oratorical devices, but most are not detectable in written form, such as pitch or rate. One variation, however, called *numeris*, may on occasion be detected in written form. A skilled orator paid attention to the *numeris*, or the succession of long and short

---

[28] Stowers, *Diatribe*, 21. Much of this discussion has been condensed from his excellent analysis.

[29] So Stowers, *Diatribe*, 75, *et alii*. Those who still assert the diatribe as a *Gattung* do so by emphasizing the common elements and explaining the differences as the result of the historical evolution of the form.
Very recently the use of the diatribe by Paul has been strongly rejected. Thomas Schmeller in a thorough investigation (400+ pp.) questioned the nature and use of the diatribe (in Bion, Rufus, and Epictetus) as well as its use by Paul in Romans (1:18–2:11; 11:1–24; also 8:31–39) and 1 Corinthians (15:29–49; also 4:6–15; 9:1–18). See Schmeller, *Paulus und die "Diatribe": eine vergleichende Stilinterpretation*, NTAbh, 19 (Munich: Aschendorffsche, 1987).

[30] So John White, "Saint Paul and the Apostlic Letter Tradition", *CBQ* 45 (1983): 436.

[31] J. B. Greenough in the introduction to *Select Orations of Cicero*, rev. ed. J. B. Greenough and G. L. Kittredge (Boston: Athenaeum Press, 1897), 43, observes that in the (common) criticism that Cicero's speeches are often carelessly redundant and tautological the critic is displaying his ignorance of ancient rhetoric.

syllables, so as to give, along with varied tones of emphasis, a pleasant musical cadence.

To incorporate rhetoric properly into a letter requires some skill and training on the part of the author (or secretary), gained either by prolonged exposure or by formal education.

bb) The Pauline Letter

Sufficient commonality between the Pauline letters and the typical Greco-Roman letter can be shown using the same general categories: purpose, structure, and content.

Purpose

Heikki Koskenniemi's three purposes (philophronesis, parousia, and homilia) are clearly evident in the Pauline letters. Problems arise only when the question of the purposes of the Pauline letters is posed using the framework of "literary epistles" versus "occasional letters". In many ways, the difficulties of characterizing the type (and hence the general purpose) of the letters of Paul have served to highlight the problems with this type of classification.[32]

If Greco-Roman letters are viewed as a spectrum with two polarities of public and private letters, then one may conclude that Paul's letters fit within the general, acceptable purposes for Greco-Roman letters, allowing room for modification and specialization.[33] His letters are more complex in purpose than most of the occasional papyrus letters; yet his letters are not as complex as the most literary epistles. As Seneca (*via* Cicero) took the colloquial Latin letter and gave it an elevated purpose, so also Paul took the koine, occasional letter and modified it to suit his purposes.[34]

---

[32] Due to the complexity of the issue this is discussed in an appendix, since for the purpose here, it is only one aspect of a comparison of Paul's "purposes" to those found generally in Greco-Roman letters. It is however treated in some detail; see Appendix G: The "Literary or Non-literary" (Deissmann) Debate: The Problem of Classifying the Letters of Paul".

[33] This is the general consensus of modern scholarship. See, *e.g.*, Doty, "Epistle", 8–20; and Stowers, *Letter Writing*, 25, 34–35.

[34] This argument is elaborated in the extended discussion in Appendix G; see esp. p. 216 n. 29.

Structure

The basic structure of the letter (opening, body, and closing) is used consistently by Paul.[35] His openings contain the usual information on the sender and addressee, and a greeting. Yet his opening is also remodeled.[36] Paul alters the traditional "χαίρειν" (cf. Acts 15:23) to a more 'Christian' "χάρις", and adds a Jewish "εἰρήνη" (שָׁלוֹם). Jewish letters tended to elaborate the names of the sender and addressee more than did Greek letters and often contained a prayer for peace as well as both the customary supplication for good health and the convention of mentioning that the writer held the addressee in his memory.[37] Paul may be reflecting this influence.

The part of the letter in which Paul handles the bulk of matters, the body, has received the least attention as to formal elements and conformity to traditional forms.[38] Nonetheless it is also used by Paul for the customary purposes, such as imparting or requesting information.

Paul is not bound tightly to the closing conventions of the Hellenistic letter. The Hellenistic letters themselves, however, are also less consistent here. Paul closes with neither the second healthwish nor a word of farewell. Rather he often uses a benediction — although one may argue that this is only a 'Christianized' healthwish — or a doxology.[39]

---

[35] Even the two extremes, Philemon, which is the most like an occasional papyrus letter, and Romans, which is perhaps the least occasional and the most like the more literary epistles, may be grouped together.

[36] V. Parkin, "Some Comments on the Pauline Prescripts", *IBS* 8 (1986): 92–99, argues that the largest modification occurred after 1 and 2 Thessalonians were written.

[37] Bezadel Porten, "Address Formulae in Aramaic Letters: a New Collation of Cowley 17", *RevB* 90 (1980): 398–413. See also the chart in Exler, *Form*, 61.

[38] Doty, *Letters*, 34, offers four reasons for this lack: "The body as a formal entity is not considered sufficiently unitary or consistent from letter to letter...; it is difficult to identify how the 'normative' forms of the body took shape; there is the difficulty seen in the several attempts to define where the body begins and ends; and finally there is confusion because several letters (1 Cor., Phil., and 2 Th.) seem to assimilate the entire body into the thanksgiving".

[39] These closing conventions are also not the final closure of the letter. See Rom. 11:36; Gal. 1:5; Phil. 4:20; Eph. 3: 20–21; 1 Tim. 1:17; 2 Tim. 4:18; *cf.* only Rom. 16:27 (perhaps placed in 'proper' form because of the secretary). Robert Funk (*Language, Hermeneutic, and the Word of God*, [New York: Harper & Row, 1966], 249) suggests that the closing was modified to increase Paul's "apostolic presence". Paul indicates his reason for writing and then his intention to send an emissary or to make a personal visit (Rom. 15:14–33; Philem. 21–22; 1 Cor. 4:14–21; 1 Th. 2:17–3:13; 2 Cor. 12:14-13:13; Gal. 4:12–20; Phil. 2:19–24; Eph. 6:21–22; Col. 4:7–9; and 2 Tim. 4:9–11). There is a progression from letter to personal visit.

Some have seen this closing section as paraenetic; *e.g.*, M. Dibelius, *From Tradition to*

Postscripts are common in the letters of Paul and, excepting their Christian terminology, are typical, containing a final salutation, an authenticating section in the author's own hand, and a closing list of greetings. Paul also adds an occasional reference to a "holy kiss" and a final blessing that, because of their uniformity, may have been liturgical.

Content

As in the previous two categories, Paul's letters contain the typical content of Greco-Roman letters, allowing for their Christian nature. His content has points of comparison in breadth and depth to the letters of Cicero.[40] He also demonstrates a knowledge and use of both stereotyped fomulae and epistolary rhetoric.

Stereotyped formulae. Paul makes frequent use of the usual Greco-Roman epistolary formulae, such as the greeting formulae. The location, length, personalization, and type of greetings are customary and typical for his time.[41] The joy formula occurs in Phil. 4:10; 2 Cor. 7:16; and 7:9. The expression of astonishment is used in Gal. 1:6. The compliance formula is found in Gal. 1:8, 9. The statement of report formula occurs in Gal. 1:13*ff.* The ironic rebuke is used in 2 Cor. 12:11−13. In all these cases, Paul uses traditional forms. He varies from typical Greco-Roman practice usually by citing a different occasion or reason for the use of the formula. For instance, his astonishment (in Gal. 1:6) is not because he has not received a letter from them.

Paul also makes frequent use of the thanksgiving formula which occurs in all of his undisputed letters except Galatians.[42] The formula follows the traditional form with the following exceptions: (1) his occasion

---

Gospel, 2d ed., trans. B. L. Woolf (New York: Charles Scribner's Sons, 1965), 233−65. Others have difficulty with a paraenesis at the close of the letter and have considered it "tacked on" and not an integral part of the letter. See H. D. Betz, *Galatians: a Commentary on Paul's Letter to the Churches in Galatia*, in the Hermeneia Commentary Series (Philadelphia: Fortress, 1979), 254, who argues against this, by asserting that the paraenesis corresponds to the customary "prescriptive" forms of arguments that come near the end of philosophical letters.

[40] So also Stowers, *Letter Writing*, 34−35.

[41] *E.g.*, in Romans all three types of greetings occur: the first person type in v. 22, the second person type in vv. 3−16, and the third person type in v. 16. See Appendix D. See also the recent discussion by F. Schnider and W. Stenger, *Studien zum neutestamentlichen Briefformular*, NTTS, no. 11 (Leiden: Brill, 1987) that the Pauline greetings can be subdivided into 'greeting instruction' and 'greeting presentation'.

[42] This may be explained in Galatians by its occasion: either because it was his first letter (*i.e.*, he has not yet established this pattern), because it was a quick letter dashed in anger,

for the thanksgiving is no longer being saved by the god(s) from danger but often the faithfulness of the congregation; (2) he tends to blend an intercession into his thanksgiving (he gives thanks and then prays it will continue); and (3) he tends to preview the contents of the letter in the thanksgiving. Therefore, although he makes frequent use of the formula, he modifies and expands it, often placing it near the beginning of the letter, a less common location.[43]

Paul Schubert, in his investigation of the Pauline thanksgiving, admits having problems determining where the thanksgiving ends.[44] Jack Sanders suggests that there is a definite ending to the Pauline thanksgiving and it is marked by a "distinctive phrase" which occurs in two styles.[45] T. Y. Mullins, however, has subsequently restructured Sander's findings.[46] He points out that he has already identified the first style as a petition formula and the second as a disclosure formula.[47] Thus Paul usually ends his thanksgiving with a petition formula, although he may on occasion use a disclosure formula, as he does elsewhere to indicate a transition.[48]

---

or because it was not a part of the rhetorical framework. In 2 Corinthians, it is not as pronounced. Titus has none.

[43] Beda Rigaux, *The Letters of St. Paul: Modern Studies*, ed. and trans. S. Yonick (Chicago: Franciscan Herald, 1968), 121–22, argues that this is a carry-over from the Jewish custom of beginning a speech with thanksgiving.

[44] P. Schubert, *Pauline Thanksgiving*.

[45] J. T. Sanders, "The Transition from Opening Epistolary Thanksgiving to Body in the Pauline Corpus", *JBL* 81 (1962): 352–62. He maintains that a formula marked the transition and it had two forms:
1. παρακαλῶ δὲ ὑμας, ἀδελφοί,
   διὰ τοῦ ὀνόματος Ἰησοῦ χριστοῦ,
   περί . . .
   ἵνα . . .
2. οὐ θέλω δὲ ὑμᾶς ἀγνοεῖν, ἀδελφοί,
   τό . . .
   ὅτι . . .

He summarizes this into seven elements: (1) a verb of enjoinment; (2) the particle δὲ; (3) the recipients in the accusative; (4) the vocative; (5) an appeal to the authority of the Lord; (6) an optional prepositional phrase, stating the topic of the injunction; and (7) the injuction itself ("Transition", 359). See 1 Cor. 1:10; Phil. 1:12; 2 Th. 2:1; Rom. 11:25*; 12:1; 15:20; 16:17; 1 Cor. 10:1*; 11:3*; 15:1–3; 16:15; 2 Cor. 2:8; 6:1; 10:1; 12:8; Phil. 4:2; 4:15; 1 Th. 3:2; 3:7; 4:10; 4:13*; 5:1; 5:12. (Those marked by an * are of the second style.)

[46] Mullins, "Disclosure: a Literary Form in the New Testament", *NovT* 7 (1964): 45.

[47] See Appendix C. Also Mullins, "Petition as a Literary Form", *NovT* 5 (1962): 48 and idem, "Disclosure", 45–46.

[48] John White, "Paul and the Apostolic Letter", 439 n. 9, suggests that Paul "prefers" the disclosure formula for introducing the letter body, using it in 5 of the 7 [undisputed]

Epistolary rhetoric. Both literary and oratorical devices are abundant in the Pauline letters.

(1) Literary devices. Paul employs all the major literary devices used commonly in Greco-Roman letters. He makes frequent use of analogy in his letters, although his particular handling of an analogy may not be as typical.[49] In the century before Paul the use of chiasmus was much in vogue but may have fallen out of use in epistolary rhetoric during Paul's time. Beda Rigaux pronounces that in the first Christian century chiasmus was "only to be noticed intermittently as a stylistic curiosity".[50] Modern interest in chiasmus, however, was revived when Jo-

---

letters. See Rom. 1:13; 2 Cor. 1:8; Gal. 1:11; Phil. 1:12; and 1 Th. 2:1. 1 Corinthians (1:10) uses a petition formula and 2 Thessalonians (2:1) uses a variation of the petition (ἐρωτῶμεν δὲ ὑμᾶς, ἀδελφοί, ὑπέρ . . .).

In the other letters, a formula is used in Col. 2:1, and, if Ephesians 1—3 is an extended thanksgiving, then also in Eph. 4:1 (petition). In the pastorals, 1 Tim. 2:1 fits Paul's usual custom. Titus has no such pattern. In 2 Tim. 1:15 there is a participial construction which serves the same purpose as a disclosure formula and falls in the proper location. This nonstandard form could be the result of poor imitation (if deutero-Pauline, although why would an imitator not merely copy one of the abundant examples in Paul?) or secretarial alteration, perhaps because the secretary was working from notes that were not verbatim.

[49] Paul has been criticized for analogical convolutions. *E.g.*, William Doty observes, "Paul may use a cluster of images to make a single point, or he may drop one image to pick up another before exhausting the possibilities of the first; the points Paul makes are not always consistent with the actual situations from which the analogies are derived" (*Letters*, 45 n. 59). Paul's analogy between a woman in marriage and man under the law in Romans 7 may be cited. Some argue that such peculiarities were the result of Paul's carelessness, whether from overenthusiastic haste or technical inexpertise, while others argue that they were deliberate, maintaining that any apparent twist in the analogy may have a Pauline 'logic'.

[50] Rigaux, *Letters*, 127. This may not be entirely accurate. The chiastic analysis of Greek texts is deficient (so John W. Welch, "Chiasmus in Ancient Greek and Latin Literature", in *Chiasmus in Antiquity: Structure, Analyses, and Exegesis*, ed. J. W. Welch [Hildesheim: Gerstenberg, 1981], 258). Chiasmus has been demonstrated in classical Latin literature. R. B. Steele lists 1257 examples of chiasmus in Livy ("Anaphora and Chiasmus in Livy", *TAPA* 32 [1901]: 166), 211 in Sallust, 365 in Caesar, 1088 in Tacitus, and 307 in Justinus (idem, *Chiasmus in Sallust, Caesar, Tacitus and Justinus* [Northfield, MN: Independent Publishing Co., 1891], 4—5). Nevertheless, most of these examples, particularly in the Latin, are composed of only pairs of words (so idem, "Anaphora and Chiasmus", 185). Complex chiasmus had apparently become rare in the first century.

Interestingly in Cicero's works chiasmus appears in those that were carefully composed. "In those epistles of Cicero which were most freely and rapidly written chiasmus does not often occur" (idem, "Chiasmus in the Epistles of Cicero, Seneca, Pliny and Fronto", in *Studies in Honor of B. L. Gildersleeve*, ed. C. A. Briggs, [Baltimore: John Hopkins, 1902], 339). The same restriction apparently applies to Pliny's letters (ibid., 346—47). Chiasmus is rare in Seneca (ibid., 342).

achim Jeremias demonstrated its frequent use by Paul.[51] What may have been viewed as redundancy and verbosity in Paul is seen now as a complex use of chiasmus, employed not only with sense-lines but also with ideas, and even major sections.[52] A corollary to Paul's use of chiasmus is his use of parallelism. As a Jew well-versed in the Old Testament Paul makes numerous uses of both synonymous and antithetic parallelism with words, phrases, ideas, and perhaps even the structuring of pericopae.[53]

Paul also employs paradoxical and metaphorical imagery and development as well as some minor literary devices, such as pleonasm,[54] tribulation lists,[55] virtue and vice lists, moral imperatives, swearing one's message is God-given, and curse pronouncements.[56]

(2) Oratorical devices. One prominent device is the paraenetic use of the *topos*. The form (injunction, rationale, optional analogous situation, and discussion) is most noticeable in Romans 13, where there are several, and in 1 Th. 4:9-5:11. Passages where there is an extended scriptural argument, notably in Galatians and Romans, show characteristics of an oration.[57] It is in this style of oral communication that the best explanation is found for the numerous examples of meiosis and litotes,[58] delibe-

---

[51] J. Jeremias, "Chiasmus in den Paulusbriefen", *ZNW* 49 (1958): 139–56.

[52] See Appendix E. Also see Turner, *Style*, 97–99, and the collected examples of chiastic passages from the New Testament discussed by John Welch, "Chiasmus in the New Testament", in *Chiasmus in Antiquity*, 211–18. He argues that chiasmus is "a basic element in the literary composition of the New Testament" (Welch, "Chiasmus in the New Testament", 248). Since chiasmus was common only in the letters of Cicero and Pliny that were carefully written (see n. 50 above), then the same may be suspected of Paul: those letters containing chiasmus were probably more carefully written.

[53] *E.g.*, Paul uses synonymous (1 Cor. 15:54; Rom. 9:2; 2 Th. 2:8; Col. 3:16), antithetic (Rom. 4:25; 2:7; 1 Cor. 1:18; 4:10; 15:42; 2 Cor. 6:4; 1 Tim. 3:16), and mixed (2 Tim. 2:11) parallelism. Rigaux, *Letters*, 127, oddly credits it to a deeply rooted need in Paul's temperament.

[54] *E.g.*, Gal. 4:10, "You observe days and months and seasons and years".

[55] See Appendix F.

[56] Interestingly, H. D. Betz, "The Literary Composition and Function of Paul's Letter to the Galatians", *NTS* 21 (1975): 378–79 (a precursor to his commentary on Galatians), argues that since the letter begins with a conditional curse, which is very carefully constructed, cursing every Christian who dares to preach a different gospel, and then ends by pronouncing a corresponding conditional blessing upon those who remain loyal to the Pauline gospel (4:16), it is to be classified as a "magical" letter, one of the "non-real" letters (see Appendix A).

[57] So John White, "Paul and the Apostolic Letter", 436.

[58] *I.e.*, the use of a negative expression for a positive meaning, as in 1 Cor. 1:25, "For the foolishness of God is wiser than men". Also see 1 Th. 2:14–16 and 2 Th. 3:2–7.

rate anacolutha,[59] and homilectic directness.[60] Yet instances like sustained numeris over a prolonged period[61] suggest that oratorical devices were a written phenomenon and not only the recording of an oral presentation.

While these oratorical devices are quite evident in Paul's letters, it is the diatribe that has received the most attention. Undeniably there are certain elements of Bultmann's description of the diatribe in Paul's letters: the use of question and answer, the use of the imaginary (?) interlocutor, the use of *exempla*, quotations from the poets, the play on sentiment, and the dialogical exchange.[62]

If the diatribe is the most discussed of the rhetorical elements, then surely the dialogue is the most discussed of the diatribe's elements. The dialogical element is contrasted to the imaginary interlocutor in that the latter has no real life counterpart but is only a representative of the view to be refuted. In the dialogue, there is assumed to be a real person(s) with whom the writer is "in dialogue". The question usually then is, which device is Paul using? The question becomes more complex. The dialog was more likely to be used independently of the diatribe, whereas the imaginary interlocutor was not. Therefore the question becomes, was Paul using a literary *Gattung* with established elements or merely some common rhetorical devices? This abstract question develops concrete results immediately. For example, when Paul addresses a Jew in Rom. 2:17*ff.*, is he speaking to a group of Jews in Rome (hence a dialogue) or is the Jew a symbol of a particular theological position (hence a diatribe)? The answer affects the nature and purpose of Romans.[63]

---

[59] *I.e.*, an abrupt change in grammatical construction within one sentence unit, as in 2 Cor. 1:23, "But I call God to witness — it was to spare you..." See also 2 Th. 2:2.

[60] As in Rom. 14:12, "So let each of us give an account to God".

[61] *E.g.*, 1 Cor. 13:1—13 and 1 Th. 5:14—22 (if not a *topos*).

[62] *E.g.*, Rom. 3:27—4:2 is a series of questions and answers, as is Epictetus (Arr. *Epict. Diss.*) 4.1—2. Elsewhere in Epictetus (1.29.3—4) an interlocutor objects and gives an *exemplum*, whom Epictetus then uses in his response. Likewise in Rom. 4:1, an interlocutor objects and cites an *exemplum* (Abraham), whom Paul uses in his response (4:1—25).

[63] Günther Bornkamm ("The Letter to the Romans as Paul's Last Will and Testament", in *The Romans Debate*, ed. K. P. Donfried [Minneapolis: Augsburg, 1977], 17—31) holds that the questions in Romans arose from Paul; hence they do not have any direct connection to a particular group or opponents in Rome. Thus Romans uses the diatribe. Karl Donfried ("False Presuppositions in the Study of Romans", in *The Romans Debate*, 132—41) strongly disagrees, arguing among other things that Bultmann never proved that the diatribe was an established genre. Thus there is nothing to prevent interpolating the situation at Rome from the opposing positions implied by Paul. Inevitably this difficult genre question is approached with preconceived ideas about the purpose of Romans, ideas that inevitably bias the conclusions about the use of a diatribe.

Preliminary Considerations 143

Many Paulinists contend that the diatribe is a questionable genre due to the lack of internal consistency.[64] Those, however, who uphold the integrity of the diatribe often argue that the style differs because of the audience.[65]

Irrespective of whether Paul uses the diatribe, he clearly makes use of epistolary rhetoric in his letters, both oratorical and literary devices.[66] With his frequent use of stereotyped formulae, his letters fall in the range of the usual content for Greco-Roman letters. Therefore since his purpose, structure, and content fit within the typical parameters of Greco-Roman letters, one may conclude that he does stand clearly within the Greco-Roman letter tradition.[67]

Any remaining question about the influences on Paul from the Greco-Roman letter tradition cannot ask whether Paul was influenced by the tradition — the parallels are too numerous — but rather must ask how this influence occurred. Was Paul formally trained in letter-writing? Because of the presence of at least some rhetorical elements, one may even ask, did Paul study under a Hellenistic teacher of rhetoric? The latter appears doubtful. Nigel Turner is probably correct when he contends that it is unlikely because:

> his anacolutha and solecisms are too numerous. There is a direct object in the nominative case (Rom. 2:8), the antecedent of *ho* (neuter) can be masculine (Eph. 5:5) or feminine (Col. 3:14). We find extraordinary grammar in 2 Cor. 12:17 and casus pendens in Rom. 8:3. Paul's periods are rarely finished off neatly, a fault which Abel ascribes to forgetfulness as to how the period began, rather than to disdain of grammatical rules; Paul allows himself to be drawn along on the wings

---

[64] So K. P. Donfried and also Robert Karris ("The Occasion of Romans: a Response to Professor Donfried", in *The Romans Debate*, 150). His disagreement with Donfried concerns another matter.

[65] *E.g.*, A. J. Malherbe, *The Social Aspects of Early Christianity*, (Baton Rouge: Louisiana State University, 1977), 50 and n. 55. See also idem, "μὴ γένοιτο in the Diatribe and Paul", *HTR* 73 (1980): 231–40. Thus the addresses of Epictetus to his students, Dio Chrysostom to the masses, Maximus of Tyre to the aristocrats, and Paul to his fellow Christians differ because of the situations.

[66] So also Wilhelm Wuellner, "Greek Rhetoric and Pauline Argumentation", in *Early Christian Literature and the Classical Intellectual Tradition: in Honorem Robert M. Grant*, ed. W. R. Schoedel and R. L. Wilken (Paris: Théologie historique, 1979), 177–88. Also see idem, "Paul's Rhetoric of Argumentation in Romans: an Alternative to the Donfried-Karris Debate over Romans", in *The Romans Debate*, 152–74 (originally published in *CBQ* 38 [1976]: 330–51). See also W. D. Davies' conclusion: "The presence of Hellenistic influences on Paul has become increasingly clear in his epistolary usages, as in his structuring of the Epistles, and in his use of Hellenistic rhetorical forms and phrases"; *Paul and Rabbinic Judaism*, 4th ed. (Philadelphia: Fortress, 1980), XXIII.

[67] So *inter permulti* O. Roller, *Formular*, 251 n. 7 and the Appendix G.

of his thoughts in sharp bursts, resulting in parentheses and discords, while particles and participles are brought in to weave over the gaps in diction.[68]

If not from a teacher of rhetoric, then where did Paul learn letter writing?

cc) The "Jerusalem or Tarsus" Debate: the Question of the Educational Background of Paul

The question of Paul's heritage is more than an issue of biographical interest. It is frequently a foundation stone for an argument as to whether Paul should be examined exclusively within a Greco-Roman framework. Often the debate takes the approach of asking at what age Paul left Tarsus for Jerusalem (if he ever did), that is, did Paul remain in Tarsus long enough to have been influenced significantly by this Hellenistic city?[69] Although a difficult problem, unless some attempt is made to determine the degree to which Paul participated in the distinctive elements of the Jewish and Greco-Roman cultures, his background and training in letter writing remain somewhat in question.

An abbreviated approach to the problem, following basically that of van Unnik in his excellent monograph,[70] is used here. First, the sources of information concerning the early life of Paul will be established, namely the pertinent passages in the Epistles and Acts,[71] weighing the texts on the basis of their relative reliability. Second, the accepted texts will be interpreted, a matter made more difficult by ambiguities in some texts. Third, based on the established heritage, Paul's educational background will be suggested, particularly with respect to letter writing.

In the letters of Paul, two autobiographical remarks bear directly upon the question:

(1) περιτομῇ ὀκταήμερος, ἐκ γένους Ἰσραήλ, φυλῆς Βενιαμίν, Ἑβραῖος ἐξ Ἑβραίων, κατὰ νομον Φαρισαῖος, κατὰ ζῆλος διώκων τὴν ἐκκλησίαν, κατὰ δικαιοσύνην τὴν ἐν νόμῳ γενόμενος ἄμεμπτος (Phil. 3:5—6), and

---

[68] Nigel Turner, *Style*, vol. 4 in *A Grammar of New Testament Greek*, ed. J. H. Moulton (Edinburgh: T & T Clark, 1976), 86.

[69] *E.g.*, A. Deissmann argues that since "the son of Tarsus spent his boyhood in the Hellenistic city of his birth ... we are bound to assume him to have been strongly influenced from his childhood by the Septuagint and the Hellenistic world surrounding him". *St. Paul*, 92—93. See also *inter alii*, Joseph Fitzmyer, "A Life of Paul", in *JBC*, esp. 2: 217.

[70] W. C. van Unnik, *Tarsus or Jerusalem: the City of Paul's Youth*, trans. G. Ogg (London: Epworth, 1962).

[71] The testimony of Jerome (*De vir. ill.* 5) is intriguing, but, in addition to its late witness, its additional strand of tradition does not contribute to the discussion.

(2) καὶ προέκοπτον ἐν τῷ Ἰουδαϊσμῷ ὑπὲρ πολλοὺς συνηλικιώτας ἐν τῷ γένει μου, περισσοτέρως ζηλωτὴς ὑπάρχων τῶν πατρικῶν μου παραδόσεων (Gal. 1:14).

The authorship of these letters generally is not questioned — they are among the "seven undisputed letters" — and concommitantly the veracity of Paul's claims usually are not disputed.

In addition to his direct references to his heritage, several indirect indications may be cited: (1) Paul has a thorough knowledge of the Old Testament and frequently cites it as an authority. (2) He apparently prefers the LXX. (3) Paul often employs Jewish exegetical techniques.[72] (4) He writes his letters in the koine Greek. (5) His letters show literary influences in letter structure, rhetorical forms and phrases.[73] (6) Paul twice quotes from Greek authors.[74] (7) Finally, Paul employs esoteric terms to describe his own mysticism.[75] Along with the obvious connections of Paul with the Greco-Roman world, these indirect indicators also support Paul's autobiographical claims to a Jewish heritage.

---

[72] See E. E. Ellis, *Paul's Use of the Old Testament* (Grand Rapids: Baker, 1957; reprint, 1981), esp. 38–82; idem, "Midrash *Pesher* in Pauline Hermeneutics", in *Grace upon Grace [for] L. Kuyper*, ed. J. I. Cook (Grand Rapids: Eerdmans, 1975), 137–42; and idem, "Exegetical Patterns in 1 Corinthians and Romans", *NTS* 2 (1955): 127–33 [the two articles have been reprinted in his collected essays, *Prophecy and Hermeneutic*]. See also R. Longenecker, *Biblical Exegesis in the Apostolic Period* (Grand Rapids: Eerdmans, 1975).

[73] See above, pp. 136–44. Also see W. D. Davies, *Paul*, XXIV.

[74] 1 Cor. 15:33 (Menander *Thaïs*) and Tit. 1:12 (Epimenides *De oraculis*, περὶ χρησμῶν). It is generally recognized, though, that these two snippets can hardly be used to argue a pervasive familiarity with Greek literature. They were probably proverbial. See R. Renehan, "Classical Greek Quotations in the New Testament", in *The Heritage of the Early Church: Essays in Honor of G. V. Florovsky on the Occasion of His Eightieth Birthday*, ed. D. Neiman and M. Schatkin, (Rome: Pontifical Institute of Oriental Studies, 1973), 33.

[75] It was common to say that Paul borrowed these ideas from the Greek Mysteries. See, *inter alii*, Richard Reitzenstein, *Hellenistic Mystery-Religions: Their Basic Ideas and Significance*, trans. J. E. Steely (Pittsburg: Pickwick, 1978) [original German ed., Berlin: Teubner, 1920] and A. Schweitzer, *The Mysticism of Paul the Apostle*, trans. Wm. Montgomery (London: Black, 1931). The source, however, may lay in Jewish mysticism. See W. D. Davies' cogent rebuttals (a) to Schweitzer's misleading distinction between Palestinian Judaism and Diaspora Hellenistic Judaism (Davies, *Paul*, VII-X), (b) to R. Reitzenstein's view of Spirit in Paul as an aspect of Hellenistic mysticism, (ibid., 193–200), and (c) to Dibelius' ["Mystic and Prophet", trans. W. Meeks, in *The Writings of St. Paul*, ed. W. Meeks (New York: Norton, 1972), 395–409; original German ed., "Paulus und die Mystik", in *Botschaft und Geschichte*, vol. 2 (Munich: E. Reinhardt, 1941)] misunderstanding of the source of Paul's "ἐν χριστῷ" [Davies, *The New Creation*, (Philadelphia: Fortress, 1971), 1–11]. See also Gershom G. Scholem, *Major Trends in Jewish Mysticism*, rev. 3d ed. (New York: Schocken, 1954), esp. 14–19 and J. W. Bowker "'Merkabah' Visions and the Visions of Paul", *Jss* 16 (1971): 157–73. (I do not think, however, that Bowker proved his position. The structures of the *Merkabah* visions and Paul's Damascus vision were both probably derived independently from Isaiah 6.)

In the secondary literature, one passage in Acts (22:3) stands out as the most significant:

ἐγώ εἰμι ἀνὴρ Ἰουδαῖος γεγεννημένος ἐν Ταρσῷ τῆς Κιλικίας, ἀνατεθραμμένος δὲ ἐν τῇ πόλει ταύτῃ, παρὰ τοὺς πόδας Γαμαλιὴλ πεπαιδευμένος κατὰ ἀκρίβειαν τοῦ πατρῴου νόμου, ζηλωτὴς ὑπάρχων τοῦ θεοῦ καθὼς πάντες ὑμεῖς ἐστε σήμερον.

Subsidiary support is added by Acts 26:4–5, where the Lukan Paul begins his defense before Herod Agrippa I with a reference to his educational background:

Τὴν μὲν οὖν βίωσίν μου [τὴν] ἐν νεότητος τὴν ἀπ' ἀρχῆς γενομένην ἐν τῷ ἔθνει μου ἔν τε Ἱεροσολύμοις ἴσασι πάντες [οἵ] Ἰουδαῖοι προγινώσκοντές με ἄνωθεν, ἐὰν θέλωσι μαρτυρεῖν, ὅτι κατὰ τὴν ἀκριβεστάτην αἵρεσιν τῆς ἡμέτερας θρησκείας ἔζησα Φαρισαῖος.

Two additional minor references remain in Acts. Paul is termed a man of Tarsus in Acts 9:11, and his Tarsan citizenship is noted in Acts 21:39. Nonetheless, it is Paul's apologetic speech following the Temple riot, Acts 22:3, that remains the pivotal passage, for it best describes his early relocation to Jerusalem and his association with Gamaliel.

Because it is Luke and not Paul *per se* who reveals this important aspect of Paul's heritage, the question of the historical reliability of Luke must be addressed. While this is clearly too large an issue to be discussed fully here, the problem may be outlined. The historicity of the Lukan speeches is frequently denied, largely because (1) they are Lukan in style, and (2) ancient historians commonly composed speeches for the lips of their characters in order to further their literary purposes.[76] This attitude of

---

[76] M. Dibelius wrote two important essays on this subject: "The Speeches of Acts and Ancient Historiography", and "Paul on the Areopagus", included in the collected essays, *Studies in the Acts of the Apostles*, ed. H. Greeven, trans. M. Ling (New York: Scribner's Sons, 1956), 26–77 and 138–85 (respectively). See also E. Schweizer, "Concerning the Speeches in Acts", *Studies in Luke-Acts: Essays Presented in Honor of Paul Schubert*, ed. L. E. Keck and J. L. Martyn (Philadelphia: Fortress, 1980), esp. 208.

Others have argued this position from a different angle, *viz.*, Paul does not show a knowledge of Palestinian Judaism as represented by its literature. See *e.g.*, C. G. Montefiore, *Judaism and St. Paul* (London: Goschen, 1914), 93, and S. Sandmel, *A Jewish Understanding of the New Testament* (New York: University Publishers, 1956), 37–51. M. Hengel and W. D. Davies have both demonstrated that a dichotomy between Palestinian and Hellenistic Judaism was false (see below, p. 150 n. 97).

Recently E. P. Sanders, in his admirable investigation of early Jewish sources, *Paul and Palestinian Judaism* (Philadelphia: Fortress, 1977), reasserted Paul's ignorance of Judaism. A full critique of Sanders is not possible here, but in addition to the recent criticisms by Judaic scholars, he may be criticized for (1) his unwillingness to allow for much influence by both Christianity and the fall of Jerusalem on post-70 Judaism, and (2) the late date of his

skepticism, however, is changing. Several recent works have reasserted Luke's reliability as an historical witness.[77] Old arguments have been revived that Luke may have written from first hand knowledge,[78] written source material,[79] or early ecclesiastical tradition.[80] Even if one maintains that Luke had his own theological agenda and has cast his protagonists' speeches in his own words (or in the most extreme, freely composed them), it does not necessarily follow that the information contained therein is false.

There is, however, one serious objection that may be raised specifically against the historicity of Acts 22:3. Paul is silent about his connection with the noted Jewish teacher when boasting elsewhere of his orthodoxy. Furthermore, it can be demonstrated easily that these particular points in the Lukan-Pauline biography are well suited to the Lukan *Tendenz*.[81] Nonetheless, if one holds the basic reliability of Luke, then the arguments specifically against this passage may be countered: (1) it is *argumentum e silentio*; (2) in Acts 22 Paul is addressing Jews from Jerusalem who would personally know and venerate the great scribe. The related Pauline passages (Rom. 11:1; Gal. 1:3—4; 2 Cor. 11:22; and Phil. 3:5—6) are addressed to mixed congregations in the diaspora; (3) the Lukan nature of the speech may indicate redaction but it cannot prove creation *ex*

---

core material. He demonstrates his covenantal nomism in post-Hadrianic sources but is unable to cite earlier sources (OT Pseudepigrapha) that demonstrate more than a *part* of his system. The only early work that contains an unmixed system (4 Ezra) presents the *opposite* position (Sanders, *Paul*, 409).

[77] See esp. the noted Tübingen scholar, Martin Hengel, *Acts and the History of Earliest Christianity*, trans. John Bowden (Philadelphia: Fortress, 1979).

[78] So Jacob Jervell, "Paul in the Acts of the Apostles: Tradition, History, Theology", in *Actes de Apôtres: tradition, redaction, théologie*, ed. J. Kremer, BETL, no. 48 (Louvan: University of Louvan, 1979), 297—306 and also idem, "Der unbekannte Paulus", in *Die Paulinische Literatüre und Theologie*, ed. Sigfred Pederson, Skandinavische Beiträge (Göttingen: Vandenhoeck & Ruprecht, 1980), 29—49. Both have been reprinted in his collected essays, *The Unknown Paul* (Minneapolis: Augsburg, 1984).

[79] See Ernst Haenchen, "The Book of Acts as Source Material for the History of Early Christianity", in *Studies in Luke-Acts*, 258—78.

[80] See, *e.g.*, J. Lambrecht, "Paul's Farewell Address at Miletus", in *Actes de Apôtres*, 327.

[81] This is cogently argued by John Knox, *Chapters in the Life of Paul*, (New York: Abingdon, 1950), 74 *ff*. A *Tendenz*, however, should be broadened to include a bias that governs the *selection* of material and not merely a bias that governs the *creation* of material as in F. C. Baur, *Kritische Untersuchung über die kanonischen Evangelien: ihre Verhältnisse zu Einander, ihren Charakter und Ursprung* (Tübingen: Fues, 1847), 71—76. See also the cautions of C. F. D. Moule, "Some Observations on *Tendenz-kritik*," in *Jesus and the Politics of His Day*, ed. Ernst Bammel and C. F. D. Moule (Cambridge: Cambridge University, 1984), 91—100.

nihilo; and (4) while it is certainly true that the claims in Acts 22:3 fit the *Tendenz* of Luke, they also suited Paul's immediate needs quite well.

The claims of the 'Lukan' Paul blend well with the claims of the 'epistolary' Paul. Paul claims to be a pharisee (Phil. 3:5–6) and to be a pharisee in the first century was to be a part of an organized and closed community, with established requirements for admission and conduct.[82] He also claims to have advanced "ἐν τῷ Ἰουδαϊσμῷ ὑπὲρ πολλοὺς συνηλικιώτας ἐν τῷ γένει μου" (Gal. 1:14). This connotes an academic setting, or surely at least a semi-established age-graded structure. Thus Paul's claims in his epistles support the Lukan assertion that Paul was educated in Jerusalem. "We know nothing of any form of organized Diaspora Judaism or of Pharisaic schools outside Jerusalem before A.D. 70".[83]

Since Paul was trained in Jerusalem, the question remains, when did Paul come to Jerusalem? Obviously the earlier his arrival in Jerusalem, the more profound would be the Palestinian influence. The crux of the issue lies in whether Acts 22:3 allows for Paul to have spent his formative years in Tarsus. The question may be expressed in terms of punctuating Acts 22:3. Should a minor stop be read after ἐν τῇ πόλει ταύτῃ or after παρὰ τοὺς πόδας Γαμαλιήλ? If the former is correct, as will be argued, then the Lukan Paul is claiming that he was (1) born (γεγεννημένος) in Tarsus, (2) brought up or nurtured (ἀνατεθραμμένος) in Jerusalem, and (3) educated (πεπαιδευμένος) under Gamaliel according to strict tradition.

Richard Longenecker argues for the alternate punctuation, pointing to a parallelism in the phrasing of the verse: each perfect participle (γεγεννημένος, ἀνατεθραμμένος, πεπαιδευμένος) begins its clause, making ἀνατεθραμμένος the temporal equivalent of πεπαιδευμένος.[84]

The deciding factor is provided by van Unnik who recognized that the triad birth (γενέσεως), nurture (τροφῆς), and education (παιδείας) was a

---

[82] J. Jeremias, *Jerusalem in the Time of Jesus*, trans. F. H. and C. H. Cave (Philadelphia: Fortress, 1969), 247. Jeremias may have slightly overstated his case; so E. P. Sanders, *Paul*, 153–55. The rules of conduct may have been primarily concerned with the observance of the dietary laws; see J. Neusner, "The Fellowship (חבורה) in the Second Jewish Commonwealth", *HTR* 53 (1960): esp. 125 n. 1 and idem, *The Rabbinic Traditions about the Pharisees before 70*, 3 vols. (Leiden: Brill, 1971). But *cf.* E. Rivkin, "Defining the Pharisees: the Tannaitic Sources", *HUCA* 41 (1970): 234–38, who considers the pharisees to have been a "scholar's class".

[83] M. Hengel, *Acts*, 82. See also J. Jeremias, *Jerusalem*, 252 n. 26, who doubts the existence of established pharisaic groups outside Jerusalem.

[84] R. Longenecker, *Paul: Apostle of Liberty* (Grand Rapids: Baker, 1964; reprint, Grand Rapids: Baker, 1976), 25–26.

"fixed literary unit".[85] From his investigations, van Unnik concludes (1) ἀνατρέφειν always occurred in the home and incorporated initial educational development; (2) παιδεύειν began when the child entered school and took place through more formal instruction under the hand of a teacher; and finally (3) these terms indicated distinct stages in life that were *sequential*.

Since Paul was brought up and educated in Jerusalem, what type of education did he likely receive? Jewish education centered primarily upon the Law. Josephus (*ca.* A.D. 100) describes Jewish education:

> We take the most trouble of all over the education of children... If one of us should be questioned about the laws, he would recite them all the more easily than his own name.[86]

The purely religious curriculum described by Josephus, who is not known for understatement, perhaps existed in the scribal schools of the early Second Temple period,[87] but very quickly thereafter a Greek influence was felt. Although many Jews opposed the more pagan aspects of Hellenism, the Hellenistic stress on education meshed well with the similar Jewish affirmation, resulting in an emphasis on widespread public education.[88] Although it is uncertain how much of the well-documented post-70 educational system existed during Paul's time, probably the same basic structure was in place.[89] Martin Hengel contends that:

---

[85] W. C. van Unnik, *Jerusalem or Tarsus*, 19. He cites numerous examples from the classics as well as early Christian writers (*e.g.*, Euseb. *HE* 6.19.7). See also Luke's prior use of the triad in Acts 7:20–22 in Stephen's speech on the life of Moses. Moses was born (ἐγεννήθη) and brought up (ἀνετράφη) for three months in his parental home. He was adopted by Pharoah's daughter who brought him up (ἀνεθρέψατο) as her own. Finally, Moses was instructed (ἐπαιδεύθη) in the wisdom of Egypt.

[86] Joseph. *Contra Apionem* 2.18; also Philo *Legat*. 31; 16.

[87] See M. Hengel, *Judaism and Hellenism*, 2 vols., trans. J. Bowden (Philadelphia: Fortress, 1974), 1: 78. Also see George F. Moore, *Judaism*, 2 vols. (Cambridge: Harvard University, 1927), 1: 283.

[88] Hengel, *Judaism and Hellenism*, 1: 81. Although Ben Sira wishes to exclude the lower classes from the study of wisdom (Sir. 38:25*ff.*), Hengel argues that Ben Sira stands at the point of transition; ibid., 2: 54 n. 168.

In some ways adopting the Hellenistic concepts of education opened the door, for Hellenism is at its heart an educational phenomenon. Even before Alexander, Isocrates declaims "The designation 'Hellene' seems no longer to be a matter of descent but of disposition, and those who share in our education have more right to be called Hellenes than those who have a common descent with us" (Isoc. *Panegyricus* 4.50).

[89] See the excellent discussion by Rainer Riesner, *Jesus als Lehrer: eine Untersuchung zum Ursprung der Evangelien-Überlieferung*, WUNT, no. 7 (Tübingen: Mohr, 1981), 153–99, esp. 198–99.

One significant consequence of the idea, which began with the Hasidic and later Pharisaic scribes and wisdom teachers, of educating the whole people in the Torah was the gradual introduction of elementary schools (bēt sēper).[90]

Pupils came to these schools around the age of six.[91] The qualified student might advance to the study of the oral tradition sometime after the age of ten,[92] judging from this later formulation:

> Such is the usual way of the world; a thousand enter the Bible school, and a hundred pass from it to the study of Mishnah; ten of them go on to Talmud study, and only one of them arrives at the doctor's degree (rabbinical ordination).[93]

With such an education in Jerusalem, it is apparent from where the Jewish influences in Paul originate. A better question may be, where does Paul receive his Greco-Roman heritage? Classical Greek education was available to Jews in the cities of the Diaspora.[94] It was, however, also available in Jerusalem as early as 175 B.C.[95] Hellenistic education remained popular even after the Maccabean revolt, particularly after the advent of Herod.[96] Thus Jewish education, even in the stronghold of Jerusalem, was profoundly Hellenized.[97] Even those who appeared to resist Hellenism most vehemently bore the mark of Greece.[98] David Daube demonstrates that the seven hermeneutical principles of Hillel, a Diaspora Jew, whose rules guided rabbinic interpretation, were derived

---

[90] Hengel, *Judaism and Hellenism*, 1: 81.

[91] 'Abot. 5.21 sets the age at five. b.Ber. 21a, however, indicates that six or seven was the proper age.

[92] 'Abot. 5.21 gives the age of ten. Moore, *Judaism*, 1: 320, suggests twelve to fifteen as more probable.

[93] Eccl. Rab. 7.28 as quoted in Moore, *Judaism*, 1: 320.

[94] M. Hengel, *Judaism and Hellenism*, 1: 65–70.

[95] 2 Macc. 4:9. Jason receives Antiochus IV's permission to establish a gymnasium and to enroll the men of Jerusalem as citizens of Antioch.

[96] M. Hengel, *Judaism and Hellenism*, 1: 75–77. See also 2 Macc. 4:10–15 and J. Jeremias, *Jerusalem*, 74.

[97] That Palestine during the time of Paul was profoundly hellenized is now a well recognized point. See, *inter alii*, W. D. Davies, "Paul and the Dead Sea Scrolls: Flesh and Spirit", in *The Scrolls and the New Testament*, ed. Krister Stendahl (New York: Harper & Bros., 1957), 157; and Martin Hengel, *Judaism and Hellenism*. Van Unnik is not correct when he tries to maintain a contrast between a Jewish education in Tarsus that was hellenistic and one in Jerusalem that was strictly rabbinic and even anti-hellenistic (*Tarsus or Jerusalem*, 3–4, 52).

[98] M. Hengel even argues that the Qumran community was influenced, adopting the popular organizational structure of a religious association based on the conversion of the individual. *Jews, Greeks, and Barbarians*, trans. J. Bowden (Philadelphia: Fortress, 1980), 123.

from Hellenistic rhetorical theory, both in presupposition and in their manner of application.[99]

If Jewish education in Jerusalem included Hellenistic elements, did Paul's Jewish education include attending any sort of Hellenistic rhetorical school, that is, a tertiary level of education?[100] While some modern writers attempt to place Paul within the class of well-trained rhetoricians,[101] Paul's letters do not display a consistent conformity to established rhetorical standards.[102] It seems unlikely that a trained rhetorician would permit such *faux pas*. Bultmann is probably correct when he maintains that Paul's use of the diatribe (and other rhetorical elements) was an unconscious, unintentional imitation.[103] The frequent use of certain formulae and conventions, as well as the lack of a large variety in rhetorical elements, support an unconsidered use by Paul, probably acquired with his preaching style and not from any formal training.[104]

The Jewish educational system included Hellenistic elements, and it may have incorporated, probably in the later secondary levels, some of the rudimentary aspects of Greco-Roman literacy, particularly those elements which were seen as mere practical preparation for participation in the larger Greco-Roman world, such as basic letter writing. The Jews had their own traditional method of writing letters, but it is not unreasonable to assume that they were given some instruction in Greco-Roman letters.

Paul also may have been Hellenized less directly. The Greek language had penetrated deeply into Palestine, so much that Hengel would claim

---

[99] D. Daube, "Rabbinic Methods of Interpretation and Hellenistic Rhetoric", *HUCA* 22 (1949): 239–64.

[100] Influence is of course a tricky problem. While probably not formally trained in rhetoric, it is not certain how much Paul's training may have included "circumcized" techniques that were unconsciously adopted. Paul's use of the formula "τι οὖν...; μὴ γένοιτο" may well be an example.

[101] *E.g.*, perhaps H. D. Betz, "Literary Composition", 377. His classification of Galatians as an apologetic letter requires the author (Paul) to have been well trained. See A. Malherbe, *Social Aspects*, 59 n. 83.

[102] *E.g.*, Paul on occasion chooses non-conventional rhetorical word-order, such as "Χριστὸς ἀπέθανεν καὶ ἔζησεν" (Rom. 14:9), "πρὸς αἷμα καὶ σάρκα" (Eph. 6:12), and "ἕνι Ἕλλην καὶ Ἰουδαῖος" (Col. 3:11). The variant readings, for instance, in Rom. 14:9 probably reflect an early recognition of the awkwardness of the construction and the scribal attempts to rectify the problem. Also see the conclusion by Nigel Turner, *Style*, 86 (quoted above, pp. 143–44).

[103] See the discussion in S. Stowers, *Diatribe*, 18–19.

[104] Perhaps picked up in the agora or, as Turner, *Style*, 87, and Doty, *Letters*, 45, maintain, in the (Diaspora) synagogue.

"anyone who sought social respect or even the reputation of being an educated man had to have an impeccable command of it".[105] Moreover, Paul's "Hellenization" probably intensified after his conversion. Assuming anything other than a radical chronology of his ministry, he spent more than *ten years* in Tarsus, Cilicia, and Antioch, which would certainly have increased his knowledge of and familiarity with the Greco-Roman world, particularly with such simple things as letter writing.

Many of the contentions from his letters that argue against a rhetorical training for Paul must also be used to argue against a rhetorical training for any Pauline secretary. The possibility of a *professional* secretary for Paul therefore is diminished because of many of these same "inelegances", such as instances of zeugma that scribes were usually quick to correct.[106] One may contend that Paul exercised tight control over his secretary. Yet surely a secretary would be permitted to alter any "unpolished" elements he noticed. Furthermore, if the secretary were so tightly restricted that he was not permitted such slight alterations (improvements), then the resulting letters should display more homogeneity of vocabulary and style.[107] The preferable explanation to a strictly controlled secretary is that the secretary, like Paul himself, was untrained in the finer aspects of rhetoric and epistolary style. The unpolished aspects of Paul's letters remained uncorrected because his secretary (or secretaries) was an amateur — probably a member of the apostolic band.

In summary then, five points may be emphasized. First, Paul's own letters indicate that Paul lived in Jerusalem prior to his conversion, and they strongly suggest that he was formally educated in Jerusalem. Se-

---

[105] M. Hengel, *Judaism and Hellenism*, 1: 58.

[106] *E.g.*, 1 Cor. 3:2; see Turner, *Style*, 82. See the zeugma in 1 Cor. 14:34 that was corrected early, predominantly in the western tradition [D K G Ψ 0243 lat(t) sy].

[107] Of course, many scholars maintain that the *authentic* letters are distinctly Pauline. Yet any supposed rejection because of theological variation is a dubious methodology. For example, 2 Corinthians is not rejected despite the apparent variation in eschatology between 2 Corinthians 5 and 1 Corinthians 15. Alternative explanations are sought that retain Pauline authorship of both letters. *E.g.*, M. J. Harris, "2 Corinthians 5:1–10: a Watershed in Paul's Eschatology?" *TynB* 22 (1971): 32–57; C. F. D. Moule, "St. Paul and 'Dualism': the Pauline Conception of Resurrection", in *Essays in New Testament Interpretation* (New York: Cambridge University, 1982), 200–21; and E. E. Ellis, "The Structure of Pauline Eschatology (2 Corinthians 5:1–10)", in *Paul and His Recent Interpreters* (Grand Rapids: Eerdmans, 1961), 35–48. Why are other (less dramatic) variations in theology used to argue that some letter is non-Pauline (such as the eschatology of 2 Thessalonians or the ecclesiology of Ephesians)? These variations are considered non-Pauline because the letters are *already* suspected to be non-Pauline on the basis of stylistic considerations. Yet it has already been argued that stylistic factors are not reliable indicators (above, pp. 92–97).

cond, the testimony of Acts 22:3 should be allowed full weight as reliable Pauline biography. It is not inconsistent with the epistolary testimonies, and the Hellenistic characteristics of Paul may be explained in other ways than by requiring a lengthy childhood or permanent residence in Tarsus. Based on Acts 22:3, one also should expect a strongly Jewish element in the heritage of Paul. Third, while it is quite unlikely that Paul received any sort of formal Greco-Roman rhetorical training, it is not improbable, because of the Hellenization of Palestine, that Paul was taught such practical matters as composing normal (Greco-Roman) letters. Moreover, even if not during his formal education, letter writing was such a common element of life that it was easily acquired. Other common aspects of Greco-Roman education, such as simple methods of argumentation, also could be learned unconsciously in the schools or in the marketplace. It must be remembered though that such levels of instruction would not be to the extent that a rhetorician or even a professional secretary would receive. Fourth, the prolonged period of time that Paul spent among Gentiles in Greco-Roman cities before he began writing his letters must not be discounted as a factor in the "education" of Paul. Fifth, the same limitations in the training of Paul probably apply to his secretary as well, unless Paul did not permit his secretary even minor *corrections*, an unlikly event.

b) Συνεργοί

The problem of the co-workers of Paul is raised because Paul frequently mentions a colleague or two in his letter address.[108] Are these co-workers active participants in the composition of the letter? As mentioned before, a letter in antiquity from co-authors is uncommon but nevertheless still known.[109] Furthermore, possibly the most common type of letter with co-authors was from religious groups, possibly to reflect the group's unanimity as to the purpose of the letter.[110] The vague reference to multiple senders in Gal. 1:1 may be a Pauline parallel, reflecting the support of Paul's associates.[111]

---

[108] 1 Cor. 1:1; 2 Cor. 1:1; Phil. 1:1; Col. 1:1; 1 Th. 1:1; 2 Th. 1:1; Philem. 1. Cf. Gal. 1:1. The actual term συνεργοί is not used in the addresses but is used for some members of the Pauline band. The term, however, serves well to introduce a discussion limited to any points of contact with the secretary.

[109] Cic. *Att.* 11.5.1. See above, p. 47 n. 139.

[110] See above, p. 47 n. 138.

[111] "Παῦλος ἀπόστολος, ... καὶ οἱ σὺν ἐμοὶ πάντες ἀδελφοί, ταῖς ἐκκλησίαις τῆς Γαλατίας·" Only this letter of Paul contains such a sweeping, non-particular inclusion of col-

It is quite unlikely, though, that Paul's references to others *by name* in his address was intended to indicate anything *less* than an *active* role in the composition of the letter. A practice of including others in the address as a "nicety" is not supported by the evidence.[112] What constitutes an active role is more debatable. The co-authors apparently are not full contributors on an equal level with Paul. On the other hand, they must have some role in the writing of the letter. Earle Ellis in his discussion of the exegetical patterns in 1 Corinthians and Romans, concludes:

> They [the exegetical patterns] probably point not only to the creative mind of the apostle but also to that of some of his co-workers, the circle of prophets and teachers whose exegetical labors Paul participated in and used.[113]

This point is also acknowledged by C. K. Barrett in his discussion of the role of Sosthenes in 1 Corinthians ("Παῦλος κλητὸς ἀπόστολος Χριστοῦ Ἰησοῦ διὰ θελήματος θεοῦ, καὶ Σωσθένης ὁ ἀδελφός"): "There is no doubt that Paul is the senior partner; or that Sosthenes genuinely is a partner".[114]

H. A. W. Meyer had earlier argued the same point:

> Modern interpreters reckon him [Sosthenes] the amanuensis of the Epistle. But the mere amanuensis as such has no share in the Epistle itself, which must, however, be the case with one who holds a place in the introductory salutation ... we must rather suppose that *Paul made his Epistle run not only in his own name, but also* (although, of course, in a subordinate sense) *in the name of Sosthenes*, so that the Corinthians were to regard the letter of the apostle as at the same time a letter of Sosthenes, who thereby signified his desire to impress upon them the same doctrines, admonitions, etc. This presupposes that Paul had previously considered and discussed with this friend the contents of the letter to be issued.[115]

---

leagues. If this was his first letter (*i.e., ca.* A.D. 49), then a desire to demonstrate support among the brethren is more understandable. Moreover, his first journey was probably seen more as a team effort, having been commissioned as a team.

[112] I found no clear evidence for merely courteously including another in one's address (*pace* Moffatt). The tradition (seen as early as Chrysostom [*fl. ca.* 390] and continuing in Theophylact [*fl. ca.* 1075]) that Paul's inclusion of others in his address, *e.g.*, Sosthenes in 1 Cor., was proof of his great modesty also has no grounds.

[113] E. E. Ellis, "Exegetical Patterns in 1 Corinthians and Romans", in his collected essays, *Prophecy and Hermeneutic in Early Christianity*, WUNT, no. 18 (Tübingen: Mohr, 1978; reprint, Grand Rapids: Eerdmans, 1980), 220.

[114] Barrett, *A Commentary on the First Epistle to the Corinthians*, HNTC (New York: Harper & Row, 1968), 31. See also the discussion, "Die Beteiligung der Mitabsender an den Paulinischen Briefen", in O. Roller, *Formular*, 153–87.

[115] Meyer, *A Critical and Exegetical Hand-book to the Epistle to the Corinthians* (New York: Funk & Wagnalls, 1884), 9 [Italics are his].

Perhaps Paul includes him because he is known and respected by the Corinthians. Whether he is the Sosthenes of Acts 18:17 is uncertain.[116] He is, though, apparently a co-author, although probably his role is subordinate and does not extend to the point of writing sections of his own.[117] His input probably is filtered through Paul as perhaps may be indicated by the immediate use of the first person, in verse four, in a thanksgiving formula: "εὐχαριστῶ τῷ θεῷ μου".[118]

Using the singular forms of the verb, though, for evidence of the singularity of authorship has difficulties. For example, the letter address in 2 Corinthians includes Timothy: "Παῦλος ἀπόστολος Χριστοῦ Ἰησοῦ διὰ θελήματος θεοῦ, καὶ Τιμόθεος ὁ ἀδελφός". What is the role of Timothy? While the body of 1 Corinthians does open with a petition formula in the *singular:* "παρακαλῶ δὲ ὑμᾶς, ἀδελφοί, διά..." [1:10], the

---

[116] The tradition identifying Sosthenes in 1 Cor. to the beaten synagogue leader in Acts 18:17 is at least as early as Theodoret [*fl. ca.* 440]. This possibility is suggested by many modern commentators (*e.g.*, F. W. Grosheide) and offers a justification for the inclusion of Sosthenes: he was a person of repute in Corinth. F. W. Grosheide, *A Commentary on the First Epistle to the Corinthians*, NICNT (Grand Rapids: Eerdmans, 1953), 22. Sosthenes, however, was a common name.

[117] Such a conclusion, however, must be supported from a study of the epistle. On the one hand the inclusion of Sosthenes in the address must be taken seriously and deserves more than the one line (almost nonsensical) dismissal by Conzelmann: "The fellow-writer is not a fellow-author; cf. the singular in v. 4". Hans Conzelmann, *1 Corinthians: a Commentary on the First Epistle to the Corinthians*, trans. J. W. Leitch, in the Hermeneia Series (Philadelphia: Fortress, 1975), 20 n. 12. Yet elsewhere Conzelmann is quite open to the possibility of Paul's participation in a 'school' dynamic. *E.g.*, he sees signs of a possible influence from a "jüdisch-hellenistischer Schul-Theologie" in 1 Cor. 1:18*ff*.; 2:6*ff*.; 10:1*ff*.; 11:2*ff*.; and 13; Conzelmann, "Paulus und die Weisheit", *NTS* 12 (1965): 231–44.

G. G. Findlay in his old commentary expresses a similar unsupported sentiment: "Sosthenes shares in this epistle not as joint-composer, but as witness and approver". Findlay, *St. Paul's First Epistle to the Corinthians*, Expositor's Greek Testament Series (Grand Rapids: Eerdmans, 1917), 758. (Findlay does not say but Paul's inclusion possibly may be a carryover from the Jewish custom of including the names of witnesses.) John Massie remarks that Sosthenes could not be a co-author — although he offers no rationale — and adds the odd observation that Sosthenes was in harmony with what Paul was writing "and more expressly so than if he were mentioned at the close of the letter". Massie, *Corinthians*, rev. ed., The Century Bible Series (London: Blackwood, Le Bas & Co., n.d. [1902?]), 137 n.

On the other hand, *cf.* Earle Ellis, "Paul and His Co-Workers", in *Prophecy and Hermeneutic*, 22: "Paul's associates also may have had a literary role. In what measure, for example, did the co-senders of his letter participate in framing their content? Do any of the pre-formed traditional pieces scattered through Paul's letters find their origin in the cooperative enterprise of Paul and his colleagues?"

[118] The variant readings concerning μου reflect only a scribal discomfort over Paul's exclusive claim to God. They wished to conform this verse to Paul's later use of ἡμῶν in the thanksgiving. The singular reading of the verb is certain.

body of *2 Corinthians* opens with a disclosure formula in the *plural:* "οὐ γὰρ θέλομεν ὑμᾶς ἀγνοεῖν, ἀδελφοί, ὑπέρ..." [1:8]. If the switch to a singular verb in 1 Corinthians indicates that Paul alone was the author, as Conzelmann implies,[119] what does the parallel but plural verb in 2 Corinthians indicate? Furthermore, 2 Corinthians repeatedly changes the number of the verb.[120] An analysis of the use of singular versus plural verbs in 2 Corinthians readily reveals that it cannot be merely a literary device (see Table 2). It has been argued that Paul has a complex theological agenda behind his alternation of "I" and "We" in 2 Corinthians.[121] There may be another, deceptively simpler, explanation: the "we" may indicate the input of Timothy.[122] According to 1 Corinthians (4:17), Timothy is sent to Corinth. It is quite possible that Paul uses Timothy's familiarity with the troubles in Corinth to write this letter.[123] The same argument may also apply to 1 Corinthians. Sosthenes is included in the address because he aides Paul in writing the letter, perhaps because he is fa-

---

[119] See n. 117 above.

[120] C. E. B. Cranfield acknowledges this problem when he argues that the "we" must refer to the co-workers mentioned in the subscription. Cranfield, "Changes in Person and Number in Paul's Epistles", in *Paul and Paulinism: Essays in Honour of C. K. Barrett*, ed. M. D. Hooker and S. B. Wilson (London: S.P.C.K., 1982), 285–86. Why Cranfield argues for the co-workers in the subscription and not Timothy in the address (the more traditional possibility) is unclear.

Vic Furnish also notes that Paul frequently alternated between the first person singular and plural; yet "the kind of shift apparent here in 2 Cor. occurs in no other Pauline letter". V. P. Furnish, *II Corinthians*, in The Anchor Bible, vol. 32A (Garden City, NY: Doubleday, 1984), 32.

[121] *E.g.*, Carrez, "Le 'nous'", 476, argues that Paul uses "we" to refer to an interaction of four different groups.

[122] The high frequency of "I" as opposed to "we" in 2 Cor. 10–13 (the opposite pattern of chs. 1–9) may strengthen the suggestion that chs. 10–13, with their accompanying severity, arose when Paul took the pen himself and the tempering influence of Timothy (the co-author) and/or the secretary was lost. *Cf.* the harshness (or abruptness) when Paul elsewhere takes the pen in 1 Cor. 16:22 and Philem. 19. Also see below, pp. 178–79.

[123] Note also the co-senders Silas and Timothy in both 1 and 2 Thessalonians. Both letters also are written in the first person plural. 1 Th. has 49 total first person verbs of which 47 are plural (or 96% plural); 2 Th. has 19 total first person verbs of which 17 are plural (or 89% plural). (But *cf.* Philemon which has the same senders; yet all the first person verbs are singular.) If inclusion in the greeting had *no* meaning other than involvement in the letter's *Sitz-im-Leben*, then one may legitimately ask why Titus was not included in the greeting in 2 Cor. He had a major role in the events preceding 2 Corinthians and Paul calls him a συνεργός in 2 Cor. 8:23. He is not included in the greeting because he was not a co-author.

miliar with the trouble in Corinth.[124] Evidently the possible role of the co-sender as a co-author must be taken seriously and examined separately for each letter in which this occurs. As H. A. W. Meyers indicates,[125] however, the co-sender (co-author?) is not to be confused with the secretary, who is never listed in the letter address.[126]

Table 2
"I" VS. "WE" Uses in 2 Corinthians

	I	We
2 Corinthians 1−9	81 (26 %)	225 (74 %)
2 Corinthians 10−13	147 (74 %)	51 (26 %)

Source: adapted from M. Carrez, "Le 'nous' en 2 Corinthiens: Contribution à l'étude de l'apostolocité dans 2 Corinthiens," *NTS* 26 (1980): 475.[127]

There is another aspect of the role of the συνεργοί in the letters of Paul. Josephus uses this same term to describe the literary assistants who helped him write the *Bellum Judaicum*:

... χρησάμενός τισι πρὸς τὴν Ἑλληνίδα φωνὴν συνεργοῖς, οὕτως ἐποιησάμην τῶν πράξεων τὴν παράδοσιν.[128]

These συνεργοί, he belatedly confesses to have used, were assistants (secretaries?) who aided him in translating his work. In fact their assistance extended beyond mere translation.[129] This raises the question, does Paul have the same connotations in mind when he describes some of his colleagues as συνεργοί? Unfortunately there is no evidence to sug-

---

[124] It is not necessary for him to be the Sosthenes of Acts 18 or a member of Chloe's household as some suggest; see the remarks by Grosheide, *First Corinthians*, 22.

[125] In the passage quoted above, p. 154.

[126] 'Never' is a strong term, but I found no instances in the (941) letters of Cicero, the (369) letters of Pliny, and the (645) private papyrus letters in the collections of *POxy.*, *PTebt.*, and *PZen*.

[127] The numbers given by Carrez have been corrected here. These frequencies present an accurate picture because the two sections contain about an equal proportion of total "I" and "We" uses; *e.g.*, 2 Cor. 1−9 has 61% of the total ("I" and "We") occurrences and comprises about 67% of the letter.

[128] Joseph. *Ap.* 1.50; "... and with the aid of some assistants for the sake of the Greek, at last I committed to writing my narrative of the events".

[129] Josephus' work on the Antiquities of the Jews displays well his lack of skill in Greek and in Hellenistic historiography. Yet the *BJ* is well written. "The immense debt which he owes to these admirable collaborators [the συνεργοί] is apparent on almost every page of the work" (so Thackeray, "Introduction", LCL xv).

gest that συνεργοί was often used as a term for secretarial assistants.[130] No doubt Josephus merely chose a more general — and less revealing — title.[131] Similarly Paul uses συνεργοί as a general (and gracious) designation for his fellow (and usually subordinate) members of the missionary team.[132]

c) Παραδόσεις and Μεμβράναι

The third and final preliminary issue to be discussed is how Paul coordinated his use of a secretary with his inclusion of preformed material, both traditions (παραδόσεις) he received and any material he himself previously composed, represented here by μεμβράναι (parchment notebooks), one common means of retaining such notes.

aa) Paul's Use of Παραδόσεις and Μεμβράναι

The reader of Paul's letters frequently encounters creed-like formulae, confessions, and metrical prose, noticeable because their context, content, rhythm and/or structure suggest that they did not originate within Paul's present composition. One concludes that such passages were composed some time prior to the rest of the text, that is, they are "preformed traditions".[133] This is not to say necessarily that Paul did not

---

[130] A related problem is the description of Luke in the anti- Marcionite prologues. In the prologue to Luke's gospel (the only one extant in Greek as well as Latin), Luke is described: "῎Εστιν ὁ ἅγιος Λουκᾶς ... μαθητὴς ἀποστόλων γενομένος καὶ ὕστερον Παύλῳ..." (Latin version: ... postea vero Paulum secutus...). The meaning is unclear. Regul argues that the prologue is implying that Luke was Paul's literary assistant, in which case the secretarial role of Luke must be considered. Jürgen Regul, Die Antimarcionitischen Evangelienprologue, Vetus Latina, no. 6 (Freiburg: Herder, 1969), 198–202. The significance of the testimony, however, is questionable. Regul (Antimarcionitischen Evangelienprologue, 202) contends that the prologues were composed at different times and from different viewpoints. Moreover, they probably date from the fourth Christian century not the second as has been argued, e.g., by D. de Bruyne, "Les plus anciens prologues latines des Evangile", RBén 40 (1928): 193–214. See also Harry Gamble, Canon, 62.

[131] The tendency to hide his sources and downplay any assistance he receives is well-attested. See Thackeray, "Introduction", XX-XXI.

[132] See, inter alii, E. E. Ellis, "Paul and his Co-Workers", 3–22. Also H. Conzelmann, "Paulus und die Weisheit", 231–44.

[133] At the suggestion of E. E. Ellis I adopted this term in an unpublished research project I did under his supervision: "Preformed Christological Traditions in the Roman and Corinthian Letters" (1985).

himself compose the preformed piece but only that the piece in question was composed at some time *before* the rest of the text.[134]

An early Christian preference for tradition can be derived by analogy from the Church's Jewish heritage, but this is unnecessary since there is ample early attestation for the use of traditional material within the Christian community. Pliny the Younger, governor of Bithynia, in a letter to the emperor Trajan describes the use of hymns in the worship practices of the early Christians:

> quod essent soliti stato die ante lucem convenire carmenque Christo quasi deo dicere...[135]

If 1 Timothy is Pauline, then a preference for traditional material may be seen in the first century in the admonition in 1 Tim. 6:20: "Ὦ Τιμόθεε, τὴν παραθήκην φύλαξον".[136] The use of Christian tradition, though, extends even further back into the first century. In 1 Corinthians Paul cites traditional pieces and explicitly calls them such.[137]

The study of traditional material in the New Testament, and specifically in Paul, has been rather sporadic.[138] Usually the presence of a pre-

---

[134] Frequently, though, the traditional material was composed by another and was in use in the church before Paul incorporated it into his text.

[135] Pliny *Ep.* 10.96; "they were in the habit of meeting on a certain fixed day before it was light, when they sang in alternate verses a hymn to Christ, as to a god..."

[136] One can deny that this refers to tradition, but it is thusly understood by Clement of Alexandria *Stromateis* 6.15: "...the trust [παραθήκη] which is given back to God is the understanding and discipline of sacred tradition, according to the teaching of the Lord through the apostles". There are also the 'πιστὸς ὁ λόγος' traditions in 2 Timothy.

[137] 1 Cor. 11:23; 15:3. Certainly παραλαμβάνω and παραδίδωμι are to be understood here as *termini technici* for the receiving and passing on of tradition. Also see 2 Th. 2:15.

[138] This lacuna in the otherwise popular field of Pauline studies originated partly from the contention that Paul was not interested in the historical Jesus, being concerned only with the 'thatness' of his existence (so R. Bultmann, "Die Bedeutung des geschichtlichen Jesus für die Theologie des Paulus", in *Glauben und Verstehen*, 2 vols. (Tübingen: Mohr, 1933), 2: 188–213; and more recently W. Schmithals, "Paulus und der historische Jesus", *ZNW* 53 (1962): 145–60.)

With the subsequent argument that Paul in fact was interested in the facts about Jesus [see *e.g.*, C. F. D. Moule, "Jesus in New Testament Kerygma", in *Verborum Veritas: Festschrift für Gustav Stählin*, ed. O. Böcher and K. Haacker (Wuppertal: Theologischer Brockhaus, 1970), 15–26; for a survey of the debate, see V. Furnish, "The Jesus-Paul Debate: From Baur to Bultmann", *BJRL* 47 (1965): 342–75], the objection arose that Paul obstinately refused to accept tradition from men (Gal. 1:12) and that his statements about tradition referred to direct personal revelation from the risen Christ (2 Cor. 5:16). This extremist position has met with widespread rejection (*e.g.*, O. Cullmann, "'*KYRIOS*' as a Designation for the Oral Tradition concerning Jesus: (*Paradosis* and *Kyrios*)", *SJT* 3 (1950): 182; R. Bultmann, *Theology of the New Testament*, trans. K. Grobel, 2 vols. (London: SCM, 1952), 1: 148–49; H. Lietzmann, *An die Korinther I. II.*, rev. W. G. Kümmel, in

formed tradition is noted only within a discussion of that particular passage. Pioneering works[139] suffered from the lack of criteria. They often asserted without justification that a particular piece is a preformed (non-Pauline) tradition. This became a pervasive problem because of the lack of well accepted criteria.[140] Recently, however, preformed traditions in Paul has received more systematic examination, and Paul's use of traditional material in his letters is now recognized.[141]

bb) Implications of the Use of Παραδόσεις and Μεμβράναι in the Composition of a Letter

In Greco-Roman times, notes[142] were traditionally taken on thin tablets (*codicilli*) of wood or ivory covered with wax, in which letters were cut — hence the use of *exarare* for "to write" on tablets — in uncial characters by a *stylus*. They were protected from defacement by a raised rim around the border of the tablet.[143] They were also called *tabellae* or *pugillares* (hand notebooks) and came in various sizes of two, three, five, or

---

HNT (Tübingen: Mohr, 1969), 57; and J. Weiss, *Der erste Korintherbrief* (Göttingen: Vandenhoeck & Ruprecht, 1910), 283).

Cullmann ("*KYRIOS,*" 184—85) also ably answers the question of how Paul could embrace the use of tradition when Jesus appears to condemn its use (Mk. 7:3—8) by distinguishing between the *use* and *misinterpretation* of tradition. That Paul had access to Christian traditions, particularly about Christ, hardly needs a defense as is indicated by Dodd's oft-quoted quip that Paul did not spend a fortnight and a day in Jerusalem talking with Peter about the weather; C. H. Dodd, *Apostolic Preaching and Its Developments*, 2d ed. (London: Hodder & Stoughton, 1944; reprint, Grand Rapids: Baker, 1980), 26. Furthermore, Paul surely learned much from his συνεργοί, Barnabas, Silas, and John Mark (a point well argued by A. Oepke, *Die Missionspredigt des Apostels Paulus* [Leipzig: Deichert, 1920], 135—36).

[139] Such as A. M. Hunter, *Paul and His Predecessors*, 2d ed. (London: SCM, 1961), who studied the pre-Pauline paradoses, hymns, words of the Lord, paraenetic traditions, collections of *testimonia*, and 'quasi-creedal' formulae.

[140] See the discussion of suggested criteria in App. H.

[141] See, *e.g.*, the excellent presentations of Markus Barth, "Traditions in Ephesians", *NTS* 30 (1984): 3—25 (esp. his list of criteria); and E. Earle Ellis, "Traditions in 1 Corinthians", *NTS* 32 (1986): 481—502 (esp. his survey of recent research).

[142] The term μεμβράναι is used to introduce a discussion of note-taking in general.

[143] An excellent brief discussion of the writing tablet is given by Roberts and Skeat, *Codex*², 11—14. See also Thompson, *Introduction*, 18, who discusses (with references) the use of tablets by Latin and Greek writers; Doty, "Epistle", 14, who offers a brief history of the development of the wax tablet; and Bahr, "Letter Writing", 470 n. 44, who presents some older bibliography on the tablets.

more tablets.[144] It appears that such tablets had three distinct but related uses in letter writing: (1) the dashing off of a quick note or brief letter, (2) the preparation of a rough draft of a letter to be rewritten later on papyrus or parchment, and (3) the recording of notes by the author (or his secretary) to be used later.

(1) Usually letters were written with a reed pen on papyrus or parchment. Those of the wealthy Cicero were usually composed with *charta* (parchment sheets), *calamus* (reed pen), and *atramentum* (ink).[145] Nevertheless, for several reasons tablets were used on occasion for brief letters. (A) Apparently *codicilli* were carried on the person and used for jotting down quick notes required at the moment frequently because of urgency or haste. Thus it is by *codicilli* that Retina sends a note to the elder Pliny when she is alarmed by the sudden eruption of Vesuvius; Acidinus informs Servius Sulpicius by *codicilli* that Marcellus is dead; Cicero sends Balbus *codicilli* when he requests immediate information about a law.[146] When Atticus desires some information as soon as possible, Cicero responds by writing it on a tablet and sending the carrier immediately back. This is discernible because it was customary to mention a previous correspondence in case it did not arrive. Thus Cicero begins his next letter by describing to Atticus this previous letter: "Quae desideras, omnia scripsi in codicillis eosque Eroti dedi".[147] Urgency can be caused by anger as well as circumstances. Apparently Cicero's brother Quintus dashed off a note in a passion. Cicero responds "Epistulam hanc convicio efflagitarunt *codicilli* tui".[148] Cicero provides another example of a note dashed in haste "... hoc litterularum exaravi egrediens e villa ante lucem".[149]

(B) A short note to a local recipient was also frequently written on a tablet, although no haste or urgency was involved, such as a quick letter

---

[144] *Duplices* (δίπτυχα), *triplices, quinquiplices,* or *multiplices*; see Cic. *Att.* 13.8 and Tyrrell and Purser, *Cicero*, 1: 55.

[145] *E.g.*, Cic. *Fam.* 7.18; *Att.* 5.4.4; *QFr.* 2.14.1.

[146] Pliny, *Ep.* 6.16.8; Cic. *Fam.* 4.12.2; 6.18.2 (respectively); see also *Att.* 12.7.1; *QFr.* 2.9.1.

[147] Cic. *Att.* 12.7; "I have scribbled a note with all you want on a tablet and given it to Eros, ..."

[148] Cic. *QFr.* 2.11.1; "This letter has been elicited by the strong and importunate language of your note". [Italics are mine.]

[149] Cic. *Att.* 12.1; "... I have scribbled these few lines while leaving my country house before daybreak". In Cicero's case some of these notes may have been written on parchment and not tablets, but such would only be another example of the frivolity of the upper classes. *Cf. Att.* 7.18.2.

to a neighbor.¹⁵⁰ Similarly, while in the Senate in 46 B.C., Cicero wrote Cornificius a note that he suddenly brought to an abrupt ending, "Plura otiosus. Haec, cum essem in senatu, exaravi".¹⁵¹

(2) The second use of a tablet — the first was writing brief letters — was for preparation of a rough draft of a letter that in final form would be written on papyrus or parchment.¹⁵² Cicero began a letter by noting "... cum ad te harum exemplum in codicillis exaravi".¹⁵³ Evidently Cicero wrote the letter and retained the draft, called a 'copy' for his records. He then had a *librarius* make a copy on *chartae* for dispatching.¹⁵⁴ Pliny described a boar hunting experience and confessed to Cornelius Tacitus:

> Non tamen ut omnino ab inertia mea et quiete discederem. Ad retia sedebam; erat in proximo non venabulum aut lancea, sed stilus et pugillares; meditabar aliquid enotabamque, ut, si manus vacuas, plenas tamen ceras reportarem.¹⁵⁵

While the captive of pirates, Caesar passed his time while awaiting the payment of his ransom "... ποιήματα γράφων καί λόγους τινὰς ἀκροαταῖς ἐκείνοις ἐχρῆτο, ..."¹⁵⁶ These "rough drafts" probably never saw a polished form and surely were written on tablets. It is unlikely that pirates provided papyrus or parchment for casual compositions doodled to pass the time.

(3) Tablets also served as "notebooks" for a writer. Evidently a writer kept notes for three distinct purposes: (a) to record the thoughts of others; (b) to keep extracts from other works; and (c) to make personal notes.

---

[150] See Sen. *Ep.* 55.11. This may account for the "silence" in the letter collections of Cicero during the later years in which both Cicero and Atticus were residing in Rome.

[151] Cic. *Fam.* 12.20; "More when I have leisure. I am in the Senate as I jot this down". Tyrrell and Purser, *Cicero*, 5: 336, also understand *exaravi* as indicating that the letter was written on *codicilli*.

[152] Tyrrell and Purser, *Cicero*, 2: 124 n. 1.

[153] Cic. *Fam.* 9.26; "... and am jotting down a copy of this letter in my note-book".

[154] Or vice versa, it is not completely clear which draft was retained. Tyrrell and Purser, *Cicero*, 4: 419, cite these as "epistolary tenses", but Cicero's wording is unclear. Economy may be the issue: since there would be little revision, his "rough" draft could serve as the copy.

[155] Pliny, *Ep.* 1.6; "However, I indulged at the same time my beloved inactivity, and whilst I sat at my nets, you would have found me, not with spear and dart, but pen and tablet by my side. I mused and wrote, being resolved if I returned with my hands empty, at least to come home with my pocket-book full".

[156] Plut. *Caes.* 1.2; "... writing poems and sundry speeches which he read aloud to them, ..."

(A) Evidently notes[157] were often taken to preserve the thoughts of others. In a (forged) Socratic letter, 'Xenophon' writes to the Friends of Socrates:

> I have written down some memoirs [ἀπομνημονεύματα] about Socrates. When I am fully satisfied with them, I shall send them to you also.[158]

Of course the forger is referring to a well-written work appropriate for a Socratic school. Yet his attempt to represent ἀπομνημονεύματα as authentic implies that taking notes of a teacher's thoughts *in situ* was not unknown.

(B) Extracts from longer works were apparently popular in the ancient world. When an ancient writer such as Pliny quotes a small extract from another writer, he frequently checked his accuracy by referring to a personal copy, often in the form of a notebook of extracts.[159]

(C) The ancient author took notes for personal use as well, as seen in W. W. Tarn's discussion of the sources of Plutarch: "Greeks compiled endless ὑπομνήματα, collections of snippets on any and every subject".[160] The younger Pliny describes his uncle at work[161] with a slave by his side holding both a book from which to read and tablets (*pugillares*) on which to take down anything that the Elder wished to be extracted or noted. According to Sherwin-White, the Younger maintained a distinction between the papyrus roll (the books) and these *pugillares* (tablets).[162] Cicero, in a quip about Pompey, reveals that other men besides prolific writers kept notes:

> Si vero id est, quod nescio an sit ut non minus longas iam in codicillorum fastis futurorum consulum paginulas habeat quam factorum, . . .[163]

---

[157] Here the term μεμβράναι has its strongest connection with the practice of note-taking.

[158] Ps-Socr. *Ep.* 18. The polished quality of these memoirs is indicated in *Ep.* 22.

[159] So argues, *e.g.*, Alan Wardman, *Rome's Debt to Greece* (New York: St. Martin's, 1976), 118: "[Pliny] refers to several speeches . . . he would hardly have looked them up for the first time, though he may have verified them from note-books". This may mean small scrolls here, but it does not matter. The "scroll vs. codex" debate is not germane to this discussion.

[160] Tarn, *Alexander the Great. II: Sources and Studies* (Cambridge: Cambridge University, 1948), 307. See also his article, "Alexander's ὑπομνήματα and the 'World-Kingdom'", *JHS* 41 (1921): 10, and Diog. *Vit. Xen.* 2.48.

[161] Pliny, *Ep.* 3.5.15–16.

[162] Sherwin-White, *Letters of Pliny*, 225, understands the *pugillares* to be a "codex notebook". See also Pliny, *Epp.* 1.6.1 and 9.6.1.

[163] Cic. *Att.* 4.8a (Autumn 56 B.C.); "But if it is true that our friend has in his notebooks as many pages of names of future consuls as of past, . . ."

By the first century parchments were beginning to usurp the place of the traditional wax tablet, since like the tablet a specially prepared parchment could be easily washed off and the sheet reused. Moreover the parchment codex was gaining in popularity as a substitute for the sets of wooden tablets. Roberts and Skeat offer ample evidence for the existence in the first Christian century of *membranae* that were parchment notebooks used in much the same form and for much the same purpose as the wooden tablets.[164] They further argue that when sources made distinctions between the *membranae* and papyrus or parchment texts, the contents of the *membranae* were for personal use and were not intended for publication. Their argument is based primarily upon the classical jurists, whom they contend are particularly good sources since as jurists they reflect more the prevailing meaning of the term rather than an idiosyncratic use by an individual author.[165] Roman lawyers, as lawyers today, were beleaguered by problems with precision in language. In the execution of a will, for instance, how did the executor distinguish between books and unpublished notes or manuscripts? Roberts and Skeat claim that *membranae* were used to designate the latter.[166] Consequently when an author wished to note for a later letter an observation, event, remark, or a passage from a work he was reading, he (or his secretary) jotted down the note on tablets or in *membranae*, whichever he was carrying.

Does the use of notes among Greco-Roman writers have any relevance for Paul? Ironically, according to C. H. Roberts and T. C. Skeat, Paul is the only Greek writer of the first century to refer to μεμβράναι, a Roman invention.[167] In 2 Tim. 4:13, he writes:

τὸν φαιλόνην ὃν ἀπέλιπον ἐν Τρῳάδι παρὰ Καρπῳ ἐρχόμενος φέρε, καὶ τὰ βιβλία, μάλιστα τὰς μεμβράνας.[168]

---

[164] Roberts and Skeat, *Codex*², 15–23. See Mart. 14.7 and *CIL* 10.6. Sherwin-White had earlier defined *pugillares* as meaning "either the usual waxed tablets or the recently introduced 'pugillares membranei'"; *Letters of Pliny*, 100. Tyrrell and Purser, *Cicero*, 1: 55, made a similar observation decades before.

[165] Roberts and Skeat, *Codex*², 30.

[166] Ibid., 21–22, 30. A work of the jurist Neratius Priscus, a contemporary of Trajan, was called *Liber sextus membranarum*. They proposed that *membranae* here was the title, that is, *membranae* were so familiar in court usage that to use it in the title of a work was equivalent to calling it *Jottings from a Lawyer's Notebook*.

[167] Roberts and Skeat, *Codex*², 22. μεμβράναι was borrowed from the Latin *membranei*. See also the short discussion in O. Roller, *Formular*, 342.

[168] T. C. Skeat argues ("Especially the Parchments: a Note on 2 Timothy IV.13", *JTS*, n.s., 30 (1979): 172–77) that μάλιστα has a particularizing function, *i.e.*, μεμβράναι *are* the βιβλία. He may be correct; see Gal. 6:10; 1 Tim. 4:10; also Phil. 4:22; Philem. 16; 1 Tim. 5:8, 17; Tit. 1:10.

Evidently Paul kept and used (judging from his request) notebooks.[169]

If Paul incorporated notes into his letters, how was this coordinated with his use of a secretary? Apparently (pre-written) notes were incorporated in much the same way as (preformed) traditional materials. Consequently they will be considered together in their relation to secretarial assistance.

Like Paul, Cicero uses traditional material in his letters. Also like Paul, he occasionally introduces such material with a formula. For instance, Cicero complains to Atticus:

O rem minime aptam meis moribus! o illud verum ἔρδοι τις ! Dices...[170]

In the next letter, Cicero observes:

Quod superest, si verum illud est οἵαπερ ἡ δέσποινα, certe permanebunt.[171]

Thus in two letters, written within a week, Cicero (or his secretary[172])

Roberts and Skeat (*Codex*², 22 n. 3) are probably correct in their assessment that Paul's initial description of the parchments as βιβλία is *not* significant because such a technical legal or literary distinction (*i.e.*, μεμβράναι vs. βιβλία) was not important to Paul nor his recipient.

[169] An interesting theory suggests itself. Harry Gamble in an unpublished paper read to the International Colloquim on Paul and the Legacies of Paul (March 1986) argued, modifying the thesis of Roberts and Skeat, that the codex first arose not from the use of the four gospels but from the early collection and use of Paul's letters. In much the same manner as Roberts and Skeat, he contends primarily for practical reasons for the early adoption of the codex. What both these theories lack is a reason for an early connection of a codex with Paul's letters (or the gospels). An *early* and quite reasonable connection is provided here. A secretary usually kept copies of the letters (see above, pp. 3–4). Copies were often kept in codices (see Cic. *Fam.* 9.26 [p. 3 n. 11] and p. 8 n. 41). Paul no doubt retained these copies with him, since he used several different secretaries. (They could even be the μεμβράναι of 2 Tim. 4:13.) Thus the first collection of Paul's letters were in codex form and arose from Paul's personal copies and *not* from collecting the letters from the various recipients. Subsequent copies of his letters would naturally retain the form of the original.

Two implications arise from such a theory: (1) The so-called "lost letters" were letters which were not copied before dispatching, perhaps due to haste, and not letters that were somehow misplaced. (2) Such a collection might easily fall into Luke's hands at the death of Paul (2 Tim. 4:11).

[170] Cic. *Att.* 5.10 (June 29, 51 B.C.); "The business is little suited to my tastes. It is a true saying, 'Cobbler, stick to your task'. You will say..."

[171] Cic. *Att.* 5.11 (July 6, 51 B.C.); "For the rest, if the saying be true, 'Like master, like man', assuredly they will stick to their good behavior".

[172] There is no explicit evidence, but judging from (1) his preference at the time and (2) internal considerations (the standardized references to minor details such as travel dates and locations of visits, and the formulaic request to keep him informed), it is likely.

used a formula to introduce a tradition-piece.[173] The use of the formula was unnecessary. The traditional material was in Greek. The mere change in language would have set the material apart. Moreover, these particular quotations were not from any special class of highly venerated material.[174] The use of formula may be mere rhetoric, serving to highlight the particular appropriateness of the saying for the current topic. Yet it may also indicate a secretarial preference for the formula. It would then have been added when the secretary converted the letter into longhand and inserted the quotation.

In the case of snippets of preformed material (either tradition or notes) Cicero and other ancient writers probably presented the material in the same manner as the rest of the letter. When Cicero quotes some material (usually Greek excerpts from Homer), he almost always gives only a line or two.[175] No doubt he quotes from memory and does not trouble to check his accuracy.[176] He does, on occasion, cite a longer passage as indicated by his request to Atticus:

> Would you please write home telling them to give me the run of your books, more especially of Varro, just as though you were there? I shall have to use some passages from these books for the works *I have in hand*, which I hope will meet with your hearty approval.[177]

When citing an extended passage (or perhaps anything more than a snippet) Cicero evidently preferred to use a text. It appears unlikely that Cicero is merely checking his accuracy or planning ahead, anticipating a need. Rather apparently Cicero has already written the work ("works I have in hand"), probably in rough draft. He must have skipped the passages in the first draft, probably leaving the insertion of the quoted material for inclusion in later drafts (when a copy of the quoted text was available).

---

[173] A parallel between Cicero's '*o illud verum*' and Paul's 'πιστὸς ὁ λόγος' is obvious. Was this a popular idiom for introducing common traditions?

[174] Cicero is quoting Aristophanes *Vespae* 1431 (ἔρδοι τις ἣν ἕκαστος εἰδείη τέχνην) [*Att.* 5.10] and Plato, *Resp.* 8.563 (οἵαπερ ἡ δέσποινα, τοία χἠ κύων) [5.11]. Yet elsewhere he quotes from Homer, Plato, *et alii*, with no such formulaic introductions. Another parallel to the pastorals suggests itself. If Cicero's use of the formula does *not* indicate a different attitude toward the traditional material than in his other letters, then the πιστὸς ὁ λόγος formula may not necessarily indicate a different (more venerated) attitude toward Christian tradition than in Paul's other letters, *e.g.*, in 1 Corinthians.

[175] Tyrrell and Purser, *Cicero*, 2: LI, call him the "chief of phrase-mongers".

[176] He might of course check a handy notebook. I noticed that Cicero usually does not cite this type of material during those times of his life characterized by extra stress or grief. Did he have no desire for casual reading, reading that provided these snippets?

[177] Cic. *Att.* 4.14 (May 10, 54 B.C.). [Italics are mine.]

Skipping quoted material, leaving its inclusion into the text until later, may have been a common practice with a secretary. The practicality of such a technique is obvious. If the material is merely to be copied, the secretary can do so while he is preparing the final draft, thus saving time and writing material.[178] For example, a long letter of Cicero to Atticus (10.8) has all the signs of being virtually *ippsissima verba Ciceroni*.[179] It concludes with the appended copies of two letters — not an uncommon practice in antiquity.[180] One would scarcely expect Cicero personally to copy these letters. Surely they are the work of a secretary.[181]

Yet these two appended letters seem to be incorporated into the text. For instance they are not introduced at the same place in his letter. After the copy of the first letter ends the second is introduced by "On the same day, Philotimus brought me a letter from Caesar of which this is a copy". Cicero's procedure with this letter was probably typical and occurred in this way. He apparently dictated the letter (*viva voce?*) to his secretary and at the end dictated a reference to the first letter to be copied and handed the secretary the letter (to be copied into his text later). He then immediately introduced the second letter and likewise handed it over to be copied. This is far more likely than contending that either (1) Cicero dictated the letter-copies as well or (2) he left the introductions of the letter-copies to the secretary. Both letter-copies contain their full epistolary garb including the letter addresses, even though they are rendered redundant because of the individual introductions.[182]

Such a practice has two implications. (1) The text often will read quite smoothly if the inserted (preformed) material (either tradition or notes)

---

[178] Secretaries were often also copyists.

[179] My analysis. The letter is generously sprinkled with short quotations and allusions, as well as the use of rhetorical questions ("Shall we then resist the fleet?" or "Could there be a crime, deeper, greater, or baser?"), interlocutors ("You will say I might..."), and other signs of this skilled rhetorician.

[180] See the discussion above, pp. 4–5.

[181] The entire letter probably was written with secretarial assistance. Dictating letters was his overwhelming preference at this time (May 49 B.C.).

[182] Surely if Cicero is dictating the letters to be copied as he dictated the main letter (with introductions), he would avoid such a blatant redundancy as "... a letter from Caesar of which this is a copy. Caesar to Cicero..." I think Cicero does, on occasion, dictate the letter to be copied while dictating the main letter. In *Att.* 10.10, he includes a copy of Anthony's letter, but it is stripped of its epistolary garb and (apparently) any redundant or superfluous details. The letter address was often removed by an author when copying it (see White, "Retrospect", 12), although the copy was often shortened by abbreviations and omissions (see idem, *Light*, 217–18).

is removed, since there was very little break in the author's thought.[183]
(2) The presence of extraneous details can be very pronounced. Some point of contact brought the material to mind and prompted the author to order the secretary to insert it. Since the author may not be re-reading the inserted material, any extraneous or tangential elements may be overlooked.[184] Details that might be edited out if the author was dictating the inserted material as well into the letter remain when the secretary transfers it into his full draft.[185] Once in the text, the author may not deem the deletion of any extraneous material to merit rewriting the tradition or the letter.

In summary, one may suggest that παραδόσεις as well as excerpts from μεμβράναι (or other notes), particularly when more than a snippet, were often left to the secretary to incorporate into his finished draft. As a result, this material can contain some of the same characteristics of later insertions, since in a sense they are later insertions.[186]

---

[183] Hence the smooth connection between 2 Cor. 6:13 and 7:2 should not be surprising. It *does* indicate an insertion but *not* necessarily a later (post-Pauline) insertion, for which there is no textual evidence.

[184] Theoretically material with an immediate point of contact could actually contain subtle presuppositions that conflict with the author's own, as some suggest concerning 2 Cor. 6:14–7:1. But *cf.* the issue of responsibility, above pp. 53–56.

[185] Secretaries often copied material without discernment. An excellent example is provided by Diogenes Laertius in his Life of Epicurus. He supplements his sources by including three letters of Epicurus. These letters appear genuine, although they are heavily encumbered by scholia, either added by Diogenes himself (a possibility according to R. D. Hicks [LCL, xxx]) or more likely indiscriminantly copied into the text of Diogenes by the secretary who was to copy the letter from a manuscript (with scholia) into his text (so H. Usener [*Epicurea* (Leipzig: University of Leipzig, 1887)] and also Hicks). Hicks concludes "the manuscript [of the letters] seems to have been entrusted to a scribe to copy, just as it was: scholia and marginal notes, even where they interrupt the thread of argument, have been faithfully reproduced. See §§ 39, 40, 43, 44, 50, 66, 71, 73, 74, 75" (LCL, 564–65 n. *e*; also see 660 n. *a*).

[186] This makes the detection of later insertions more difficult. Certainly external evidence is still decisive, as, *e.g.*, in the pericope on adultery. When external evidence is lacking, an exegete must be more tenuous in a conclusion based on extraneous details (or theology) or disruption of context. This is in direct contrast to the position of William Walker, "The Burden of Proof in Identifying Interpolations in the Pauline Letters", *NTS* 33 (1987): 610–18, and especially his presentation to the SBL Southwest Regional Conference, March 12, 1988.

2. Paul's Employment of a Secretary

Since most ancient letter writers availed themselves of a professional secretary,[187] it is not surprising that Paul did the same. An understanding of when and possibly how[188] he employs his secretary needs examination. To ascertain when Paul uses a secretary, his letters will be searched for evidence of the criteria developed in the preceding chapter.[189]

a) Explicit Evidence

There is explicit evidence in some of his letters for his use of a secretary, and this makes it certain in those letters. It can be seen by examining the previously established categories: (1) references by the author; (2) references by the secretary; and (3) changes in handwriting.

aa) References by the Author

Although Cicero commonly comments "I am dictating this letter...", Paul never speaks directly of the way in which his letters were taken down.

bb) References by the Secretary

The most common types of secretarial remarks in antiquity were the illiteracy formulae. Yet no letter of Paul contains one. This offers two implications. (1) His letters were not viewed as having any official or business connotation. They were, strictly speaking, private letters. Therefore the secretary was not required to identify himself.[190] (2) Concomitantly the *lack* of any illiteracy formula does not necessarily indicate that Paul was literate — of course, there are many other indications that he was — only that the letters were private and needed no formula.[191]

---

[187] So, *e.g.*, McKenzie, *Light*, 14.

[188] *Cf.* the skepticism of Wm. Doty, *Letters*, 41: "I am not as convinced as some writers that we may identify the manner in which Paul composed his letters". Nevertheless he has not, perhaps, considered all the evidence.

[189] The results of this investigation will be summarized in Table 4 below, p. 190.

[190] Even his letters that clearly evidence a secretary do not contain any illiteracy formulae. When Tertius names himself in Romans (16:22), it was not in any sense an official identification.

[191] Were Deissmann's assessment (*Light*, 174, 246) of Paul's ability with a reed pen ac-

The other type of reference by a secretary that gives clear evidence of his presence are secretarial remarks in the text of the letter. One letter of Paul contains such a secretarial remark. Among the list of closing greetings in Romans 16, the following is found (v. 22): ἀσπάζομαι ὑμᾶς ἐγὼ Τέρτιος ὁ γράψας τὴν ἐπιστολὴν ἐν κυρίῳ. That Tertius is the secretary is certain. This type of remark was not uncommon.[192] The secretary appears most likely to include such a remark when (1) he is known to the recipient(s), and (2) his status with the author (and perhaps the recipient(s)) is more than that of a mere slave or employee, perhaps even that of a friend or colleague, although certainly in a subordinate sense. Thus Alexis, Atticus' secretary, feels confident enough to include a personal greeting to Cicero,[193] because he has a good relationship with both Atticus and Cicero.

This suggests two relationships. First, Tertius was not unknown to Paul, that is, he was not merely contracted in the agora. Even if Tertius was well-known in Rome, he probably would not have felt the freedom to insert a greeting *into Paul's letter*, unless he also knew Paul well. Otherwise an appended greeting would perhaps have been used. Second, Tertius was also known to the recipients in Rome (or Ephesus, if one favors the theory that chapter 16 was a separate *litterae commendaticae* for Phoebe sent to Ephesus appended to a copy of the letter [chs. 1–15] to Rome[194]).

One final observation may be made here. Who is this Tertius? To be mentioned by name only once among the Pauline letters is common, especially in this letter. Yet usually these people are only the recipients of greetings or are named for a particular occasion (*e.g.*, Syntyche and Euodia). The names of people who are more closely associated with Paul, that is, not the mere recipients of greetings, have a strong tendency to re-surface in other letters of Paul. It seems odd that someone who is

---

curate, a formula could have been used, such as the one given by the secretary who wrote for Herma because "he writeth somewhat slowly" (see above, p. 74).

[192] See the discussion above, p. 76.

[193] *Vid.* from Cic. *Att.* 5.20.

[194] See *e.g.*, the discussion "Der sogenannte 'kleine Römer- oder Epheserbrief'" in O. Roller, *Formular*, 195–99. But see Harry Gamble, *The Textual History of the Letter to the Romans: a Study in Textual and Literary Criticism*, SD, no. 42 (Grand Rapids: Eerdmans, 1977). While a discussion of this theory is hardly possible here, one point may be made. According to the custom of other ancient letter writers, copies of letters were commonly appended to the end, even if they were significantly longer than the actual letter. Moreover they were also customarily marked as a copy. It is possible, but less likely, that Paul was re-using material in a letter to another, a quite typical activity; see the brief discussion above, p. 5.

familiar enough with Paul to insert his own greeting in Paul's letter does not reappear elsewhere, unless Tertius only had strong ties with Rome (or Ephesus).

Why is Tertius, who never appears as a member of the Pauline band, used as a secretary here? It may not be mere coincidence that he is also used to write down the longest letter of Paul,[195] the letter that contains the strongest oral features,[196] that contains such a high frequency of oratorical rhetoric, that perhaps has the strongest possibility of being all or partly *ipsissima verba Pauli viva voce*.[197] If Tertius was a tachygraphist, it may explain why he was used to record this long letter — or perhaps even why this letter is so long.[198] It may also shed light on Tertius' apparent affiliation with Rome: this city was perhaps the most likely to house a tachygraphist.[199]

A tachygraphist would, of course, also be well trained in other secretarial skills. This may explain Paul's singular use of a well-written *litterae commendaticae* (Romans 16).[200] Converting the (usually oral) instructions of an author into a polished, standardized, letter of recommendation was a common assignment for a *professional* secretary. If Tertius was a trained secretary, then this reconstruction is possible. Paul dictated the letter and then told Tertius to write a commendation for Phoebe and to greet the important people in the Roman church. In addition to writing a proper recommendation for Phoebe, Tertius displayed another secretarial trait: the tendency to include details and to be exhaustive.[201] Either Tertius knew the people to greet or he collected a list.

---

[195] Assuming that chapter 16 (where the greeting of Tertius appears) is part of the original letter and hence he was the secretary for the entire letter.

[196] And thus, if the idiom of Romans does resemble Epictetus' discourses at times, it may be because *both* are recordings of preachers speaking *viva voce*.

[197] Aside from the use of the diatribe (or oration), the energy carried over extended arguments, etc., makes a laborious syllable-by-syllable composition quite unlikely. O. Roller, *Formular*, 8–14, is certainly correct here that it is completely unreasonable to imagine Romans being composed extemporaneously while being recorded *syllabatim*. Interestingly, it is also the only letter among the undisputed seven not to mention a co-sender (co-author).

[198] Paul was a long-winded speaker, if Luke may be trusted (*e.g.*, Acts 20:7–12).

[199] The wealthy Roman aristocracy, according to the evidence, were the major users of tachygraphists. Still this is, of course, a tenuous assertion because of the nature of the evidence; yet most ancient references to tachygraphists around the first century are from Rome. Incidentally Tertius is a Latin name.

[200] *Cf.* Chan-Hie Kim, *The Form and Structure of the Familiar Greek Letter of Recommendation*, SBLDS, no. 4 (Missoula, MT: Scholars, 1972).

[201] This is illustrated by Cicero (discussed at length above, p. 116). He briefly thanks

Since Tertius was not a regular member of the Pauline band (arguing *e silentio*), his skills as a tachygraphist may explain why Paul chose to use him. That the Roman letter was recorded <u>*viva voce* can be maintained finally only by a study of the epistle itself;</u> nevertheless the possibility that Tertius was a professional secretary deserves a future investigation.[202]

cc) Changes in Handwriting

This last form of explicit evidence for the use of a secretary can be detected three ways: from autographs, annotated copies, and remarks in the text. Unfortunately no autographs of Paul are extant today. Nor are there any annotated copies of his letters.[203] Nevertheless the largest amount of evidence for the use of a secretary is found in this category. Five letters contain explicit remarks by Paul evidencing a change in handwriting.

1. In 1 Cor. 16:21 Paul states Ὁ ἀσπασμὸς τῇ ἐμῇ χειρὶ Παύλου.
2. In Gal. 6:11 Paul remarks Ἴδετε πηλίκοις ὑμῖν γράμμασιν ἔγραψα τῇ ἐμῇ χειρί.

Atticus for some library slaves. A second letter (written the same day) by his secretary is a more official thank-you and includes the names of the slaves and a detailed description of their accomplishments.

[202] Space prevents it here. That Tertius was also a Christian (ἐν κυρίῳ) does not preclude his being a secretary.
Incidentally, there is some dispute over whether ἐν κυρίῳ is to be read with the subject [so in Living Bible and in Goodspeed's translation: "I, Tertius ... send my greetings as a fellow Christian"] or with the verb [so in TEV, NIV, RSV, JB: "... greet you in the Lord"]. Gordon Bahr, "Letter Writing", 465, argues that ἐν κυρίῳ is to be read with the participial phrase, ὁ γράψας τὴν ἐπιστολήν. He adds that ἐν κυρίῳ can often mean 'in the service of (the) master' (Rom. 16:8, 12, 13; 1 Cor. 7:22; 9:1, 2; 15:58; Eph. 4:1; 6:21; 1 Th. 4:1; 5:12; also [*cf.*] Mt. 9:34; Mk. 3:22; 11:28, 29, 33; Lk. 11:15, 18–20; Acts 4:7, 9, 10, 12). Thus Bahr translates Rom. 16:22: "I, Tertius, who write this letter in the service of (my) master [Paul], greet you".
Bahr's position has several problems. (1) ἐν κυρίῳ always refers to Jesus in the passages Bahr cites. (2) ἐν κυρίῳ means much more than 'in the service of the Lord' in the passages he cites in Paul. Although the *non-Pauline* passages he cites may carry this meaning, none use the word 'κύριος'. (3) I know of no parallels to a secretary using such a construction or anything similar. (4) ἐν κυρίῳ is used extensively in Romans 16 – six times excluding v. 22 and the variant in v. 9 – and always as a Christian formula. Finally (5) it is very unlikely that Paul, the self-proclaimed δοῦλος, would permit himself to be called κύριος.

[203] The lengthy explanatory subscriptions found in most minuscules scarcely deserve mention for they are unquestionably late and have no link to authentic tradition. *E.g.*, the *subscriptio* to Romans that is found in most minuscules (according to NA^{26}) is "επιστολη προς Ρωμαιους εγραφη δια Φοιβης" and actually contradicts the testimony of the letter itself (which explains the discerning alteration in MS 337).

3. Col. 4:18 similarly states Ὁ ἀσπασμὸς τῇ ἐμῇ χειρὶ Παύλου.
4. In like manner Paul writes in 2 Th. 3:17 Ὁ ἀσπασμὸς τῇ ἐμῇ χειρὶ Παύλου, ὅ ἐστιν σημεῖον ἐν πάσῃ ἐπιστολῇ· οὕτως γράφω.
5. Finally in the same manner Paul concludes his letter to Philemon (v. 19) ἐγὼ Παῦλος ἔγραψα τῇ ἐμῇ χειρί.

Several observations may be made. First, Paul discloses his use of a secretary with what is apparently a typical formula: τῇ ἐμῇ χειρί.[204] He uses it in every instance. This is also a preferred formula for Cicero (*mea manu*). It was apparently a standard means in personal letters of signalling the use of a secretary for the preceding part of the letter.

Second, the use of ἔγραψα in Galatians and Philemon has been argued to refer to the entire letters.[205] Usually this is countered by citing the parallels in his other letter. Thus the ἔγραψα must be an epistolary aorist.[206] There is, however, a much stronger argument. The evidence in antiquity strongly indicates that such authorial references *always begin* the autographed section.[207]

---

[204] That χείρ refers to handwriting is not questioned. See e.g., Philo *Spec. leg.* 4.160.

[205] D. Guthrie, *Galatians*, Century Bible Commentary, New Series (London: Th. Nelson, 1969), 158, suggests that ἔγραψα may refer to the entire letter; so also George Duncan, *The Epistle of Paul to the Galatians*, MNTC (London: Hodder & Stoughton, 1934), 189; and W. F. Adeney, *A Commentary of Paul's Epistle to the Galatians*, in the Century Bible Commentary, o.s. (London: Caxton, 1911), 335 [although only in Philem. 19]. Aside from its apparent formulaic nature, it is scarcely plausible that Paul would have written the entire epistle in 'large letters'.

[206] They are so classified by some grammarians, e.g., A. T. Robertson, *A Grammar of the Greek New Testament in the Light of Historical Research*, 3d ed. (New York: Hodder & Stoughton, 1919), 846; W. D. Chamberlain, *An Exegetical Grammar of the Greek New Testament* (New York: Macmillan, 1941), 78; and (possibly) N. Turner, *Syntax*, vol. 3 in *A Grammar of New Testament Greek*, ed. J. H. Moulton (Edinburgh: T & T Clark, 1963), 73. But cf., e.g., F. B. Blass, *Grammar of New Testament Greek*, trans. H. St. J. Thackeray (London: Macmillan & Co., 1898), 194, who claims that in the New Testament ἔγραψα *always* refers to an earlier letter or an earlier portion of the letter. The epistolary aorist, however, is well-attested in antiquity (esp. Latin) and quite probably here (so Roberston and Turner).

Many commentators translate this as an epistolary aorist; see, e.g., Betz, *Galatians*, 314; E. DeW. Burton, *A Critical and Exegetical Commentary on the Epistle to the Galatians*, in the ICC (New York: Scribner's Sons, 1920), 347-48; A. L. Williams, *The Epistle of Paul the Apostle to the Galatians*, in the Cambridge Greek Testament for Schools and Colleges Series (Cambridge: University Press, 1910), 136-37; Adeney, *Galatians*, 335 [not including Philemon]; and G. G. Findlay, *St. Paul's Epistle to the Galatians*, in the Expositor's Greek Testament Series (New York: Hodder & Stoughton, 1888), 422-22.

[207] See the discussion above, p. 69. There are just no grounds for Bahr to begin the autographed sections earlier. Bahr, "Subscriptions", 33-41.

Third, the added remark in 2 Thessalonians (ὅ ἐστιν σημεῖον ἐν πάσῃ ἐπιστολῇ) needs more examination. It probably was added by Paul here to protect the Thessalonians from forgeries (2 Thes. 2:2). Yet it is unclear what Paul means by ἐν πάσῃ ἐπιστολῇ. Clearly it cannot mean explicit citations, for 2 Corinthians, 1 Thessalonians, Ephesians, 1 and 2 Timothy, and Titus have none. Does Paul mean all letters to the Thessalonians? Yet again 1 Thessalonians has no explicit indication of ἀσπασμὸς τῇ χειρὶ Παύλου.[208] There is *no* way to ascertain if *all* of his letters contained an autograph postscript. His remark, however, leaves only two conclusions: (1) Paul was inconsistent about using an autographed postscript. Apparently Cicero did not intend for his similar remark to be taken 'carte blanche'.[209] Or (2) Paul was inconsistent about *explicitly* mentioning the postscript. This is a much less serious accusation since it does not invalidate his claim in 2 Th. 3:17. The change in handwriting was a sufficient indication to his readers. Perhaps A. Deissmann is correct that it is a sheer *petitio principii* to say that only the letters that explicitly state so have a postscript in Paul's own hand.[210] This however would make secretarial mediation a possibility in all of his letters — a factor to be considered.

Finally, Paul's remark in Gal. 6:11 ("Ἴδετε πηλίκοις ὑμῖν γράμμασιν ἔγραψα τῇ ἐμῇ χειρί) clearly indicates that Paul's handwriting stands in marked contrast to the handwriting of the secretary.[211] The implication is that the secretary's script was small (or perhaps cursive[212]). What is the implication from Paul's writing in large letters is less clear. Deissmann asserts:

> The apostle's 'large letters' are best explained as the clumsy, awkward writing of a workman's hand deformed by toil, and hence... St. Paul dictated his letters by preference, writing was not particularly easy to him.[213]

Paul's motivation may have been more complex.[214] Deissmann elsewhere suggests that Paul may be engaging in some good-natured irony

---

[208] It could mean all previous letters if 2 Thessalonians were written first, but this would include, at the most, Galatians.

[209] Cic. *Att.* 2.23.1.

[210] Deissmann, *Light*, 167 n. 7, argues that it means all the letters. He cites an example of a (autograph) letter that contains a postscript in the writer's own hand, although the writer does not expressly state this.

[211] His remark in 2 Th. 3:17 implies his handwriting may have been somewhat distinctive.

[212] See the excellent discussion in Williams, *Galatians*, 136.

[213] Deissmann, *St. Paul*, 51; *Light*, 174, 246.

[214] There is no connotation of ill-shapen letters here. See Williams, *Galatians*, 136. This

by signing his name in big block letters such as would be used to insure that children could read it.[215] Yet there are no parallels for this very subtle practice.[216] There is evidence from Pisidian Antioch and Pompeii that writing in large letters was used to accentuate in much the same way as italics today and thus Paul was drawing attention to his postscript.[217]

The inclusion of an autographed closing is understood traditionally as an ancient indicator of authenticity (or simulated authenticity in pseudonymous letters). Quite recently this has been disputed from a genre-critical perspective.[218] Franz Schnider and Werner Stenger contend that this autographed section should be seen in a juridical sense. The letter is the written presence of the apostle; the present words of an absent authority. The autographed section, as part of the '*eschatocoll*', served to enforce the letter's contents. Yet this distinction seems rather artificial. If the autograph insured its authenticity, then it also insured its authority. Only a summary postscript could provide additional authentication. Yet since summary postscripts were not used in private letters, the letter's content was assumed the author's by nature of the author's accountability. He checked the draft.

b) Implicit Indicators

In addition to the explicit signs of Paul's use of a secretary, there may be some implicit indicators. Obviously their greatest value is for those letters of Paul that contain no explicit evidence, for these indicators can do no more than suggest the possibility of a secretary, and they have varying degrees of reliability and validity.[219] As in the preceding chapter, these indicators are examined in the ascending order of value (beginning with the least helpful): (1) the presence of a postscript; (2) the preference of Paul; (3) the particular letter-type; and (4) stylistic variations in an authentic letter.

---

is not to say, however, that such a point would not be relevant. Were Paul a poor writer, then the possible use of a secretary where not clearly evident is greatly increased. This is considered, however, under the indicator "preference of the author".

[215] Deissmann, *Bible Studies*, 2d ed., trans. A. Grieve (Edinburgh: T & T Clark, 1909), 348.

[216] Wm. Ramsey, *A Historical Commentary on St. Paul's Epistle to the Galatians* (London: Hodder & Stoughton, 1900), 466, dismisses it as belonging "to the region of pure comedy".

[217] See Williams, *Galatians*, 136. The preponderance of commentators understand it similarly.

[218] F. Schnider and W. Stenger, *Studien zum neutestamentlichen Briefformular*.

[219] These terms are used in their technical senses; see below, App. H, p. 218 n. 8.

aa) The Presence of a Postscript

Since there are two forms of postscripts, summary subscriptions and postscripts of additional material, and since these have different values and difficulties, they will be discussed separately.

Summary Subscriptions

Gordon Bahr's argument that Paul used a secretary is not new and is certainly not disputed here.[220] His contribution lies in his theory as to *how much* Paul used a secretary in a letter, that is, how much of the letter did the secretary write versus how much did Paul write in his own hand.[221] Bahr contends that Paul may have frequently written much more in his own hand than has been assumed traditionally. For example, Paul is writing in his own hand in Gal. 6:11. Bahr however argues that Paul actually began writing in his own hand at Gal. 5:2. Galatians is not the only instance. His analysis of the ten Pauline letters (he excludes the Pastorals) shows that he repeatedly moves up the beginning of the postscript (see Table 3). Why he begins the postscripts earlier is directly related to his definition of summary subscriptions.

Bahr's analysis of the nature and purpose of summary subscriptions in Greco-Roman *records* is quite accurate.[222] His error lies in his application of the material to private letters: "One can also find *letters* in which the signature [*i.e.*, the postscript] refers to material in the body of the letter, and these may be called subscriptions because they seem to have essentially the same function as the subscriptions in records".[223] He then argues that there was no sharp distinction in antiquity between letters and records. Thus private letters could contain summary subscriptions as well. This innocent observation is then converted into a criterion. Whenever a letter of Paul begins to recapitulate, he assumes that it is the be-

---

[220] Bahr, "Subscriptions", 27–41. He also sees the secretarial role as a continuum with four major distinctions. His conclusions about Paul differ only because of his analysis of the subscriptions.

[221] Although Bahr recognizes the existence of shorthand in the first century ("Letter Writing", 475–76) he does not consider it a possibility for Paul. Yet he offers no rationale other than citing Roller's (*Formular*, 333) conclusion that dictation was a rarity. Roller however meant dictation *syllabatim*. Since Bahr does not think Paul could have dictated *viva voce*, he argues that Paul used his secretary – to use my term – as a co-author, although perhaps on occasion as an editor or a composer.

[222] See the earlier description above, pp. 81–83.

[223] Bahr, "Subscriptions", 33.

Table 3
A Presentation of Gordon Bahr's Analysis of the Letter Body Written by the Secretary to the Postscript Written by Paul

	Written by a Secretary	Written by Paul
Rom.	1:1–11:36 (&16) (78.9 %) [5191 (& 423) words]	12:1–15:33 (21.1 %) [1500 words]
1 Cor.	1:1–16:14 (98.2 %) [6717 words]	16:15–24 (1.8 %) [123 words]
2 Cor.	1:1–9:15 (67.6 %) [3033 words]	10:1–13:14 (13?) (32.4 %) [1455 words]
Gal.	1:1–5:1 (75.3 %) [1681 words]	5:2–6:18 (24.7 %) [552 words]
Eph.	1:1–3:21 (45 %) [1091 words]	4:1–6:24 (55 %) [1332 words]
Phil.	1:1–2:30 (57.1 %) [932 words]	3:1–4:23 (42.9 %) [699 words]
Col.	1:1–2:7 (41.3 %) [654 words]	2:8–4:18 (58.7 %) [928 words]
1 Thes.	1:1–3:13 (58.3 %) [864 words]	4:1–5:28 (41.7 %) [619 words]
2 Thes.	1:1–2:17 (66.7 %) [549 words]	3:1–18 (33.3 %) [274 words]
Philem.	1–16 (69.3 %) [232 words]	17–25 (30.7 %) [103 words]

Source: The information was abstracted from Bahr, "Subscriptions", 34–40. A similar table was used by A. J. Bandstra, "Paul, the Letter Writer", *Calvin Theological Journal* 3 (1968): 176–80, in his critique of Bahr. Percentages (based on the number of words in the NA^{26} text) are given for the purpose of comparison. Approximate percentages for someone like Cicero are needed.

ginning of a summary subscription. A. J. Bandstra in his critique of Bahr rightly notes the problem:

> there does seem to be sufficient evidence that 'records' contained the kind of subscriptions which Bahr contends is present in Paul's letters. But is there sufficient evidence that real letters or epistles had such subscriptions?[224]

---

[224] Bandstra, "Paul, the Letter Writer", 179.

Bandstra only raises the question. But Bahr has apparently forgotten that summary subscriptions had a *legal* etiology,[225] something irrelevant in private letters. If private letters did not require an illiteracy formula, they certainly would not need an authenticating summary. And there is no evidence that *letter* writers summarized the content of their letters when they took the pen from their secretary. Although there are numerous letters with 'subscriptions', such as in the letters of Cicero, they are not *summary* subscriptions but postscripts of additional material. Consequently Bahr's criterion for determining the beginning of the Pauline subscriptions is not valid. He may be correct that the Pauline letters contain postscripts, but he is incorrect that a summarizing of the letter could mark the end of the secretarial assistance and the beginning of the (autographed) postscript.

Two more observations may be made before leaving the discussion of summary subscriptions. First, there is one more critique that may be made against Bahr. The evidence strongly suggests that remarks like "I am writing this in my own hand" *begin* the autographed section.[226] Thus without his criterion of 'summarization', all the evidence is against beginning the postscript any earlier than when Paul indicates that he is now writing "τῇ ἐμῇ χειρί".

Second, there appears to be one private letter with a summary subscription — a letter of Paul. In Philem. 19 Paul indicates that he has begun writing in his own hand. What follows could be loosely termed a summary subscription, because Paul repeats the matter about Philemon's indebtedness to him. This however does not support Bahr's thesis. (1) It is the remark of Paul not the summarizing of content that indicates a postscript. (2) Bahr begins the summary too early (v. 17). (3) In such a single-minded and short letter, a repetition of the main point is not surprising. (4) Paul may be engaging perhaps in an amiable jest, concluding the letter like an official letter. (5) The postscript has an abrupt and stern tone not found in the letter body. Possibly when Paul checked the secretarial draft of the letter, he decided that his wishes might be lost in all of the

---

[225] O. Roller, *Formular*, 286 n. 83, also notes their strictly legal function: "Sonst spielt die Eigenhändigkeit in dem Urkundenwesen der Alten nur bei der Unterschrift eine Rolle, und war in den übrigen Teilen der Urkunden ebensowenig ein rechtliches Erfordernis wie bei uns".

[226] See the discussion above, p. 69. Also see, *e.g.*, Cic. *Att.* 12.32.1. In the one exception I found in Cicero (Cic. *QFr.* 3.1.19) he very plainly indicates that the preceding section was autographed and that (for situational reasons) he was using a secretary for the next section. Apparently Cicero felt that because the remark was not at the beginning, it required an explanation.

secretary's circumlocutions. Therefore the more direct, less tactful, Paul (as seen in Galatians and 2 Corinthians 10—13) picks up the pen to 'sign' the letter and then adds a stiffer reminder to Philemon (perhaps to the chagrin of the secretary who had worked to tone down the letter body).[227] Although the category of summary subscriptions is inappropriate for the letters of Paul, there are some indications that Paul employed the other type of postscript.

Additional Material

Postscripts could contain material that had been forgotten during the course of writing the letter body, material that was newly acquired since the letter body was finished, or material that was secretive or sensitive. Although Bahr blends all postscripts into summary subscriptions, he notes the use of this other type of postscript.

> One has the impression that now, after the secretary has completed the letter which the author wished to send, the author himself writes to the addressee in personal, intimate terms; the items discussed in signatures of this type are usually of a very personal nature.[228]

For example, Cicero in a letter to Atticus (12.32.1) apparently draws the letter to a close with his final greetings but then adds: "Piliae it Atticae salutem... Haec ad te mea manu". He then writes in his own hand a postscript that is five times longer than the original letter. This extensive section is very personal.

Does Paul engage in personal postscripts? Obviously he does, at least in those letters that indicate by his personal remarks that he has begun writing in his own hand.[229] Other than these letters there is little indication. Romans, Ephesians, Philippians, and the Pastorals have no indications of a postscript. 1 Thessalonians may have the slightest clue. Throughout the letter, the stereotyped formulae[230] are always in the plural. After the final greetings, however, in verse 26, there is a request in the singular ('Ἐνορκίζω ὑμᾶς...). Moreover, the previous requests have been rather abstract and 'spiritual', but this request is very prag-

---

[227] In 1 Cor. 16:22—24 there is obviously a postscript (but not a summary subscription), and it also has a sterner tone.
[228] Bahr, "Subscriptions", 33.
[229] *E.g.*, 1 Cor. 16:21—24; Col. 3:18; 2 Th. 3:17—18; and esp. Philem. 19—25 and Gal. 6:11—18.
[230] *E.g.*, thanksgiving (1:2 and 2:13); disclosure (2:1; 4:9; 4:13; and 5:1) and petition (4:1 and 5:14) formulae.

matic and stands in contrast to the rest of the epistle. Perhaps it is an indication of Paul taking the pen to affix a closing greeting (v. 28) and adding a personal request as well.

2 Corinthians may also have an indication of a postscript. The difference between chs. 1—9 and 10—13 has long been noted, and the suggestion that 10—13 was once a separate letter[231] has gained followers because of among other things the shift in tone at the beginning of 10:1. Certainly the wording of this verse, αὐτὸς δὲ ἐγὼ Παῦλος παρακαλῶ..., must be taken seriously. Yet it is not a typical beginning for a letter. If its original epistolary garb had been stripped away, what (besides later redaction) can explain the double emphasis on Paul as the author?[232] Another explanation is possible. The wording is not that unusual for a postscript — they usually begin with an emphasis on the unmediated input of the author[233] — nor is the relative length (33%) inappropriate. Cicero commonly has postscripts that are relatively longer. Nor is the abrupt change in tone inexplicable. Cicero has demonstrated that much of a situation can change between the writing of a letter and the appending of a postscript.[234] Moreover, there are indications in other (undisputed) Pauline postscripts[235] that Paul tends to be more abrupt or

---

[231] The difference is first noted in the work of J. S. Semler, *Paraphrasis II. Epistulae ad Corinthos*, Vetus Latina (Halae: Hammerdiani, 1776). That chs. 10—13 is a separate letter has two major variations: either written after chs. 1—9 (thus Semler; Bruce; Barrett; Windisch; and Jülicher- Fascher) or written between 1 and 2 Corinthians as the intermediate letter (first proposed by A. Hausrath, *Der Vier-Capitelbrief des Paulus an die Korinther* (Heidelberg: F. Bassermann, 1870), and held by T. W. Manson; Filson; Héring; Marxsen; Sparks; de Zwaan; Bultmann; Dodd; Georgi; Nickle; Schmithals; Klijn; Goguel; Cleary; et al.). See the discussion in Werner Kümmel, *Introduction to the New Testament*, rev. ed., trans. H. C. Kee (Nashville: Abingdon, 1975), 289—90.

[232] To answer my own question, it could *possibly* be explained two ways: (1) It could mean that Paul alone, *i.e.*, without his co-author Timothy, authored the remaining section. Yet why would Paul choose to leave Timothy out and *indicate* it, unless Paul wanted to be more to the point than he felt that Timothy was permitting, or Timothy wanted it clear that he was not a part of the stern reprimand that was coming. Or (2) it could be an example of the ancient practice of abbreviating and omitting parts of the epistolary address in an appended copy of another letter (see White, *Light*, 217—18 for a brief discussion of the practice). Yet no examples apparently exist where it is so abbreviated that it is no longer clear that it is an appended copy.

[233] Cicero begins his postscripts by indicating that he personally is now writing. He does not, though, use any Latin parallel to this particular construction.

[234] See the discussion above, pp. 83—85.

[235] 1 Cor. 16:22—24; Philem. 20—25; and possibly Gal. 6:12—18 and Col. 4:18.

stern in his personal postscripts. It is quite possible that chs. 10–13 represent a Pauline postscript appended to the secretarial draft.[236]

Nevertheless, the use of postscripts for determining the presence of secretarial assistance, as stated at the outset, is the weakest indicator.[237] As a result, without additional indicators, the use of a secretary for 2 Corinthians and 1 Thessalonians may be listed as only 'possible'.

bb) The Preference of Paul

The indicated preference of the author is a more reliable indicator than the use of postscripts. Since we have seen that evidently Paul does use a secretary in some of his letters, the question that must be answered is why he chose to do so. For example, Cicero occasionally writes that inflammation of the eyes has forced his use of a secretary.[238] Such a problem, however, was variable. Why does Paul use a secretary? If he employs one for convenience only, then this criterion is of less value. A secretary is used unless one is not available. Paul's confession in 2 Cor. 10:10 is probably rhetoric and his remark in Gal. 6:11 probably does not mean that he is a poor writer. Consequently, his preference for a secretary must be sought in the situations of his correspondences.

If the use of a secretary can be demonstrated in one letter, then another letter that was written from the same situation is more likely also to have used a secretary. The problem with this approach is that it requires ascertaining that the author's situation has not changed significantly enough to disallow a comparison. For example, 1 and 2 Corinthians may have been written within a short time of each other. Paul used a secretary in

---

[236] It is not a new idea to argue that 10–13 is a conclusion by Paul, either caused by his writing in his own hand (so Feine-Behm; Bates; Dibelius), by the receipt of new information (so R. M. Grant; Harrington; Jülicher- Fascher; Price; Munck), by a sleepless night (so Lietzmann), or a sudden change of mind by Paul concerning the genuineness of the repentance of the Corinthians (so Guthrie). See Kümmel, *Introduction*, 289–90; and Vic Furnish, *II Corinthians*, AB, vol. 32A (Garden City, NY: Doubleday, 1984), 36.

Cicero provides an example of a letter written in the heat of emotion and yet still sent (and regretted later): "I had written you a letter not quite in a brotherly spirit, upset as I was... I had written it in a fit of temper, and was anxious to recall it. Such a letter, though written in an unbrotherly way, you ought as a brother to forgive" (*QFr.* 1.2.12). Incidently this letter was no doubt written in Cicero's own hand, for he indicates in a subsequent letter to his brother (2.2.1) that writing in his own hand had been his custom for previous letters to his brother.

[237] A stylometric analysis of the postscripts is planned for the future. If indeed they are from the unmediated hand of Paul, then they should show greater homogeneity.

[238] *E.g.*, Cic. *Att.* 7.13a and 8.13.

1 Corinthians. Does this preference transfer to 2 Corinthians, or has the epistolary situation changed too much? There may well have been an intervening letter, possibly written without secretarial assistance. Paul was perhaps forced to leave Ephesus unexpectedly before writing 2 Corinthians.[239] Thus his personal situation may have changed too dramatically to permit a simple comparison. With other letters, however, his situation may not have changed so dramatically between their writing. If Paul was in prison — certainly a sufficient inconvenience to justify the use of a secretary — and he evidently used a secretary for some of his prison letters (*e.g.*, Colossians and Philemon), then he probably used a secretary for the others (*e.g.*, Ephesians and Philippians). Again, this criterion may only suggest because there are many other variables. A relocation from Caesarea to Rome, for example, could alter the entire situation.[240]

cc) The Particular Letter-Type[241]

The letter-types in Paul possibly calling for a secretary are the *litterae commendaticae* in Romans 16 and the apologetic letter (if H. D. Betz's interpretation of Galatians is accurate).[242] One must first show that the *litterae commendaticae* was a form with which Paul was unlikely to be familiar, and only then is the possibility of a secretary greatly increased. Yet the presence of a secretary in Romans is already evident at Rom. 16:22. Similarly the presence of the secretary in Galatians is already clear because of his remark in Gal. 6:11.[243]

---

[239] *Cf.* 1 Cor. 16:8 and Acts 20:16. See, *e.g.*, the reconstruction of Kümmel, *Introduction*, 293.

[240] Assuming any of the prison letters had a Caesarean origin.

[241] It is an appropriate question: did Paul ask himself 'What letter form shall I use?' Although perhaps unconsciously, even we consider this as we pick up the pen. What is this letter's purpose: recommendation, business, personal, love, defense, information? The answer may affect the letter form we use.

[242] See H. D. Betz, *Galatians*, esp. 16–23.

[243] Without the evidence from 6:11, the case is quite weak. For the letter-type to indicate a secretary, the argument must run: Galatians is an example of a highly structured form of classical rhetoric, such as an apologetic letter. Paul was unable to write such a letter — arguing from his background and perhaps a literal interpretation of 2 Cor. 10:10. Therefore a secretary must be responsible for the structure of the letter, acting in the role of an extensive editor, or probably a co-author, or possibly even a composer.

This example also illustrates the major problem with the criterion. Betz's classification of Galatians is disputed. For example, Robert Hall ("The Rhetorical Outline for Galatians: a Reconsideration", *JBL* 106 (1987): 277–87), a former student of George Kennedy, recently argued that Betz has placed Galatians into the wrong rhetorical category entirely!

dd) Stylistic Variations in an Authentic Letter

Although this is the most reliable implicit indicator of a secretary, it is also the most disputed. The purpose of this indicator, however, is *not* to determine authenticity which must be demonstrated by other means.[244] Its purpose is to say that *if* a letter is deemed authentic and also meets one of these two conditions, then secretarial mediation is a likely explanation.[245]

Establishing a Pauline Standard of Form, Style, and Diction

Determining the writing style of Paul from such a limited sample and a sample that has such diverse occasions is a very troublesome problem.

He maintains that Galatians is not part of the judicial species of rhetoric but of the deliberative. As a result, he proposes a different outline:

H. D. Betz:	Robert Hall:
1. Epistolary Prescript (1:1−5)	1. Salutation (1:1−5)
2. Exordium (1:6−11)	2. Proposition (1:6−9)
3. Narratio (1:12−2:14)	3. Proof [Probatio] (1:10−6:10)
4. Propositio (2:15−21)	A. Narration (1:10−2:21)
5. Probatio (3:1−4:31)	B. Further Headings (3:1−6:10)
6. Exhortatio (5:1−6:10)	
7. Epistolary Postscript (6:11−18)	4. Epilogue (6:11−18)

See also G. Kennedy, *New Testament Interpretation Through Rhetorical Criticism*, Studies in Religion Series (Chapel Hill: University of North Carolina, 1984), 144−52. *Cf.* also, quite recently, J. Smit, "The Letter of Paul to the Galatians: a Deliberative Speech", NTS 35 (1989): 1−26.

[244] The opposite starting point (inauthenticity) is not considered because if the letter is assumed pseudonymous, then the issue of secretarial mediation is not significant.

[245] The problem becomes more complex. The role of a secretary can account for many − although perhaps not all − of the factors used to argue for the rejection of a letter. *E.g.*, Leander Keck and Victor Furnish, *The Pauline Letters*, Interpreting Biblical Texts Series (Nashville: Abingdon, 1984), 56, typify the arguments for rejection: (1) there are numerous differences in form, function, style, vocabulary, and theological point of view; (2) in at least one case (2 Th.) there is clear literary dependence on the Apostle's own writing; (3) certain issues and situations addressed in these letters do not correspond with those Paul is likely to have confronted; and (4) it is virtually impossible to fit some of these letters (notably the Pastorals) into the chronology implied by the authentic letters.

The last two issues are certainly disputed and usually are maintained only if the letters are already considered inauthentic. The first problem is certainly real (although I would dispute whether there are significant differences in form and function). A secretary, however, can easily account for all these differences. I am not sure why the second item is considered a problem. It has already been demonstrated that writers reused material from previous letters (see the discussion above, p. 5).

Nonetheless there have been reasonably successful efforts to establish a Pauline style.[246] Even the use of statistical procedures probably has some validity.[247] The major work in this area, by A. Q. Morton and James McLeman,[248] has been severly criticized.[249] The same approach but with a better text and technique has been taken recently by Anthony Kenny.[250]

A few words should be said about using the conclusions of these statistical procedures. First, they may all be faulted for failing to recognized preformed tradition-pieces within the Pauline letters. These must be eliminated or the data will be skewed.[251] Of course, this creates the possibility of a circular method (eliminate everything non-Pauline and the remainder comes out Pauline), but there are passages that are recognized widely enough as preformed material that they can be safely eliminated.

Second, although Morton and McLeman recognize the possible influence of a secretary, they dismiss it without any true consideration.[252] To the assertion that Paul used a secretary they reply: "The rejoinder to this assertion is that this is something which we do not know". Yet we do know that Paul used a secretary. They further argue "Homer was blind

---

[246] See, *e.g.*, N. Turner, *Style*, 80.

[247] The first major work to use statistical analysis to determine style was P. N. Harrison, *The Problem of the Pastorals* (London: Oxford University, 1921).

[248] *Paul, the Man and the Myth: a Study in the Authorship of Greek Prose* (London: Hodder & Stoughton, 1966).

[249] The approach of Morton (as seen in a summary article by S. Michaelson and A. Q. Morton, "Last Words: a Test of Authorship for Greek Writers", *NTS* 18 [1972]: 192–208) has been criticized strongly by P. F. Johnson, "The Use of Statistics in the Analysis of the Characteristics of Pauline Writing", *NTS* 20 (1973): 92–100.

G. U. Yule, *The Statistical Study of Literary Vocabulary* (Cambridge: Cambridge University, 1944), 281, sounded what has been the rallying cry of many who oppose statistical methodologies: for a proper comparison, the samples must be larger than 10, 000 words and be similar in length and subject matter; see, *e.g.*, E. E. Ellis, "The Authorship of the Pastorals: a Résumé and Assessment of Recent Trends", in *Paul and His Recent Interpreters* (Grand Rapids: Eerdmans, 1961), 54. More recent works have profited from Type-Token-Ratio analysis used in other fields and have avoided some of the pitfalls of the older analyses. *E.g.*, W. C. Wake, "Numbers, Paul and Rational Dissent", *Faith and Freedom* [Oxford] 37 (1984): 59–72, uses statistical criteria like sentence length, distribution of καί, and position of words. His work is not without problems, however; see the critique by P. Trudinger, "Computers and the Authorship of the Pauline Epistles", *Faith and Freedom* 39 (1986): 24–27.

[250] *A Stylometric Study of the New Testament* (Oxford: Clarendon, 1986). It remains to be seen if Kenny's work has answered the objections to his predecessors.

[251] Obviously the more that a letter cites traditional material the greater will be its overall divergence from Paul.

[252] Morton and McLeman, *Paul*, 94–95.

and must have used one but no Homeric scholar has felt obliged to defend the purity of the text against the amanuensis". *If* Homer were blind, he must have used a secretary throughout his work. There would be no variances because there are no texts from Homer's hand alone. Josephus does use a secretary in various roles, and the secretary *is* used to explain some differences.[253] Why are Morton and McLeman so eager to dismiss the possible influence of a secretary? Is it because they found no divergences among the letters of Paul? They found numerous ones. They wish to dismiss the secretary because he can ruin their thesis. Since there are numerous differences among the letters of Paul — and this is their thesis — the differences can be explained only by different authors. Thus Paul did not author many of the letters.[254] The problems with their methodology are too numerous to discuss here and have been corrected largely in the subsequent work of Anthony Kenny.

Third, the work of Anthony Kenny has produced remarkably different conclusions.[255] (1) There is a great deal of diversity among the thirteen letters.[256] Yet they all contain about the same amount of commonality.

> There is no support given by [the data] to the idea that a single group of Epistles (say the four major Tübingen Epistles) stand out as uniquely comfortable with one another; or that a singe group (such as the Pastoral Epistles) stand out as uniquely diverse from the surrounding context.[257]

(2) If one takes a rough measure of how well each letter is 'at home' in the Pauline corpus, the following ranking results (from the most comfortable to the least): Romans, Philippians, 2 Timothy, 2 Corinthians, Galatians, 2 Thessalonians, 1 Thessalonians, Colossians, Ephesians, 1 Timothy, Philemon, 1 Corinthians, and Titus. Most would expect Romans and Philippians to be near the top and Titus to be near the bottom,

---

[253] See the discussion above, pp. 157—58.

[254] They assert Pauline authorship for the *Hauptbriefe* only. The rest came from six different hands (Morton and McLeman, *Paul*, 94). Actually they can only demonstrate commonality among these four letters by eliminating a large number of "anomalies", places where they diverge from each other.

[255] This is due evidently to the use of a better text (Aland's) and technique (*e.g.*, see Kenny, *Stylometric*, 80, and (his) table 14.2, also 107—110). His lack of the hostility so quickly evident in Morton and McLeman also enables him to be more objective. He may be further contrasted to them by his hesitancy to make sweeping conclusions even when he has considerably more data (*e.g.*, p. 95).

[256] How the removal of any traditional material from the raw data might alter the degree of commonality is worth research.

[257] Kenny, *Stylometric*, 99—100.

but much of the rest of the list is surprising, such as finding 2 Timothy as near the center as 2 Corinthians.

Kenny makes no attempt to explain why the letters have such divergences — he is not a New Testament scholar — except to say that if there was one author (and not thirteen) then he must have been rather versatile (but not unreasonably so).[258] If there was not one author, then statistically there is *no case* for arguing that one man was responsible for a certain group of letters.

There are two possible explanations: (1) Kenny's stylistic analysis is not precise enough to discriminate authorship, or (2) somehow one man produced some very different letters. A major purpose of stylometry (stylistic analysis) is to determine authorship, and it has been argued to be rather reliable.[259] Therefore the second possibility should be considered. Multiple authors is not a reasonable alternative. There is such divergence that in order to assume that there were less than thirteen authors one must group together letters that are diverse enough that all the letters would fit (with the possible exception of Titus).[260] The more reasonable option is to assume that "... twelve of the Pauline Epistles are the work of a single, unusually versatile author".[261]

Certainly the outstanding apostle of early Christianity qualifies as versatile, but the wide variation among the letters may have a simpler explanation: a secretary can explain both the commonalities and the differences.[262] There is enough commonality to maintain that they probably had the same author. Yet there are enough differences to require some type of mediating element, and a secretary was the most common type in antiquity. One preliminary means to test this explanation is to compare the letters that are most likely to have been written without secretarial mediation. They should have a high degree of commonality. Unfortunately only Philippians has any chance of being from the hand of Paul himself.[263] Yet Romans may also qualify. If it was dictated,[264] then it should resemble Philippians stylometrically. This is in fact the case. "Romans and Philippians can therefore be regarded as at the centre of the

---

[258] Ibid., 95. He later entertains the theory that Paul's style changed as he grew older (pp. 109–10).

[259] Kenny defends the reliability and validity of his method; ibid., 1–4.

[260] Ibid., 92, 95. Co-authorship could explain the differences in some of the letters but not all.

[261] Ibid., 100.

[262] See the brief discussion of this possibility in Ellis, "Authorship", 55–56.

[263] This possibility is discussed below, pp. 189–90.

[264] As argued above, pp. 170–72.

constellation".[265] The possibility that the secretary's influence can be demonstrated stylometrically in Paul deserves future attention.[266]

Deviating Letters that Contain Argumentation, Tone, or Content Suggesting Paul

As discussed previously, a letter was accepted as authentic if it purported to be from the author (and had a reasonable chance of being so) and contained larger aspects, such as argumentation, tone, or content, that was consistent with the author, *because* a secretary could account for the other differences.[267] Consequently, if a Pauline letter is considered authentic, perhaps because it claims to be Pauline and contains larger elements that suggest Pauline authorship, then a secretary may account for the differences.[268]

Deviating Letters that Match the Style of a Trusted Colleague

When Cicero received a letter from Pompey that he recognized as actually written by Sestius, he still did not question the letter's authenticity, that is, he assumed that the purpose and general content of the letter must still have been what Pompey wanted.[269] This was assumed by virtue of the trust that existed between Pompey and Sestius. Likewise, it was the trust between Cicero and Brutus that prevented Cicero from writing pseudonymously in Brutus' name.[270]

A parallel exists for the the Pauline letters, if the Pastorals do indeed have great similarity to the writings of Luke.[271] While usually any simi-

---

[265] Kenny, *Stylometric*, 98. Their slight variance may have resulted from (1) a slight influence from Tertius, or more likely (2) the difference between dictating (*viva voce*) and either writing personally or dictating more slowly.

[266] Further work should include a new analysis of the letters after eliminating the preformed tradition-pieces.

[267] See the discussion above, pp. 92—97.

[268] The role of a co-author, *i.e.*, one named in the address, should also be considered in any explanation.

[269] Cic. *Att.* 7.17. See the discussion above, pp. 96—97.

[270] Cic. *Att.* 15.3—4; or above, p. 96.

[271] See H. J. Holtzmann, *Die Pastoralbriefe* (Leipzig: Engelmann, 1880), 92*ff*. Robert Scott, *The Pastoral Epistles* (Edinburgh: T & T Clark, 1909), 329—71, argues for Lukan authorship (after the death of Paul) because (1) a similarity of general vocabulary; (2) passages that suggest interdependence with Lukan writings; (3) the use of medical terminology [probably not a valid point]; (4) the familiarity with the religious ideas of Greece; and (5) a similar use of favorite words, idioms and terms. (He does allow for Luke as a secretary,

larity is used to argue that Luke wrote for Paul after his death, the more likely argument is that Luke was writing as Paul's secretary. Otto Roller suggests that the rigorous conditions of Roman imprisonment would make the use of a secretary necessary.[272] C. Spicq, contends, however, that the "rigors" of prison should not be overdone, since Ignatius and others were able to write from imprisonments as well.[273] Yet Ignatius apparently used a secretary.[274] Moreover, Paul evidently uses a secretary during his (first?) imprisonment in Rome (Col. 4:18).

If Luke was Paul's secretary, he may perhaps be compared with an established example: Eumenes, the secretary of Alexander the Great. First, Eumenes was a trusted friend and advisor of Alexander, in addition to being his personal secretary.[275] Second, he was given a share in the affairs of Alexander, even given command of troops when the need or opportunity arose.[276] Thus he was allowed to take an active part in the mission of Alexander. Finally, he wrote a descriptive account of the exploits of Alexander, called the *Ephemerides of Alexander*. Plutarch mentions this work as he discusses the final days of Alexander and states that "Most of this account [Plutarch's] is word for word as written in the *Ephemerides*."[277] Plutarch's account is narrative, speaking of Alexander in the third person and, assuming the rest of the the *Ephemerides* is the same, has similarities to the book of Acts.[278] Of course this discussion begins with the debatable issue of whether Luke's style is discernible in the Pastoral letters.

All four implicit indicators suggest the presence of the secretary in letters of Paul where there is not explicit evidence.[279] Unfortunately the

---

p. 353). But *cf.* James Moffatt, *Introduction to the Literature of the New Testament*, The International Theological Library Series (New York: Scribner's Sons, 1911), 414.

[272] Roller, *Formular*, 20—21. He means using the secretary as an editor or a co-author. Also see J. Jeremias, *Briefe an Timotheus und Titus*, 2d ed. (Göttingen: Vandenhoeck & Ruprecht, 1981), 5—6. J. A. Eschlimann, "La rédaction", 188—89, asserts that dictation *syllabatim* was not possible but that using the secretary as a co-author was [using my terms]. So generally also A. Nairne, *The Faith of the New Testament* (London: Longmans, Green & Co., 1920), 60—61.

[273] Spicq, *Les epîtres pastorales*, 2 vols., 4th ed., (Paris: Études bibliques, 1947), 1: CXIX.

[274] See the discussion above, pp. 70—72.

[275] Cornelius Nepos *De Viris Illustribus* 18.1.4—6; Plut. *Eum.* 1.

[276] Plut. *Eum.* 1.

[277] Plut. *Alex.* 76—77.

[278] Is there another point of similarity between Eumenes the secretary and Luke. As a good secretary Eumenes kept copies of the letters he wrote (see the discussion above, p. 6 n. 30). Did the various secretaries of Paul retain copies that Paul kept with him? Also see the discussion above, pp. 6—7 and 165 n. 169.

[279] All the results are summarized in Table 4, p. 190.

more reliable indicators are less relevant to the letters of Paul, because they begin with debated starting points.

3. An Evaluation of Paul's Use of a Secretary

It has been ascertained *with certainty* that Paul frequently used a secretary.[280] Unfortunately it cannot be ascertained *with certainty* in what role he used him. Nevertheless, enough is known of secretarial practices in general and the situational factors of Paul in specific to allow for some probable conclusions.

a) The Pauline Letters Written With Secretarial Assistance

The results of the foregoing application of the criteria to the letters of Paul appears in Table 4 in which his use of a secretary is ranked for each letter on a scale of 'certain', 'probable', 'possible', 'improbable', and 'unascertainable'.

From the table it is clear that six of the letters were certainly written with secretarial assistance: Romans, 1 Corinthians, Galatians, 2 Thessalonians, Colossians, and Philemon. All six contain explicit evidence (and many have implicit indicators). Their use of a secretary is rated 'certain'.

Two other letters, 2 Corinthians and 1 Thessalonians, contain two strong implicit indications of a secretary. (1) Both probably have autographed postscripts.[281] (2) Both have a precedent for secretarial use from the same geographical area and chronological period (*i.e.*, 1 Corinthians and 2 Thessalonians). Although the case for 1 Thessalonians is stronger than for 2 Corinthians, a secretary is considered 'probable' for both letters.

Philippians contains no evidence of a secretary nor any implicit indicators.[282] It is quite confessional and discloses an unusual amount of personal compassion for the recipients.[283] If the use of a secretary did imply even a slight sense of a lack of personal concern for the recipients,[284] then

---

[280] See the discussion above, pp. 169–75.

[281] The additional remarks in the postscript of 2 Thessalonians about his custom of autographing a postscript implies that *at least* the previous postscript (1 Th. 5:27–28?) also was autographed.

[282] I am not taking into account Paul's remark in 2 Th. 3:17, which makes a secretary possible in any letter.

[283] See *e.g.*, Kümmel, *Introduction*, 322–23.

[284] *E.g.*, Cicero appears to apologize to his brother (*QFr.* 2.2.1) for using a secretary ra-

Table 4

The Evidence for the Use of a Secretary in the Letters of Paul

	Explicit Evidence				Implicit Indicators		
	Co-sender	References by the author	References by the Secretary	Changes in Handwriting	Post-Scripts[a]	Preferences of the Author	Particular Letter Type	Stylistic Variations in an Authentic Letter
Rom.		16:22				Ch. 16?		
1 Cor.	1			16:21	16:22–24			
2 Cor.	1				Chs. 10–13?	1 Cor. ?		
Gal.	?			6:11	6:12–18		Rhet. ?	
Eph.							Cycl. ?	
Phil.	1							
Col.	1			4:18	4:18b			
1 Th.	2				5:27–28?	2 Th.?[b]		
2 Th.	2			3:17	3:17–18			
1 Tim.						In prison?		Lukan?
2 Tim.						In prison?		Lukan?
Tit.						In prison?		Lukan?
Philem.	1			19	20–25			

[a] 2 Th. 3:17 makes postscripts possible in all of Paul's letters (see above, p. 174), but this is not included in the table.

[b] The matter of mere preferences may be strengthened because of the close chronological and geographical origins of these letters. Also, do the forgery in 2 Th. 2:2 and the explicit noting of the look of his handwriting (οὕτως γράφω) imply that the Thessalonians were not familiar with his handwriting? If 1 Thessalonians was written first, then this strongly implies the use of a secretary with 1 Thessalonians.

Paul may have chosen to write personally in his own hand to this church to whom he was so indebted (Phil. 4). Yet this is hardly convincing. For the common man who lacked the leisure to write personally, the use of a secretary probably carried no ill connotations. Because of the lack of indicators, however, the use of a secretary for this letter is rated 'unascertainable'.[285]

---

ther than writing in his own hand. The clear implication is that Quintus would interpret the secretarial mediation as a sign of Cicero's unwillingness (and not his inability) to write personally. See p. 69.

[285] This, however, does *not* take into account two additional factors which greatly increase the probability of secretarial use in *all* the letters of Paul: (1) the implication that all of his letters contained an autographed postscript whether explicitly mentioned or not

If Ephesians was a cyclical letter derived generally from the letter to the Colossians,[286] then this may be an implicit indicator. A secretary was clearly used for Colossians, and secretaries were certainly used to prepare additional copies. If this was the case, then the secretary was probably told to take a copy of the letter to the Colossians and to make certain changes as specified by Paul.

This suggestion is hardly original and traditionally is rejected for several reasons. (1) The secretary would hardly have access to all the Pauline letters with which Ephesians has contacts. (2) His work would not have reflected the same kind of literary relationship with Colossians. The similarity would have been more in phraseology. (3) He would not have enlarged the ethical sections as Ephesians has done. (4) This theory does not explain the author's references to himself (*i.e.*, first person references) in Ephesians. (5) Finally, there is no motive for Paul to have adopted so unusual a procedure.

There is, however, some response against each argument. (1) There is actually a higher probability that a secretary would have access to the letters of Paul during Paul's lifetime than would a disciple after the death of Paul and before A.D. 120 (the *terminus ad quem*, for Ignatius and Polycarp clearly know Ephesians). It is quite likely that Paul retained personal copies of his letters; it was common for a writer to keep copies of even ordinary letters.[287] For a collection to be available to a later disciple implies an early collection (and veneration?) of Paul's letters in the last half of the first century,[288] which is less likely. (2) This second objection has validity if the secretary was a contracted professional. If the secretary was

---

(2 Th. 3:17); and (2) the sheer tedium, effort (skill), and time required to write personally letters of such length (for 'tedium', see, *e.g.*, Wikenhauser, *Einleitung*, 245–46).

[286] Based either upon a "gap" in the letter address (so Schlier, Albertz, Harrington, Henshaw, Klijn, Percy) or upon the letter containing only the generic address (so Feine-Behm, Guthrie, Michaelis; M. Goguel, "Esquisse d'une solution nouvelle du problème de l'épître aux Ephésiens", *RHR* 111 (1935): 254*ff.*; and Cadbury, "The Dilemma of Ephesians", *NTS* 5 (1958): 91–102.). See D. Guthrie, *New Testament Introduction* (Downers Grove, IL: Inter-Varsity, 1970), 128 n. 1. See also the discussion, "Die Epheseradresse und die Zirkularbriefhypothese," in O. Roller, *Formular*, 199–212.

[287] This is argued above, pp. 3–4. The specific problem of the parallel endorsements of Tychicus in Eph. 6:21–22 and Col. 4:7–8 is not so difficult. Such a routine endorsement is quite likely to be reused by a secretary in another letter, particularly if the letter has a different destination but is to be delivered by the same carrier. *Cf.* the frequent repetitions of routine endorsements of the carriers in Ignatius' letters. The situations are quite parallel (discussed above, pp. 70–72), and his endorsements have a stereotypical tone. It may be less likely that a *forger* would so blatantly reveal his pattern-source.

[288] See the discussion by Harry Gamble, *Canon*, 36–43.

allowed some freedom and he was member of the Pauline band, he easily might add material he has heard from Paul's preaching or even from his own theology. He would have been a contributing colleague of Paul, a συνεργός. (3) Actually the opposite point is likely: if the secretary was going to add material, he is more likely to add it in the paraenetic sections, based either upon *topoi* common in the Pauline band or perhaps his personal preference for material from the Hellenistic-Jewish *Haustafeln* or Qumran.[289] (4) If he is writing as Paul's secretary, regardless of the amount of material he himself may insert, he must still write from the viewpoint of Paul as author (since Paul ultimately must assume responsibility for the content[290]). (5) Finally, the procedure was not as unusual as some suggest.[291] Irrespective of these responses, this theory has not received widespread acceptance,[292] and thus Paul's use of a secretary in Ephesians is considered only 'possible'.

If one accepts the Pastorals as Pauline,[293] then a secretary can explain some of their differences from the other Pauline correspondence.[294] Al-

---

[289] See Kümmel, *Introduction*, 365; also see J. Murphy-O'Conner, "La 'vérité' chez Saint Paul et à Qumrān", *RB* 72 (1965): 50—60; Herbert Braun, *Qumran und das Neue Testament* (Tübingen: Mohr, 1966), 1: 286—300; E. Käsemann, "Das Interpretationsproblem des Epheserbriefes", *TLZ* 86 (1961): 1—8; and K. G. Kuhn, "Der Epheserbrief im Lichte der Qumrantexte", *NTS* 7 (1961): 346.

[290] See the discussion of responsibility above, pp. 53—56.

[291] *E.g.*, E. Percy, *Die Probleme der Kolosser- und Epheserbriefe*, (Lund: Gleerup, 1946), 421—22.

[292] I am not fully persuaded by the theory despite the counterarguments. M. Barth briefly summarizes the four modern opinions on the authorship of Ephesians: (a) Paul, (b) an outline or impulse was provided by Paul and fleshed out by another, (c) non-Paul, (d) a cautious suspension of judgment (*Ephesians*, AB 1:38). He also briefly discusses the possibility of a secretary using basically the same four roles (1: 40—41). A secretary would fall under the first two options. M. Barth, however, will apparently argue for the priority of Colossians in his forthcoming work on Colossians in the AB.

[293] As do, *e.g.*, D. Guthrie, *The Pastoral Epistles*, Tyndale New Testament Commentary Series (London: Tyndale, 1957), 584-624; J. N. D. Kelly, *A Commentary on the Pastoral Epistles*, HNTC (London: Harper, 1963; reprint, Thornapple Commentary Series, Grand Rapids: Baker, 1981), 3—36; and perhaps most thoroughly C. Spicq, *Les épîtres pastorales*. See also Ellis, "Authorship", 49—57. More recently, see Gordon Fee, *1 and 2 Timothy, Titus*, Good News Commentary Series (San Francisco: Harper & Row, 1984); and the cautious evaluation by Luke Johnson, *Writings of the New Testament: an Interpretation* (Philadelphia: Fortress, 1986), 381—89. But *cf.* Kümmel, *Introduction*, 367—87.

[294] Its best early defender was O. Roller, *Formular*. It has recently been revived by J. Jeremias, *Die Briefe an Timotheus und Titus*; W. Metzger, *Die letzte Reise des Apostels Paulus* (Stuttgart: Calwer, 1976); and tentatively by C. F. D. Moule, "The Problem of the Pastoral Epistles: a Reappraisal", *BJRL* 47 (1965): 450—2. B. M. Metzger has perhaps softened his stance from a defense ("A Reconsideration of Certain Arguments against Pauline Au-

though not necessary for the thesis, the supporters of this view often attempt to identify the secretary. For example, Jeremias believes it may have been Tychicus. A large group, however, favor Luke, although often it is argued that he composed the letters after Paul's death.[295] The most thorough attempt to identify Luke's hand in the Pastorals has been done by S. G. Wilson,[296] although he favors Luke as a composing disciple and not as a secretary.

It is unnecessary to critique the secretary theory in general or Wilson's identification of Luke in specific here, but three general issues about the role of the secretary as an explanation for the Pastoral letters resurface frequently and deserve attention. A. T. Hanson in his newer commentary on the Pastoral letters, notes that "there are grave difficulties facing the secretary hypothesis".[297] (1) Hanson argues that 2 Timothy fits the secretary hypothesis much better than the other two, since for example it has Paul in the rigors of prison. Yet, in response to this "difficulty", this problem is not directly related to the role of the secretary. The hypothesis should not be built from a proposed epistolary situation but from the letters themselves. (2) Hanson argues that if the secretary is given credit for much of the letters then the whole purpose of the secretary theory (to defend Pauline authorship) is defeated. Yet, in response, to what purpose the theory is put is irrelevant. Furthermore his contention is just not the case. He and others who fail to see much difference between the secretary and the fragmentary hypotheses[298] have not recognized the issue of authorial responsibility. As demonstrated previously,[299] when using a secretary, even as a composer, the author assumed complete responsibility for the content and exercised this duty usually by checking, editing, or even correcting the draft. Finally, (3) Hanson asks incredulously, "Are we to envisage a secretary who

---

thorship of the Pastoral Epistles", *ExpTim* 70 (1958): 91–92) to an uncontested reporting of the popular theories (*The New Testament: Its Background, Growth, and Content*, 2d ed. enl. (Nashville: Abingdon, 1983), 238–39). The theory merits more than the casual rejection it usually receives; *e.g.*, in M. Dibelius and H. Conzelmann, *The Pastoral Epistles*, 5.

[295] *E.g.*, see A. Strobel, "Schreiben des Lukas? Zum sprachlichen Problem der Pastoralbriefe", *NTS* 15 (1969): 191–210.

[296] *Luke and the Pastoral Epistles* (London: S.P.C.K., 1979).

[297] *The Pastoral Epistles*, The New Century Bible Commentary Series (Grand Rapids: Eerdmans, 1982), 8–10. In his earlier commentary, *The Pastoral Letters: a Commentary on the First and Second Letters to Timothy and the Letter to Titus*, The Cambridge Bible Commentary Series (Cambridge: Cambridge University, 1966), he had adopted the fragment theory.

[298] *E.g.*, Dibelius and Conzelmann, *Pastoral Epistles*, 5.

[299] See above, pp. 53–56.

wrote largely on his own initiative what he thought Paul would have said?" Even to such an extreme instance, the answer given by Cicero is 'yes'. Cicero repeatedly asks Atticus — not Tiro — to do that very thing, because at that moment he had not the time nor the heart for letter writing.[300] Secretaries, however, were not usually used in such a 'carte blanche' manner. Hanson's question should be reworded into a form that is more suited to the evidence: "are we to envisage a secretary who developed out the major point or points suggested by Paul?" Again the answer may be 'yes'.

Be all this as it may, this criterion neither proves nor disproves Pauline authorship for the Pastoral epistles.[301] This is not the purpose. If however the letters are accepted as Pauline, then the variations in style and somewhat in viewpoint and theology may be explained by the influence of a secretary. Therefore, if the Pastorals are Pauline, then the presence of a secretary should be considered very 'probable'.

b) Toward an Analysis of Paul's Method of Using a Secretary

How does Paul use his secretary? Not only in what role does the secretary act, but also how would Paul likely integrate his use of a secretary into his other missionary activities? One may even ask, when would he likely not use a secretary?[302] Two general areas should be discussed. (1) First and most importantly, in what role did the secretary function for Paul? This must be examined on a letter by letter basis and even then may suffer from over- simplification, because there is nothing to prevent Paul from using a secretary in several ways within the same letter. The following suggestions are only preliminary. (2) The second area of analysis is a comparison of some of the attributes of other secretary-assisted letters to his letters.

---

[300] See Cic. Att. 11.5; 11.11 (above, p. 50).

[301] Pauline authorship for the Pastorals does, however, merit serious reconsideration because (as has been noted): (a) the mediating role of the secretary; (b) the possible influence of the co-senders; and (c) their large use of preformed tradition-pieces. Prof. Earle Ellis has mentioned (in a private conversation) that over 41% of 1 Tim., 46% of Tit., and 16% of 2 Tim. are preformed traditions. (Note how A. Kenny's stylometric analysis coincides with this, in that 2 Tim is placed significantly nearer the Pauline 'center' than 1 Tim. or Tit. See above, pp. 185−86.)

[302] Because Cicero used personal secretaries whom he trusted, as likely did Paul, their preferences have some commonality. Cicero apparently does not use a secretary when the matter was secret or urgent, or when a secretary was not available. Such possibilities in Paul merit future attention.

The first investigation begins by setting the parameters within which Paul's secretary probably operated. On the one extreme, there is dictation *viva voce*. Because special training was required for this skill, it is unlikely that Paul had a tachygraphist available for him to use as he travelled. This is not to exclude the possibility for any particular letter. As argued previously, it is possible that Tertius, the secretary for the Roman letter, was able to take dictation *viva voce*.[303] Nevertheless, the odds are against such a luxury for the majority of Paul's letters.[304] On the other extreme, there is the use of a secretary as a composer. As also indicated previously,[305] such a use was rare – if not unpracticed – in antiquity and appears to have occurred in only two ways (at least among Cicero and his friends): (a) the author specifically mentions the matter and was apparently motivated by practicality; or (b) the author *deceptively* omitted any notification and was apparently motivated by an unwillingness to write himself (with Cicero it was caused by depression) but nonetheless a desire (or need) to send a letter. It is unlikely that Paul permitted such a practice, arguing situationally not ethically. Only perhaps during a second Roman imprisonment could an analogous situation be pictured for Paul. Interestingly, in every case where the ancient private letter did not indicate that the secretary composed it, the 'composing secretary' was *never* a mere secretary but a known and trusted associate of the author.

One may then assume that most of Paul's letters were written with a secretary acting as a recorder *syllabatim*, an editor, or a co-author. Since an editorial role was the most common, this is likely the role for Paul's secretary. A letter by letter (perhaps even a section by section) analysis is needed before further differentiation can be made.[306]

In the second area, certain characteristics of other secretary-assisted letters may have similarities to Paul's. Paul's use of the κοινή Greek has been cited as indicating his poorer educational level and concommitantly

---

[303] See the discussion above, pp. 170–72.

[304] 'Luxury' is not meant merely to connote money. It is very unlikely Paul paid for secretarial help. His secretaries were probably volunteers or their services were provided by a wealthy benefactor.

[305] See above, pp. 107–111.

[306] This is done to a limited extent in the preceding section. A much more detailed examination is needed along the lines of the analysis done by E. I. Robson, "Composition and Dictation", 289–300. He works through the Roman letter but only attempts to differentiate those passages that were dictated extemporaneously from those that were first composed in rough draft.

his lower social status. Yet Cicero[307] and Seneca[308] argue that *letters* should be in the everyday speech.

Letters could be used to speak more boldly than would be done in person. In a letter to Lucceius, who was planning to write a history of Rome, Cicero is attempting to persuade Lucceius to include him, a rather bold request. Interestingly Cicero comments that in presence he is unimpressive but in a letter he will be bold.[309] Comparisons to Paul suggest themselves.[310]

The author's mood has affected a letter even when filtered through a secretary. This was seen not only in the content of the letter[311] but in the quality as well. When Cicero was in exile, he claimed literary incompetence and listlessness, unable – actually unwilling – to write up to the level of his ability.[312] Perhaps it is unreasonable to expect a 'Romans' or another *Hauptbrief* from Paul during an imprisonment.

Letters in antiquity could have an interval of time hidden within them. Cicero composed a letter and after some time, picked up the letter again. Cicero specifically stated that he has done this but apparently only because the situation had changed, rendering a remark in the first part of the letter obsolete.[313] It was not worth rewriting the letter. Several observations made be made. (1) Apparently some time had elapsed during the writing of the two parts of the letter. (2) The letter was probably not detained awaiting the further news, since the matter was merely one of minor gossip. (3) Lastly, he noted the passage of time *because* it has rendered obsolete a remark earlier in the letter. Presumably, had nothing significant changed, no notation would have been made. An interval of

---

[307] *Fam.* 9.21.1: "how do I strike you in my letters? Don't I seem to talk to you in the language of common folk? ... What similarity is there between a letter and a speech in court or at a public meeting? ... but my letters I generally compose in the language of everyday life".

[308] *Ep.* 75.1: "I prefer that my letters should be just what my conversation would be ... for my letters have nothing strained or artificial about them".

[309] Cic. *Fam.* 5.12; "Often when I have attempted to discuss this topic with you face to face, I have been deterred by a sort of almost boorish bashfulness; but now that I am away from you I shall bring it all out with greater boldness; for a letter does not blush".

[310] 1 Cor. 2:3 and 2 Cor. 10:10. In the case of Cicero at least, this may not be all rhetoric. Plutarch records that it was said of Cicero that he was weak in his delivery and that he often trembled and shook with fear as he spoke (Plut. *Cic.* 5.3–4 and 35.3).

[311] See Cic. *Att.* 3.8; "From these rambling notes of mine, you can see the perturbed state of my wits". He was currently "crushed and overwhelmed with grief".

[312] See Cic. *Att.* 3.7.8 and Tyrell and Purser, *Cicero*, 1: 77.

[313] Cic. *Fam.* 8.6.5; "I wrote to you above that Curio was very cold; well, he is warm enough now; ... he had not done so before I wrote the first part of this letter".

time, however, can have many more results than merely rendering facts obsolete, such as the changing of moods or attitudes.[314]

Paul and Cicero shared a method of letter response, suggesting that it was a standard procedure. In a responding letter, Cicero addressed each issue in turn,[315] using the same pattern as Paul's περὶ δέ in 1 Cor. 7:1, 25; 8:1. Notably, both examples occur in letters written with the use of a secretary.

Secretary-assisted letters often included details that the author would not trouble to add if writing himself. For example, Cicero's letter via a secretary included a long flattering description of the work of some library slaves, mentioning them by name.[316] Similarly, the secretary for the letter to the Romans could account for the long list of greetings. As a good secretary he included details for which Paul himself elsewhere displays little concern. Galatians has no greetings nor does 2 Thessalonians. Philippians has only a generic greeting "Ἀσπάσασθε πάντα ἅγιον ἐν χριστῷ Ἰησοῦ," as does 1 Thessalonians. Yet Colossians has a long list of greetings *before* Paul picked up the pen (in v. 18). 1 Cor. 16:20 and 2 Cor. 13:12 have only generic greetings, and these are also before the Pauline postscript.

Some pragmatic restrictions inferred from other secretary-assisted letters may have applications to Paul. Cicero remarked in a note that he cannot write a decent letter while their ship was out to sea.[317] Presumably Paul also did not write during his times aboard ship.

Cicero warned Atticus:

> You must not expect long letters from me nor always letters in my own handwriting; till I have settled down somewhere. When I have time I will guarantee both. I am now engaged on a hot and dusty journey.[318]

Elsewhere in the letter he indicated that he was dictating in the evening during an overnight stop at Tralles. Evidently the rigors of travelling (and Cicero usually travelled in a carriage) prevented an overnight stop from being sufficiently conducive for writing long letters even when dic-

---

[314] *Cf.* the note on 2 Cor. 10–13 above, p. 181 n. 236.
[315] Cic. *Fam.* 3.8.2, 4, 10; *Fam.* 12.30 (*de . . . de . . .*).
[316] Cic. *Att.* 4.8. See the discussion above, p. 116.
[317] Cic. *Att.* 5.12. This may exclude personal notes that might be used in a later letter.
[318] Cic. *Att.* 5.14. Incidentally, here and elsewhere, it may be that Cicero's remarks about using a secretary were precipitated by complaints from Atticus. Cicero mentions it in the form of a defense: "I am dictating because . . ." Note also the clear defense in Cic. *Att.* 1.19.

tating. Since Paul did not travel in a carriage, it is even less likely that any of his letters were dashed off during a brief stop-over. The leisure time necessary for writing required a stop that was long enough to recuperate, to become settled, and probably to take care of the immediate missionary tasks.[319] If Cicero with all the accouterments of luxury was unable to write while travelling, then it is all the more unlikely for the footsore apostle.

---

[319] Cicero does on occasion answer a letter while actually on the road, but he indicates the unusual circumstances:
> Though the tax-farmers' messengers are actually on their road and I am travelling, still I think I must snatch a moment for fear you may imagine I have forgotten your commission. So I sit down on the high road to scribble you a summary of what really calls for a long epistle" (Cic. *Att.* 5.16).

The relevance to Paul is obviously minimal. Paul was unlikely to meet a messenger who was unable at least to follow him to the next town. Cicero a few days later writes a brief letter without pausing to stop, dictating while riding in the carriage (Cic. *Att.* 5.17).

Conclusion

There is more than sufficient evidence from Greco-Roman antiquity to describe the role of the secretary in letter writing. Both from (1) literarily-transmitted texts, such as descriptions in ancient handbooks of rhetorical letter writing, impromptu explanations from authors concerning their use of a secretary in a letter, and the information that can be inferred from these texts, and from (2) extant texts from the period surrounding the first Christian century, a picture emerges of the ancient secretary toiling in the service of his letter writing master. The implications of this image may be applied to the great letter writer and missionary of the first century, the Apostle Paul.

1. The Role of the Secretary in Greco-Roman Antiquity

The ancient secretary was not a tightly restricted servant. His duties and influences were loosely defined and were controlled largely by the abilities and desires of his employer. He was asked at times merely to *record* a letter that was dictated to him. Depending on his training and proficiency as well as the desire of the author, he recorded the dictation either at the speed of normal writing (*e.g.*, syllable-by-syllable, or phrase-by-phrase) or at the speed of normal speech (using shorthand, tachygraphy). In both cases the author (and thus the letter) was affected by the rate of delivery.

If the secretary was unskilled in shorthand (or if the author wished to present an incomplete draft), he could still accept the letter at the speed of speech. From his (incomplete) notes and with his knowledge of proper letter writing, the he drafted a finished letter, a letter that invariably contained some *editing*, whether deliberate or accidental. He could follow the same procedure if working from a written rough draft by the author.

On occasion the secretary received only a skeleton of a draft or with only brief instructions, perhaps because the author considered the letter routine or unimportant, or perhaps because the author considered himself to be less skilled in the proper content and form for that type of letter or less informed about the subject or situation. The secretary was left to complete the letter. Thus in some ways he became a *co-author* of the letter, contributing content (usually stereotypical material) as well as organization and form. The difference between this co-authorship and editing is only in the amount of content and direction the author offered and the amount of control and material he relinquished to his secretary. When he delegated much, then the secretary controlled the letter, at least until the draft was finished. Ultimately, however, the author assumed responsibility for what was written (and even what was omitted) and customarily checked the draft.

In rare circumstances an author could relinguish complete control to a secretary to *compose* a letter for him without any direction or specification of content, even without an indication of the exact recipient. Nevertheless the evidence for this practice in personal letters (*i.e.*, not in routine government or business correspondence) indicates that this secretarial role was very rare and given only to trusted colleagues of the author.[1] These men were not secretaries by vocation but peers of the author who were asked to compose letters in his stead.[2]

Thus great diversity existed in the various secretarial roles in personal letter writing, although the 'editorial' role was the most prominent. These roles, however, were not independent and distinct. They are actually artificial guideposts along a spectrum. The lines of distinction are blurred and were frequently crossed. Within one letter a secretary could serve in a hybrid of roles.

The ancient secretary was often a trained professional; yet he could be an amateur as well. Even an obliging friend or family member could serve as a secretary for another's letter. Thus among secretaries there was great variance in training and experience as well as in roles. All these variables must be considered when examining Paul's secretaries.

---

[1] The only exception I know is the 'letter' of Rufus to Cicero. Yet it is not a true letter but a compilation of newsworthy events. Even so, Rufus is at great pains to explain why he allowed a mere secretary such a role. See the discussion above, pp. 51–52.

[2] This does not automatically eliminate the possibility in the Pauline letters. Paul had his συνεργοί in the mission.

2. The Role of the Secretary in the Letters of Paul

That Paul employed a secretary on occasion is unquestionable. Six letters certainly were written with secretarial assistance (Rom., 1 Cor., Gal., Col., 2 Th., Philem.), three more probably were (2 Cor., Eph., 1 Th.), one remains possible (Phil.), and the Pastorals, if Pauline, probably were.[3]

The more significant question is in what role did Paul's secretaries act. Obviously there could be wide variation with so many letters and in so many different epistolary occasions, even if only one secretary was used for all the letters — an unlikely event. Since Paul never revealed in what capacity he was using his secretary,[4] the answers must be extracted from an examination of his letters. Nevertheless the problem must be addressed. It is not acceptable to sideline the issue and proceed as if the letters were solely the words and thoughts of Paul. In view of the diverse yet recognized and acceptable ways of using a secretary, there are far-reaching consequences on such issues as how completely 'Pauline' are the letters' thoughts, contents, argumentation, organization, style, or vocabulary. If one does not attempt the secretary question, then he must beware of speaking of items in the letters as 'non-Pauline'.[5] Even if Paul exercised much control over his secretary, there was more influence possible from a secretary than many modern exegetes have allowed.

---

[3] See Table 4 above, p. 190.

[4] There is no intention to deceive; the use of a secretary was typical. He does not mention it, because unlike writers such as Cicero who wrote of the most trivial of matters, he always had serious issues to discuss.

[5] *I.e.*, if no attempt is made to determine the secretarial role, then anything apparently 'non-Pauline' could be the secretary's. And if the secretary's, then ultimately it must be Paul's: he permitted it to remain in his letter. Subsequently only external evidence could indicate an interpolation.

Appendix

A. Types of Letters

Business. Hundreds of contracts, surveys, wills, etc., were composed in letter form. These were usually written by secretaries who were trained in the proper conventions.

Official. Letters were often used by Hellenistic rulers to establish a new situation or convey directions to a large group of people. The letter in a sense carried the presence of the ruler, for it was his decree in epistolary form.[1]

Public. Formal letters of apology or persuasion were often framed as a personal letter that had become public. This type of letter suggests intimacy and lends credence to the ideas expressed therein.

Non-Real. By 'non-real' are meant pseudonymous letters, letters "from heaven", epistolary novels, and "magical" letters.

Discursive. Nearest to the literary essay in content, the discursive letter usually had a briefer length and a slightly less elevated style.

Ostraca. Any smooth surface was used for writing. Broken bits of pottery were often used for brief letters, such as receipts, short orders, or personal greetings accompanying a gift. Ostraca texts are distinctive because of their reduction of the message to an unpolished minimum, although they still contained most epistolary features. Since the major motivations for writing on ostraca were convenience, speed, and economy, one would not expect secretarial assistance in an ostracon.

Source: Doty, *Letters*, 4–8 with modifications.

---

[1] A parallel to Paul's letters is apparent. The leader (Paul) is sending directions to a Christian community and is doing so as one who has the authority. The letters are his presence in letter form.

B. Examples of Various Locations for Introductory Formulae

At the Beginning:

Disclosure[1]	*POxy.* 1155, 1481
Petition	*POxy.* 292
Ironic Rebuke	*POxy.* 1223, 1348
Thanksgiving	*POxy.* 1299
Greeting	*POxy.* 531, 1160, 1679

In the Middle:

Disclosure	*POxy.* 1670
Petition	*POxy.* 1480
Ironic Rebuke	*POxy.* 113
Thanksgiving	*POxy.* 1070
Greeting	*POxy.* 1765, 1070, 1679

At the End:

Petition	*POxy.* 1666
Thanksgiving	*POxy.* 1481
Greeting	*POxy.* 1216, 1679

Source: Compiled from Mullins, "Formulas," 386.

---

[1] The categories of formulae are defined in Appendix C.

C. Various Types of Stereotyped Formulae

1. The Disclosure Formulae:[1]
   a) a verb of disclosure (e.g., a verb of desire, θέλω or βούλομαι in the first person indicative with a noetic verb, γινώσκω, in the infinitive);
   b) the person addressed (which may include the vocative); and
   c) the information to be disclosed (which is usually introduced by ὅτι).

2) The Request or Petition Formula:
   a) an introduction of the request;
   b) a verb of request (usually παρακαλῶ);
   c) the vocative; and
   d) the content of the request (which is usually introduced by the ἵνα clause of purpose or περί and the aorist infinitive).

3. The Joy Expression:
   a) either χαίρω in the aorist or ἔχω χαριν;
   b) an adverb of magnitude (e.g., μεγάλως);
   c) a temporal statement (usually regarding the arrival of a letter or some news); and
   d) the object of the joy (which is usually introduced by ὅτι).

4. The Expression of Astonishment:
   a) a verb of astonishment (e.g., θαυμάζω); and
   b) the object of the astonishment (which was usually a failure to write on the part of the addressee) introduced by ὅτι or πῶς.

5. The Statement of Compliance (either the sender reminding the addressee of some instruction that the addressee has failed to do or the sender informing the addressee that he has complied with his instructions):
   a) an introductory adverb (e.g., ὡς, καθώς, or καθότι);
   b) a verb of instruction (usually ἐντέλλω in a past tense);
   c) the instruction (usually introduced by περί); and
   d) a statement concerning either the fulfillment of the instructions or an assertion of the sender's confidence in the addressee's compliance.

---

[1] The usual order is noetic verb, person addressed, disclosure verb, and information; e.g., POxy. 1493: "γινώσκειν σε θέλω, ἀδελφέ, ὅτι..." Mullins, "Disclosure", 47–48 gives many more examples. POslo. 50, however, reads: "θέλω σε γεινώσκειν ὅτι παραγενόμενος εἰς τὴν πόλιν..." This word order (disclosure verb, person addressed, noetic verb, and information) is the order customarily used by Paul.

6. The Statement of Report, with a formulaic use of "hearing" or "learning":

   a) an adverb denoting the degree of grief;
   b) the aorist of either λυπέω or ἀγωνιάω;
   c) the verb ἀκουώ or ἐπιγινώσκω (frequently in participial form); and
   d) the subject of the report.

7. The Ironic Rebuke:

   a) the sender rebukes the addressee through some rhetorical device like an imaginary interlocutor; or
   b) the sender rebukes himself for some failure of his own.

8. The Thanksgiving Formula:

   a) a verb of thanks (usually εὐχαριστέω) in the first person indicative;
   b) the person being thanked (usually a god(s) or goddess(es)); and
   c) the reason for the thanksgiving (usually good news concerning the addressee's safety, health, etc.).

9. The Greeting Formula:[2]

   a) the verb of greeting (which is some form of ἀσπαζεσθαι);
   b) an indication of the person(s) who is (are) giving the greeting;
   c) an indication of the person(s) who is (are) being greeted; and
   d) an optional phrase to elaborate any of the above elements.

10. Transition Indicators:

    a) δε καί ... ;
    b) ὁμοίως δὲ καί (or ὁμοίως καί, or ὡσαύτως δὲ καί);
    c) περὶ δέ with the genitive absolute;[3]
    d) ἔτι οὖν (δὲ) καὶ νῦν; and
    e) an abrupt question (e.g., τί οὖν).[4]

Source: The table was compiled from J. White, "Introductory Formulae", 93–97; idem, "Epistolary Formulas and Cliches", 307; and T. Y. Mullins, "Disclosure: a Literary Form in the New Testament", *NovTest* 7 (1964): 45–47.

---

[2] See Appendix D.

[3] The transition indicators described in 'a' and 'b' are the usual means of turning to a new subject within the letter, while 'c' is used usually to indicate a response to an earlier subject or a subject of another correspondence.

[4] See R. Bultmann, *Der Stil der paulinischen Predigt und die kynisch-stoische Diatribe*, 45. The formula "τί οὖν ... μὴ γενοῖτο" was, however, probably a common oratorical device by Paul's day, learnable in the market place, and not necessarily an indication of Cynic-Stoic influence.

D. The Greeting Formulae

There are three types of greeting formulae,[1] based on the three persons of the verb:

1. The First Person Greeting. The author of the letter greets someone. *E.g.*, *PTebt.* 415: "ἀσπάζομαι πολλὰ τὸν πατέρα σου καὶ τοὺς ἐνοίκους πάντας."
2. The Second Person Greeting. The author tells the addressee to greet someone for him. *E.g.*, *PTebt.* 412: "ἀσπάζου τὴν ματέρα σου καὶ τὸν πατέρα σου".
3. The Third Person Greeting. The author relays to the addressee that a third party greets someone (either the addressee or a fourth party). *E.g.*, *POxy.* 114: "ἀσπαζεται Ξάνθιλλα καὶ πάντας τοὺς αὐτῆς".

Frequently the greeting formula will include an elaborating phrase that either

a) modifies the verb (usually πολλά),
b) describes, often complimenting, the person being greeted (*e.g.*, ἀγαπητός), or
c) identifies the greeter, as in *POxy.* 1582: "ἀσπάζεται σε Σαραπίων ὁ υἱός μου".

It was very common in the non-literary papyri to include many greetings accompanied by personal descriptions. For example, in *POxy.* 533 the final ten percent of the letter is greetings, with many personal descriptions. Paul's letter to the Romans contains a long section of greetings, but they still comprise only 5.9 % of the total letter.

---

[1] Exler, *Form*, 116, first noted this in a more general, non-organized manner. H. Koskenniemi, *Studien*, 148–50, suggested three different forms: (1) writer greets addressee; (2) writer greets others than addressee; and (3) writer sends greetings from another to addressee.

E. Examples of Chiasmus in Paul[1]

I. Chiasmus of Sense-Lines

A. Rom. 10:9–10[2]

ὁμολογήσῃς... στόματι...	A – B
πιστεύσῃς... καρδίᾳ...	C – D
καρδίᾳ... πιστεύεται...	D – C
στόματι... ὁμολογεῖται...	B – A

B. Col. 1:13–20[3]

brought from darkness into Kingdom	A
redemption	B
image of God	C
first-born	D
creation	E
the heavenly hierarchy	F
ALL IN CHRIST	
the church below	F
the Beginning (Gen. 1:1)	E
first-born	D
God dwelt in him	C
reconciliation	B
making peace by the cross	A

C. Eph. 2:11–22 (an elaborate treble chiasmus)[4]
vv. 11–13 A-B-C-D-*D-C-B-A*
   A. once B. gentiles C. flesh
   D. uncircumcision *D. circumcision*
   C. flesh B. blood of Christ A. now
vv. 13–17 A-B-C-D-E-F-G-*G-F-E-D-C-B-A*
   A. far-off:near B. blood of Christ
   C. both one D. middle wall E. hostility
   F. his flesh G. Law *G. commandments*
   F. new man E. peace D. reconcile
   C. one body B. cross A. far-off:near

---

[1] Like most citations of chiasmus in the New Testament, any of these particular examples may be disputed, but see, *e.g*, Jeremias, "Chiasmus in den Paulusbriefen" *ZNW* 49 (1958): 139–56; and J. W. Welch, "Chiasmus in the New Testament", in *Chiasmus in Antiquity: Structure, Analyses, and Exegesis*, 211–49 (Hildesheim: Gerstenberg, 1981).

[2] See, *inter alii*, Bruce Corley, "The Significance of Romans 9–11: a Study in Pauline Theology" (Ph.D. diss., Southwestern Baptist Theological Seminary, 1975), 97.

[3] Turner, *Style*, 98.

[4] Ibid., 98–99.

vv. 18—22 A-B-C-D-E-F-*F-E-D-C-B-A*
    A. Spirit B. Father C. strangers
    D. house of God E. built F. foundation
    F. corner-stone E. building D. holy temple.
    C. built together B. God A. Spirit

C. Other examples

    1 Cor. 5:2—6 A B (ab*b*a) C (ab*b*a) *B* (ab*b*a) *A*
    Col. 3:3—4 A-B-C-D-*D-C-B-A*
    Col. 3:11 A-B-*B-A*
    Phil. 1:15—16 A-B-C-*C-B-A*
    Phil. 3:10 A-B-*B-A*

II. Chiamus of Major Sections

Galatians (the entire book is one large chiasmus that is centered around a smaller one [4:1—10])[5]

Prologue	A
Autobiography	B
Justification by faith	C
Scriptural argument	D
CENTER CHIASMUS	
Scriptural argument	*D*
Justification by faith	*C*
Paraenesis	*B*
Epilogue	*A*

---

[5] Derived from Bligh's commentary on Galatians in the *Householder Commentaries* (London: T & T Clark, 1969). Needless to say, this particular example is disputed by many, and reflects more the creativity of Prof. Bligh than of Paul.

F. Examples of Tribulation Lists

I. Tribulation lists in the Pauline letters

   A. Simple lists

   1. Rom. 8:35; affliction, anguish, persecution, famine, nakedness, danger, sword.
   2. 2 Cor. 6:4–5; afflictions, hardships, anguishes, blows, imprisonments, riots, fatigues, watchings, fastings.
   3. 2 Cor. 11:23–29; fatigues, imprisonments, blows, deadly circumstances, thirty-nine lashes, struck with rods, stonings, shipwreck, adrift at sea, dangers from rivers, robbers, own people, Gentiles, danger in town, in countryside, on the sea, from false brethren, fatigue, toil, watchings, hunger, thirst, fastings, cold, nakedness, anxiety, concern for the churches,[1] weakness, scandal.
   4. 2 Cor. 12:10 - weakness, insults, hardships, persecutions, anguishes.

   B. Antithetical lists

   1. 1 Cor. 4:10–13; we are fools, you are wise; we are weak, you are strong; you are honored, we are despised; we are hungry and thirsty and naked; we are maltreated and homeless; we labor...
   2. 2 Cor. 4:8–9; we are hemmed in, but not crushed; perplexed, but not despairing; persecuted, but not overtaken; overwhelmed, but not annihilated.
   3. 2 Cor. 6:8–10; [considered] for imposters, though true; for unknown, though known well; as dying, though we live; as punished, though not killed...
   4. Phil. 4:12; how to be abased, how to abound; plenty and hunger; abundance and want.

II. Parallels in non-Biblical texts

   A. Epictetus: "Is there any other danger but death, or a prison, or bodily pain, or exile, or defamation?" (Arr. *Epict. Diss.* 2.10.2); "Show me one who is sick, yet happy; in danger, yet happy; dying, yet happy; exiled, yet happy; disgraced, yet happy" (2.10.3); "The instrument of destruction is a sword, or a wheel, or the sea,..." (6.4.2).
   B. 2 Enoch 66:6; "Walk my children, in long-suffering, in meekness, in affliction, in distress, in faithfulness, in truth, in hope, in weakness, in derision, in assaults, in temptation, in deprivation, in nakedness".

---

[1] This is an interesting item for a tribulation list.

C. See also TJos. 1:4–7; Sir. 39:28–34;[2] Jos. *BJ* 4.3.10 and *Ant.* 10.7.3; Nag Hammadi text of *The Thunder, Perfect Mind* 6.2.13–18.30 [trans. George MacRae and Douglas Parrott, in *The Nag Hammadi Library*, ed. James M. Robinson (New York: Harper & Row, 1977), 271–77];[3] and Plut. *Alex.* 327.A-C.

Source: R. Hodgson, "Paul the Apostle and First Century Tribulation Lists", *ZNW* 74 (1983): 59–80

---

[2] This may be a tribulation list, but it is more clearly the antithetic parallel to vv. 21–27 and forms part of a theodicy.

[3] Again, the tribulations here are the antithetic parallels to blessings. Antithesis, as the translators note, is a major element in this work.

G. The "Literary or Non-Literary" (Deissmann) Debate: The Problem of Classifying the Letters of Paul

Late nineteenth century philologists and historians of Hellenistic literature attempted to classify the letters of Paul with the literary epistles.[1] Although men like Ulrich von Wilamowitz-Moellendorff and Martin Dibelius considered Paul one of the great letter writers of antiquity, most others, including Franz Overbeck, Paul Wendland, and Eduard Norden, tended to compare Paul unfavorably with the ancient rhetoricians or to rule him unworthy of any consideration.[2]

Literary epistles, judging from the remains, comprise only a small percentage of the letters. Thousands of personal and business letters have been found that were written on papyrus and pottery fragments. These more occasional letters were not intended necessarily to be preserved and were found in the remains of trash heaps, domestic ruins, old libraries, and official depositories of records. They provided a view of Hellenistic life not previously available, including business contracts and arrangements, family matters, and correspondence between friends. With the discovery and publication of numerous papyrus letters during this century, similarities were noticed with Paul, particulary in diction, style, and references to everyday life.

Adolf Deissmann[3] carefully differentiated between these occasional papyrus letters and the literary epistles or treatises. The natural, daily, situational letters (*Briefe*) were to be understood differently from the artificial, artistic literary epistles (*Episteln*). The epistles were written for anyone who was able and willing to read them. They were addressed to an individual, usually a friend or a patron of the writer and were written in prose or verse. Although they may be communicating to the recipient, their real and recognized purpose was to state a fact or an opinion to the general public.[4] They were written for preservation and enlightenment. On the other hand, the (occasional) letters were intended to be read by no one but the addressee. They were not intended necessarily to be preserved for future use. A 'letter' could become 'epistle' if the persons involved and the topic of the letter were of general interest, but it was still not written originally for the general public.

---

[1] *E.g.*, there are the letters of Plato and Isocrates (some of which are geniune), Aristotle, Demosthenes, and Epicurus. Horace wrote poetic epistles on various topics. In Paul's time, Seneca, the younger Pliny, and Quintilian wrote brief treatises that have epistolary qualities. The letters of Apollonius of Tyana (b. 4 B.C.) which were (probably) written by his disciples have affinities to Paul in that they espouse a religio-philosophical teaching to be followed.

[2] U. v. Wilamowitz-Moellendorff, *Antigonos von Karystos*, Philologische Untersuchungen, no. 4 (Berlin: Weidmann, 1881); M. Dibelius, *An Philemon*, 3d ed., ed. H. Greeven, HNT (Tübingen: Mohr, 1953); P. Wendland, *Die hellenistische-römische Kultur in ihren Beziehungen zu Judentum und Christentum*, 2d ed. (Tübingen: Mohr, 1912); and esp. E. Norden, *Kunstprosa*, 1: 499 (Paul's style is totally "unhellenic"). Thus Paul's confession, "εἰ δὲ καὶ ἰδιώτης τῷ λόγῳ", in 2 Cor. 11:6 was taken literally.

[3] A. Deissmann, *Light*, 290–301.

[4] McKenzie, *Light*, 11–12.

Deissmann emphasized the close relationship between Paul and these occasional papyrus letters, freeing Paul from the previous, unfavorable comparisons to classical literature. Once he established this "obvious" relationship, Deissmann made several conclusions. (1) These letters (*Briefe*) of Paul represented his genuine religious impulse at a given moment and contained none of the artificiality of the sophists. They are artless and unpremeditated. (2) They were concerned with matters of private (confidential, secret, individual, personal) interest and were not intended to be seen by the general public.[5] The fact that the readers may have shared them with others, with or without the bidding of Paul, does not change their purpose and definition. (3) They were a substitute for direct oral confrontation. They were a conversation halved with no essential difference between the letter and oral dialogue.

One problem of Deissmann's classification of Paul's letters with the occasional papyrus letters[6] is that it has led to the mistaken conclusion that since Paul's letters are not "literary epistles" they should not be treated as theological treatises, even if they later received canonical status.[7]

Deissmann was certainly correct that the letters of Paul were similar to the occasional papyrus letters, especially in diction. Yet the early letter theorists recog-

---

[5] McKenzie, *Light*, 12, carried this to an extreme: "The moral principle involved illustrates the problems of reading the letters of perfect strangers, which is what Paul and the church of Corinth are to modern readers. We know little about them except from their letters. An epistle is addressed to us; a letter is written from a naturally private situation. If the situation is not known, the letter is unintelligible unless the letter itself discloses enough of the situation... We may call it exegesis, but the common name for reading other people's mail is snooping".

[6] William Doty, "Epistle", 19, offers a convenient summary of Deissmann's categorization of *Brief* vs. *Epistel* in the form of a table. O. Roller, *Formular*, 32–33, decides for classfying the letters as "wirkliche Briefe".

A related problem is that such a classification seems automatically to place Paul (and usually the other New Testament writers) with the members of the lower ranks of society and not with the cultured upper classes (So Deissmann, *Light*, 8, and idem, *New Light*, 25). While such an evaluation is probably correct (see *e.g.*, Mary E. Andrews, "Paul, Philo, and the Intellectuals", *JBL* 53 (1934): 166, who states: "Paul cannot be rated among the intellectuals of his day"), it must be demonstrated from the letters themselves.

[7] Deissmann, *Light*, 147; see also idem, *Paul*, 12. It seems that Deissmann has made a classification that requires the reinterpretation of the original function and modern usage of Paul's letters. It is more likely, however, that the reverse is true: due to an *a priori* bias of Deissmann—and others of his time—to hesitate to see "theology" in Paul, he readily grouped the Pauline letters in a class that did not contain "theologies", a class that Paul's letters did not fit as well as he implied.

More recently Beda Rigaux also has argued for the classification of Paul's letters as occasional. In opposition to Deissmann, however, he does assert that merely because they are letters and not epistles, this "does not mean that the Pauline letters should be regarded as ephemeral compositions intended to be read once to the community and subsequently forgotten. Such letters are also apostolic acts, and like preaching, are truly the words of God" B. Rigaux, *Letters*, 118. Thus Rigaux is arguing for a canonical principle that overrides the original, occasional, nature (and purpose) of the letter.

nized there were differences even among the occasional letters. Cicero, for example, maintained a difference between letters that were written purely to convey information (as in most of the extant papyrus letters) and those intended to communicate also the emotional or intellectual state and personality of the writer (as in his own letters). If he considered his letters distinct from the ordinary papyrus letter, Paul's letters also should not be placed with the papyri. Even a poor qualifier like letter length illustrates this.[8] In the approximately 14, 000 private letters from Greco-Roman antiquity, the average length was about 87 words, ranging in length from about 18 to 209 words. Yet the letters of more literary men like Cicero and Seneca differed considerably. Cicero averaged 295 words per letter, ranging from 22 to 2, 530 words, and Seneca averaged 995, ranging from 149 to 4134. By both standards, though, Paul's letters were quite long. The thirteen letters bearing his name average 2, 495 words, ranging from 335 (Philemon) to 7, 114 (Romans).

If the letters of Paul were atypically long, do they still deserve a place among the papyri solely because of their occasional nature? William Doty rightly noted that the key factor in distinguishing these occasional letters from the literary epistles was merely the "intent-to-publish".[9] Discerning "original intention" is a very dubious task.[10] Moreover Paul's letters strictly speaking are not private letters. They were written to be read before the congregation.[11]

Are Paul's letters to be classified strictly with the papyri because they are "non-literary"? As Otto Roller argued,[12] aesthetic judgment becomes a factor in any de-

---

[8] The following familiar approximations were originally from Wikenhauser, *Einleitung*, 245, and are sufficiently accurate. (The figures for the Pauline letters have been corrected to correspond to the text of NA^{26}.)

[9] Doty, "Epistle," 21.

[10] Cicero indicated by his comments to Tiro that he *later* made the decision to publish his letters; Cic. *Fam.* 16.1. A statement made elsewhere to Trebonius is seemingly to the contrary but is mere rhetoric; Cic. *Fam.* 15.21.4: "In the first place, when I sent [*ego . . . misi*] that letter to Calvus, I had no idea that it would get abroad any more than the one you are now reading. You see, I have one way of writing [*scribimus*] what I think will be read by those to whom I address my letter [*mittimus*], and another way of writing what I think will be read by many [*putamus*]".

There is an odd change to the first person plural at this one point in the letter. An editorial "we" seems unlikely in light of the "ego . . . misi" in the preceding sentence. Perhaps it is an inclusive "we", meaning that both he and Trebonius had this habit. It is possible, however, that he was including the secretary—perhaps not so unusual custom for Cicero (*pace* Tyrrell and Purser, *Cicero*, 1: 84-85)—and means that he and his secretary had a different procedure when writing for publication.

[11] 1 Th. 5:27; also Col. 4:16. A parallel may be seen in the use of Clement's letter; see Eus. *H.E.* 4.23. L. Hartman, "On Reading Other's Letters", 145, contends that Paul's letters were to be shared. D. J. Selby also argues for their intended use as a group communication, arguing from the use of the second person plural, the allusions to various persons, and the multiple greetings. Selby, *Toward an Understanding of St. Paul*, (Englewood Cliffs, NJ: Prentice-Hall, 1962), 239. Yet literary epistles addressed to one person also used these.

[12] Roller, *Formular*, 345–47.

cision as to what was "acceptable" at any particular time. Moreover, Deissmann has been criticized for giving too "literary" a definition of an epistle[13] and for denying too far the literary worth of Paul's letters.[14] In fact, Deissmann's entire distinction between letter and epistle is too strained.[15]

Do Paul's letters belong with the papyrus letters because of their overwhelming commonalities? W. G. Kümmel observed that they do not fit perfectly the form of the occasional letter. The praescript, proem, formulae, and paraenesis have been modified too much to remain in this category.[16] There are elements in Paul's letters, however, that are similar to the occasional letters: the opening,[17] the closing salutation, the use of stereotyped formulae.[18] These elements certainly are more common to occasional letters than to literary epistles, but they are not without changes in Paul.

If Paul's letters do not belong with the non-literary, occasional, papyrus letter, should they then be returned to the category of the literary epistles? Paul's letters contain some of the elements found in the higher style of these literary epistles. His use of chiasmus, allegory, metaphor, ellipse, and parallelism is not an aspect of an unpremeditated letter.[19] Hans Dieter Betz interpreted Galatians as a literary work, considering it an example of the "apologetic letter" genre, structured after the rhetorical model of a written forensic speech of defense.[20] He outlines Galatians—a difficult task—by using the rhetorical outline.[21]

The literary epistles also do not furnish an acceptable paradigm. Aside from the various—usually negative—evaluations of Paul's literary expertise, Stan Stowers has recently reminded us of the sociological differences:

> The social context for such literary letters is a small circle of intimate aristocratic friends who share advanced rhetorical educations. The purpose is aesthetic entertainment. As [the younger] Pliny remarks, the first requirement for this kind of literary activity is leisure

---

[13] So A. T. Robertson, *Grammar*, 88.

[14] So, *inter alii*, Paul Wendland, *Neutestamentliche Grammatik: das Griechisch der neuen Testaments im Zusammenhang mit der Volkssprache dargestellt*, vol. 2: *der urchristliche Literaturformen* (Tübingen: Mohr, 1912), 344; Henry G. Meecham, *Light*, 101; and William Doty, "Epistle", 18.

[15] So, *inter alii*, George Milligan, *New Testament Documents: Their Origin and Early History* (London: Macmillan & Co., 1913), 95; and Klaus Thraede, *Brieftopik*, 1—4. Doty, "Epistle", 9—22, offers a thorough analysis and critique of Deissmann.

[16] Kümmel, *Introduction*, 248.

[17] See the discussion by V. Parkin, "Pauline Prescripts", 92—99, who argues for a modification after 1 and 2 Thessalonians.

[18] The similarities are discussed under the section on "content"; see above, pp. 138—39.

[19] Paul's use of these elements is discussed above, pp. 140—43.

[20] Betz, *Galatians*, 14—25, esp. 14, 24. A helpful, shorter discussion is given by Benoît Standaert, "La rhetorique antique et l'épître aux Galates", *Foi et Vie* 84/5 (Sept. 1985): 33—40. But *cf.* the discussion above, p. 182 n. 243.

[21] This is not to say that I think Betz is correct. Nevertheless, the point remains that a *literary* model is used for a comparison with Paul. Nigel Turner noted that the epistles of Epicurus and Polemon of Ilion have been considered as models for Paul's letters; *Style*, 82—83.

(7.2). Pliny notes that such letters should usually be brief and employ simple vocabulary in a direct style (7.9.8). The paradox is that Pliny employs elaborate structure and studied prose rhythm in order to achieve this simplicity and directness. Pliny refers to the gathering of friends where such literary gems were shared.[22]

He continued by noting "that such aestheticism belonged to an extremely small group of writers, who lived in a rarefied world of elite sensitivities". While Gregory of Nazianzus or Jerome may fit this category, Paul certainly does not.

The lack of a clear classification for Paul has prompted some to forsake the task and declare the New Testament as distinct from and unaffected by the Greco-Roman categories: "Our point is that our early Christian literary arts were different from those that ancient paganism produced, and that Greek and traditional humanist categories are inadequate as measuring rods".[23] The Pauline letters are also separated in a more subtle way. Deissmann's description of occasional letters as "an artless and casual surrogate for what he would have said had he been present"[24] is further developed. Paul's letters were not true letters at all; therefore naturally they defy classification.

Nevertheless the solution is not to be found in any "escapist" approach. The better approach lies not in removing Paul from the debate but in altering the debate's framework. The difficulty has arisen from an underlying assumption concerning these two general categories of literary and non-literary: they are mutually exclusive. In other words, the classification of a letter as one type precluded the possibility of it having any characteristics of the other.[25] Rather than viewing a letter as *either* literary *or* non-literary, it should be placed on a spectrum ranging from the more literary epistles to the more occasional letters.[26] Scholarship may now have reached a cautious balance between occasional and literary, between:

> treating Paul's letters as purely occasional, contextual writings, directed only to specific situations, and as attempts to express a Christian understanding of life which had ramifications for theological expression beyond the particular historical situation".[27]

---

[22] Stowers, *Letter Writing*, 34–35.

[23] Amos Wilder, *Early Christian Rhetoric: the Language of the Gospel*, 2d ed. (Cambridge: Harvard University, 1971), 44.

[24] Deissmann, *Light*, 147. He does not pursue this line of argument.

[25] The approach that something must always be "either-or" and never "both-and" is a recurring problem in New Testament studies and has been termed "the Hegelian captivity of the Church".

[26] This is the conclusion of William Doty, "Epistle", 8–11, who favors a "public" versus "private" polarity within a common definition for the letter.

[27] Doty, *Letters*, 26. He concludes: (1) Paul never writes in impersonal epistolary convention but speaks from concrete situations, (2) his letters are more substitutes for oral presence and frequently indicates more of the oral looseness, and (3) his style lies between the flat, graceless papyrus letters and the polished elements of the rhetorical treatises. So also S. Stowers, *Letter Writing*, 25: "There is considerable variation among New Testament letters. But taken as a whole, they resemble neither the common papyri from the very lowest levels of culture and education nor the works of those with the highest levels of rhetorical training. They fall somewhere in between and have the cast of a Jewish subculture".

If the Pauline letters are hybrids, what prompted the metamorphosis? Is it merely that Paul was more educated than the common man but not educated enough to compose a true literary epistle? W. G. Kümmel argued that the Pauline letters are different because they were the instruments by which Paul conducted his missionary work. They were occasioned, but the tasks needed in missions, edification, the care of souls, the warnings against heresy, and the guarantees of ecclesiastical order required more than the stylistic limitations of the more occasional letters could supply.[28] Therefore Paul altered the letter[29] into a form of internal Christian communication to suit his purposes.[30]

---

[28] Kümmel, *Introduction*, esp. 249.

[29] Paul's adaptation of the occasional letter to a "loftier" purpose may not be without precedent. Salles ("Le genre littéraire", 41–47) discussed the development of the Latin familiar letter genre. She maintained that there was a gradual transformation occurring in Latin letter writing. Cicero took what in Greek was a non-literary form and elevated it somewhat while nonetheless retaining the vitality and spontaneity of the Greek letter. "... le génie particulier de Ciceron [a] dû au jaillissement perpétuel de l'improvisation, ce qui donne à cette correspondance une place tout à fait originale dans la littérature antique" (p. 45). The elevation of the letter to an art form is best represented by the younger Pliny (p. 46). Seneca combined the two. In the guise of casual letters to his disciple and friend, Lucilius, Seneca was able, by reflecting on daily life, to describe and discuss his philosophy. Thus he was able to combine the philosophical treatise with the casual and spontaneous letter. Two conclusions may be made: (1) the nature and purpose of the letter was flexible and could be altered to fit the needs of a creative individual; and (2) by analogy from Seneca, ancient casual letters could be used to discuss "theology" by casting it against the backdrop of the concrete matters of daily (Christian) life.

[30] An interesting turn has occurred. It was anticipated that a classification of the Pauline letters as either literary epistles or occasional letters would help to settle the questions concerning their *Sitz-im-Leben*, that is, whether Paul dashed the letter off as a purely occasional letter amidst the flurry of other activities (*e.g.*, Deissmann), or carefully constructed the letter as a rhetorical treatise (*e.g.*, Betz). It now appears that an assumed *Sitz-im-Leben* (missions) was used to determine the classification.

H. Criteria for Detecting Παραδόσεις in the Pauline Letters

Since Paul evidently chooses not to indicate always when he is citing preformed pieces, one is left with the task of distilling them from his letters. Some rather obvious pieces of tradition are those introduced by confessional, kerygmatic, or didactic verbs. Yet other traditions are more problematic. For instance, the traditional confession, Jesus is Lord,[1] was taken over by Paul.[2] Because of its brevity, it is easily incorporated into Paul's own thought, becoming so integrated with his theology that it is no longer a 'borrowed' (traditional) piece. There are other "bits" that also perhaps began as traditions that are too brief or perhaps too assimilated into Paul's thought to be labelled as the citation of a tradition every place they occur, such as Χριστὸς ἀπέθανεν (ὑπερ),[3] εἷς θεός,[4] the clothing metaphors (doffing vices[5] and donning Christ), εἰκὼν τοῦ θεοῦ, and deliverance formulae.[6] Not only do these elusive fragments indicate the need for a more objec-

---

[1] Cullmann considers the fundamental confession to be κύριος Χριστός; O. Cullmann, *Die ersten christlichen Glaubensbekenntnisse* (Zürich: Evangelischer, 1949), 55–61. Perhaps the more fundamental confession is κύριος Ἰησοῦς (1 Cor. 12:3; Rom. 10:9; and perhaps Rom. 1:4; 1 Cor. 11:23, and the Aramaic *maranatha*). M. Hengel, ("Erwägungen zum Sprachgebrauch von Χριστός bei Paulus und in der 'vorpaulinischen' Überlieferung", in *Paul and Paulinism: Essays in Honour of C. K. Barrett*, ed. M. D. Hooker and S. G. Wilson [London: S.P.C.K., 1982], 137–38) argues that while Paul's use of the term 'Christ' was extensive ('promiscuous' ["Erwägungen", 140]), it was only in the titular and never in the formulaic or confessional sense. Perhaps my examples above are debatable, but surely 1 Cor. 3:11 is confessional and not merely titular (so also J. A. Fitzmyer, *Pauline Theology* [Englewood Cliffs: Prentice-Hall, 1967], 12).

[2] Perhaps from a baptismal (1 Cor. 6:11; Acts 8:16; 19:5) or a liturgical (Phil. 2:11) use.

[3] Rom. 5:6, 8; 14:15; 1 Cor. 8:11; 2 Cor. 5:14–15. Note, though, the use of Χριστός rather than his more customary Ἰησοῦς or Ἰησοῦς Χριστός. V. H. Neufeld (*The Earliest Christian Confessions*, NTTS, no. 5 [Grand Rapids: Eerdmans, 1963], 48) is probably correct in seeing a Jewish-Christian origin for this formula, but he is perhaps incorrect in seeing all the variations as separate formulae.

[4] Rom. 3:30; 1 Cor. 8:4, 6; Gal. 3:20; Eph. 4:6; 1 Tim. 2:5; *cf.* Mt. 19:17 (*et p.*); Mk. 12:29; Jn. 8:41; Jas. 2:19.

[5] The vice lists themselves (Rom. 1:29–31; 13:13; 1 Cor. 6:9–11; 2 Cor. 12:20–21; Gal. 5:19–22; Eph. 5:3–5; Col. 3:5–8) are probably traditional. See E. Schweizer, "Traditional Ethical Patterns in the Pauline and Post-Pauline Letters and Their Development (Lists of Vices and House-Tables)", in *Text and Interpretation: Studies in the New Testament Presented to Matthew Black*, ed. E. Best and R. McL. Wilson (Cambridge: Cambridge University, 1979), 195–200, 207; and E. E. Ellis, "Traditions in 1 Corinthians", 483–84.

[6] Rom. 2:16; Gal. 1:3–4; 1 Th. 1:10. W. D. Davies, *Paul*, 136–41, calls these "fragments of kerygma".

Other "bits" may include: words of the Lord (1 Cor. 7:10; 9:14; 13:2; Rom. 12:14; 13:9; 16:19; 1 Th. 4:2, 15), liturgical elements, like 'amen' (1 Cor. 14:16; 2 Cor. 1:20), '*abba*'

tive approach to determining pre-formed pieces, but so also do other disputed passages.[7]

Establishing criteria can be an evanescent task. The best approach is to examine passages that are already widely accepted as traditional and to distill some characteristic criteria from them, that is, literary indicators that can then be taken to the texts to test their reliability and validity.[8] My cursory examination produced the following criteria, which are divided into two general categories based on whether they rely on content or form.[9]

a) Criteria related to content

1. A formula may introduce material as a tradition. Often *termini technici*, such as παραλαμβάνω and παραδίδωμι, or less technical formulae, like πιστὸς ὁ λόγος, are employed. In the case of ὁμολογία traditions more specialized vocabulary may be used, such as ὁμολογεῖν with a recitative ὅτι, a double accusative, or an infinitive.[10]

2. The omission of the names of Him who is praised, which are often replaced with a relative pronoun.[11]

(Rom. 8:15; Gal. 4:6), and the triad 'faith, hope, and love' (1 Th. 1:3; 5:8; Col. 1:4—5; Eph. 4:2—5; Gal. 5:5—6; Rom. 5:1—5; and esp. 1 Cor. 13:13; *cf.* Heb. 6:10—12; 10:22—24; and 1 Pet. 1:3—8, 21—22). See also Hunter, *Paul*, 33—34.

[7] *E.g.*, Eph. 1:3—14 is quite possibly a Christological hymn, but it is usually not included with the accepted ones; see J. T. Sanders, *The New Testament Christological Hymns*, SNTSMS, no. 15 (Cambridge: University Press, 1971). It is, however, strongly asserted to be a tradition by Felice Montagnini, "Christological Features in Eph. 1:3—14", in *Paul de Tarse: Apôtre du notre temps*, ed. L. De Lorenzi (Rome: Abbey of St. Paul, 1979), esp. 538—39.

[8] This is not a circular method. It is a common procedure in such diverse disciplines as sociology, chemistry, and geometry.

'Reliability' and 'validity' are used with their technical meanings. Reliability is the ability of a criterion to produce consistent results. Validity is the ability of a criterion to measure what it claims to measure.

[9] My initial search for criteria was aided considerably by gathering suggestions from the casual observations of a host of writers. Three works, though, were especially helpful: R. Jewett, "The Redaction and Use of an Early Christian Confession in Romans 1:3—4", in *The Living Text*, ed. D. E. Groh (Lauham, MD: University Press of America, 1985), 100—2; C. L. Palmer, "The Use of Traditional Materials in Hebrews, James, and 1 Peter", (Ph.D. diss., Southwestern Baptist Theological Seminary, 1985), 6—8; and Markus Barth, "Traditions in Ephesians", 9—10.

[10] See Neufeld, *Confessions*, 20.

[11] See M. Barth, "Traditions in Ephesians", 10. He also notes that "whether hymns sung in praise of God actually are older than obvious Christ-hymns (W. Bousset; R. Deichgräber) does not affect the fact that both types stem from traditions".

3. Multiple attestation[12] can indicate a pre-formed tradition, especially if there is little probability of direct literary dependence.[13]

4. The frequent occurance in a brief pericope of peculiar idioms or infrequent words or concepts can suggest traditional material. When attempting to isolate non-Pauline traditions, this criterion becomes more important. It can be used, however, for any type of preformed material since the genre of the literature affects diction and idiom. A piece composed originally as a different type of literature, such as a hymn, may still bear some marks of its original genre. This criterion, though, must be applied with caution.[14]

5. Traditional material may be indicated by the presence of extraneous details, that is, details that are an integral part of the tradition but extraneous in its present context. A tradition-piece is cited because one element of the tradition fits the context well. Yet when the entire unit is quoted, parts of the material may not fit well because its original *Sitz-im-Leben* was probably not the same as its present context. Thus a piece may in one part be congruent with the context, but in other parts be superfluous or tangential.[15]

6. Occasionally the actual content of the piece may indicate that it is a preformed tradition.[16]

---

[12] To adapt a criterion from source criticism in the gospels. D. R. Catchpole, "Tradition History", in *New Testament Interpretation: Essays on Principles and Methods*, ed. I. H. Marshall (Grand Rapids: Eerdmans, 1972), 174—76, may be justified in his rejection of this for gospel studies, but for the present application, 'multiple attestation' may be valid. The criterion of 'coherence' (p. 177) may be useful for determining traditional *concepts*; e.g., Paul's teaching on divorce (1 Cor. 7:10) is likely traditional, being coherent with Jesus' (Mk. 10:2—9; Lk. 16:18; Mt. 8:22 [=Lk. 9:60]), especially since this particular teaching may be disconsonant with the establishment. Coherence, though, is insufficient to indicate more than a traditional *concept*.

[13] See, *e.g.*, Ellis' use of this for determining the traditional nature of (1) certain OT expositions. (2) the virtue/vice lists, and (3) the *Haustafeln*. E. E. Ellis, "Traditions in 1 Corinthians", 482—83.

[14] The role of the secretary can easily account for many of these differences.

[15] *E.g.*, the tradition in 1 Cor. 8:6. Idols are nothing, Paul argues, because there is only one God and the food offered to them is clean because Christ created all things. The piece is cited because it speaks of God as one and Christ as creator (δι' οὗ τὰ πάντα). Yet the piece goes on to speak of Christ as savior, a point unnecessary — even irrelevant — to the argument. Incidently, this passage also meets other criteria, *viz.*, nos. 4, 7, 8, and possibly 9 (see below). On the traditional character of 1 Cor. 8:6, also see E. E. Ellis, "Traditions in 1 Corinthians", 494—95. Although Markus Barth notes its subjective nature, he nonetheless considers this a valid indicator: an "interruption of the context, perhaps even contradiction to it which, however, is toned down by interpolations". Barth, "Traditions in Ephesians", 10.

[16] M. Barth suggests two: (a) a summary presentation of the gospel's substance, without concern for historical details or witnesses, and (b) an emphasis on the cosmic extension of Christ's realm — in his pre-existence, at the present time and at the parousia — coupled with (or, by supposed interpolations corrected to describe) his specific care for the Church; "Traditions in Ephesians", 10.

b) Criteria related to form

7. The insertion of traditional material may interrupt the syntax or thought flow of the author, that is, the larger passage may read quite smoothly when the material is removed. The smooth continuation of thought may have been more likely if the tradition-piece was not written out in full until a later draft, that is, that author merely marked the text for insertion later.[17]

8. Traditional material in the Pauline literature often takes a rhythmic form, as evidenced by the ability to arrange it in parallel sense-lines or stanzas and occasionally by *homoiarcha* or *homoiteleuta*.[18] Parallelism is a strong indicator. Although less common, the content may also be arranged in parallelism (synonymously, antithetically, or chiastically).[19]

9. Certain syntactical features appear to be common in the traditional material in the New Testament: the use of appositives, predicate nominatives, participial[20] and relative clauses (frequently in parallel), changes in person and number, and anarthrous nouns where the article often is used[21].

No one criterion is decisive by itself. Yet material that meets several criteria, especially if in both content and form, may be called traditional with reasonable certainty.[22] The use of the ambiguous phrase "several criteria" is unavoidable.

---

[17] *E.g.*, Rom. 1:3–4. The Pauline introduction reads smoothly without the material, perhaps following more closely the typical Pauline form: "...the gospel concerning his son, [deletion] Jesus Christ our Lord, through whom we have received grace and apostleship..." This piece also meets criteria nos. 2, 4, 8, and 9.

[18] *E.g.*, see Rom. 14:7–9. A suggested arrangement is offered below, n. 22. Also see M. Barth, "Traditions in Ephesians", 10.

[19] *E.g.*, see Rom. 10:9–10. Also see the discussion of chiasmus in Paul, above, pp. 140–41, esp. nn. 50–52, and App. E; and M. Barth, "Traditions in Ephesians", 10.

[20] See Jewett, "Confession", 100. Participles at the beginning of subordinate clauses may be a strong indicator; see K. Wengst, *Christologische Formeln und Lieder der Urchristentum*, 2d ed., SNT, no. 7 (Gütersloh: Mohn, 1973), 112; esp. 3rd person singular aorists, so M. Barth, "Traditions in Ephesians", 10.

[21] See H. Zimmermann, *Neutestamentliche Methodenlehre* (Stuttgart: Katholisches Bibelwerk, 1967), 198. Also see Jewett, "Confession", 101. M. Barth generalizes this into a criterion of "brevity achieved by the use of anarthrous abstract nouns – sometimes coupled with repetitions and pleonasms in the form of synonyms or genitive appositives; "Traditions in Ephesians", 10.

[22] *E.g.*, I applied these to a passage that has not been not considered traditional material, [I know of noone who cites this as traditional material, including, *e.g.*, (*e silentio*), U. Wilckens, *Der Brief an die Römer*, 3 vols., in EKKNT (Zurich: Neukirchener, 1978–82), 3: 84–85; Conzelmann, *An Outline of the Theology of the New Testament* (New York: Harper & Row, 1969), 279; and *vid. NA*[26]]: Rom. 14:7–9:

Appendix 221

They are not equal in value; hence the number of necessary criteria vary. The decision as to whether the evidence is sufficient to warrant calling the material traditional unfortunately remains somewhat subjective.[23]

οὐδεὶς γὰρ (ἡμῶν) ἑαυτῷ ζῇ
καὶ οὐδεὶς ἑαυτῷ ἀποθνῄσκει
    ἐάν τε γὰρ ζῶμεν, τῷ κυρίῳ ζῶμεν,
    ἐάν τε ἀποθνῄσκωμεν, τῷ κυρίῳ ἀποθνῄσκομεν,
        ἐάν τε οὖν ζῶμεν
        ἐάν τε ἀποθνῄσκωμεν
            τοῦ κυρίου ἐσμέν.
εἰς τοῦτο γὰρ
    Χριστὸς ἀπέθανεν καὶ ἔζησεν
    ἵνα καὶ νεκρῶν καὶ ζώντων κυριεύσῃ.

Several criteria are evident here. (1) There are details, like lording over the living and the dead, that are an integral part of the piece (note the consistent contrast of 'living' and 'dying' throughout) but are extraneous here. Actually the entire piece is slightly off the theme of the context. (2) The flow of Paul's argument reads well with this piece removed, although v. 7 may have been written to lead into the piece. (3) The use of Χριστός alone. (4) The abrupt change in person and number. And (5) the parallelism, rhythm, and *homoiteleuta*, although based on a common Pauline idiom, are striking, and — not wishing to disparage the spontaneous creativity of the apostle — probably indicate a prior composition.

[23] This problem, however, does not render the criteria useless. Compare the parallel procedure in textual criticism.
An intriguing possibility arises: might the various criteria be assigned numerical values based upon their relative importance? A required minimum total could be determined, perhaps making the process more objective.

Sources Consulted

Adeney, W. F.: *A Commentary on Paul's Epistle to the Galatians*. The Century Bible Commentary Series. London: Caxton, 1911.
Albert, Paul: *Le genre epistolaire chez le Anciens*. Paris: Librairie Hachette, 1896.
Alon, Gedalyahu: *Jews, Judaism and the Classical World*. Translated by Israel Abrahams. Jerusalem: Magnes, 1977.
Amherst Papyri. Edited by B. P. Grenfell and A. S. Hunt. 2 vols. London: H. Frowde, 1900–01.
Andrews, Mary: "Paul, Philo, and the Intellectuals". *Journal of Biblical Literature* 53 (1934): 150–66.
The Apostolic Fathers. Edited and translated by Kirsopp Lake. 2 vols. The Loeb Classical Library, Greek Series. Cambridge: Harvard University, 1976–77.
Arrian: *Anabasis Alexandri*. Edited and translated by P. A. Brunt. 2 vols. The Loeb Classical Library, Greek Series. Cambridge: Harvard University, 1976.
Attridge, Harold: *First Century Cynicism in the Epistles of Heraclitus*. Harvard Theological Studies, no. 29. Missoula, MT: Scholars, 1976.
Backus, D.: "Some Sources of Graeco-Roman Features in the New Testament". *Concordia Theological Monthly* 38 (1967): 655–57.
Baer, G.: "Zur iraelitisch-jüdischen Briefliteratur". In *Alttestamentliche Studien Rudolf Kittel zum 60. Geburtstag dargebracht*, ed. A. Alt, 20–41. Leipzig: Hinrichs, 1913.
Bagnall, Roger S. and Peter Derow, eds.: *Greek Historical Documents: the Hellenistic Period*. Society of Biblical Literature Sources for Biblical Study Series, no. 16. Chico, CA: Scholars, 1981.
Bahr, Gordon J.: "Paul and Letter Writing in the First Century". *Catholic Biblical Quarterly* 28 (1966): 465–77.
–, "The Subscriptions in the Pauline Letters". *Journal of Biblical Literature* 87 (1968): 27–41.
Bailey, David Roy Shackleton: *Cicero*. Classical Life and Letters Series. New York: Scribners, 1971.
Bailey, John A.: "Who Wrote II Thessalonians?" *New Testament Studies* 25 (1979): 131–45.
Bakir, ᶜabd el-Mohsen: *Egyptian Epistolography from the Eighteenth to the Twenty-first Dynasty*. Cairo: L'institut français d'archéologie orientale, 1970.
Bandstra, A. J.: "Paul, the Letter Writer". *Calvin Theological Journal* 3 (1968): 176–80.
Barrett, C. K.: *A Commentary on the First Epistle to the Corinthians*. Harper's New Testament Commentary Series. New York: Harper & Row, 1968.
Barth, Markus: *Ephesians*. The Anchor Bible Commentary Series. Garden City, NY: Doubleday, 1974.
–, "Traditions in Ephesians". *New Testament Studies* 30 (1984): 3–25.
Bauer, Walter: *Die Briefe des Ignatius von Antiochia und der Polykarpbrief*. Vol. 2 in *Die Apostolischen Väter*. 3 vols. in 1. Handbuch zum Neuen Testament Supplement Series. Tübingen: Mohr, 1920.

–, ed.: *A Greek-English Lexicon of the New Testament*. Translated by W. F. Arndt. Edited by F. W. Gingrich, and F. W. Danker. Chicago: University of Chicago, 1979.

Baur, Ferdinand Christian: *Kritische Untersuchung über die kanonischen Evangelien: ihre Verhältnisse zu Einander, ihren Charakter und Ursprung*. Tübingen: Fues, 1847.

Bell, H. I.: "Some Private Letters of the Roman Period from the London Collection". *Revue egyptologique*, n.s., 1 (1919): 203–6.

Benoit, P., J. T. Milik, and R. de Vaux: *Les grottes de Murabba'ât*. Discoveries in the Judean Desert Series, no. 2. Oxford: Oxford University, 1961.

Bereńyi, Gabriella: "Gal. 2:20: a Pre-Pauline or Pauline Text?" *Biblica* 65 (1984): 490–537.

Berger, K.: "Apostelbriefe und apostolische Rede: zum Formular frühchristlicher Briefe". *Zeitschrift für die neutestamentliche Wissenschaft* 65 (1974): 190–231.

Betz, Hans Dieter: *Der Apostel Paulus und die sokratische Tradition: eine exegetische Untersuchung zu seiner 'Apologie' 2 Korinther 10–13*. Beiträge zur historischen Theologie, no. 45. Tübingen: Mohr, 1972.

–, *Galatians: a Commentary on Paul's Letter to the Churches in Galatia*. Hermeneia Commentary Series. Philadelphia: Fortress, 1979.

–, ed.: *The Greek Magical Papyri in Translation*. Chicago: University of Chicago, 1986.

–, "The Literary Composition and Function of Paul's Letter to the Galatians". *New Testament Studies* 21 (1975): 353–79.

–, *2 Corinthians 8 and 9*. Philadelphia: Fortress, 1985.

Blass, F. B.: *A Grammar of New Testament Greek*. Translated by H. St. J. Thackeray. London: Macmillan & Co., 1898.

Böhlig, Hans: "En Kyriō". In *Neutestamentliche Studien Georg Heinrici zu seinem 70. Geburtstag dargebracht*, ed. Hans Windisch, 170–75. Untersuchungen zum Neuen Testament, no. 6. Leipzig: Hinrichs, 1914.

Bornkamm, Günther: "The Letter to the Romans as Paul's Last Will and Testament". In *The Romans Debate*, ed. Karl P. Donfried, 17–31. Minneapolis: Augsburg, 1977.

–, "Der Philipperbrief als paulinische Briefsammlung". In *Neotestamentica et Patristica: eine Freundesgabe, Herrn Professor Dr. Oscar Cullmann zu seinem 60. Geburtstag überreicht*, ed. W. C. van Unnik, 192–202. Supplements to Novum Testamentum Series, no. 6. Leiden: Brill, 1962.

Bowersock, G. W.: *Greek Sophists in the Roman Empire*. Oxford: Clarendon, 1969.

Bowker, J. W.: "'Merkabah' Visions and the Visions of Paul". *Journal of Semitic Studies* 16 (1971): 157–73.

Bradley, David: "The Topos as a Form in the Pauline Paraenesis". *Journal of Biblical Literature* 72 (1953): 238–46.

Braun, Herbert: *Qumran und das Neue Testament*. Tübingen: Mohr, 1966.

Brinkmann, L.: "Die ältesten Briefsteller". *Rheinisches Museum für Philologie*, n.s., 64 (1909): 310–17.

Bruce, F. F.: "The Romans Debate – Continued". *Bulletin of the John Rylands Library* 64 (1982): 334–59.

–, "St. Paul in Macedonia, 3: the Philippian Correspondence". *Bulletin of the John Rylands University Library of Manchester* 63 (1981): 260–84.

Bruyne, D. de.: "Les plus anciens prologues latines des Evangile". *Revue bénédictine* 40 (1928): 193–214.

Bultmann, Rudolf: "Die Bedeutung des geschichtlichen Jesus für die Theologie des Paulus". In *Glauben und Verstehen*, 2: 188–213. Tübingen: Mohr, 1933.

–, *Der Stil der paulinischen Predigt und die kynisch-stoische Diatribe*. Göttingen: Vandenhoeck & Ruprecht, 1910.

–, *Theology of the New Testament*. Translated by K. Grobel. 2 vols. London: SCM, 1952.
Burstein, Stanley M. ed.: *The Hellenistic Age from the Battle of Ipsos to the Death of Kleopatra VII*. Translated Documents of Greece and Rome Series, no. 3. Cambridge: Cambridge University, 1985.
Burton, Ernest DeWitt: *A Critical and Exegetical Commentary on the Epistle to the Galatians*. The International Critical Commentary, New Testament Series. New York: Scribner's Sons, 1920.
Cadbury, H. J.: "The Dilemma of Ephesians". *New Testament Studies* 5 (1958): 91–102.
Calderine, Aristide: "Pensiero e sentimento nelle lettere private greche dei papiri". *Studi Della Scuolo Papirologica* 2 (1980): 2–28.
Cancik, Hildegard: *Untersuchungen zu Senecas Epistolas morales*. Spudasmata Series, no. 18. Hildesheim: Georg Olms, 1967.
Cannon, George E.: *The Use of Traditional Materials in Colossians*. Macon: Mercer University, 1983.
Carrez, M.: "Le 'nous' en 2 Corinthiens: Contribution à l'étude de l'apostolicité dans 2 Corinthiens". *New Testament Studies* 26 (1980): 474–86.
Catchpole, D. R.: "Tradition History". In *New Testatment Interpretation: Essays on Principles and Methods*, ed. I. H. Marshall, 165–80. Grand Rapids: Eerdmans, 1972.
Chamberlain, W. D.: *An Exegetical Grammar of the Greek New Testament*. New York: Macmillan, 1941.
Charlesworth, James H., ed.: *The Old Testament Pseudepigrapha*. 2 vols. Garden City, NY: Double Day & Co., 1983–85.
Church, F. Forrester: "Rhetorical Structure and Design in Paul's Letter to Philemon". *Harvard Theological Review* 71 (1978): 17–33.
Cicero, Marcus Tullius: *Letters to Atticus [Epistulae ad Atticum]*. Edited and translated by E. O. Winstedt. 3 vols. The Loeb Classical Library, Latin Series. Cambridge: Harvard University, 1966–70.
–, *Letters to His Friends [Epistulae ad Familiares]*. Edited and translated by W. Glynn Williams. 3 vols. The Loeb Classical Library, Latin Series. Cambridge: Harvard University, 1965–72.
–, *Letters to Quintus [Epistulae ad Quintum Fratrem]*, *Brutus [ad Brutum]*; *Comment. Petit.*; *Ep. ad Octav*. Edited and translated by William Armistead Falconer. Enlarged edition. The Loeb Classical Library, Latin Series. Cambridge: Harvard University, 1972.
–, *Select Letters*. Edited and translated by D. R. S. Bailey. Cambridge Greek and Latin Classic Series. New York: Cambridge University, 1979.
–, *Select Orations*. Rev. ed. Edited and translated by J. B. Greenough and G. L. Kittredge. Boston: Athenaeum, 1897.
Clark, Donald L.: *Rhetoric in Greco-Roman Education*. New York: Colombia University, 1957.
Clark, Gillian, "The Social Status of Paul". *Expository Times* 96 (1985): 110–11.
Coetzer, Wentzel, "The Literary Genre of Paranesis in the Pauline Letters". *Theologica Evangelica* 17 (1984): 36–42.
Collins, Raymond F.: "The Unity of Paul's Paraenesis in 1 Thess 4:3–8 and 1 Cor 7:1–7: a Significant Parallel". *New Testament Studies* 29 (1983): 420–29.
Conzelmann, Hans: *1 Corinthians: a Commentary on the First Epistle to the Corinthians*. Translated by J. W. Leitch. Hermeneia Commentary Series. Philadelphia: Fortress, 1975.
–, *An Outline of the Theology of the New Testament*. New York: Harper & Row, 1969.
–, "Paulus und die Weisheit". *New Testament Studies* 12 (1965): 231–44.

Cook, David: "The Pastoral Fragments Reconsidered". *Journal of Theological Studies*, n.s., 35 (1984): 120–31.
Corpus Inscriptionum Graecarum. 4 vols. Edited by Augustus Boeckhius (vols. 1–2), Ioannes Franzius (vol. 3), and Ernestus Curtius and Adolphus Kirchoff (vol. 4). Studia Epigraphica: Auellen und Abhandlungen zur griechischen Epigraphik. New York: Georg Olms, 1977.
Corpus Inscriptionum Herodianum I: Introduction, Bibliography, and Historical Analysis. Edited by E. Jerry Vardaman. Waco, TX: Baylor University, 1974.
Corpus Inscriptionum Iudaicarum. Edited by Jean Baptiste Frey. Rome: Pontificio Istituto di Archeologia Cristiana, 1925–36.
Corpus Inscriptionum Latinarum. Edited by Attilio Degrassi. Berolini: De Gruyter, 1965.
Cotton, Hannah: "Greek and Latin Epistolary Formulae: Some Light on Cicero's Letter Writing". *American Journal of Philology* 105 (1984): 409–25.
Cranfield, C. E. B.: "Changes in Person and Number in Paul's Epistles". *Paul and Paulinism: Essays in Honour of C. K. Barrett*, ed. M. D. Hooker and S. B. Wilson, 280–89. London: S.P.C.K., 1982.
Cullmann, Oscar: *Die ersten christlichen Glaubensbekenntnisse*. Zürich: Evangelischer, 1949.
–, "'*KYRIOS*' as Designation for the Oral Tradition Concerning Jesus: (*Paradosis* and *Kyrios*)". *Scottish Journal of Theology* 3 (1950): 180–97.
Dahl, N. A.: "The Particularity of the Pauline Epistles as a Problem in the Ancient Church". In *Neotestamentica et Patristica: eine Freundesgabe, Herrn Professor Dr. Oscar Cullmann zu seinem 60. Geburtstag überreicht*, ed. W. C. van Unnik, 261–71. Supplements to Novum Testamentum Series, no. 6. Leiden: Brill, 1962.
Daube, David: "Rabbinic Methods of Interpretation and Hellenistic Rhetoric". *Hebrew Union College Annual* 22 (1949): 239–64.
Davies, William David: *The New Creation*. Philadelphia: Fortress, 1971.
–, "Paul and the Dead Sea Scrolls: Flesh and Spirit". In *The Scrolls and the New Testament*, ed. Krister Stendahl, 157–82. New York: Harper & Bros., 1957.
–, *Paul and Rabbinic Judaism*. 4th ed. Philadelphia: Fortress, 1980.
Davies, W. D.: and Louis Finkelstein, eds. *The Cambridge History of Judaism*. Vol. 1. *Introduction: the Persian Period*. Cambridge: Cambridge University, 1984.
Davis, W. Hershey: *Greek Papyri of the First Century*. New York: Harper & Bros., 1933.
Deissmann, Adolf: *Bible Studies*. 2d ed. Translated by Alexander Grieve. Edinburgh: T & T Clark, 1909.
–, "Epistolary Literature". In *Encyclopaedia Biblica: a Critical Dictionary of the Literary, Political, and Religious History, the Archaeology, Geography, and Natural History of the Bible*, 4 vols., ed. T. K. Cheyne and J. Sutherland Black, cols. 1323–29. London: Adams and Charles Black, 1899–1903.
–, *Light from the Ancient East: the New Testament Illustrated by Recently Discovered Texts of the Graeco-Roman World*. Translated by Lionel R. M. Strachan. London: Hodder & Stoughton, 1910.
–, *St. Paul: a Study in Social and Religious History*. Translated by L. R. M. Strachan. London: Hodder & Stoughton, 1912.
Demetrius of Phaleron: *On Style*. Translated by W. R. Roberts. In *Demetrius of Phaleron: Spurious and Doubtful Works*. The Loeb Classical Library, Greek Series. New York: Putnam's Sons, 1927.
Dibelius, Martin: *An Philemon*. 3d ed. Edited by Heinrich Greeven. Handbuch zum Neuen Testament Series. Tübingen: Mohr, 1953.
–, *From Tradition to Gospel*. 2d ed. Translated by B. L. Woolf. New York: Scribner's Sons, 1965.

—, "Mystic and Prophet". Translated by Wayne Meeks. In *The Writings of St. Paul*, ed. W. Meeks, 395—409. New York: Norton, 1972; original German edition, "Paulus und die Mystik". In *Botschaft und Geschichte*, vol. 2. Munich: E. Reinhardt, 1941.

—, "Paul on the Areopagus". In *Studies in the Acts of the Apostles*, ed. Heinrich Greeven, 138—85. Translated by Mary Ling. New York: Scribners, 1956.

—, "The Speeches of Acts and Ancient Historiography". In *Studies in the Acts of the Apostles*, ed. Heinrich Greeven, 26—77. Translated by Mary Ling. New York: Scribners, 1956.

Dibelius, Martin, and Hans Conzelmann: *The Pastoral Epistles*. Rev. ed. Translated by P. Buttolph and A. Yarbro. Hermeneia Commentary Series. Philadelphia: Fortress, 1972.

Dio Cassius Cocceianus: *Roman History*. Edited and translated by Earnest Cary. 9 vols. The Loeb Classical Library, Greek Series. (vols. 1—6) New York: Putnam's Sons; (vols. 7—9) Cambridge: Harvard University, 1914—55.

Diogenes Laertius: *Lives of Eminent Philosophers*. Edited and translated by R. D. Hicks. The Loeb Classical Library, Greek Series. Cambridge: Harvard University, 1925.

Dion, Paul E.: "The Aramaic 'Family Letter' and Related Epistolary Forms in Other Oriental Languages and in Hellenistic Greek". *Semeia* 22 (1981): 59—76.

—, "Aramaic Words for 'Letter'". *Semeia* 22 (1981): 77—88.

—, "Tentative Classification of Aramaic Letter Types". *Society of Biblical Literature Abstracts and Seminar Papers* 11 (1977): 415—41.

Dion, Paul E., Dennis Pardee, and James D. Whitehead: "La lettre araméenne passe-partout et ses sous-espèces". *Revue biblique* 89 (1982): 528—75.

—, "Les types épistolaires hébréo-araméens jusqu'au temps de Bar- Kokhbah". *Revue biblique* 86 (1979): 544—79.

Dodd, C. H.: *Apostolic Preaching and Its Developments*. 2d ed. London: Hodder & Stoughton, 1944; reprint, Grand Rapids: Baker, 1980.

Donfried, Karl Paul: "False Presuppositons in the Study of Romans". In *The Romans Debate*, ed. K. P. Donfried, 120—48. Minneapolis: Augsburg, 1977.

—, "A Look at Letters". *Interpretation* 29 (1975): 427—31.

—, "A Short Note on Romans 16". In *The Romans Debate*, ed. K. P. Donfried, 50—60. Minneapolis: Augsburg, 1977.

Doty, William G.: "Classification of Epistolary Literature". *Catholic Biblical Quarterly* 31 (1969): 183—99.

—, "The Epistle in Late Hellenism and Early Christianity: Developments, Influences, and Literary Form". Ph.D. diss., Drew University, 1966.

—, *Letters in Primitive Christianity*. Guides to Biblical Scholarship, New Testament Series. Philadelphia: Fortress, 1973.

Dugas, Ludwic: *L'amitié antique d'après les moeurs populaires et les théories des philosophes*. Paris: Felix Alcon, 1894.

Duncan, George: *The Epistle of Paul to the Galatians*. Moffatt New Testament Commentary Series. London: Hodder & Stoughton, 1934.

Dziatzko, C.: "Der Brief". In *Pauly's Real-Encyclopädie der classischen Altertumswissenschaft*, ed. August Friedrich von Pauly, Georg Wissowa, and Wilhelm Kroll, 24 vols. and supplements, 3: 836—38. Stuttgart: Druckenmuller, 1893—1963.

Easterling, P. E., and B. M. W. Knox, eds.: *The Cambridge History of Classical Literature*. Vol. 1, *Greek Literature*. New York: Cambridge University, 1985.

Ehrenberg, Victor, and A. H. M. Jones, eds.: *Documents Illustrating the Reigns of Augustus and Tiberius*. Rev. 2d ed. Oxford: Clarendon, 1954; reprint, Oxford: Clarendon, 1976.

Ellis, E. E.: "The Authorship of the Pastorals: a Résumé and Assessment of Recent Trends". In *Paul and His Recent Interpreters*, 49–57. Grand Rapids: Eerdmans, 1961.
–, "Exegetical Patterns in 1 Corinthians and Romans". In *Prophecy and Hermeneutic in Early Christianity: New Testament Essays*, 213–20. Wissenschaftliche Untersuchungen zum Neuen Testament, no. 18. Tübingen: Mohr, 1978; reprint, Grand Rapids: Eerdmans, 1980.
–, "Midrash Pēsher in Pauline Hermeneutics". In *Prophecy and Hermeneutic in Early Christianity: New Testament Essays*, 173–81. Wissenschaftliche Untersuchungen zum Neuen Testament, no. 18. Tübingen: Mohr, 1978; reprint, Grand Rapids: Eerdmans, 1980.
–, "Paul and His Co-Workers". In *Prophecy and Hermeneutic in Early Christianity: New Testament Essays*, 3–22. Wissenschaftliche Untersuchungen zum Neuen Testament, no. 18. Tübingen: Mohr, 1978; reprint, Grand Rapids: Eerdmans, 1980.
–, *Paul's Use of the Old Testament*. Grand Rapids: Baker, 1957; reprint, Grand Rapids: Baker, 1981.
–, "The Structure of Pauline Eschatology (2 Corinthians 5:1–10)". In *Paul and His Recent Interpreters*, 35–48. Grand Rapids: Eerdmans, 1961.
–, "Traditions in First Corinthians". *New Testament Studies* 32 (1986): 481–502.
Epictetus: *The Discourses as Reported by Arrian [Epicteti Dissertationes], the Manual, and Fragments*. Edited and translated by W. A. Oldfather. 2 vols. The Loeb Classical Library, Greek Series. Cambridge: Harvard University, 1925–28.
Epicurus: *Epicurus: the Extant Remains*. Edited and translated by Cyril Bailey. Oxford: Oxford University, 1926.
Erman, A.: *Die Literatur der Aegypter*. Leipzig: Teubner, 1923.
Eschlimann, J. A.: "La rédaction des epîtres pauliniennes: d'aprés une comparison avec les lettres profanes de son temps". *Revue biblique* 53 (1946): 185–96.
Eusebius: *The Ecclesiastical History [Historia ecclesiastica]*. Edited and translated by Kirsopp Lake (vol. 1) and J. E. L. Oulton (vol. 2). 2 vols. The Loeb Classical Library, Greek Series. Cambridge: Harvard University, 1980.
Exler, Francis X. J.: *The Form of the Ancient Greek Letter: a Study in Greek Epistolography*. Washington, DC: Catholic University of America, 1922.
Fee, Gordon: *1 and 2 Timothy, Titus*. Good News Commentary Series. San Francisco: Harper & Row, 1984.
Findlay, G. G.: *St. Paul's Epistle to the Galatians*. Expositor's Greek Testament Series. London: Hodder & Stoughton, 1888.
–, *St. Paul's First Epistle to the Corinthians*. Expositor's Greek Testament Series. London: Hodder & Stoughton, 1917.
Fiore, Benjamin: "'Covert Allusion' in 1 Corinthians 1–4". *Catholic Biblical Quarterly* 47 (1985): 85–102.
–, *The Function of Personal Example in the Socratic and Pastoral Letters*. Analecta Biblica Series, no. 105. Rome: Biblical Institute, 1986.
Fischer, James A.: "Pauline Literary Forms and Thought Patterns". *Catholic Biblical Quarterly* 39 (1977): 209–23.
Fitzmyer, Joseph A.: "Aramaic Epistolography". *Semeia* 22 (1981): 25–57.
–, "A Life of Paul". In *The Jerome Biblical Commentary*, ed. R. E. Brown, J. A. Fitzmyer, and R. E. Murphy, 2: 215–222. 2 vols in 1. Englewood Cliffs, NJ: Prentice-Hall, 1968.
–, "New Testament Epistles". In *The Jerome Biblical Commentary*, ed. R. E. Brown, J. A. Fitzmyer, and R. E. Murphy, 2: 223–26. 2 vols in 1. Englewood Cliffs, NJ: Prentice-Hall, 1968.
–, *Pauline Theology*. Englewood Cliffs, NJ: PrenticeHall, 1967.

–, "Some Notes on Aramaic Epistolography". *Journal of Biblical Literature* 93 (1974): 201–25.
Foat, F. W. G.: "On Old Greek Tachygraphy". *Journal of Hellenic Studies* 21 (1901): 238–67.
Francis, F. O.: "The Form and Function of the Opening and Closing Paragraphs of James and 1 John". *Zeitschrift für die neutestamentliche Wissenschaft* 61 (1970): 110–26.
Freeman, Kenneth J.: *The Schools of Hellas: an Essay on the Practice and Theory of Ancient Greek Education from 600 to 300 B.C.* Edited by M. J. Rendall. London: Macmillan, 1932.
Fronto: *The Correspondence of Marcus Cornelius Fronto*. Edited and translated by C. R. Haines. 2 vols. The Loeb Classical Library, Latin Series. Cambridge: Harvard University, 1919–20.
Fuhrman, Manfred: *Das systematische Lehrbuch: ein Beitrag zur Geschichte der Wissenschaft in der Antike*. Göttingen: Vandenhoeck & Ruprecht, 1960.
Funk, R. W.: "The Form and Structure of II and III John". *Journal of Biblical Literature* 86 (1967): 424–30.
–, *Language, Hermeneutic, and the Word of God*. New York: Harper & Row, 1966.
Furnish, Victor.: "The Jesus-Paul Debate: From Baur to Bultmann". *Bulletin of the John Rylands University Library of Manchester* 47 (1965): 342–75.
–, *II Corinthians*. In The Anchor Bible Commentary Series. Garden City, NY: Doubleday, 1984.
Gamble, Harry: *New Testament Canon: Its Making and Meaning*. Guides to Biblical Scholarship, New Testament Series. Philadelphia: Fortress, 1985.
–, "The Redaction of the Pauline Letters and the Formation of the Pauline Corpus". *Journal of Biblical Literature* 94 (1975): 403–18.
–, *The Textual History of the Letter to the Romans: a Study in Textual and Literary Criticism*. Studies and Documents Series, no. 42. Grand Rapids: Eerdmans, 1977.
Gardthausen, V.: "Tachygraphie oder Brachygraphie des Akropolis- Steines". *Archiv für Stenographie* 56 (1905): 81–84.
–, "Zur Tachygraphie der Griechen". *Hermes* 2 (1876): 444–45.
Garland, David E.: "The Composition and Unity of Philippians: Some Neglected Literary Factors". *Novum Testamentum* 27 (1985): 141–73.
Georgi, Dieter, ed.: *Concordance to the Corpus Hermeticum*. The Concordances to Patristic and Late Classical Texts Series. Cambridge: Boston Theological Institute, 1971.
–, *Die Gegner des Paulus im 2 Korintherbrief: Studien zur religiösen Propaganda in der Spät-Antike*. Wissenschaftliche Monographien zum Alten und Neuen Testament, no. 11. Neukirchen-Vluyn: Neukirchen, 1964.
Gerhard, G. A.: "Untersuchungen zur Geschichte des griechischen Briefes, I. Die Angangsformel". *Philologus* 64 (1905): 27–65.
Gitlbauer, Michael: *Die drei Systeme der griechische Tachygraphie*, Denkschriften der daiserliche Akademie der Wissenschaften, no. 44. Vienna: C. Gerold's Son, 1896.
Goguel, M.: "Esquisse d'une solution nouvelle du problème de l'épître aux Ephésiens". *Revue de l'histoire des religions* 111 (1935): 254ff.
Goldstein, Jonathan: *The Letters of Demosthenes*. New York: Colombia University, 1968.
Goodspeed, Edgar J.: *Index patristicus*. Leipzig: Hinrich, 1907; reprint (with corrections), Naperville, IL: Allenson, 1960.
–, *New Chapters in New Testament Study*. New York: Macmillan, 1937.
Gradenwitz, Otto: *Einführung in die Papyruskunde*. Erklärung ausgewählter Urkunden, no. 1. Leipzig: S. Hirzel, 1900.
Grant, Robert McQueen: "Paul, Galen, and Origen". *Journal of Theological Studies*, n.s., 34 (1983): 533–36.

Grosheide, F. W.: *A Commentary on the First Epistle to the Corinthians*. The New International Commentary on the New Testament Series. Grand Rapids: Eerdmans, 1953.
Gruen, Erich: *The Hellenistic World and the Coming of Rome*. Berkeley: University of California, 1984.
Gulak, Asher: *Das Urkundenwesen im Talmud im Lichte der griechischen-aegyptischen Papyri und des griechischen und römischen Rechts*. Jerusalem: R. Mars, 1935.
Guthrie, Donald: *Galatians*. The Century Bible Commentary, New Series. London: Th. Nelson, 1969.
–, *New Testament Introduction*. Downers Grove, IL: Inter-Varsity, 1970.
–, *The Pastoral Epistles*. The Tyndale New Testament Commentary Series. London: Tyndale, 1957.
Haelst, Joseph van: *Catalogue des papyrus littéraires juifs et chrétiens*. Paris: Sorbonne, 1976.
Haenchen, Ernst: *Die Apostelgeschichte*. Göttingen: Vandenhoeck & Ruprecht, 1959.
–, "The Book of Acts as Source Material for the History of Early Christianity". In *Studies in Luke-Acts: Essays Presented in Honor of Paul Schubert*, ed. L. E. Keck and J. L. Martyn, 258–78. Philadelphia: Fortress, 1980.
Hall, Robert: "The Rhetorical Outline for Galatians: a Reconsideration". *Journal of Biblical Literature* 106 (1987): 277–87.
Hammer, Paul. L.: "Canon and Theological Variety: a Study in the Pauline Tradition". *Zeitschrift für die neutestamentliche Wissenschaft* 67 (1976): 83–89.
Hammond Bammel, C. P.: "Ignatian Problems". *Journal of Theological Studies*, n.s., 33 (1982): 62–97.
Hanson, A. T.: *The Pastoral Epistles*. The New Century Bible Commentary Series. London: Marshall, Morgan, & Scott, 1982.
–, *The Pastoral Letters: a Commentary on the First and Second Letters to Timothy and the Letter to Titus*. Cambridge Bible Commentary Series. Cambridge: Cambridge University, 1966.
Hapel, Norman C.: "Appeal to Ancient Tradition as a Literary Form". *Zeitschrift für die alttestamentliche Wissenschaft* 88 (1976): 253–72.
Harper's Latin Dictionary. Revised and enlarged by C. T. Lewis and C. Short. New York: Harper & Bros., 1879.
Harris, Murray J.: "2 Corinthians 5:1–10: a Watershed in Paul's Eschatology?" *Tyndale Bulletin [TynB]* 22 (1971): 32–57.
Harrison, Percy Neal: *The Problem of the Pastorals*. London: Oxford University, 1921.
Hartman, L.: "On Reading Others' Letters". *Harvard Theological Review* 79 (1986): 137–46.
Hartmann, Karl: "Arrian und Epiktet". *Neue Jahrbücher für das klassische Altertum, Geschichte, und deutsche Literatur und für Pädagogik* 8 (1905): 248–75.
Hata, Gohei: "Is the Greek Version of Josephus' 'Jewish War' a Translation or a Rewriting of the First Version?" *Jewish Quarterly Review* 66 (1975): 89–108.
Hausrath, A.: *Der Vier-Capitelbrief des Paulus an die Korinther*. Heidelberg: F. Bassermann, 1870.
Havener, Ivan: "The Pre-Pauline Christological Creedal Formulae of 1 Thessalonians". *Society of Biblical Literature Abstracts and Seminar Papers* 20 (1981): 105–28.
Heard, R. G.: "The apomnēmoneumata in Papias, Justin, and Irenaeus". *New Testament Studies* 1 (1954): 130–34.
Hengel, Martin: *Acts and the History of Earliest Christianity*. Translated by John Bowden. Philadelphia: Fortress, 1979.

–, "Erwägungen zum Sprachgebrauch von χριστός bei Paulus und in der 'vorpaulinischen' Überlieferung". In *Paul and Paulinism: Essays in Honor of C. K. Barrett*, ed. M. D. Hooker and S. G. Wilson, 135–159. London: S.P.C.K., 1982.
–, *Jews, Greeks, and Barbarians*. Translated by John Bowden. Philadelphia: Fortress, 1980.
–, *Judaism and Hellenism*. Translated by J. Bowden. 2 vols. Philadelphia: Fortress, 1974.
Hennecke, Edgar: *New Testament Apocrypha*. Edited by Wilhelm Schneemelcher. Translated by R. M. Wilson. 2 vols. Philadelphia: Westminster, 1963–65.
Henneman, A.: "Der äußere und innere Stil in Traians Briefen". Ph.D. diss, Giessen, 1935.
Henshaw, T.: *New Testament Literature*. London: Hodder & Stoughton, 1963.
Hester, James D.: "The Rhetorical Structure of Galatians 1:11–2:14". *Journal of Biblical Literature* 103 (1984): 223–33.
Hirzel, Rudolf: *Der Dialog: ein literarhistorischer Versuch*. 2 vols. Stuttgart: S. Hirzel, 1895; reprint, Hildesheim, Geroge Olms, 1963.
Hitchcock, F. R. Montgomery: "The Use of *graphein*". *Journal of Theological Studies*, o.s., 31 (1930): 271–75.
Hock, Ronald F.: "Paul's Tentmaking and the Problem of his Social Class". *Journal of Biblical Literature* 97 (1978): 555–64.
–, "Simon the Shoemaker as the Ideal Cynic". *Greek, Roman, and Byzantine Studies* 17 (1976): 41–53.
Hock, Ronald F. and Edward N. O'Neil: *The Chreia in Ancient Rhetoric; Vol. 1: The Progymnasmata*. Society of Biblical Literature Texts and Translation Series, no. 27. Chico, CA: Scholars, 1986.
Hodgson, Robert: "Paul the Apostle and First Century Tribulation Lists". *Zeitschrift für die neutestamentliche Wissenschaft* 74 (1983): 1–2, 59–80.
Holladay, Carl R.: *Fragments from Hellenistic Jewish Authors*. Society of Biblical Literature Pseudepigrapha Series, no. 10. Chico, CA: Scholars, 1983.
Holtzmann, Heinrich Julius: *Pastoralbriefe*. Leipzig: Engelmann, 1880.
Horn, R. C.: "Life and Letters in the Papyri". *Classical Journal* 17 (1922): 487–502.
Howard, G. E. and J. C. Shelton: "The Bar-Kokhba Letters and Palestinian Greek". *Israel Exploration Journal* 23 (1973): 101–2.
Hubner, Hans: "Der Galaterbrief und das Verhältnis von antiker Rhetorik und Epistolographie". *Theologische Literaturzeitung* 109 (1984): 241–50.
Hunter, A. M.: *Paul and His Predecessors*. 2d ed. London: SCM, 1961.
Ignatius of Antioch: *Ignace d'Antioche*. 4th (corrected) ed. Translated by P. Th. Camelot. Sources chrétiennes, no. 10. Paris: Cerf, 1969.
–, *The Letters of Ignatius*. In *The Apostolic Fathers*. 2 vols. Translated by Kirsopp Lake. The Loeb Classical Library, Greek Series. Cambridge: Harvard University, 1977.
Isenberg, Sheldon R.: "Some Uses and Limitations of Social Scientific Methodology in the Study of Early Christianity". *Society of Biblical Literature Abstracts and Seminar Papers* 19 (1980): 29–49.
Jeremias, Joachim: *Briefe an Timotheus und Titus*. 2d ed. Göttingen: Vandenhoeck & Ruprecht, 1981.
–, "Chiasmus in den Paulusbriefen". *Zeitschrift für die neutestamentliche Wissenschaft* 49 (1958): 139–56.
–, *Jerusalem in the Time of Jesus*. Translated by F. H. and C. H. Cave. Philadelphia: Fortress, 1969.
Jervell, Jacob: "The Letter to Jerusalem". In *The Romans Debate*, ed. K. P. Donfried, 61–74. Minneapolis: Augsburg, 1977.

–, *The Unknown Paul: Essays on Luke-Acts and Early Christian History*. Minneapolis: Augsburg, 1984.
Jewett, Robert: "The Redaction and Use of an Early Christian Confession in Romans 1:3–4". In *The Living Text*, ed. D. E. Groh, 99–122. Lanham, MD: University Press of America, 1985.
Johnen, Chr.: *Allgemeine Geschichte der Kurzschrift*. 4th ed. Berlin: F. Schrey, 1940.
–, *Geschichte der Stenographie: im Zusammenhang mit der allgemeinen Entwicklung der Schrift und der Schriftkürzung*. Berlin: F. Schrey, 1911.
Johnson, Luke: *The Writings of the New Testament: an Interpretation*. Philadelphia: Fortress, 1986.
Johnson, P. F.: "The Use of Statistics in the Analysis of the Characteristics of Pauline Writing". *New Testament Studies* 20 (1973): 92–100.
Johnston, Harold W.: *Latin Manuscripts: an Elementary Introduction to the Use of Critical Editions*. The InterCollegiate Latin Series. Chicago: Scott, Foresman, & Co., 1897.
Josephus: *The Life, Against Apion, and the Jewish War [Bellum Judaicum]*. Edited and translated by H. St. J. Thackeray. 3 vols. The Loeb Classical Library, Greek Series. Cambridge: Harvard University, 1976.
Joxe, Friedrich: "Le Christianisme et l'évolution des sentiments familiaux dans les lettres privées sur papyrus". *Acta antiqua academiae scientiarum Hungaricae* 7 (1980): 411–20.
Judge, Edwin A.: *Rank and Status in the World of the Caesars and St. Paul*. University of Cantebury Series, no. 29. Christchurch, NZ: University of Cantebury, 1982.
–, "The Reaction against Classical Education in the New Testament". *Journal of Christian Education Papers* 77 (1983): 7–14.
Julian: *Letters*. Edited and translated by W. C. Wright. The Loeb Classical Library, Greek Series. Cambridge: Harvard University, 1923.
Karris, Robert J.: "The Occasion of Romans: a Response to Prof. Donfried". In *The Romans Debate*, ed. K. P. Donfried, 149–51. Minneapolis: Augsburg, 1977.
–, "Romans 14:1–15:13 and the Occasion of Romans". In *The Romans Debate*, ed. K. P. Donfried, 75–99. Minneapolis: Augsburg, 1977.
Käsemann, Ernst: "Das Interpretationsproblem des Epheserbriefes". *Theologische Literaturzeitung* 86 (1961): 1–8.
Kassel, Rudolph: *Untersuchungen zur griechischen und römischen Konsolationsliteratur*. Munich: Beck, 1958.
Keck, Leander, and Victor Furnish: *The Pauline Letters*. The Interpreting Biblical Texts Series. Nashville: Abingdon, 1984.
Kelly, John Maurice: *Roman Litigation*. Oxford: Clarendon, 1966.
Kelly, J. N. D.: *A Commentary on the Pastoral Epistles*. Harpers New Testament Commentary Series. New York: Harper, 1963; reprint, Grand Rapids: Baker, Thornapple Commentary Series, 1981.
Kennedy, George A.: *New Testament Interpretation through Rhetorical Criticism*. Studies in Religion Series. Chapel Hill: University of North Carolina, 1984.
Kenney, E. J. and W. V. Clausen, eds.: *The Cambridge History of Classical Literature: Latin Literature*. New York: Cambridge University, 1982.
Kenny, Anthony: *A Stylometric Study of the New Testament*. Oxford: Clarendon, 1986.
Kenyon, Frederic G.: *Books and Readers in Ancient Greece and Rome*. 2d ed. Oxford: Clarendon, 1951.
–, *The Paleography of Greek Papyri*. Oxford: Clarendon, 1899; reprint, Chicago: Argonaut, 1970.
Keyes, Clinton: "The Greek Letter of Introduction". *American Journal of Philology* 56 (1935): 28–44.

Kim, Chan-Hie: *The Form and Structure of the Familiar Greek Letter of Recommendation*. The Society of Biblical Literature Dissertation Series, no. 4. Missoula, MT: Scholars, 1972.
–, "Index of Greek Papyrus Letters". *Semeia* 22 (1981): 107–12.
–, "Papyrus Invitation". *Journal of Biblical Literature* 94 (1975): 391–402.
Kittel, Gerhard, and Gerhard Friedrich, eds.: *The Theological Dictionary of the New Testament*. Edited and translated by W. Bromiley. 10 vols. Grand Rapids: Eerdmans, 1964–76. S.v. "γραμματεύς", by Joachim Jeremias.
Klein, Günter: "Paul's Purpose in Writing the Epistle to the Romans". In *The Romans Debate*, ed. K. P. Donfried, 32–49. Minneapolis: Augsburg, 1977.
Knox, John: *Chapters in the Life of Paul*. New York: Abingdon, 1950.
Koch, Dietrich-Alexander: "Beobachtungen zum christologischen Schriftgebrauch in den vorpaulinischen Gemeinden". *Zeitschrift für neutestamentliche Wissenschaft* 71 (1980): 174–91.
Koskenniemi, Heikki: "Cicero über die Briefarten (*genera epistularum*)". *Arctos* (1954): 97–102.
–, *Studien zur Idee und Phraseologie des griechischen Briefes bis 400 n. Chr.* Helsinki: Suomalainen Tiedeakatemia, 1956.
Kuhn, K. G.: "Der Epheserbrief im Lichte der Qumrantexte". *New Testament Studies* 7 (1961): 334–46.
Kümmel, W. Georg: *Introduction to the New Testament*. Rev. ed. Translated by H. C. Kee. Nashville: Abingdon, 1975.
–, "Das literarische und geschichtliche Problem des ersten Thessalonischerbriefes". In *Neotestamentica et Patristica: eine Freundesgabe, Herrn Professor Dr. Oscar Cullmann zu seinem 60. Geburtstag überreicht*, ed. W. C. van Unnik, 213–27. Supplements to Novum Testamentum Series, no. 6. Leiden: Brill, 1962.
Ladd, George Eldon: "Paul's Friends in Colossians 4:7–16". *Review and Expositor* 70 (1973): 507–14.
Ladouceur, David J.: "The Language of Josephus". *Journal for the Study of Judaism in the Persian, Hellenistic and Roman Period* 14 (1983): 18–38.
Lambrecht, J.: "Paul's Farewell Address at Miletus". In *Actes de Apôtres: tradition, redaction, théologie*, ed. J. Kremer. Bibliotheca ephemeridum theologicarum louvaniensium, no. 48. Louvan: University of Louvan, 1979.
Lampe, Peter: "Zur Textgeschichte des Römerbriefes". *Novum Testamentum* 27 (1985): 273–77.
Lausberg, Heinrich: *Handbuch der literarischen Rhetorik: eine Grundlegung der Literaturwissenschaft*. Munich: M. Huebner, 1960.
Lebreton, M. Jules: *Études sur la langue et la grammaire de Cicéron*. Paris: Bloud & Gay, 1901.
Levy, Matthias: *The History of Short-hand Writing*. London: Trübner & Co., 1862.
Lewis, Naphtali: *Life in Egypt under Roman Rule*. Oxford: Clarendon, 1983.
Liddell, H. G., and R. Scott, eds.: *A Greek-English Lexicon*. Revised by H. S. Jones and R. McKenzie. Oxford: Clarendon, 1968.
Lietzmann, D. H.: *An die Korinther I. II*. Handbuch zum Neuen Testament Series. Tübingen: Mohr, 1969.
Lillie, William: "Pauline House-Tables". *Expository Times* 86 (1975): 179–83.
Lindemann, Andreas: "Bemerkungen zu den Adressaten und zum Anlasse des Epheserbriefes". *Zeitschrift für die neutestamentliche Wissenschaft* 67 (1976): 235–51.
Livius, Titus: *History of Rome*. Edited and translated by B. O. Foster, F. G. Moore, E. T. Sage, and A. C. Schlesinger. 14 vols. The Loeb Classical Library, Latin Series. Cambridge: Harvard University, 1962–76.

Longenecker, Richard N.: *Biblical Exegesis in the Apostolic Period*. Grand Rapids: Eerdmans, 1975.
–, *Paul: Apostle of Liberty*. Grand Rapids: Baker, 1964; reprint, Grand Rapids: Baker, 1976.
Lossmann, Friedrich: *Cicero und Caesar im Jahre 54: Studien zur Theorie und Praxis der römischen Freundschaft*. Hermes Einzelschrift Series, no. 17. Wiesbaden: Steiner, 1962.
Lund, Nils Wilhelm: *Chiasmus in the New Testament: a Study in Formgeschichte*. Chapel Hill: University of North Carolina, 1942.
Malherbe, Abraham: "Ancient Epistolary Theorists". *Ohio Journal of Religious Studies* 5 (1977): 3–77.
–, *The Cynic Epistles: a Study Edition*. The Society of Biblical Literature Sources for Biblical Study Series, no. 12. Missoula, MT: Scholars, 1977.
–, "Exhortation in First Thessalonians". *Novum Testamentum* 25 (1983): 238–56.
–, *Moral Exhortation: a Greco-Roman Sourcebook*. Library of Early Christianity Series. Philadelphia: Westminster, 1986.
–, "μὴ γένοιτο in the Diatribe and Paul". *Harvard Theological Review* 73 (1980): 231–40.
–, *The Social Aspects of Early Christianity*. Baton Rouge: Louisiana State University, 1977.
Manson, T. W.: "St. Paul's Letter to the Romans – and Others". In *The Romans Debate*, ed. P. K. Donfried, 1–16. Minneapolis: Augsburg, 1977.
Manus, Chris Ukachukwa: "The 'Amanuensis Hypothesis': a Key to the Understanding of Paul's Epistles in the New Testament". *Bible Bhashyam* 10 (1984): 160–74.
Marrou, H. I.: *A History of Education in Antiquity*. Translated by George Lamb. New York: Sheed & Ward, 1956.
Martialis, Marcus Valerius: *Epigrammata*. Edited and translated by W. M. Lindsay. Scriptorum classicorum bibliotheca Oxoniensis Series. Oxford: Clarendon, 1902.
Marty, Jacques: "Contribution a l'étude de fragments épistolaires antiques, conservé principalement dans la Bible hebräiques: les formules de salutation". In *Mélanges syriens offerts à Monsieur René Dussaud secrétaire perpétual de l'académie des inscriptions et belles-lettres par ses amis et ses élèves*, 2 vols., 845–55. Bibliotheque archeologique de historique Series, no. 30. Paris: Geuthner, 1939.
Massie, John: *Corinthians: Introduction*. Rev. ed. The Century Bible Commentary Series. London: Blackwood, Le Bas & Co., n.d. [1902?].
Mayer, Gunther: *Index Philoneus*. Berlin: de Gruyter, 1974.
McArthur, H. K.: "Kai Frequency in Greek Letters". *New Testament Studies* 15 (1969): 339–49.
McDonald, J. I. H.: "Was Romans XVI a Separate Letter?" *New Testament Studies* 16 (1970): 369–72.
McEleney, Neil J.: "The Vice Lists of the Pastoral Epistles". *Catholic Biblical Quarterly* 36 (1974): 203–19.
McKenzie, John L.: *Light on the Epistles: a Reader's Guide*. Chicago: Thomas More, 1975.
Meecham, H. G.: *Light from Ancient Letters*. New York: Macmillan, 1923.
Meeks, Wayne A., and Robert L. Wilken: *Jews and Christians in Antioch in the First Four Centuries of the Common Era*. The Society of Biblical Literature Sources for Biblical Study Series, no. 13. Missoula, MT: Scholars, 1978.
Mentz, Arthur: *Die Geschichte der Kurzschrift*. Wolfenbüttel: Heckners, 1949.
–, *Geschichte der Stenographie*. 2d ed. Berlin: Gerdes & Hödel, 1907.
–, *Geschichte und Systeme der griechischen Tachygraphie*. Berlin: Gerdes & Hödel, 1907.
–, "Die Grabschrift eines griechischen Tachygraphen". *Archiv für Stenographie* 54 (1902): 49–53.

"Römische und griechische Stenographie". *Archiv für Schreib- und Buchwesen* 4 (1930): 67–70.

–, *Die tironischen Noten: eine Geschichte der römischen Kurzschrift.* Berlin: de Gruyter, 1944.

Metzger, Bruce Manning: *The New Testament: Its Background, Growth, and Content.* 2d ed. Nashville: Abingdon, 1983.

–, *New Testament Studies: Philogical, Versional, and Patristic.* New Testament Tools and Studies Series, no. 10. Leiden: Brill, 1980.

–, "A Reconsideration of Certain Arguments against Pauline Authorship of the Pastoral Epistles". *Expository Times* 70 (1958): 91–92.

Metzger, Wolfgang: *Die letzte Reise des Apostels Paulus.* Stuttgart: Calwer, 1976.

Meyer, H. A. W.: *A Critical and Exegetical Hand-book to the Epistle to the Corinthians.* New York: Funk & Wagnalls, 1884.

Michaelson, S., and A. Q. Morton: "Last Words: a Test for Authorship for Greek Writers". *New Testament Studies* 18 (1972): 192–208.

Millard, Alan R.: "In Praise of Ancient Scribes". *The Biblical Archaeologist* 45 (1982): 143–53.

Milligan, George: *New Testament Documents: Their Origin and Early History.* London: Macmillan & Co., 1913.

Milne, H. J. M.: *Greek Shorthand Manuals: Syllabary and Commentary.* London: Oxford University, 1934.

Mitteis, Ludwig: *Römisches Privatrecht bis auf die Zeit Diokletians.* 2 vols. Leipzig: Duncker & Humblot, 1908.

Moffatt, James: *An Introduction to the Literature of the New Testament.* The International Theological Library Series. 3d ed. Edinburgh: T & T Clark, 1949.

Mondini, Maria: "Lettere femminili nei papiri greco-egizi". *Studi Della Scuola Papirologica* 2 (1980): 29–50.

Montagnini, Felice: "Christological Features in Eph. 1:3–14". In *Paul de Tarse: Apôtre du notre temps*, ed. L. de Lorenzi, 538–39. Rome: Abbey of St. Paul, 1979.

Montefiore, C. G.: *Judaism and St. Paul.* London: Goschen, 1914.

Montfaucon, Bernard de: *Palaeographia graeca: sive de ortu et progressu literarum graecarum.* Paris: la communaute des libraires et imprimeurs de Paris, 1708; reprint (by photo-reproduction), Westmead, GB: Gregg International, 1970.

Moore, George Foote: *Judaism.* 2 vols. Cambridge: Harvard University, 1927.

Morgenstern, Otto: "Cicero und die Stenographie". *Archiv für Stenographie* 56 (1905): 1–6.

Morrow, G. R.: *Plato's Epistles: a Translation with Critical Essays and Notes.* Indianapolis: Bobbs & Merrill, 1962.

Morton, A. Q.: "The Authorship of the Pauline Corpus". In *The New Testament in Historical and Contemporary Perspective: Essays in Memory of G. H. C. Macgregor*, ed. H. Anderson and Wm. Barclay, 209–35. Oxford: B. Blackwell, 1965.

Morton, A. Q. and James McLeman: *Paul, the Man and the Myth: a Study in the Authorship of Greek Prose.* London: Hodder & Stoughton, 1966.

Motto, Anna Lydia: *Seneca.* New York: Twayne, 1973.

Moule, C. F. D.: *The Birth of the New Testament.* 3d rev. ed. San Francisco: Harper & Row, 1982.

–, "Jesus in New Testament Kerygma". In *Verborum Veritas: Festschrift für Gustav Stählin zu 70. Geburtstag*, ed. O. Böcher and K. Haacker, 15–26. Wuppertal: Theologischer Brockhaus, 1970.

–, "The Problem of the Pastoral Epistles: a Reappraisal". *Bulletin of the John Rylands University Library of Manchester* 47 (1965): 450–2.

–, "Saint Paul and 'Dualism': the Pauline Conception of Resurrection". *Essays in New Testament Interpretation*, 200–221. New York: Cambridge University, 1982.
–, "Some Observations on *Tendenzkritik*". In *Jesus and the Politics of His Day*, ed. Ernst Bammel and C. F. D. Moule, 91–100. Cambridge: Cambridge University, 1984.
Moulton, James Hope, and George Milligan: "Lexical Notes from the Papyri". *The Expositor*, 7th ser., 6 (1908): 84–93.
Mullins, Terrence Y.: "Ascription as a Literary Form". *NewTestament Studies* 19 (1973): 194–205.
–, "Disclosure: a Literary Form in the New Testament". *Novum Testamentum* 7 (1972): 44–50.
–, "Formulas in New Testament Epistles". *Journal of Biblical Literature* 91 (1972): 380–90.
–, "Greeting as a New Testament Form". *Journal of Biblical Literature* 87 (1968): 418–26.
–, "Petition as a Literary Form". *Novum Testamentum* 5 (1962): 48.
–, "The Thanksgivings of Philemon and Colossians". *New Testament Studies* 30 (1984): 288–93.
–, "Topos as a New Testament Form". *Journal of Biblical Literature* 99 (1980): 541–47.
–, "Visit Talk in New Testament Letters". *Catholic Biblical Quarterly* 35 (1973): 350–58.
Murphy-O'Conner, Jerome: "La 'vérité' chez saint Paul et à Qumrān". *Revue biblique* 72 (1965): 29–76.
Nairne, A.: *The Faith of the New Testament*. London: Longmans, Green & Co., 1920.
Neufeld, V. H.: *The Earliest Christian Confessions*. New Testament Tools and Studies Series, no. 5. Grand Rapids: Eerdmans, 1963.
Neusner, Jacob: "The Fellowship (חבורה) in the Second Jewish Commonwealth". *Harvard Theological Review* 53 (1960): 125–42.
–, *The Rabbinic Traditions about the Pharisees before 70*. 3 vols. Leiden: Brill, 1971.
Newman, Barclay M., Jr.: "Some Suggested Restructurings for the New Testament Letter Openings and Closings". *The Bible Translator* 25 (1974): 240–45.
Nieboer, M. C.: "The Statistical Analysis of A. Q. Morton and the Authenticity of the Pauline Epistles". *Calvin Theological Journal* 5 (1970): 64–80.
Norden, Eduard: *Die antike Kunstprosa*. 2 vols. Leipzig: Weidmann, 1898; reprint, Leipzig: Weidmann, 1958.
Oates, Whitney J., ed. and trans.: *The Stoic and Epicurean Philosophers: the Complete Extant Writings of Epicurus, Epictetus, Lucretius, Marcus Aurelius*. New York: Random House, 1940.
Oepke, A.: *Die Missionspredigt des Apostels Paulus*. Leipzig: Deichert, 1920.
Ogilvie, Robert Maxwell: *A Commentary on Livy: Books 1–5*. Oxford: Clarendon, 1965.
Oikonomides, Alexander N., ed.: *Abbreviations in Greek Inscriptions: Papyri, Manuscripts, and Early Printed Books*. Chicago: Ares, 1965.
Olson, Stanley N.: "Epistolary Uses of Expressions of Self-Confidence". *Journal of Biblical Literature* 103 (1984): 585–97.
–, "Pauline Expressions of Confidence in His Addressees". *Catholic Biblical Quarterly* 47 (1985): 282–95.
O'Rourke, J. J.: "Some Considerations about Attempts at Statistical Analysis of the Pauline Corpus". *Catholic Biblical Quarterly* 35 (1973): 483–90.
Ovid: *Tristia and Ex Ponto*. Edited and translated by A. L. Wheeler. Rev. ed. The Loeb Classical Library, Latin Series. Cambridge: Harvard University, 1985.
Oxford Classical Dictionary. 2d ed. Edited by N. G. L. Hammond, and H. H. Scullard. Oxford: Clarendon, 1970.
Oxford Latin Dictionary. Edited by P. G. W. Glare. Oxford: Clarendon, 1968–82.

The Oxyrhynchus Papyri. Edited by B. P. Grenfell and A. S. Hunt. 51 vols. London: Oxford University, 1898–1951.
Palmer, C. L.: "The Use of Traditional Materials in Hebrews, James, and 1 Peter". Ph.D. diss., Southwestern Baptist Theological Seminary, 1985.
Papyri. Literary-Poetry: Texts, Translations, and Notes. Edited and translated by Denys L. Page. The Loeb Classical Library, Greek Series. Cambridge: Harvard University, 1970.
Papyri. Non-Literary. Edited and translated by A. S. Hunt and C. C. Edgar. 2 vols. The Loeb Classical Library, Greek Series. Cambridge: Harvard University, 1932–34.
Pardee, Dennis: Handbook of Ancient Hebrew Letters: a Study Edition. The Society of Biblical Literature Sources for Biblical Study Series, no. 15. Chico, CA: Scholars, 1982.
Pardee, Dennis, J. David Whitehead, and Paul E. Dion: "Overview of Ancient Hebrew Epistolography". Journal of Biblical Literature 97 (1978): 321–46.
Parkin, V.: "Some Comments on the Pauline Prescripts". Irish Biblical Studies 8 (1986): 92–99.
Pauly, August Friedrich von, ed.: Der kleine Pauly: Lexikon der Antike auf der Grundlage von Pauly's Real-Encyclopädie der classischen Altertumswissenschaft. Edited by K. Ziegler and W. Sontheimer. 5 vols. Stuttgart: Druckenmuller, 1964–72.
Pauly, August Friedrich von, and Georg Wissowa, eds.: Pauly's Real- Encyclopädie der classischen Altertumswissenschaft. 24 vols. with supps. Revised by Wilhelm Kroll. Stuttgart: Druckenmuller, 1893–1963.
Penna, Romano: "Les juifs à Rome au temps de l'apôtre Paul". New Testament Studies 28 (1982): 321–47.
Percy, E.: Die Probleme der Kolosser- und Epheserbriefe. Lund: Gleerup, 1946.
Peter, Hermann Wilhelm Gottlob: Der Brief in der römischen Literatur: literargeschichtliche Untersuchungen und Zusammenfassungen. Abhandlungen der philologisch-historischen Classe der Königlichen Sächsischen Gesellschaft der Wissenschaften, no. 20. Leipzig: Teubner, 1901.
–, Die Quellen Plutarchs in die Biographien der Römer. Halle: Waisenhaus, 1865.
Philo of Alexandria: Works. Edited and translated by F. H. Colson and G. H. Whitaker. 10 vols. The Loeb Classical Library, Greek Series. Cambridge: Harvard University, 1929–62.
Philostratus of Lemnos: Flavii Philostrati Opera. Edited by C. L. Kayser. 2 vols. Leipzig: Teubner, 1871.
–, Life of Apollonius of Tyana; Epistles of Apollonius. Edited and translated by F. C. Conybeare. 3 vols. The Loeb Classical Library, Greek Series. Cambridge: Harvard University, 1912.
Pitman, Isaac: A History of Shorthand. 3d ed. London: Isaac Pitman & Sons, 1895.
Plato: The Epistles of Plato. Vol. 7 in The Works of Plato. Edited and translated by R. G. Bury. The Loeb Classical Library, Greek Series. Cambridge: Harvard University, 1929.
Pliny the Elder: Natural History [Naturalis Historia]. Edited and translated by H. Rackham. 10 vols. The Loeb Classical Library, Latin Series. Cambridge: Harvard University, 1960–68.
Pliny the Younger: Letters [Epistulae] and Panegyricus. Edited and translated by Betty Radice. 2 vols. The Loeb Classical Library, Latin Series. Cambridge: Harvard University, 1972–75.
Plutarch: The Parallel Lives. Edited and translated by Bernadotte Perrin. The Loeb Classical Library, Greek Series. Cambridge: Harvard University, 1967–70.

Porten, Bezadel: "Address Formulae in Aramaic Letters: a New Collation of Cowley 17". *Revue biblique* 90 (1980): 398–413.
Pottier, Bernard, ed.: *La paléographie grecque et byzantine*. Colloques internationaux de centre national de la recherche scientifique, no. 559. Paris: Editions du centre national de la recherche scientifique, 1977.
Pseudo-Anacharsis: *Epistles*. Edited and translated by Anne M. McGuire. In *The Cynic Epistles*, ed. Abraham Malherbe, 35–52. Missoula, MT: Scholars, 1977.
Pseudo-Crates: *Epistles*. Edited and translated by Ronald Hock. In *The Cynic Epistles*, ed. Abraham Malherbe, 53–90. Missoula, MT: Scholars, 1977.
Pseudo-Diogenes: *Epistles*. Edited and translated by Benjamin Fiore. In *The Cynic Epistles*, ed. Abraham Malherbe, 91–184. Missoula, MT: Scholars, 1977.
Pseudo-Heraclitus: *Epistles*. Edited and translated by David Worley. In *The Cynic Epistles*, ed. Abraham Malherbe, 186–215. Missoula, MT: Scholars, 1977.
Pseudo-Socrates and the Socratics: *Epistles*. Edited and translated by Stanley Stowers. In *The Cynic Epistles*, ed. Abraham Malherbe, 217–308. Missoula, MT: Scholars, 1977.
Quintilianus, Marcus Fabius: *Institutio oratoria*. Edited and translated by J. S. Watson. 4 vols. The Loeb Classical Library, Latin Series. New York: Putnam's Sons, 1921–22.
Rabe, H.: "Aus Rhetoren-Handschriften". *Rheinisches Museum für Philologie*, n.s., 64 (1909): 288*ff*.
Radl, Walter: "Der Sinn von γνωρίζω im 1 Kor 15:1". *Biblische Zeitschrift*, n.s., 28 (1984): 243–45.
Ramsay, Sir William: *A Historical Commentary on St. Paul's Epistle to the Galatians*. 2d ed. London: Hodder & Stoughton, 1900.
Regul, Jurgen: *Die antimarcionitischen Evangelienprologue*. Vetus Latina: die Reste der altlateinischen Bible; aus der Geschichte der lateinischen Bibel, no. 6. Freiburg: Herder, 1969.
Reitzenstein, Richard: *Hellenistic-Mystery Religions: Their Basic Ideas and Significance*. Translated by J. E. Steely. Pittsburg: Pickwick, 1978; original German edition, Berlin: Teubner, 1920.
Renehan, Robert: "Classical Greek Quotations in the New Testament". In *The Heritage of the Early Church: Essays in Honor of G. V. Florovsky on the Occasion of His Eightieth Birthday*, ed. David Neiman and Margaret Schatkin, 17–46. Rome: Pontifical Institute of Oriental Studies, 1973.
Rengstorf, Karl Heinrich, ed.: *A Complete Concordance to Flavius Josephus*. 4 vols and a supp. Leiden: Brill, 1973–83.
Riesner, Rainer: *Jesus als Lehrer: eine Untersuchung zum Ursprung der Evangelien-Überlieferung*. Wissenschaftliche Untersuchungen zum Neuen Testament, no. 7. Tübingen: Mohr, 1981.
Rigaux, Beda: *The Letters of St. Paul: Modern Studies*. Edited and translated by Stephen Yonick. The Herald Scriptural Library Series. Chicago: Franciscan Herald, 1968.
Rist, Martin: "Pseudepigraphy and the Early Christians". In *Studies in New Testament and Early Literature: Essays in Honor of Allen P. Wikgren*, ed. David Edward Aune, 75–91. Supplements to Novum Testamentum Series, no. 33. Leiden: Brill, 1972.
Rivkin, E.: "Defining the Pharisees: the Tannaitic Sources". *Hebrew Union College Annual* 41 (1970): 234–38.
Roberts, Colin H., and T. C. Skeat: *The Birth of the Codex* [*Codex²*]. London: Oxford University, 1983.
Roberts, William Rhys: *Greek Rhetoric and Literary Criticism*. New York: Longmans, Green and Co., 1928.

Robertson, A. T.: *A Grammar of the Greek New Testament in the Light of Historical Research.* 3d ed. New York: Hodder & Stoughton, 1919.

Robinson, C. E.: *Everyday Life in Ancient Greece.* Oxford: Clarendon, 1933.

Robinson, Thomas Arthur: "Grayston and Herdan's 'C' Quantity Formula and the Authorship of the Pastoral Epistles". *New Testament Studies* 30 (1984): 282–88.

Robson, E. Iliff: "Composition and Dictation in the New Testament Books". *Journal of Theological Studies,* o.s.:, 18 (1917): 288–301.

Roetzel, Calvin J.: *The Letters of Paul: Conversations in Context.* 2d ed. Atlanta: John Knox, 1982.

Roller, Otto: *Das Formular der paulinischen Briefe.* Stuttgart: W. Kohlhammer, 1933.

Roon, A. van: *The Authenticity of Ephesians.* Translated by S. Prescod-Jokel. Supplements to Novum Testamentum Series, no. 39. Leiden: Brill, 1974.

Russell, Ronald: "The Pauline Letter Structure in Philippians". *Journal of the Evangelical Theological Society* 25 (1982): 295–306.

Salles, Catherine, "Le genre littéraire de la lettre dans l'antiquité". *Foi et Vie* 84/5 (1985): 41–47.

Sanders, E. P.: *Paul and Palestinian Judaism.* Philadelphia: Fortress, 1977.

Sanders, Jack T.: *The New Testament Christological Hymns.* Society for New Testament Studies Monograph Series, no. 15. Cambridge: Cambridge University, 1971.

–, "The Transition from Opening Epistolary Thanksgiving to Body in the Pauline Corpus". *Journal of Biblical Literature* 81 (1962): 352–62.

Sandmel, S.: *A Jewish Understanding of the New Testament.* New York: University Publishers, 1956.

Schmeller, Thomas: *Paulus und die "Diatribe": eine vergleichende Stilinterpretation.* Neutestamentliche Abhandlungen, n.s., no. 19. Munich: Aschendorffsche, 1987.

Schmidt, Daryl: "The Authenticity of 2 Thessalonians: Linguistic Arguments", *The Society of Biblical Literature Abstracts and Seminar Papers* 22 (1983): 289–96.

Schmidt, Peter L.: "Epistolographie". *Der kleine Pauly,* ed. Konrat Ziegler and Walther Sontheimer, 2: 324–27. Stuttgart: A. Druckenmüller, 1967.

Schmithals, W.: "Paulus und der historische Jesus". *Zeitschrift für die neutestamentliche Wissenschaft* 53 (1962): 145–60.

Schnider, Franz, and Werner Stenger: *Studien zum Neutestamentlichen Briefformular.* New Testament Tools and Studies, no. 11. Leiden: Brill, 1987.

Schoedel, William R.: *Ignatius of Antioch.* Hermeneia Series. Philadelphia: Fortress, 1985.

Scholem, Gershom G.: *Major Trends in Jewish Mysticism.* 3d rev. ed. New York: Schocken, 1954.

Schreibner, A.: "An Autograph Letter by Eliyahu b Shelomo". *Jewish Quarterly Review* 73 (1982): 152–54.

Schubart, W.: *Einführung in die Papyruskunde.* Berlin: Weidmann, 1918.

Schubert, Paul: *The Form and Function of the Pauline Thanksgiving.* Berlin: Alfred Topelmann, 1939.

Schweitzer, A.: *The Mysticism of Paul the Apostle.* Translated by Wm. Montgomery. London: Black, 1931.

–, *Paul and His Interpreters.* Translated by Wm. Montgomery. London: Black, 1912.

Schweizer, Eduard: "Concerning the Speeches in Acts". In *Studies in Luke-Acts: Essays Presented in Honor of Paul Schubert,* ed. L. E. Keck and J. L. Martyn, 208–16. Philadelphia: Fortress, 1980.

–, "Traditional Ethical Patterns in the Pauline and Post-Pauline Letters and Their Development (Lists of Vices and House-Tables)". In *Text and Interpretation: Studies in the New Testament Presented to Matthew Black*, ed. E. Best and R. M. Wilson, 195–210. Cambridge: Cambridge University, 1979.

Scott, Robert: *The Pastoral Epistles*. Edinburgh: T & T Clark, 1909.

Selby, D. J.: *Toward an Understanding of St. Paul*. Englewood Cliffs, NJ: Prentice-Hall, 1962.

Selwyn, E. G.: *The First Epistle of St. Peter: the Greek Text with Introduction, Notes and Essays*. 2d ed. London: Macmillan & Co., 1947; reprint, Grand Rapids: Baker, Thornapple Commentary Series, 1981.

Semler, J. S.: *Paraphrasis II. Epistulae ad Corinthos*. Vetus Latina. Halae: Hammerdiani, 1776.

Seneca the Elder: *Controversiae*. Edited and translated by M. Winterbottom. 2 vols. The Loeb Classical Library, Latin Series. Cambridge: Harvard University, 1974.

Seneca, Lucius Annaeus: *Ad Lucilium epistulae morales*. Edited and translated by Richard M. Bummere. 3 vols. The Loeb Classical Library, Latin Series. New York: Putnam's Sons, 1920–25; rev. ed., John W. Basore. 3 vols. Cambridge: Harvard University, 1970.

–, *Apocolocyntosis*. Rev. ed. Edited and translated by W. H. D. Rouse. The Loeb Classical Library, Latin Series. Cambridge: Harvard University, 1961.

Sevenster, J. N.: *Do You Know Greek? How Much Greek Could the First Jewish Christians Have Known?* Supplements to Novum Testamentum Series, no. 19. Leiden: Brill, 1968.

–, *Paul and Seneca*. Supplements to Novum Testamentum Series, no. 4. Leiden: Brill, 1961.

Sharp, Douglas Simmonds: *Epictetus and the New Testament*. London: Kelly, 1914.

Sherwin-White, A. N.: *The Letters of Pliny: a Historical and Social Commentary*. Oxford: Oxford University, 1966; reprint (with corrections), Oxford: Oxford University, 1985.

Siegert, Folker: *Argumentation bei Paulus: gezeigt an Röm 9–11*. Wissenschaftliche Untersuchungen zum Neuen Testament, no. 34. Tübingen: Mohr, 1985.

Skeat, T. C.: "Especially the Parchments: a Note on 2 Timothy IV.13". *Journal of Theological Studies*, n.s.: 30 (1979): 173–77.

Soden, Hermann von: *Griechisches Neues Testament*. 2 vols. Göttingen: Vandenhoeck & Ruprecht, 1913.

Spicq, C.: *Les épîtres pastorales*. 2 vols. 4th ed. Paris: Études bibliques, 1947.

Standaert, Benoît: "La Rhétorique antique et l'épître aux Galates". *Foi et Vie* 84/5 (1985): 33–40.

Steele, Robert Brown: "Anaphora and Chiasmus in Livy". *Transactions of the American Philological Association* 32 (1901): 166ff.

–, "Chiasmus in the Epistles of Cicero, Seneca, Pliny, and Fronto". *Studies in Honor of B. L. Gildersleeve*, ed. C. A. Briggs, 339–52. Baltimore, MD: John Hopkins, 1902.

–, *Chaismus in Sallust, Caesar, Tacitus, and Justinus*. Northfield, MN: Independent Publishing Co., 1891.

Stein, Arthur: "Die Stenographie im römischen Senat". *Archiv für Stenographie* 56 (1905): 177–86.

Stenger, Werner: "Timotheus und Titus als literarische Gestalten: Beobachtungen zur Form und Funktion der Pastoralbriefe". *Kairos* 16 (1974): 252–67.

Stirewalt, Martin Luther, Jr.: "The Form and Function of the Greek Letter-Essay". In *The Romans Debate*, ed. P. K. Donfried, 175–206. Minneapolis: Augsburg, 1977.

Stone, Michael Edward, ed.: *Jewish Writings of the Second Temple Period*. Compendia rerum Iudaicarum ad Novum Testamentum, sec. 2, vol. 2. Philadelphia: Fortress, 1984.

Stowers, Stanley Kent: *The Diatribe and Paul's Letter to the Romans*. The Society of Biblical Literature Dissertation Series, no. 57. Chico, CA: Scholars, 1981.

–, *Letter Writing in Greco-Roman Antiquity*. Library of Early Christianity Series. Philadelphia: Westminster, 1986.

–, "Paul's Dialogue with a Fellow Jew in Romans 3:1–9". *Catholic Biblical Quarterly* 46 (1984): 707–22.

–, "Social Status, Public Speaking and Private Teaching: the Circumstances of Paul's Preaching Activity". *Novum Testamentum* 26 (1984): 59–82.

Strange, E.: "Diktierpausen in den Paulusbriefen". *Zeitschrift für die neutestamentliche Wissenschaft* 18 (1918): 109–17.

Strauss, J. A.: "Notes sur quelques papyrus concernant l'escalvage dans l'Egypt romaine". *Zeitschrift für Papyrologie und Epigraphik* 32 (1978): 259–62.

Strobel, A.: "Schreiben des Lukas? Zum sprachlichen Problem der Pastoralbriefe". *New Testament Studies* 15 (1969): 191–210.

Suetonius Tranquillus, C.: *Lives of the Caesars*. Edited and translated by J. C. Rolfe. 2 vols. The Loeb Classical Library, Latin Series. Cambridge: Harvard University, 1935.

Sykutris, J.: "Epistolographie". In *Pauly's Real-Encyclopädie der classischen Altertumswissenschaft*, ed. August Friedrich von Pauly, Georg Wissowa, and Wilhelm Kroll, 24 vols. and supplements, supp. 5: 185–220. Stuttgart: Druckenmüller, 1893–1963.

Tarn, W. W.: *Alexander the Great. II: Sources and Studies*. Cambridge: Cambridge University, 1948.

–, "Alexander's ὑπομνήματα and the World-Kingdom". *Journal of Hellenic Studies* 41 (1921): 1–17.

The Tebtunis Papyri. Edited by B. P. Grenfell, A. S. Hunt, and J. Gilbert Smyly. 3 vols in 4. University of California Graeco-Roman Archaeological Series. London: Oxford University, 1902–38.

Thayer, J. H., ed.: *A Greek-English Lexicon of the New Testament*. New York: Haper & Bros., 1887.

Thompson, Edward Maunde: *An Introduction to Greek and Latin Palaeography*. Oxford: Oxford University, 1912; reprint, New York: Burt Franklin, 1973.

Thraede, Klaus: *Grundzüge griechisch-römischer Brieftopik*. Monographien zur klassischen Altertumswissenschaft, no. 48. Munich: Beck, 1970.

Thrall, Margaret E.: "A Second Thanksgiving Period in II Corinthians". *Journal for the Study of the New Testament* 16 (1982): 101–24.

Trudinger, P.: "Computers and the Authorship of the Pauline Epistles". *Faith and Freedom* [Oxford] 39 (1986): 24–27.

Turner, Eric Gardiner: *Greek Papyri: an Introduction*. Oxford: Clarendon, 1968; reprint, Oxford: Clarendon, 1980.

–, *The Typology of the Early Codex*. Haney Foundation Series, no. 18. Philadelphia: University of Pennsylvania, 1977.

Turner, Nigel: *Style*. Vol. 4 in *A Grammar of New Testament Greek*, ed. J. H. Moulton. Edinburgh: T & T Clark, 1976.

–, *Syntax*. Vol. 3 in *A Grammar of New Testament Greek*, ed. J. H. Moulton. Edinburgh: T & T Clark, 1963.

Tyrrell, R. Y. and L. C. Purser: *The Correspondence of M. Tullius Cicero*. 7 vols. 3d rev. ed. London: Longmans, Green, & Co., 1901–33.

Unnik, W. C. van: *Tarsus or Jerusalem: the City of Paul's Youth*. Translated by G. Ogg. London: Epworth, 1962.

Usener, H.: *Epicurea*. Leipzig: University, 1887.
Wake, W. C.: "Numbers, Paul and Rational Dissent". *Faith and Freedom* [Oxford] 37 (1984): 59–72.
Walker, William O., Jr.: "The Burden of Proof in Identifying Interpolations in the Pauline Letters". *New Testament Studies* 33 (1987): 610–18.
Wardman, Alan: *Rome's Debt to Greece*. New York: St. Martin's, 1976.
Watson, Francis: "2 Cor 10–13 and Paul's Painful Letter to the Corinthians". *Journal of Theological Studies*, n.s., 35 (1984): 324–46.
Weber, E.: *De dione Chrysostomo synicorum sectatore*. Leipziger Studien, no. 9. Leipzig: University, 1887.
Wedderburn, Alexander J.: "Hellenistic Christian Traditions in Romans 6?" *New Testament Studies* 29 (1983): 337–55.
Weiss, J.: *Der erste Korintherbrief*. Göttingen: Vandenhoeck & Ruprecht, 1910.
Welch, John W.: "Chiasmus in Ancient Greek and Latin Literature". In *Chiasmus in Antiquity: Structure, Analyses, and Exegesis*, ed. J. W. Welch, 250–68. Hildesheim: Gerstenberg, 1981.
—, "Chiasmus in the New Testament". In *Chiasmus in Antiquity: Structure, Analyses, and Exegesis*, ed. J. W. Welch, 211–49. Hildesheim: Gerstenberg, 1981.
Wendland, Paul: *Die hellenistisch-römische Kultur in ihren Beziehungen zu Judentum und Christentum*. 2d ed. Tübingen: Mohr, 1912.
—, *Neutestamentliche Grammatik: das Griechisch der neuen Testaments im zusammenhang mit der Volkssprache dargestellt*. Vol. 2: *Die urchristlichen Literaturformen*. Tübingen: Mohr, 1912.
Wengst, Klaus: "Der Apostel und die Tradition". *Zeitschrift für Theologie und Kirche* 69 (1972): 145–62.
—, *Christologische Formeln und Lieder der Urchristentums*. 2d ed. Studien zum Neuen Testaments Series, no. 7. Gütersloh: Mohn, 1973.
White, John Lee: "The Ancient Epistolography Group in Retrospect". *Semeia* 22 (1981): 1–14.
—, "Epistolary Formulas and Cliches in Greek Papyrus Letters". *Society of Biblical Literature Abstracts and Seminar Papers* 14 (1978): 289–319.
—, *The Form and Function of the Body of the Greek Letter*. The Society of Biblical Literature Dissertation Series, no. 2. Missoula, MT: Scholars, 1972.
—, *The Form and Structure of the Official Petition: a Study in Greek Epistolography*. The Society of Biblical Literature Disseration Series, no. 5. Missoula, MT: Scholars, 1972.
—, "The Greek Documentary Letter Tradition, Third Century B.C.E. to Third Century C.E". *Semeia* 22 (1981): 89–106.
—, "Introductory Formulae in the Body of the Pauline Letter". *Journal of Biblical Literature* 90 (1971): 91–97.
—, *Light from Ancient Letters*. Foundation and Facets Series. Philadelphia: Fortress, 1986.
—, "Saint Paul and the Apostolic Letter Tradition". *Catholic Biblical Quarterly* 45 (1983): 433–44.
Whitehead, John David, "Early Aramaic Epistolography: the Arsames Correspondence". Ph.D. diss., University of Chicago, 1974.
Wilamowitz-Moellendorf, Ulrich von: *Antigonos von Karystos*. Philologische Untersuchungen Series, no. 4. Berlin: Weidmann, 1881.
—, *Geschichte der Philogie*. 3d ed. Leipzig: Teubner, 1959.
Wilckens, U.: *Der Brief an die Römer*. 3 vols. Evangelisch- katholischer Kommentar zum Neuen Testament Series. Zürich: Neukirchener, 1978–82.
Wilder, Amos: *Early Christian Rhetoric: the Language of the Gospel*. 2d ed. Cambridge: Harvard University, 1971.

Williams, A. Lukyn: *The Epistle of Paul the Apostle to the Galatians.* The Cambridge Greek Testament for Schools and Colleges Series. Cambridge: Cambridge University, 1910.
Wilson, S. G.: *Luke and the Pastoral Epistles.* London: S.P.C.K., 1979.
Winter, John G.: *Life and Letters in the Papyri.* Ann Arbor: University of Michigan, 1933.
Wuellner, Wilhelm: "Greek Rhetoric and Pauline Argumentation". In *Early Christian Literature and the Classical Intellectual Tradition: in Honorem Robert M. Grant,* ed. W. R. Schoedel and R. L. Wilken, 177–88. Paris: Théologie historique, 1979.
–, "Paul's Rhetoric of Argumentation in Romans: an Alternative to the Donfried-Karris Debate over Romans". *Catholic Biblical Quarterly* 38 (1976): 330–51; reprint, in *The Romans Debate,* ed. P. K. Donfried, 152–74. Minneapolis: Augsburg, 1977.
Young, Norman H.: "Did St. Paul Compose Romans 3:24ff.?" *Australian Biblical Review* 22 (1974): 23–32.
Yule, George Undy: *The Statistical Study of Literary Vocabulary.* Cambridge: Cambridge University, 1944.
The Zenon Papyri: Business Papers of the Third Century B.C. *Dealing with Palestine and Egypt.* 2 vols. Edited by W. L. Westermann, E. S. Hasenoehrl (vol. 1), C. W. Keyes (vol. 2), and H. Liebesny (vol. 2). Colombia Papyri, Greek Series, nos. 3–4. New York: Colombia University, 1934–40.
Zieliński, Tadeusz: *Das Clauselgesetz in Ciceros Reden: Grundzüge einer oratorischen Rhythmik.* Philologus, Supplementband, no. 13/1a. Leipzig: Dieterich, 1904.
Zimmerman, H.: *Neutestamentliche Methodenlehre.* Stuttgart: Katholisches Bibelwerk, 1967.

Indices

Subjects

amanuensis 1, 11, 29, 72, 89, 154, 185

carriers (also *tabellarius*) 3, 5, 7–10, 23, 56, 70–73, 87, 113–14, 115, 161, 191, 198
chiasmus 133, 140–41, 207–8, 214, 220
ψειρί 76, 172–73, 174, 178
codicilli 3, 160–63
collection of Paul's letters 6–8, 165, 191
copy 2–7, 44, 58, 74, 79, 83–84, 94, 99, 102, 103, 140, 162, 163, 165–67, 168, 170, 180, 188, 191
corpus, Pauline (see 'collection of Paul's letters')
co-worker 129, 153–58

diatribe 133–35, 142–43, 151, 171
dictation 23–44, 45, 48, 53, 62, 63, 66, 69, 78, 79, 90, 91, 99, 100, 101, 102, 112, 113, 114, 118, 119, 123, 166–67, 168, 169, 171, 174, 186, 187, 195, 197, 198, 199

Eumenes 6, 17, 46, 47, 63, 188

formulae, illiteracy 18, 22, 42, 73–76, 103, 132, 169, 178
formulae, stereotyped 91, 104, 131–32, 138–39, 143, 151, 155–56, 179–80, 203–6, 214

γραμματεύς 2, 3, 11, 15, 16, 19, 29, 66
grammaticus 57–58, 61
γράφω διά 69–73
greeting 76, 130, 132, 137, 138, 156, 170–71, 197, 205, 206

Haustafeln 192, 219
Homer 27, 54, 166, 184–85

Ignatius, Letters of 8, 70–72, 188, 191
inscription 16–17

κανών 45–46, 105

lector 10, 45, 64, 65, 117
letters of recommendation (see '*letterae commendaticae*')
librarius 2, 7, 11, 25, 62, 78, 80, 89, 100, 103, 113, 162
lists, tribulation 133, 141, 209–10
lists, vice 133, 141, 219
litterae commendaticae 5, 49, 71, 107, 170–71, 182

mea manu 62, 78, 80, 89, 90, 100, 114, 173, 179
μεμβράναι 5, 129, 158–60

notarius 11, 28, 64, 65
notebook (see also *codicilli* and μεμβράναι) 3, 5, 129, 158–68

paraenesis 133, 137–38, 141, 160, 192, 208, 214
philophronesis 23, 49, 51, 106, 107, 130, 136
Plato 86–87, 166, 211
Pompey 4, 46, 80, 85, 96, 107, 163, 187
postscript 19, 77, 80–90, 114, 116, 117, 118, 119, 120, 123, 138, 175–81, 183, 189, 190, 197
progymnasmata 61
prosopoeia 61
rhetoric 132–36, 140–44, 145, 151, 152, 153, 171, 181, 182–83, 196, 199, 211, 213, 214, 215
Rufus 30, 51–52, 107, 108, 111, 200

seal 5, 55, 64, 84, 93, 114, 117, 118

secret 6, 83, 88–90, 98, 117, 179, 194, 212
secretarial mediation, iii, 86, 126, 174, 181, 183, 186, 190, 194
shorthand 11, 26–43, 44, 45, 65, 99–103, 115, 171–72, 176, 195, 199
style 23, 24, 37, 48, 49, 60, 62, 80, 92–97, 105, 113, 115, 116, 120–27, 132, 134, 140, 151, 183–88, 194, 201, 211
stylometry 181, 184–87, 194
syllabatim 24, 25, 29, 41, 42, 44, 45, 48, 99–101, 171, 176, 188, 195

tachygraphy (see 'shorthand')

Tertius 169–72, 187, 195
testimonia 5, 160
Tiro 4, 6, 26, 31, 33, 35, 38, 43, 45, 46, 48, 56, 61, 63, 76, 77, 78, 99, 100, 103, 105, 113, 114, 115, 116, 120, 122, 194, 213
topos 133, 141, 142, 192
traditions 127, 129, 158–68, 194, 217–21

verbatim 21, 23, 29, 33, 35, 42, 43, 100, 119, 124
viva voce 24–26, 28, 29, 33, 37, 41, 43, 44, 48, 100–2, 113, 133, 167, 171, 172, 176, 187, 195

Modern Authors

Adeney, W. F., 173
Andrews, M., 212
Attridge, H., 117

Bagnall, R. S., 15
Bahr, G. J., "Letter Writing", 20, 25, 26, 30, 31, 34, 39, 41, 47, 48, 69, 81, 91, 100, 108, 112, 160, 172
–, "Subscriptions", 81–82, 173, 176–79
Bandstra, A. J., 177–78
Barrett, C. K., 154, 180
Barth, M., *Ephesians*, 192
–, "Traditions in Ephesians", 160, 218–20
Bauer, W., *Die Apostolischen Väter*, 71, 72
–, *Lexicon [BAG]*, 11
Baur, F. C., 147
Bell, H. I., 20
Benoit, P., 40, 41
Betz, H., D., *Galatians*, 92, 138, 173, 182, 214
–, "Galatians" *NTS*, 141, 151
Blass, F. B., 173
Bligh, 208
Bornkamm, G., "Romans", 142
Bowersock, G. W., 59
Bowker, J. W., 145
Bradley, D., 133
Braun, H., 192
Brinkmann, L., 60
Bruce, F. F., 180

Brunt, P. A., 37
Bruyne, D. de., 158
Bultmann, R., 180; "Bedeutung des geschichtlichen Jesus", 159
–, *kynisch-stoische Diatribe*, 134, 205
–, *Theology of the New Testament*, 159
Burstein, S. M., 16
Burton, E. D., 173
Bury, R. G., 86–87

Cadbury, H. J., 191
Camelot, P. Th., 71
Carrez, M., 156–57
Catchpole, D. R., 219
Chamberlain, W. D., 173
Clark, D. L., 58
Conzelmann, H., *Pastoral Epistles*, 128, 193
–, "Paulus und die Weisheit", 155, 158
–, *Theology of the New Testament*, 220
–, *1 Corinthians*, 155
Cranfield, C. E. B., 156
Cullmann, O., *Glaubensbekenntnisse*, 217
–, "*KYRIOS*", 159–60

Daube, D., 151
Davies, W. D., *New Creation*, 145
–, "Paul and the Dead Sea Scrolls", 150
–, *Paul and Rabbinic Judaism*, 143, 145, 217
Davis, W. H., 12
Deissmann, A., *Bible Studies*, 175

–, *Light*, 1, 12, 14, 74, 78, 100, 136, 169, 174, 211, 212, 215
–, *New Light*, 212
–, *St. Paul*, 100, 144, 174, 212
Dibelius, M., 181; *An Philemon*, 211
–, "Areopagus", 146
–, "Mystic", 145
–, *Pastoral Epistles*, 128, 193
–, "Speeches of Acts", 146
–, *Tradition*, 137
Dion, P. E., "Aramaic Family Letter", 49
–, "Aramaic Letter Types", 50
Dodd, C. H., 160, 180
Donfried, K. P, "Presuppositons", 142, 143
Doty, William G. "Epistle" (Ph.D. diss.), 11, 12, 14, 86, 129, 136, 160, 212, 213, 214, 215
–, *Letters*, 1, 49, 129, 131, 133, 137, 140, 151, 169, 202, 215
Duncan, G., 173
Dziatzko, C. 1

Ellis, E. E., 194; "Authorship", 184, 192
–, "Co-Workers", 155 158
–, "Exegetical Patterns", 145, 154
–, "Midrash Pesher", 145
–, "Pauline Eschatology", 152
–, *Paul's Use of OT*, 145
–, "Traditions in 1 Cor.", 160, 217, 219
Erman, A., 58
Eschlimann, J. A., 21, 188
Exler, F. X. J., 1, 20, 73, 74, 75, 132, 206

Fee, G., 192
Findlay, G. G., *Galatians*, 173
–, *1 Corinthians*, 155
Fitzmyer, J. A., "A Life of Paul", 144
–, *Pauline Theology*, 217
Foat, F. W. G., 26, 27, 32, 33, 35, 38
Fuhrman, M., 59
Funk, R. W., *Language*, 137
Furnish, V., "Jesus-Paul Debate", 159
–, *II Corinthians*, 156, 181
–, *Pauline Letters*, 183

Gamble, H., 165; *NT Canon*, 6, 158, 191
–, "Pauline Corpus", 6
–, *Textual History of Romans*, 170

Gardthausen, V., "Akropolis-Steines", 32
–, "Tachygraphie", 34
Georgi, D., 180
Gerhard, G. A., 58
Gitlbauer, M., 27
Goguel, M., 180, 191
Gradenwitz, O., 81–82
Grant, R. M., 181
Greenough, 135
Grosheide, F. W., 155, 157
Gummere, R., 119
Guthrie, D., *Galatians*, 173
–, *Introduction*, 181, 191
–, *Pastorals*, 192

Haenchen, E., *Apostelgeschichte*, 39
–, "Acts as Source Material", 147
Hanson, A. T., *Pastoral Epistles* (NCB), 193
–, *Pastoral Letters* (CBCS), 193
Harris, M. J., 152
Harrison, P. N., 184
Hartman, L., 6, 213
Hartmann, K., 36–37
Hausrath, A., 180
Hengel, M., *Acts*, 147–48
–, *Barbarians*, 150
–, *Judaism and Hellenism*, 149, 150, 152
–, "χριστός", 217
Henneman, A., 124–25
Henshaw, T., 6
Hicks, R. D., 168
Hirzel, R., 132
Hitchcock, F. R. M., 41
Hock, R. F., *Chreia*, 61
–, "Cynic", 87
Hodgson, R., 133, 210
Holtzmann, H. J., 187
Hunter, A. M., 160

Jeremias, J., *an Timotheus und Titus*, 188, 192
–, "Chiasmus", 141, 207
–, *Jerusalem*, 148, 150
–, "γραμματεύς", 3, 11
Jervell, J., *Unknown Paul*, 147
Jewett, R., 218, 220
Johnen, Chr., *Kurzschrift*, 34
–, *Stenographie*, 28, 34
Johnson, L., 192

Johnson, P. F., 184
Johnston, H. W., 28
Judge, E. A., *Rank,* 12, 21

Karris, R. J., "Occasion", 143
Käsemann, E., 192
Keck, L., 183
Kelly, J. N. D., 192
Kennedy, G. A., 183
Kenny, A., 184–87, 194
Kenyon, F. G., "Tachygraphy", 33, 39
Kim, C.-H., *Recommendation,* 171
Knox, J., 147
Koskenniemi, H., "Cicero", 12
–, *Studien,* 1, 12, 49, 59, 130, 206
Kuhn, K. G., 192
Kümmel, W. G., *Introduction,* 180, 181, 182, 189, 192, 214, 215

Lambrecht, J., 147
Lake, K., 71
Lebreton, M. J., 120–21
Liddell, H. G. *[LSJ],* 11, 28, 34
Lietzmann, D. H., 159, 181
Longenecker, R. N., *Exegesis,* 145
–, *Paul,* 148

Malherbe, A., *Cynic Epistles,* 19, 42, 117
–, "Theorists", 12, 52, 57, 58, 59, 60, 61
–, *Social Aspects,* 143, 151
–, "μὴ γένοιτο", 143
Manson, T. W., 180
Marrou, H. I., 58, 61
Massie, J., 155
McKenzie, J. L., 23, 24, 41, 44, 103–4, 169, 211, 212
McLeman, J., 184–85
Meecham, H. G., 12, 84, 214
Mentz, A., "Grabschrift", 32, 39
–, *Kurzschrift,* 31, 32, 39, 43
–, *Stenographie,* 39
–, *Tachygraphie,* 43
–, *Tironischen Noten,* 28, 30, 32
Metzger, B. M., *New Testament* (Intro.), 193
–, "Pastorals", 192
Metzger, W., 192
Meyer, H. A. W., 82, 154
Michaelson, S., 184
Milligan, G., *Documents,* 214
Milne, H. J. M., 33–34, 41, 43

Mitteis, L., 83
Moffatt, J., 154, 188
Montagnini, F., 218
Montefiore, C. G., 146
Moore, G. F., 149, 150
Morgenstern, O., 30, 48
Morrow, G. R., 86–87
Morton, A. Q., "Last Words", 184
–, *Paul,* 184–85
Moule, C. F. D., "Dualism", 152
–, "NT Kerygma", 159
–, "Pastorals", 192
–, *"Tendenzkritik",* 147
Moulton, J. H., 78
Mullins, T. Y., "Disclosure", 139
–, "Formulas", 132, 203
–, "Petition", 139
–, "Topos", 133
Murphy-O'Conner, J., 192

Nairne, A., 188
Neufeld, V. H., 217–18
Neusner, J., "Fellowship", 148
–, *Rabbinic Traditions,* 148
Norden, E., 134, 211

Oates, W. J., 37
Oepke, A., 160
Oldfather, W. A., 36

Palmer, C. L., 218
Parkin, V., 137, 214
Pauly, A. F. v., *Pauly's,* 28
Percy, E., 192
Peter, H. W. G., *Brief,* 59, 124
–, *Quellen Plutarchs,* 30
Pitman, I., 32
Porten, B., 137

Rabe, H., 58
Ramsay, Wm., 175
Regul, J., 158
Reitzenstein, R., 145
Renehan, R., 145
Riesner, R., 149
Rigaux, B., 139, 140, 141, 212
Rivkin, E., 148
Roberts, C. H. and T. C. Skeat, *Codex*[2], 12, 160, 164–65
Robertson, A. T., 173, 214
Robinson, C. E., 25,

Robson, E. I., 24, 195
Roller, O., 1, 6, 7, 23, 39, 41, 48, 75, 97, 128, 143, 154, 164, 170, 171, 176, 178, 188, 191, 192, 212—13

Salles, C., 13, 216
Samuel, Alan, 9
Sanders, E. P., 146, 148
Sanders, J. T., *Hymns,* 218
—, "Transition", 139
Sandmel, S., 146
Schmeller, T., 135
Schmidt, P. L., 14
Schmithals, W., 159, 180
Schnider, F., 138, 175
Schoedel, W. R., 72, 120
Scholem, G. G., 145
Schubart, W., 58, 61
Schubert, P., 1, 139
Schweitzer, A., *Mysticism,* 145
—, *Paul,* 128
Schweizer, E., "Patterns", 217
—, "Speeches", 146
Scott, R., *Pastorals,* 187
Selby, D. J., 213
Selwyn, E. G., 73
Semler, J. S., 180
Sevenster, J. N., *Greek?,* 111
Sherwin-White, A. N., 10, 12, 17, 45, 65, 123—26, 163, 164
Skeat, T. C., "Parchments", 164
Smit, J., 183
Soden H. v., 6
Spicq, C., 188, 192
Standaert, B., 214
Steele, R. B., "Cicero", 140
—, *Chaismus,* 140
—, "Livy", 140
Steen, H., 131
Stein, A., 28, 30
Stenger, W., *Briefformular,* 138, 175
Stowers, S. K., *Diatribe,* 134—35, 151
—, *Letter Writing,* 1, 11, 12, 14, 49, 51, 57, 58, 60, 101, 129, 136, 138, 215
Strauss, J. A., 18
Strobel, A., 193
Sykutris, J., 1, 86

Tarn, W. W., *Alexander,* 35, 163
—, "ὑπομνήματα", 163
Thackeray, H. St. J., 157, 158
Thayer, J. H., 11
Thompson, E. M., 28, 160
Thraede, K., 12, 214
Trudinger, P., 184
Turner, N., *Style,* 141, 144, 151, 152, 207, 214
—, *Syntax,* 173
Tyrrell, R. Y. and L. C. Purser, 4, 6, 84, 93, 99, 110, 119, 120—22, 161, 162, 164, 166, 196, 213

Unnik, W. C. v., 144—49
Usener, H., 168

Wake, W. C., 184
Walker, W. O., 168
Wardman, A., 163
Weber, E., 134
Weiss J., 160
Welch, J. W., 140, 141, 207
Wendland, P., *Grammatik,* 214
—, *Kultur,* 211
Wengst, K., *Formeln,* 220
White, J. L., "Cliches", 130
—, "Documentary Letter", 7, 49, 57, 61, 75, 132
—, "Introductory Formulae", 132
—, *Light,* 7, 9, 10, 132, 167, 180
—, "Paul", 135, 139, 141
—, "Retrospect", 10, 14, 49, 57, 167
Wikenhauser, A., 128, 191, 213
Wilamowitz-Moellendorf, U. v., *Antigonos,* 211,
Wilckens, U., 92, 220
Wilder, A., 215
Williams, A. L., 173—75
Wilson, S. G., 193
Winter, J. G., 20, 74, 92
Wuellner, W., "Argumentation", 143
—, "Romans", 143

Yule, G. U., 184

Zahn, T., 73
Zielinski, T., 121
Zimmerman, H., 220

Ancient Authors

Apuleius, *Apologia 69*, 83
Aristophanes, *Vespae 1431*, 166
Arrian, *Epict. Diss. 1.10*, 134; *1.29*, 142; *2.16*, 133; *4.1–2*, 142; *4.11*, 134
Asconius Pedianus, *In Milonianum 36.27–28*, 31
Catullus *44*, 96

Cicero
ad Atticum, Book 1: 1.7, 8; *1.10*, 50; *1.13*, 9; *1.16*, 4, 119; *1.17*, 4; *1.18*, 7; *1.19*, 46, 112, 197
–, Book 2: *2.1*, 46; *2.2*, 31; *2.8*, 8; *2.12*, 8; *2.13*, 8; *2.16*, 46; *2.19*, 9, 93; *2.20*, 93; *2.23*, 20, 42, 62, 69, 80, 90, 100, 174
–, Book 3: *3.7*, 196; *3.8*, 196; *3.9*, 4; *3.10–17*, 90; *3.12*, 94; *3.15*, 24, 50, 94, 108, 109
–, Book 4: *4.5*, 116; *4.6*, 4; *4.8*, 116, 197; *4.8a*, 13, 163; *4.14*, 166; *4.16*, 42, 62, 69, 80, 100; *4.17*, 89
–, Book 5: *5.4*, 161; *5.10*, 165, 166; *5.11*, 62, 117, 165; *5.12*, 23, 24, 69, 113, 119, 197; *5.14*, 197; *5.16*, 198; *5.17*, 42, 69, 101, 198; *5.19*, 84; *5.20*, 46, 76, 170
–, Book 6: *6.6*, 42, 69, 77, 91, 110; *6.9* 62, 91
–, Book 7: *7.2*, 46, 62, 91; *7.3*, 56, 91, 100; *7.13a*, 23, 24, 42, 62, 69, 80, 112, 181; *7.17*, 96, 187; *7.18*, 161
–, Book 8: *8.1*, 80, 85; *8.9*, 6; *8.11*, 89, 96; *8.12*, 42, 62, 69, 79, 80, 89; *8.13*, 11, 42, 62, 69, 80, 113, 181; *8.15*, 23, 24, 69, 112
–, Book 9: *9.4*, 115; *9.6*, 118
–, Book 10: *10.3a*, 42, 69, 91; *10.8*, 31; *10.10*, 167; *10.14*, 62; *10.17*, 62, 80
–, Book 11: *11.2*, 50, 77, 108; *11.3*, 24, 108, 109; *11.4*, 7; *11.5*, 24, 47, 50, 106, 108, 153, 194; *11.7*, 50, 108; *11.9*, 9, 84, 93, 110, 118; *11.11*, 108, 194; *11.16*, 94; *11.24*, 88
–, Book 12: *12.1*, 161; *12.4*, 35; *12.7*, 161; *12.10*, 46; *12.18*, 84; *12.18a*, 84; *12.32*, 23, 24, 69, 80, 178
–, Book 13: *13.6*, 4; *13.8*, 161; *13.14*, 99; *13.21*, 99; *13.21a*, 6; *13.22*, 79; *13.23*, 2, 99, 103; *13.25*, 25, 42, 69, 99; *13.29*, 5; *13.32*, 23, 24, 34, 43, 69
–, Book 14: *14.18*, 56; *14.21*, 42, 69, 79, 101
–, Book 15: *15.3*, 96, 109, 187; *15.4*, 61, 96; *15.13*, 101; *15.20*, 89
–, Book 16: *16.5*, 4; *16.6*, 5; *16.15*, 42, 62, 69; *16.16*, 79
–, Book 19: *19.14*, 80
–, Book 27: *27.3*, 101
ad Familiares
–, Book 1: *1.8*, 9; *1.9*, 8, 85
–, Book 2: *2.3*, 101; *2.4*, 13, 92; *2.5*, 88; *2.7*, 7; *2.13*, 84; *2.29*, 7
–, Book 3: *3.1*, 9, 71; *3.3*, 4; *3.5*, 9; *3.6*, 62; *3.7*, 115; *3.8*, 197; *3.9*, 53; *3.11*, 54
–, Book 4: *4.2*, 9; *4.9*, 50; *4.10*, 50; *4.12*, 161; *4.13*, 59
–, Book 5: *5.4*, 7; *5.5*, 98; *5.6*, 7; *5.7*, 54; *5.12*, 121; *5.20*, 56
–, Book 6: *6.8*, 5; *6.18*, 161
–, Book 7: *7.18*, 3, 9, 85, 89, 161; *7.25*, 3; *7.29*, 4, 76
–, Book 8: *8.1*, 51, 107, 108; *8.6*, 196; *8.9*, 98; *8.12*, 8; *8.14*, 101
–, Book 9: *9.6*, 48; *9.12*, 3; *9.15*, 7, 10; *9.16*, 5; *9.21*, 196; *9.26*, 3, 162, 165
–, Book 10: *10.5*, 5; *10.7*, 9; *10.8*, 133; *10.12*, 4; *10.28*, 5; *10.31*, 9; *10.33*, 4; *10.32*, 4
–, Book 11: *11.11*, 5; *11.20*, 9; *11.23*, 89; *11.26*, 9; *11.32*, 23, 24, 69
–, Book 12: *12.4*, 5; *12.12*, 5, 83; *12.30*, 5, 162, 197
–, Book 13: *13.6a*, 71; *13.27*, 49; *13.68*, 49; *13.69*, 49
–, Book 14: *14.1*, 7; *14.7*, 66, 113; *14.18*, 7
–, Book 15: *15.7*, 85; *15.8*, 62; *15.12*, 196; *15.14*, 8; *15.17*, 71; 115; *15.21*, 213
–, Book 16: *16.1*, 213; *16.3*, 45; *16.4*, 45, 46; *16.10*, 46; *16.11*, 45; *16.15*, 78, 80; *16.17*, 45, 105; *16.21*, 71, 103; *16.22*, 78, 103
–, Book 19: *19.9*, 85
ad Quintum Fratrem
–, Book 1: *1.1*, 8, 88, 121; *1.2*, 4, 51, 55, 79, 181

–, Book 2: 2.2, 23, 24, 42, 62, 69, 80, 100, 117, 181, 189; *2.6*, 120; *2.9*, 161; *2.11*, 161; *2.12*, 3, 8, 88; *2.14*, 161; *2.15b*, 23, 24, 54, 69, 118; *2.16*, 23, 24, 53, 62, 69, 80, 100, 112, 120; *2.23*, 100
–, Book 3: *3.1*, 23, 24, 42, 53, 56, 69, 80, 101, 113, 114, 178; *3.3*, 42, 62, 69, 80, 100; *3.6*, 2; *3.9* 55
ad Brutum *1.2*, 84; *1.16*, 4

Clement of Alexandria *Stromateis* 6.15, 159
Cornelius Nepos *De vir. ill.* 18.1, 188

Demetrius of Phaleron *Style*, 60, 130, 133
Dio Cassius Cocceianus *Roman History*, 31
Diogenes Laertius *Vit. Epic.*, 168; *Vit. Xen.*, 33, 36

Epictetus, 133
Epicurus, 168, 211
Epimenides, 145
Eusebius *Chronica*, 31; *H.E.*, 70, 149

Ignatius *Eph.*, 70; *Magn.*, 71; *Phld.*, 70, 72; *Rom.*, 71; *Smyrn.*, 70, 71, 72
Isocrates, 133, 149

Jerome *De vir. ill.*, 5
Josephus *Ant.*, 157; *Ap.*, 149, 157; *B.J.*, 118, 157

Menander *Thais*, 145

Ovid *Tristia*, 77

Paulus *Digesta* 29.1, 28
Philo, 149, 173
Philostratus of Lemnos, 52, 59, 115
Plato *Epp.*, 86-87; *Resp.*, 166
Pliny the Elder *Naturalis Historia* 7.21, 26; *7.25*, 11, 25
Pliny the Younger *De orat.* 2.51, 102; *Epp. 1.6*, 162; *3.5*, 11, 24, 27, 64, 101, 102, 163; *6.16*, 161; *6.20*, 64; *7.2*, 215; *7.9*, 215; *8.1*, 10; *9.6*, 162; *9.29*, 64; *9.36*, 101; *10.96*, 159; *36.2*, 64; *38*, 125; *40.3*, 125; *75.1*, 196; *82*, 125; *117*, 125
Plutarch *Alex.*, 6, 10, 17, 188; *Caes.*, 24, 29, 64, 66, 162; *Cat. Min.*, 19, 29, 30, 34, 45, 77, 78; *Cic.*, 9, 34, 35, 196; *Dem.*, 20; *Eum.*, 6, 17, 47, 63, 188
Polycarpus *Phil.*, 73
Pseudo-Heraclitus, 117
Pseudo-Socrates, 42, 87, 163

Quintilianus, Marcus Fabius *Inst.*, 20, 28, 42, 111, 113, 115

Scriptores Historiae Augustae (S.H.A.), 123
Seneca, Lucius Annaeus *Epp. 8.1*, 91; *26.8*, 20, 91; *40.10*, 25; *40.25*, 28; *55.11*, 162; *56.1*, 111; *75.1*, 119, 130, 196; *90.25*, 28; *Apocol. 9.2*, 11, 28, 30
Suetonius Tranquillus, C., *Caes. 55*, 30; *56.6*, 89; *Nero 10.2*, 123; *Tit. 3.2*, 11, 28, 29, 77, 118; *6.1*, 123; *Vesp. 6*, 118; *21* 17, 55, 123

Papyri and Inscriptions

BGU, 82
CIG 3902d, 39
Greek Historical Documents [inscriptions], 15, 16
PBon. 5, 58, 59
PCol. 3.6, 9
PGiess. 97, 82
PMich. *8.490*, 10; *188*, 20; *482*, 130
PMur. *164*, 40–41
POslo *50*, 204

POxy. *42*, 39; *113*, 20, 22, 83 203; *114*, 206; *116*, 84; *117*, 84; *118*, 22, 47; *119*, 59, 103; *123*, 9; *255*, 82; *264*, 82; *292*, 203; *294*, 20, 22; *394*, 20, 22, 83; *526*, 22; *528*, 20, 22, 84; *530*, 20, 33, 83; *531*, 20, 22 203; *533*, 206; *724*, 38, 43, 61; *928*, 92; *932*, 84; *1062*, 84; *1070*, 203; *1155*, 203; *1158*, 47; *1160*, 203; *1167*, 47; *1216*, 203; *1223*, 203; *1293*, 84; *1299*, 203; *1348*, 203; *1453*, 83;

1480, 203; *1481*, 203; *1484*–*1487*, 21, 55; *1491*, 21; *1493*, 204; *1582*, 206; *1666*, 203; *1670*, 203; *1677*, 84; *1679*, 203; *1785*, 203; *1837*, 92; *2860*, 22; *2983*, 22; *2985*, 22, 83; *3036*, 22; *3057*, 20, 22; *3064*, 47; *3066*, 22; *3094*, 47; *3273*, 18; *3313*, 21, 47; *3314*, 19, 85
PParis *63*, 58
PRain. *3.9,10*, 33; *13.444*, 33; *215*, 78
PSel. *51*, 82
PTebt. *13*, 24, 107; *32*, 79; *412*, 206; *415*, 206
PZen. *6*, 20, 22; *35*, 47; *56*, 16; *57*, 24, 107; *66*, 20, 22; *74*, 22; *88*, 22; *111*, 24, 107; *122*, 16

References

Old Testament
1 Kings 21:8, 84
Nehemiah 9:38, 84
Isaiah 6, 145
Jeremiah 32:14, 84
Daniel 6:17, 84

New Testament
(by chapters only)
Matthew
  Ch. *8*, 219; Ch. *9*, 172; Ch. *19*, 217; Ch. *27*, 84
Mark
  Ch. *3*, 172; Ch. *7*, 160; Ch. *10*, 219; Ch. *11*, 172; Ch. *12*, 217
Luke
  Ch. *9*, 219; Ch. *11*, 172; Ch. *16*, 219
John
  Ch. *8*, 217
Acts
  Ch. *4*, 172; Ch. *7*, 149; Ch. *8*, 217; Ch. *9*, 146; Ch. *15*, 73; Ch. *18*, 155, 157; Ch. *19*, 217; Ch. *20*, 171, 182; Ch. *21*, 146; Ch. *22*, 146–48, 153; Ch. *26*, 146
Romans
  134–35, 137, 141, 177, 179, 213; Ch. *1*, 140, 217, 220; Ch. *2*, 142–43, 217; Ch. *3*, 142, 217; Ch. *4*, 84, 141–42; Ch. *5*, 217, 218; Ch. *7*, 140; Ch. *8*, 143, 209, 218; Ch. *9*, 141; Ch. *10*, 207, 217, 220; Ch. *11*, 137, 139, 147; Ch. *12*, 139, 217; Ch. *13*, 141, 217; Ch. *14*, 142, 151, 217, 220; Ch. *15*, 137, 139; Ch. *16*, 137–39, 169–72, 182, 197, 206, 217

1 Corinthians
  114, 135, 166, 177; Ch. *1*, 139–41, 153–56; Ch. *2*, 196; Ch. *3*, 152, 217; Ch. *4*, 137, 141, 156, 209; Ch. *5*, 208; Ch. *6*, 217; Ch. *7*, 172, 197, 217, 219; Ch. *8*, 197, 217, 219; Ch. *9*, 84, 172, 217; Ch. *10*, 139, 155; Ch. *11*, 139, 155, 159, 217; Ch. *12*, 217; Ch. *13*, 142, 155, 217–18; Ch. *14*, 152, 217; Ch. *15*, 139, 141, 145, 152, 159, 172; Ch. *16*, 156, 172, 179–80, 182, 197
2 Corinthians
  6, 139, 156–57, 177; Ch. *1*, 84, 140, 142, 153, 155–56, 217; Ch. *2*, 139; Ch. *4*, 209; Ch. *5*, 152, 159, 217; Ch. *6*, 139, 141, 168, 209; Ch. *7*, 138, 168; Ch. *8*, 156; Ch. *10*, 115, 126, 139, 156, 179, 180–81, 196–97; Ch. *11*, 147, 156, 179, 196–97, 209, 211; Ch. *12*, 137–39, 143, 156, 179, 196–97, 209, 217; Ch. *13*, 197
Galatians
  92, 138, 141, 177, 179, 208; Ch. *1*, 137–38, 140, 145, 147–48, 153, 159, 217; Ch. *3*, 126, 217; Ch. *4*, 137, 141, 218; Ch. *5*, 176, 217–18; Ch. *6*, 100, 164, 172, 174, 176, 179–80, 182, 197
Ephesians
  5, 152, 177, 179; Ch. *1*, 84, 140, 218; Ch. *2*, 140, 207; Ch. *3*, 137, 140; Ch. *4*, 140, 172, 217–18; Ch. *5*, 143, 217; Ch. *6*, 137, 151, 172, 191
Philippians
  177; Ch. *1*, 139–40, 153, 179, 208; Ch. *2*, 137, 217; Ch. *3*, 144, 147–48, 208; Ch. *4*, 137–39, 164, 190, 197, 209

Colossians
5, 177, 218; *Ch. 1*, 153, 207; *Ch. 2*, 140; *Ch. 3*, 141, 143, 151, 179, 208, 217; *Ch. 4*, 137, 173, 180, 188, 191, 197, 213

1 Thessalonians
156, 177; *Ch. 1*, 153, 179, 217–18; *Ch. 2*, 137, 140–41, 179; *Ch. 3*, 139; *Ch. 4*, 139, 141, 172, 179, 217; *Ch. 5* 139, 142, 172, 179, 189, 197, 213, 218

2 Thessalonians
152, 156, 177; *Ch. 1*, 153; *Ch. 2*, 139–42, 159, 174; *Ch. 3*, 91, 141, 173–74, 179, 189, 191, 197

1 Timothy
179; *Ch. 1*, 137; *Ch. 2*, 140, 217; *Ch. 3*, 141; *Ch. 4*, 164; *Ch. 5*, 164; *Ch. 6*, 159

2 Timothy
179; *Ch. 1*, 140; *Ch. 2*, 84, 140–41; *Ch. 4*, 5, 7, 137, 140–41, 164–65

Titus
139–40, 164, 179

Philemon
137, 153, 156, 164, 173, 177–80, 213

Hebrews
Ch. 6, 218; *Ch. 10*, 218

James
Ch. 2, 217

1 Peter
Ch. 1, 218; *Ch. 5*, 72–73

Revelation
Ch. 10, 84; *Ch. 22*, 84

Apocrypha and Pseudepigrapha
4 Ezra, 145
2 Maccabees 4:9, 150
Sirach 31:25–30, 133; *38:25ff*, 149
Anti-Marcionite Prologues, 158

The Babylonian Talmud
Ab. 5:21, 150

The Midrash Rabba
Eccl.R. 7.28, 150

Wissenschaftliche Untersuchungen zum Neuen Testament

Alphabetical index of
the first and the second series

APPOLD, MARK L.: The Oneness Motif in the Fourth Gospel. 1976. *Volume II/1.*
BAMMEL, ERNST: Judaica. 1986. *Volume 37.*
BAUERNFEIND, OTTO: Kommentar und Studien zur Apostelgeschichte. 1980. *Volume 22.*
BAYER, HANS FRIEDRICH: Jesus' Predictions of Vindication and Resurrection. 1986. *Volume II/20.*
BETZ, OTTO: Jesus, der Messias Israels. 1987. *Volume 42.*
– Jesus, der Herr der Kirche. 1990. *Volume 52.*
BEYSCHLAG, KARLMANN: Simon Magnus und die christliche Gnosis. 1974. *Volume 16.*
BITTNER, WOLFGANG J.: Jesu Zeichen im Johannesevangelium. 1987. *Volume II/26.*
BJERKELUND, CARL J.: Tauta Egeneto. 1987. *Volume 40.*
BLACKBURN, BARRY LEE: 'Theios Anēr' and the Markan Miracle Traditions. 1991. *Volume II/40.*
BOCKMUEHL, MARKUS N. A.: Revelation and Mystery in Ancient Judaism and Pauline Christianity. 1990. *Volume II/36.*
BÖHLIG, ALEXANDER: Gnosis und Synkretismus Part 1. 1989. *Volume 47* – Part 2. 1989. *Volume 48*
BÜCHLI, JÖRG: Der Poimandres – ein paganisiertes Evangelium. 1987. *Volume II/27.*
BÜHNER, JAN A.: Der Gesandte und sein Weg im 4. Evangelium. 1977. *Volume II/2.*
BURCHARD, CHRISTOPH: Untersuchungen zu Joseph und Aseneth. 1965. *Volume 8.*
CANCIK, HUBERT (Hrsg.): Markus-Philologie. 1984. *Volume 33.*
CARAGOUNIS, CHRYS C.: The Son of Man. 1986. *Volume 38.*
DOBBELER, AXEL VON: Glaube als Teilhabe. 1987. *Volume II/22.*
EBERTZ, MICHAEL N.: Das Charisma des Gekreuzigten. 1987. *Volume 45.*
ECKSTEIN, HANS-JOACHIM: Der Begriff der Syneidesis bei Paulus. 1983. *Volume II/10.*
EGO, BEATE: Im Himmel wie auf Erden. 1989. *Volume II/34.*
ELLIS, E. EARLE: Prophecy and Hermeneutic in Early Christianity. 1978. *Volume 18.*
– The Old Testament in Early Christianity. 1991. *Volume 54.*
FELDMEIER, REINHARD: Die Krisis des Gottessohnes. 1987. *Volume II/21.*
FOSSUM, JARL E.: The Name of God and the Angel of the Lord. 1985. *Volume 36.*
GARLINGTON, DON B.: The Obedience of Faith. 1991. *Volume II/38.*
GARNET, PAUL: Salvation and Atonement in the Qumran Scrolls. 1977. *Volume II/3.*
GRÄSSER, ERICH: Der Alte Bund im Neuen. 1985. *Volume 35.*
GREEN, JOEL B.: The Death of Jesus. 1988. *Volume II/33.*
GUNDRY VOLF, JUDITH M.: Paul and Perseverance. 1990. *Volume II/37.*
HAFEMANN, SCOTT J.: Suffering and the Spirit. 1986. *Volume II/19.*
HEILIGENTHAL, ROMAN: Werke als Zeichen. 1983. *Volume II/9.*
HEMER, COLIN J.: The Book of Acts in the Setting of Hellenistic History. 1989. *Volume 49.*
HENGEL, MARTIN und A. M. SCHWEMER (Hrsg.): Königsherrschaft Gottes und himmlischer Kult. 1991. *Volume 55.*
HENGEL, MARTIN: Judentum und Hellenismus. 1969, ^{3}1988. *Volume 10.*
HERRENBRÜCK, FRITZ: Jesus und die Zöllner. 1990. *Volume II/41.*
HOFIUS, OTFRIED: Katapausis. 1970. *Volume 11.*
– Der Vorhang vor dem Thron Gottes. 1972. *Volume 14.*
– Der Christushymnus Philipper 2,6 – 11. 1976, ^{2}1991. *Volume 17.*
– Paulusstudien. 1989. *Volume 51.*
HOMMEL, HILDEBRECHT: Sebasmata. Volume 1. 1983. *Volume 31.* – Volume 2. 1984. *Volume 32.*
KAMLAH, EHRHARD: Die Form der katalogischen Paränese im Neuen Testament. 1964. *Volume 7.*
KIM, SEYOON: The Origin of Paul's Gospel. ^{2}1984. *Volume II/4.*
– »The ›Son of Man‹« as the Son of God. 1983. *Volume 30.*
KLEINKNECHT, KARL TH.: Der leidende Gerechtfertigte. 1984, ^{2}1988. *Volume II/13.*
KLINGHARDT, MATTHIAS: Gesetz und Volk Gottes. 1988. *Volume II/32.*
KÖHLER, WOLF-DIETRICH: Rezeption des Matthäusevangeliums in der Zeit vor Irenäus. 1987. *Volume II/24.*

Wissenschaftliche Untersuchungen zum Neuen Testament

KUHN, KARL G.: Achtzehngebet und Vaterunser und der Reim. 1950. *Volume 1.*
LAMPE, PETER: Die stadtrömischen Christen in den ersten beiden Jahrhunderten. 1987, ²1989. *Volume II/18.*
MAIER, GERHARD: Mensch und freier Wille. 1971. *Volume 12.*
- Die Johannesoffenbarung und die Kirche. 1981. *Volume 25.*
MARSHALL, PETER: Enmity in Corinth: Social Conventions in Paul's Relations with the Corinthians. 1987. *Volume II/23.*
MEADE, DAVID G.: Pseudonymity and Canon. 1986. *Volume 39.*
MENGEL, BERTHOLD: Studien zum Philipperbrief. 1982. *Volume II/8.*
MERKEL, HELMUT: Die Widersprüche zwischen den Evangelien. 1971. *Volume 13.*
MERKLEIN, HELMUT: Studien zu Jesus und Paulus. 1987. *Volume 43.*
METZLER, KARIN: Der griechische Begriff des Verzeihens. 1991. *Volume II/44.*
NIEBUHR, KARL-WILHELM: Gesetz und Paränese. 1987. *Volume II/28.*
NISSEN, ANDREAS: Gott und der Nächste im antiken Judentum. 1974. *Volume 15.*
OKURE, TERESA: The Johannine Approach to Mission. 1988. *Volume II/31.*
PILHOFER, PETER: Presbyterion Kreitton. 1990. *Volume II/39.*
RÄISÄNEN, HEIKKI: Paul and the Law. 1983, ²1987. *Volume 29.*
REHKOPF, FRIEDRICH: Die lukanische Sonderquelle. 1959. *Volume 5.*
REISER, MARIUS: Syntax und Stil des Markusevangeliums. 1984. *Volume II/11.*
RICHARDS, E. RANDOLPH: The Secretary in the Letters of Paul. 1991. *Volume II/42.*
RIESNER, RAINER: Jesus als Lehrer. 1981, ³1988. *Volume II/7.*
RISSI, MATHIAS: Die Theologie des Hebräerbriefs. 1987. *Volume 41.*
RÖHSER, GÜNTER: Metaphorik und Personifikation der Sünde. 1987. *Volume II/25.*
RÜGER, HANS PETER: Die Weisheitsschrift aus der Kairoer Geniza. 1991. *Volume 53.*
SÄNGER, DIETER: Antikes Judentum und die Mysterien. 1980. *Volume II/5.*
SANDNES, KARL OLAV: Paul – One of the Prophets? 1991. *Volume II/43.*
SATO, MIGAKU: Q und Prophetie. 1988. *Volume II/29.*
SCHIMANOWSKI, GOTTFRIED: Weisheit und Messias. 1985. *Volume II/17.*
SCHLICHTING, GÜNTER: Ein jüdisches Leben Jesu. 1982. *Volume 24.*
SCHNABEL, ECKHARD J.: Law and Wisdom from Ben Sira to Paul. 1985. *Volume II/16.*
SCHUTTER, WILLIAM L.: Hermeneutic and Composition in I Peter. 1989. *Volume II/30.*
SCHWEMER, A. M. – see HENGEL.
SIEGERT, FOLKER: Drei hellenistisch-jüdische Predigten. 1980. *Volume 20.*
- Nag-Hammadi-Register. 1982. *Volume 26.*
- Argumentation bei Paulus. 1985. *Volume 34.*
- Philon von Alexandrien. 1988. *Volume 46.*
SIMON, MARCEL: Le christianisme antique et son contexte religieux I/II. 1981. *Volume 23.*
SNODGRASS, KLYNE: The Parable of the Wicked Tenants. 1983. *Volume 27.*
SPEYER, WOLFGANG: Frühes Christentum im antiken Strahlungsfeld. 1989. *Volume 50.*
STADELMANN, HELGE: Ben Sira als Schriftgelehrter. 1980. *Volume II/6.*
STROBEL, AUGUST: Die Studie der Wahrheit. 1980. *Volume 21.*
STUHLMACHER, PETER (Hrsg.): Das Evangelium und die Evangelien. 1983. *Volume 28.*
TAJRA, HARRY W.: The Trial of St. Paul. 1989. *Volume II/35.*
THEISSEN, GERD: Studien zur Soziologie des Urchristentums. 1979, ³1989. *Volume 19.*
WEDDERBURN, A. J. M.: Baptism and Resurrection. 1987. *Volume 44.*
WEGNER, UWE: Der Hauptmann von Kafarnaum. 1985. *Volume II/14.*
ZIMMERMANN, ALFRED E.: Die urchristlichen Lehrer. 1984, ²1988. *Volume II/12.*

For a complete catalogue please write to
J. C. B. Mohr (Paul Siebeck), P. O. Box 2040, D-7400 Tübingen